C0-DKM-449
SOUTH
AFRICAN
HISTORY
ONLINE

Shifting Selves

Post-apartheid Essays on Mass Media, Culture and Identity

Edited by
Herman Wasserman and Sean Jacobs

KWELA BOOKS

Kwela Books
40 Heerengracht, Cape Town 8001;
P.O. Box 6525, Roggebaai 8012
kwela@kwela.com
http://www.kwela.com

Cover design by Louw Venter
Book design by Nazli Jacobs
Set in Simoncini Garamond
Printed and bound by Paarl Print, Oosterland Street, Paarl, South Africa

First edition, first printing 2003

ISBN 0-7957-0164-0

Social Identities South Africa

Series Editor: Abebe Zegeye

The identities of South Africa and its citizens have been undergoing crucial changes since 1994, when the first democratic elections resulted in the demise of statutory apartheid. This has led to an emerging ethos of democratic rule among all citizens of South Africa. But, although changes in South African society are clearly visible in increased social mobility, migration, access to jobs, training and educational and general reform in South Africa, the nature and influence of the identities being formed in response is as yet less clear. The SISA project aims to determine the nature of some of these new identities.

The project is shaped by research that indicates the South Africans, while going through flux and transformation in their personal and group identities, have a shared concern about the stability of their democracy and their economic future.

Other titles in the SISA Series:

Social Identities in the New South Africa
After Apartheid – Volume One
Edited by Abebe Zegeye

Culture in the New South Africa
After Apartheid – Volume Two
Edited by Robert Kriger and Abebe Zegeye

Kala Pani
Caste and Colour in South Africa
Rehana Ebr.-Vally

Coloured by History, Shaped by Place
New Perspectives on Coloured Identities in Cape Town
Edited by Zimitri Erasmus

The I of the Beholder
Identity formation in the art and writing of Breyten Breytenbach
Marilet Sienaert

Contents

Acknowledgements

We would like to thank Annari van der Merwe and Abebe Zegeye for believing in our project.

Keyan Tomaselli at the University of Natal-Durban's Centre for Media and Cultural Studies commented on earlier drafts of the manuscript. So did Krista Johnson at DePaul University, who also acted as discussant when some of the chapters were presented as part of a panel at the Annual Meeting of the African Studies Association in Washington DC, 5-8 November 2002. Krista also commented on the introduction.

Sean Jacobs wishes to thank his partner Jessica Blatt, for her support and companionship (and editing skills). He would also like to thank his friends and colleagues in New York, London and Cape Town, especially Wendy Willems, Farzanah Badsha, Ntone Edjambe (at Chimurenga), Suren Pillay, Mike Metelits, Barbara Lipietz, and Ron Krabill for stimulating exchanges around some of the ideas that made it into the introduction.

Herman Wasserman would like to thank Helena for her encouragement and interest in the project. He is also indebted to all those who commented on the work in progress, as well as to Sean Jacobs, who came up with the initial idea that resulted in this book. He extends his appreciation to the University of Stellenbosch and the Department of Journalism for support granted to do the research and final editing of the manuscript.

The chapters by Sean Jacobs, Herman Wasserman and Gabeba Baderoon appeared in a previous format in *African and Asian Studies* 1(4). A previous version of Stephanie Marlin-Curiel's chapter appeared in *TDR* (*The Drama Review*) 45, 3 (2001).

Herman Wasserman and Sean Jacobs
Cape Town, February 2003

Contributors

GABEBA BADEROON is a media scholar and poet. She holds a John Sainsbury/Linbury Trust Doctoral Fellowship at the University of Cape Town, and is a visiting student in the Department of English Language and Linguistics at the University of Sheffield. She has written recently on Orientalism in the media, on art and Islam in South Africa, and on cultural meanings of food. She was a SHARE Fellow at Pennsylvania State University in 1999 and an Associate in the African Gender Institute at the University of Cape Town in 2002. Her poetry has been published in South Africa and the United States.

FARZANAH BADSHA is doing her masters in Historical Studies at the University of Cape Town with a focus on visual history. Her research is on South African documentary photography during the 1980s and the Afrapix photographic collective in particular. She was the recipient of A.W. Mellon Fellowships for both her honours and masters degrees.

KEITH BAIN is currently co-authoring a travel guidebook on India, where he spent most of 2002. He has a DPhil in Contemporary Cinema from the University of Stellenbosch Drama Department where he teaches film, media and drama theory. A Chief Examiner with the Film and Publication Board of South Africa, he has dabbled in playwriting, stage acting, copy-editing, public relations and even teaching English in Taiwan. He has written several articles about Grahamstown's National Arts Festival and has most recently co-authored an article about the state of the local theatre industry for the *South African Theatre Journal*.

JANE BATTERSBY has recently completed a DPhil on education and Coloured identities in post-apartheid South Africa at the School of Geography and the Environment, Oxford University and is currently a post-doctoral research fellow at the University of Cape Town. She received her MA in International Cultural Change from the University of Newcastle-upon-Tyne. Her main research interest is identity constructions in South Africa, with particular focus on the relationship between constructions of space, place and identities.

MARTHINUS BEUKES is a senior lecturer in Afrikaans literature at the Rand Afrikaans University. He obtained his doctorate from the University of the North-West (1993) on the topic "Gynogenesis as discourse of power: the configuration of the New Woman in texts by Antjie Krog, Marieta Van der Vyver and Jeanne Goosen". He specialises in Afrikaans poetry, in particular the work of Antjie Krog, T.T. Cloete and Tom Gouws.

GIBSON BOLOKA teaches media economics and audience research in South Africa. His other fields of interest include: Political Economy of the Media, Media and Cultural Studies, Black Economic Empowerment and Mass Media, and Communication theory and research.

SEAN JACOBS is a researcher and journalist. He is completing his doctorate in politics at Birkbeck College, University of London. He is a former Fulbright Scholar, and held fellowships at Harvard University and the New School for Social Research. In 2002, he co-edited *Thabo Mbeki's World: The Ideology and Politics of the South African President* (University of Natal Press/Zed Books, 2002) with Richard Calland. He is also an editor of *Chimurenga Online*, a Pan-African magazine of arts, culture and politics.

JULIAN JONKER is a writer, researcher and cultural worker. He is currently completing a masters dissertation at the University of Cape Town's Faculty of Law on cultural studies of intellectual property. His other main research interest is the indigenous music of South Africa, which he is able to pursue as co-ordinator of the District Six Museum's Public Education Programme. He runs the liberation chabalala music/media project and is a DJ with the Fong Kong Bantu Sound System.

PATRICE KABEYA-MWEPU, born in Ngandanjika in the Democratic Republic of the Congo (then Zaire), lectured in the department of French language and literature at the University of Cape Town. He obtained an MA in French Language and Literature (1994), and an "Agrégation" (1994) at the University of Lubumbashi, DRC, as well as a PhD at the University of Cape Town (2001). He is currently researching on Congolese literature after 1990.

STEPHANIE MARLIN-CURIEL is an adjunct professor in the Departments of Drama, Performance Studies and Art and Public Policy at New York University's Tisch School of the Arts, where she recently received her PhD. Her dissertation, "Performing Memory, Rehearsing Reconciliation: The Art of Truth in the 'New' South Africa", analyses cultural responses to the Truth and Reconciliation Commission in South Africa. Her other published work appears in *TDR: The Drama Review, South African Theatre Journal, Theatre Research International,* and *Art and the Performance of Memory: Sounds and Gestures of Recollection*, edited by Richard Candida Smith (Routledge, 2002).

PHASWANE MPE has published short stories and poems in *Modern South African Stories* (2002), *Unity In Flight: Short Fiction* (2001), *Botsotso: Contemporary South African Culture* (2000), *English Academy Review* (1999) and *New Coin* (1998). He is the author of the novel *Welcome To Our Hillbrow* (2001). He is currently a Doctoral Fellow at the Wits Institute for Social and Economic Research, University of the Witwatersrand.

LENE ØVERLAND is a Geographer. She has a MPhil from the University of Bergen, Norway where she was an associate at the Centre for Development Studies. She is currently working as freelance journalist, researcher and media and communications consultant. When she wrote her chapter she was Programme Director at Women's Media Watch, South Africa. Her research interests are generally in the field of construction of gender identities and power relations in various spatial contexts. She has a general interest in contemporary feminist theoretical debates.

SUREN PILLAY teaches in the Department of Political Studies at the University of the Western Cape. He is currently a doctoral candidate in the Department of Anthropology at Columbia University where his research focuses on the relationship between discourses of security and political violence in South Africa under late apartheid.

RENÉ SMITH is a lecturer in media studies and communication. She has an MA in Cultural and Media Studies from the University of Natal, Durban, and is currently pursuing a PhD on the relationship between television viewing and identities of black South African youths. She is a member of the South African Film and Publication Review Board. She writes in her personal capacity.

MELISSA STEYN is director of the Institute for Intercultural and Diversity Studies at the University of Cape Town. She has published on many aspects of diversity, including race, culture, gender and sexuality. She is the author of *Whiteness just isn't what is used to be: White identity in a changing South Africa* (2001) Albany: SUNY press; and co-editor of *Cultural Synergy in South Africa: Weaving strands of Africa and Europe* (1996) Randburg: Knowledge resources.

HERMAN WASSERMAN is senior lecturer in the Department of Journalism at the University of Stellenbosch. He was awarded a doctorate from the same university for a dissertation on postcolonial identity construction in Afrikaans short fiction after 1994. He has published and presented papers locally and internationally. His current research interest is discourses of identity in South African media texts. He has worked as a journalist and has published two volumes of short stories.

CHAPTER ONE

Introduction

Herman Wasserman and Sean Jacobs[1]

Formally April 27, 1994 saw the birth of the "new" South Africa; in its wake social configurations have started to shift, identities are in the process of being renegotiated and cultural borders are being transgressed. While it could be expected that the new political, economic and cultural situation in post-apartheid South Africa might render obsolete the old binaries of "self" and "other", opening up new possibilities and a variety of new themes (Oliphant 1999:8), past oppositions have not completely disappeared. Material power relations mitigate against a boundless reshaping of the cultural landscape.

When outlining the social changes that occurred in South Africa in recent years and how these changes have been mediated in a variety of spheres, it is fascinating to note the emergence of what Nuttall and Michael (2000:2) call "new forms of imagining". On one level, hybrid constructions of identity challenge the fixity of identities under apartheid and undermine the cultural hierarchy and imposed ethnicities (Zegeye 2001:3) on which the discourse of racial discrimination was based. Identities seen in this way are fluid rather than fixed, constantly in the process of being constructed and deconstructed as the social context changes (Zegeye 2001:3). As Stuart Hall (1994:393) pointed out, cultural identities can be seen as involved in a process of becoming rather than a state of being, if it is accepted that identities are not pre-given but come into being within representation. However, identity construction in post-apartheid South Africa does not only take place as creolisation or hybridity. Exclusionary notions of identity, based on race and ethnicity, are still operative among certain sectors of post-apartheid South African society (Zegeye 2001:3). The reaffirmation of the same identities that in the past were discriminated against, in a process of postcolonial identity reconstruction similar to what Spivak (1990:11) termed "strategic essentialism", should also be recognised. The rehabilitation of a shared history of oppression and a collective self, which people with a shared history and genealogy have in common (Hall 1994:393), also forms part of the postcolonial identity project.

Moreover, in focusing on the movements taking place across the boundaries or on the margins of culture, the impact of past legacies should not be neglected. One of the more recent works exploring these issues in South Africa and one which has attracted considerable attention, is that of Nuttall and Michael (2000). They employ the term "creolisation" to describe the cultural dynamic of post-apartheid South Africa. Creolisation, they contend, is a process "whereby individuals of different cultures, languages, and religions are thrown together and invent a new language, Creole, a new culture, and a new social organisation" (2000:6). What one should not lose sight of in this celebration of cultural mobility and identity invention, is the determining impact of material factors and power relations. Creolisation, while a novel way of describing the new forms of identity formation that have arisen, does not take place in a space devoid of power struggles, nor does it signify a complete break with the past. South African society still largely reflects, for instance, economic inequalities that coincide with the racial divides of the past. Despite the emergence of cultural mixing evident for example in kwaito music, creolisation is not a free-for-all. Serious faultlines inherited from the past still exist in South Africa, hampering cross-cultural movement.[2]

This book, therefore, is an attempt to theorise the processes of mediated change in South Africa from this perspective. While investigating the emergence of new identities, renegotiations of cultural boundaries and the manifestation of hybridity in a variety of forms, this book starts out from the understanding that any theory that deals with post-apartheid South Africa would have to be rooted in local specificity. In outlining the process of cultural shifts, one should therefore attempt to remain true to the particularity of history and engage with South African localities. This does not mean that the impact of larger processes can be ignored. South Africa cannot escape the era of accelerated globalisation that on the one hand impacts on the ways in which culture and identity are being worlded, and on the other, hegemonises locally dominant political and societal discourses. This means that culture and identity have been privatised, commodified, branded and become a function of a distinct form of economic organisation, namely market capitalism, with profound impacts for forms of social and political order. One consequence of the pervasive quality of globalisation for scholarship is that the tools of enquiry already in use or prevalent elsewhere around the world are often transplanted to the local context to help re-view and re-understand our society. The contributors to this book have, however, attempted to ground such theories within the locality of South Africa, adapting and redefining these theoretical approaches where necessary.

We see the social and political changes that South Africa is undergoing as mediated – by media in a broad sense, thereby including mass media, art and cultural expression. But this mediation takes place within a complex and ever-changing set of power relations, both global and local. While this mediation is subject to the constraints imposed by past legacies, it also creates the possibility for agents to overturn them. This process is played out on a variety of fronts, ranging from the mass media and new media to mainstream art forms such as theatre or the urban aesthetics of graffiti art, poetry, intellectual property, and hip-hop, kwaito, television drama, or the claiming of the airwaves by refugees.

Critics of this volume might want to dismiss it as merely another book of case studies. Yet the writers have come together through their varied contributions to grapple with the theoretical conundrum of making sense of change post-1994 without falling into the trap of what Nuttall and Michael correctly term the "over-determination of the political, the inflation of resistance, and the fixation on race [. . .] as a determinant of identity" (2000:1) in South African cultural studies. We are, however, of the opinion that political questions surrounding hegemony, resistance and "race" still need to form part of investigations into post-apartheid society. Race (and class) have been the master narratives of most South African texts in the post-apartheid context, and although there have been attempts to break with it, this seems easier said than done. While care should therefore be taken not to afford race and class over-determining importance, they remain key determinants in the formation of cultural and social identities and can therefore not be taken out of the equation completely.

Contributions to *Shifting Selves* are written, for the most part, by relatively young authors. The majority of contributors were born at the end of the 1960s and after; the two editors were both born in 1969. The youngest of the contributors was born in the aftermath of the 1976 Soweto uprising, which symbolically also signalled a new era in South African politics, that of increased resistance, extreme state repression, and the start of the end-game of apartheid. We bring a wide range of perspectives and experiences. We do so as subjects situated within diverse contexts and coming from different backgrounds, and therefore cannot claim to put forward a homogenous approach regarding the analysis of identity construction or cultural politics. We have taken note of academic responses to the changes that the South African social and political landscape has undergone. Our own experiences as young people have however brought us some new perspectives on these changes. As a result our approach to questions of identity and culture might not always correspond with the dominant academic discourses on these topics, often diverging and sometimes differing profoundly from what has gone before. But we do not always agree with one another and bring with us different experiences. We carry with us contradictions, different backgrounds and physical spaces. Our backgrounds are South African, Congolese, Norwegian, British and American; we are from Cape Town, Johannesburg, Durban, Polokwane, London, New York; we are Afrikaner, black, coloured, women, men, activists, academics, journalists, disk jockeys, lawyers. What we have in common is our lived experiences of a changing country and an intellectual interest in how these changes are mediated.

The book starts off with a chapter by one of the editors, Sean Jacobs, which sketches the broader political outline in which this mediation is taking place. In outlining the process of identity formation and cultural shifts after apartheid, researchers and social scientists must engage with the particularities of history and with the South African localities. Jacobs's chapter locates the role and impact of mass media in South African cultural life in the context of its broader political and economic transition. It examines the main approaches to the transition in South Africa and tries to clarify their understandings of media and its relationship to broader societal changes. Jacobs argues that debates about mass media in South Africa are simultaneously debates about the nature of social change, and that they refer back to the still-unresolved questions about the transition, usually without quite saying so and sometimes while appearing to have nothing to do with mass media.

Several contributors to this book touch upon the ways in which popular art forms such as hip-hop, kwaito and techno trance music contribute to identity formation. The first of these, Stephanie Marlin-Curiel, also examines the relationship between identity and popular music, in this case Afrikaner identity and electronic music. She writes about the performances of one Heine du Toit, who borrows the name of the Afrikaner poet D.J. Opperman as his stage name, and samples the words and voices of apartheid prime ministers, an Afrikaans storyteller, and a well-known rugby commentator, among others. He also uses visual images evocative of traditional Afrikaner identity. The result is "a journey at once critical, celebratory, and healing". Marlin-Curiel suggests that in this combination of stimuli, Du Toit/Opperman "succeeded in submerging the revellers in the dream space of their youth, while propping one eye open to a sardonic vision of the past". The largely white, Afrikaans-speaking rave-goers were also exposed to a hip-hop group from the Cape Flats and kwaito music in Afrikaans. Bringing together Afrikaans-speaking musicians from varied racial and cultural backgrounds, Marlin-Curiel argues, the rave sought to reposition Afrikaans from its place as the "language of the oppressor" to the lingua franca of alternative youth culture, establishing an Afrikaner identity that is both Afrikaans and African. The party acknowledged black speakers of Afrikaans (mainly coloured) but also raised a number of questions. As a result, emerging cultural expressions such as this one must be evaluated with an eye that is both hopeful and skeptical. The current identity crisis of Afrikaans speakers, black and white, is not an entirely new phenomenon. While the 1980s "Alternatiewe Afrikaans" movement fought against the deployment of Afrikaans as a symbol of Afrikaner power, the current alternative Afrikaans movement tries to rescue Afrikaans from the present cultural stigmatisation of Afrikaans and moral stigmatisation of Afrikaner youth. In Marlin-Curiel's view, democratisation may seem like an opportunity for plural identity and equal cultural representation, but if democratisation is ultimately to rectify material inequalities inherited from an apartheid past, then the urge to formulate a "new" South African identity must take on, rather than omit, the wrongs of the past.

Gibson Boloka highlights the intersection between popular music and societal change. His chapter explores the genealogy of kwaito music, tracing its origin both to processes of globalisation as well as to its particular local political, social and economic context. The chapter demonstrates how culture has changed from being just a nucleus of society to an instrument of change through which social relations are transformed. Boloka uses a cultural studies approach to examine the changing patterns in the production, distribution and consumption of kwaito and how that impacts on social relations. He comments on three aspects of kwaito, namely kwaito as a disengagement with sociopolitical discourse; kwaito as a break with tradition; and kwaito as a reflection of post-apartheid society. In South Africa, these three developments mark the end of the political struggle through the creation of a new society. It also demonstrates how media recreate a new society by implanting a new "common" culture based on consumption. It is through this culture that new identities are forged. Boloka demonstrates that culture is a means through which societies reflect on and make sense of their experiences. Since these experiences vary as shaped by different classes, gender, ethnicity, race and so forth, they will inevitably be contested. The chapter furthermore points to the significance of the political transition in shaping the development of kwaito in South Africa that in turn created new identities based on consumption. The evolution of kwaito, Boloka argues, marks the dawn of a democratic era bringing with it freedom of expression, and various genres of popular music consumed in South Africa therefore have to be interpreted within the freedom of expression paradigm. He also points out that consumer taste shifts constantly and thus makes the consumption of popular music unpredictable.

Jane Battersby argues in her chapter that South African hip-hop as a genre is a form of postcolonial text and as such offers opportunities for new identities by the South African coloured community. She is of the opinion that popular music can be a tool for developing a powerful and common language of resistance against the legacies of colonialism that continue to haunt the globe. Having recognised popular culture as a potential tool for the expression of views counter to those of the powerful in society, it is vital to recognise that this apparent challenge to power is not unproblematic. By referring to four different relationships that situate popular music in the neo-colonialism debate, Battersby outlines the way in which cultural transmission takes place in hip-hop music. The adoption of rap music as a means of expression by South Africa's coloured population, she argues, is part of a powerful local and worldwide culture of resistance. Rap and its broader art form, hip-hop, can be seen as a continuation of the process of postcolonial production. By focusing on the works of the groups Prophets of da City (POC), Black Noise and Brasse Vannie Kaap (BVK), Battersby uncovers four major forms of "blackness" that have been adopted by Cape Town-based coloured hip-hoppers. The importance of locality and specific histories in the analysis of identity construction, as we argued above, is again brought to the fore when Battersby emphasises that coloured youth identities are rooted in local historical experiences of the population from the constructed shame associated with miscegenation, their gradual political disenfranchisement, the Group Areas Act and the current experiences of marginalisation. These and other factors unique to Cape Town's coloured population have had implications for identity that are now being expressed through hip-hop.

The complex relationship between the old and the new in cultural expression also forms a central part of the chapter by Farzanah Badsha. She uses a case study of the hip-hop scene in Cape Town in the late 1990s to show the many and vibrant negotiations of identity that have been facilitated by South Africa's headlong rush into hypermodernity. Badsha warns, however, that in the rush to rethink things we should not forget that change is never a simple process and that it never occurs in a logical order with the old simply being replaced by the new. In discussing different "schools" of hip-hop, Badsha touches upon a central thesis of this book, namely that in examining the new forms of identity coming into being through cultural expression, one should not lose sight of the ways in which this renegotiation of identity is still informed by old configurations and conditions. Badsha shows that in a country such as South Africa, where because of the policies of apartheid there are such vast differences in the levels of development, different moments of modernity co-exist with one another. For this reason it would be problematic to ignore or dramatically downplay "the political", "resistance" and especially the notions of race and class while uncritically embracing the concepts of multiculturalism, hybridity or creolisation. Instead, as Badsha convincingly demonstrates in her chapter, one needs to be flexible and open enough to be able to see how the past and the present are in constant negotiation and that it is within this negotiation that many of the most exciting and creative innovations occur.

Through a discussion of the conflict and contestation in the Cape Town hip-hop scene around authenticity, Badsha makes it evident that this sort of discourse is not about rigid boundaries between old and new or the commodified and uncommodified, but is instead a negotiation of the changes that South African youth culture has had to adapt to since the early 1990s. Rather than it being about a break between old and new, it is about having to renegotiate identities in the context of much more rapid change and easier flows of information and meanings. Badsha argues that it is imperative, when reconsidering South African culture and youth culture in particular, to broaden the field of inquiry beyond the narrow and restrictive tools of politics, resistance, race and class. At the same time, though, these tools for helping to understand the society cannot be totally discarded, because what is needed is an approach that can take into account the many levels of complexity and meaning which people are negotiating every day to navigate through their identities as well as their everyday practices of life. It is for this reason that there has to be sufficient space to accommodate ambiguity and sometimes confusing complexity.

In his discussion of the presence of South African languages on the Internet, Herman Wasserman points out how material factors inherited from the past have an impact on this new medium. Wasserman is of the opinion that the "digital divide", a term that has gained popular currency in indicating the economic disparities correlating with lack of access to global new media, hampers the realisation in cyberspace of the post-apartheid ideal of multilingualism. He outlines how the Internet opens up new possibilities for cultural empowerment, but at the same time to a large extent still mimics the divisions of the past. While the Internet has benefited sections of the Afrikaans community, especially at a time in which their language has lost much of its public functions and is now considered as one of the minority languages in South Africa, the same cannot be said of other South African languages other than English. Wasserman points out that examples of other indigenous South African languages on the Internet are hard to find and links this to the fact that inequalities regarding Internet access in South Africa are still largely in line with the economic divisions created by apartheid. However, he also notes positive developments, such as the cross-cultural activity on certain South African websites where new hybrid identities are being negotiated.

The performing arts sector in South Africa has undergone radical changes since the demise of apartheid. In his chapter, Keith Bain argues that many of these changes are not simply related to the new sociopolitical environment, but have their roots in global developments as well as revitalised thinking with regards to what constitutes "theatre" or "performance". Some of the more interesting developments, Bain points out, relate to a rediscovery of indigenous cultural traditions which have infused contemporary performance forms in order to produce something unique, fresh and potentially appealing to both local and international markets. To discuss in a few pages the many faces of South African theatre would be an impossible task. His chapter, then, is not an overview of the performing arts scene, but a brief investigation, tracing some of the effects of the post-apartheid climate on the way in which South African theatre is being created for local audiences.

Bain indicates how the Western emphasis on literary culture that has dominated colonial South Africa has effectively erased thousands of years of indigenous history and limited perceptions of sociocultural life in the region. More specifically, indigenous theatre (or performance) – which existed as a structured and formal system before the arrival of European colonisers – has been mostly forgotten since it had never been reduced to the written word. In recent years, the development of a form of theatre that is uniquely South African, that blends and integrates the performance styles of two distinct traditions – those of Africa and those brought to the subcontinent from the Western world – has emerged as an area of significant interest. "Syncretic" theatre or "hybrid" and "crossover" theatre are terms given to performance forms which make use of thematic and formal elements from a range of traditional as well as imported forms, giving rise to something that is original and potentially unique. To the concept of a hybridised theatrical form, Bain adds the notion of "total theatre", and, more radically, "hyper-theatricality", or the idea of performance that surpasses the framework of any theatrical forebear. Such "theatre" is necessarily eclectic, drawing on diverse and even disparate styles in order to produce work that might well be termed postmodern. It is a merger between old and new, Western and African, ritual and commercial performance cultures.

Within this framework of theatre and performance, Bain looks at a number of issues regarding the development of the local theatre industry. From his discussion of these issues and recent examples of theatrical performances, Bain concludes that the real challenge for South African theatre practitioners lies in the rediscovery of a tradition in which performance is a part of everyday life, and not merely a part of marginal or fringe culture.

The recent societal changes that South Africa underwent can also be observed in South African literature. Not only does literature reflect changes in society, but it also discursively constructs new identities and positions subjects within these changed contexts. In their respective chapters, Phaswane Mpe and Marthinus Beukes investigate recent examples of literary texts which can be read from this point of view. Mpe discusses the representation of cities undergoing transformation in the post-apartheid era and Beukes looks at the construction of a new gender identity in a post-patriarchal context. In his chapter, Mpe reminds us that change often catches the imagination of writers, and provides impetus for their writing. In many instances, change – whether social, political, economic or cultural – is accompanied by dramatic acts of violence and acute feelings of dislocation, insecurity and anxiety. These feelings can simultaneously be accompanied by a sense of hope for the future, while a successful management of change can lead to much joy and happiness, Mpe argues. How writers engage with the nature of change, and the intensity of the feelings it engenders in them and their respective communities, depends on how individual writers perceive the change, on what they see as its most compelling challenges and possible prospects. According to Mpe, literature often focuses on cities – or pockets of them – because they are an embodiment of a major change, one or some of its aspects, or a significant exception to a general rule or expectation. One of the reasons that Sophiatown loomed large in South African literature, for example, has been the fact that it was one of the *mixed* areas in a country in which, during the apartheid days, places were defined in terms of only white, Indian, coloured or black. This is to say that Sophiatown was something of a glaring *anomaly*. In his analysis of the way the city is being represented in recent literary texts, Mpe focuses on the Johannesburg suburb of Hillbrow. This suburb has in recent years been associated with degeneration, decay and violent crime. Mpe shows, with reference to recent texts, that the popular stereotype of the neighbourhood as nothing but evil and dangerous is being interrogated in literature. In his view, this trend is in line with the role of literature in a changing society: to ask questions, to wonder, to challenge and, when appropriate, to contradict, to reinforce, to celebrate and to entertain.

Antjie Krog is one of the foremost poets in Afrikaans. As a social commentator and journalist covering the Truth and Reconciliation Commission, the experience of which resulted in an award-winning book, *Country of My Skull*, Krog has also gained wider influence locally and internationally. Recently, a selection of her poems has also been translated into English (*Down to My Last Skin*, Random House). Although her importance is therefore not limited to an Afrikaans audience, it is especially within this literature that she has brought renewal. In his chapter, Marthinus Beukes focuses on her work in the context of gender identity. In her poetry we find a recording of the woman who has reconquered her body, but who has also recovered the text as metaphor for the body. It can indeed be said that her poetry becomes a narrative of that woman who has undergone a new birth, a rebirth in body and text.

"Gynogenesis" as a discourse of power is a corrective on the patriarchal discourse of power, but also on the militancy of extreme feminism. Krog's poetry becomes a report of this changing content of consciousness whereby gynogenesis as a transforming situation is written in ink and blood. In this way she formulates an ideolectic style characteristic of the woman who discovers herself in writing and proclaims herself as human being, therefore more than woman. The impact of gynogenesis as a social condition can be related to the changing contents of social consciousness. Change has therefore also taken place in the field of literature where the dehumanising patriarchal ideology of power was dealt with by feminism. Gynogenesis as a discourse of power expands feminist views and affirms a new image for the woman in literature: that of the New Woman. Through the analysis of a poem by Krog, Beukes shows how Krog uses language to confirm gynogenesis. Not only does Krog emphasise the woman's need for a self-directed sexual expectation, but also the use of language to reinforce her new image. It is indeed a bodily conversation with the self and fellow women. By way of a textual analysis, Beukes indicates how Krog ingenuously demonstrates the woman's living in a new guise – the image of a recolonised figure.

Still on the topic of identity, but in a different sphere, is the chapter of Julian Jonker. On April 14, 1996, not quite two years after South Africa's first democratic elections, the South African National Gallery hosted the opening of an exhibition by artist and fine art lecturer Pippa Skotnes. The exhibition was titled *Miscast: Negotiating Khoisan History and Material Culture*, and was an attempt by Skotnes to portray, not Khoisan history and material culture, but the representations of the Khoisan that were constructed during the encounters between Khoisan and colonist, and what these representations tell about both European and Khoisan. While the exhibition was praised by some, it also met with vociferous criticism. The fiercest opposition to the exhibition was voiced by Yvette Abrahams, at the time in the History Department of the University of Cape Town (UCT) and a member of the !Hurikamma Cultural Movement. Abrahams entered into a debate with Skotnes in the pages of the *Southern African Review of Books*. Their debate concerned the representations of the Khoisan people and the right to represent Khoisan history and culture. This tug of war over the power of representation pivots about two focal issues: cultural ownership and social identity. What Jonker attempts in this chapter is the beginnings of a formulation of the relationship between, on the one hand, the ownership of cultural forms of expression, and on the other hand, the discourses of identity accompanying such expression. In this way he seeks to develop a framework that could apply to legal and cultural discourses in post-apartheid South Africa. He outlines a framework in terms of which norms of ownership and discourses of identity can be seen to be interrelated in the practice of culture, and indicates how the theoretical work on law and society might be used practically to extend the imagination of legal scholarship.

The creation and perpetuation of stereotypes by the media is also the topic of Patrice Kabeya-Mwepu and Sean Jacobs's chapter. While migration to South Africa is not a new phenomenon, a new wave of wars and violent conflicts in West, Central and East Africa have brought a new wave of refugees to South Africa, from countries as diverse as Nigeria, Sierra Leone, Congo (both the Democratic Republic or former Zaire as well as Congo-Brazzaville), Angola, Somalia, Ethiopia and Eritrea. Similarly, the demise of formal apartheid has created new and as yet only partially understood opportunities for migration to South Africa. Their discussion deals with the overwhelmingly negative media coverage of immigrants and refugees, and the way media reports uncritically reproduce problematic statistics and assumptions about cross-border migration. By referring to literature on the subject as well as a study conducted among refugees and migrants living in Cape Town's townships, they find that the mainstream media do not engage critically with the dominant human rights framework as it relates to refugees and immigrants. However, some media have contributed to a counter-discourse regarding migrants and refugees, aimed at breaking down xenophobia by spreading information and challenging stereotypes and assumptions. The chapter goes on to discuss these media, among them publications produced by refugees themselves. Kabeya-Mwepu and Jacobs conclude that media campaigns are not enough to deal with attitudes about refugees and migrants in South Africa and emphasise the limitation of an intellectual approach to combating xenophobia. They suggest that further research be done on the role of the media in anti-xenophobia campaigns and how this might include a more emotional rather than intellectual approach to the problem.

The question of gender representation also forms the focus of Lene Øverland's chapter, but where Beukes examined the birth of the new woman in Krog's poetry, Øverland examines the perpetuation of the dominant patriarchal ideology in advertising. Her chapter focuses on advertising content and represents a snapshot case study of gender representations in contemporary post-apartheid South African advertising campaigns in the mainstream media. The main objective of this chapter is to investigate how advertising content reproduce and reflect gender and sexual stereotypes in post-apartheid South Africa. The chapter further elaborates on the following questions: Do race and class mediate messages that reflect gender and sexual stereotypes? How do members of various communities read and reflect around gendered and sexual stereotypes and what impact do these messages have on people's lives? In doing so, the chapter places the specific case study within a historical framework that explores the development and structure of the South African advertising industry.

Two chapters deal with questions of media and identity in the Muslim community in South Africa. Both essays take as their focus developments around the emergence in 1995 of the vigilante group, People Against Gangsterism and Drugs (Pagad). Its stated aims were to remove gangsters and end the sale of drugs in communities on the Cape Flats. Although it claimed a diverse support base, it had an overwhelmingly Muslim face. In 1996, a group of Pagad supporters publicly executed one of Cape Town's most notorious gang leaders, catapulting the organisation, and the presence of gangs, into the public space. The first of the two contributions, by Suren Pillay, is an attempt to problematise representations of both Pagad and gangs in the media and academic studies. Pillay suggests that the representations and studies were based on a set of politico-philosophical assumptions that led to the generic categorisations of these phenomena. From these categorisations derivative discourses offering programmatic solutions arose. His findings are that the identity of the gangster in Cape Town – as derivative of poverty, as anti-social, as a result of the Group Areas Act – and that of Pagad – as representative of a homogenous Islam and as the local incarnation of a global "Islamic threat" – obscure their particularity and specificity. Instead, argues Pillay, a richer grasp of their constitutive dynamics will be obtained if we explore their identities as nonstatic "processes". These processes involve locating identity formation within the interface of globality and locality: the symbolic borderlands of a structured contingency, which brings to the fore the constitutive conditions of ambiguity and hybridity.

The intersection between Muslim identity and media is also explored in Gabeba Baderoon's chapter. Baderoon departs from colonial discourse theory and Edward Said's thesis of Orientalism. She argues that an unacknowledged level of fantasy informs journalism, and that this becomes evident in the analysis of coverage of "race". After outlining earlier patterns of representation of Muslims in South African newspapers, she goes on to focus on the reporting surrounding a specific incident that occurred in Cape Town during late 1996 which represented a crisis on several levels. This incident, the public murder of gang leader Rashaad Staggie, was widely reported in the media. Baderoon explains how the coverage of this incident ties into Western fantasies about the Orient. In doing this, she discusses the image of the veiled woman and its place in the Western imagination, but also the stereotypical representation of the Muslim man and its significance in fulfilling discursive needs in the media. By using images of the veiled Muslim woman and the masked Muslim man, Baderoon argues, the newspapers in question created a blank space upon which Oriental clichés could be written. She concludes that media representations of the Staggie incident linked images of Muslims and Islam unremittingly with violence, threat and exoticism. The complex history, subjectivities and politics of varied Muslim communities were subsumed under a stereotype of violence and threat. The challenge that faces the media, Baderoon concludes, is to find new ways of speaking about Islam without reverting to binary thought. There are a great many complexities, many of them local, which need to be explored if we are to understand events like this in the Western Cape that have to do with organisations such as Pagad and criminal gangs. The organisation is made up of a diverse range of competing elements. Amongst these elements are contested meanings of Islam, its role in a plural society, party-political legitimacy, a normative disdain for drug abuse and gangsterism, and elements of gung-ho machismo. It is also one narrative within a wider range of Islamic narratives, which are being constructed using global and local symbols, which produce specific and hybridised Muslim identities. These are intimately connected to the "routes" of these symbols produced within colonialism, globalisation and the post-apartheid period. It presents us with an assemblage of tensions that are intensely internal and local, while at the same time being external and global.

We have noted above that identities are fluid and constantly changing with the social context and old identities are challenged, renegotiated or contested. In her chapter, Melissa Steyn notes how Eurocentric constructions of modernity are increasingly being challenged. A growing community of scholars emphasises that a critical examination of how "white" people experience their *own* racialisation – analyses which expose the inner workings of racially privileged positions – is crucial to the task of dismantling the power which "race" has to structure unequal societies. The aftermath of South Africa's first democratic elections of 1994 did not only see the end of official white rule, but also the beginnings of processes of reconciliation and reconstruction. However, these are being undertaken within the legacy of deep-seated intercultural and racial conflict, and the societal deformation left by the structures of apartheid and three hundred years of hegemonic colonial discourses. Major re-alignments are taking place and a new power balance between the cultural groupings in South Africa is being established. The African majority has gained political power, and for the first time in the history of the country, white people are losing the position from which they have been able to define both self and other.

The defence of the practices of whiteness – always somewhat precariously maintained in a country in which whites were numerically a small minority – depends largely on psychological misrecognition, personal inflation and denial, Steyn argues. Since the early 1990s, white South Africans have been adapting to a situation where white "self and other" constructions are challenged by the society that is evolving around them. The dominant societal dynamics are inimical to the perpetuation of privileged whiteness and a new sense of self consequently has to be forged on different terms. Studying how white South Africans represent this new situation is therefore interesting in terms of how the loss of racial entitlement is experienced subjectively. In her chapter Steyn does this by analysing two films that were screened on the popular film circuit in the immediate post-1994 period. The chapter examines the portrayal of whiteness in these films, and what these representations suggest about how the broader white society was responding to being socially repositioned. Steyn's analysis brings to light that these films seem to reflect a deep-seated ambivalence and inner conflict in white society in relation to the changes to which they were being asked to adjust. The impulse towards escapism, denial, withdrawal, and even passive aggression is evident, creating a tension that pulls against the need, whether idealistic or pragmatic in inspiration, to be reconciled with new realities. Her analysis suggests that the prognosis circa 1994 was that if white society was to contribute with commitment to reconciliation and reconstruction within the broader society, a great deal of emotional work would need to be done to enable white people to find ways of imagining what it means to be "white" differently.

In another discussion of visual art and the construction of identity, René Smith looks at a popular television series and its sequel that have been broadcast on South African television since the late nineties. The series, *Yizo Yizo,* deals with the culture of learning and teaching and attempts to address the crisis in education by exposing a barrage of issues impacting on the learning process for many young people. These include rape, harassment, lack of educational materials, problems relating to motivation of learners and educators, corporal punishment, drug abuse, crime and corruption. Smith points out that the synergy between "exposing" and "challenging" these issues is extremely contentious in itself. This is particularly problematic when assessed within the precise "real-life" context which *Yizo Yizo* purports to represent. In relation to representations of violence against women, for example, the series exists within the context of an extremely high rate of sexual violence against women.

Smith notes that *Yizo Yizo* is an important text, which has contributed to, if not instigated, extensive debate around the crisis in South African schools. Smith interrogates *Yizo Yizo* by examining issues of genre and "reality", in particular representations of women and gender-based violence. She suggests that (mis)representations of young women in the series perpetuate the dominant patriarchal ideology, thereby obliterating the series' counter-hegemonic potential. Furthermore, she argues that in neglecting to challenge the existing order and to interrogate issues relating to violence against women in particular (accepting that this constitutes a significant part of the series), *Yizo Yizo* contributes to naturalising existing gender relations and perceptions of violence against women. Smith is of the opinion that the series falls short of its (potential) counter-hegemonic narrative in so far as it refrains from exposing the myth of the "conditions" of township high schools. In so doing the viewer is left with the dominant ideological positioning of the forces of evil as responsible for a state of disequilibrium.

It is our hope that this book might lead to a better understanding of some of the complexities that arise when one starts analysing the processes of mediation that contribute to the formation of identity in South Africa today. For us, especially the editors, it was an exciting project, and we hope that others will share in this excitement.

The book is not intended as the final word on media, culture and identity in post-apartheid South Africa. On the contrary, it seeks to indicate the manifold ways in which one can look at these issues and tries to convey a sense of the speed with which they change – and yet how certain legacies still remain. The most we can hope for is that the contributions contained in this book might be the starting point for debate and discussion. If a critical re-evaluation of our society, our identities and the process by which these come into being could result from this debate, this book would have succeeded in its aim.

Notes

1 Krista Johnson and Keyan Tomaselli provided comments on the main arguments of this introduction.

2 See the exchange between one of the editors and Nuttall on these issues on the S-Africa Listserv of the webportal, Humanities-Net (http://www.h-net.msu).

References

Hall, Stuart. 1994. Cultural Identity and Diaspora. In: Williams, Patrick en Laura Chrisman. 1994 (1993). *Colonial Discourse and Post-Colonial Theory. A Reader.* New York, London etc: Harvester Wheatsheaf. 392-403.

Nuttall, Sarah and Michael, Cheryl-Ann. 2000. Introduction to *Senses of Culture: South African Culture Studies.* Cape Town: Oxford University Press. 1-27.

Spivak, Gayatri. 1990. *The Post-Colonial Critic. Interviews, Strategies, Dialogues.* (ed. Sarah Harasym). London: Routledge.

Oliphant, Andries Walter (ed.). 1999. Introduction to *At the Rendezvous of Victory and Other Stories.* Cape Town: Kwela Books.

Zegeye, Abebe. 2001. Imposed ethnicity. In: Zegeye, Abebe. 2001. *Social Identities in the New South Africa.* Cape Town and Maroelana: Kwela Books and South African History Online.

CHAPTER TWO

Reading Politics, Reading Media

Sean Jacobs[1]

Introduction

Identity and cultural transformation cannot be divorced from material factors and historical legacies. As is argued elsewhere in this book, academic responses to the profound changes currently experienced in South Africa are often characterised by the transplanting of the tools of enquiry already in use around the world to the local context to re-view and re-understand our society (cf. Nuttall and Michael 2000). While investigating the emergence of new identities, the renegotiation of cultural boundaries and the manifestation of hybridity in a variety of forms, this book departs from the understanding that any theory that deals with post-apartheid South Africa would have to be rooted first of all in local specificity, while simultaneously locating change and transformations in a global and continental setting. In outlining the process of identity formation and cultural shifts after apartheid, researchers and social scientists must engage with the particularities of history and engage with the South African localities. For this reason, this chapter locates the role and impact of mass media in South African cultural life in the context of its broader political and economic transition. It examines the main approaches to the transition in South Africa and tries to clarify their understandings of media and its relationship to broader societal changes. That is, I argue that debates about mass media in South Africa are simultaneously debates about the nature of social change, and that they refer back to the still-unresolved questions about the transition, usually without quite saying so and sometimes while appearing to have nothing to do with mass media. I look at ways in which contending approaches to the transition understand (or imply an understanding of) the relationship between politics and mass media in order to clear up what is really at stake in debates about the South African media: the nature of the transition and the workings of post-1994 South African society.

There is as yet no consensus about the fundamental cause, nature and meaning of South Africa's ongoing democratic transition. Scholars, mainly political scientists and historians, have approached these questions in a number of ways. Among the most prominent of these approaches are what I will refer to as the political-legal approach, which encompasses institutionalism, rational choice and "pactology", and opposed to it, neo-Marxist analysis and its variants. Each of these orientations has specific implications for the role and impact of mass media on the transition and in post-1994 democratic South Africa, and for the construction and renegotiation of identity as well as cultural transformations.

In my view, the political-legal approach to the transition risks over-personalising history and obscuring the structural underpinnings of the transition and, by implication, the role and place of the mass media in it. The rational choice approach, for its part, fails to deal with real political phenomena; similarly pactology, while breaking somewhat with rational choice, also relies primarily on ahistorical schemas without making adequate provision for the specificity of the South African case. Finally, the neo-Marxist approach, while it avoids these other pitfalls, is prone to reductionism – failing, for example, to adequately understand the role of the media in forming and reflecting public opinion. I will outline these objections, and then show how debates about media as such are linked to these distinct understandings of the transition. I will then offer a preliminary outline of an approach that I believe synthesises the strengths of these approaches while avoiding some of their weaknesses and offer an approach that can background approaches to social phenomena, like cultural change and identity construction in South Africa at the beginning of the twenty-first century, but also in other spheres or topics. I will suggest that the approaches to media reviewed here, rarely, if ever, interrogate the political character and effects of mass media in the post-1994 political and cultural life or its interaction with changes to the broader political system. The political-legal approach predictably offers overly optimistic views of the South African media landscape; the Marxist approach is content to deliver unrealistic policy prescriptions that ignore demand for commercial media and often at the expense of diversity. While correct in identifying a close relationship between media and democracy, both "families" of approaches reduce that relationship too much: either "pluralism leads to free media" or "free media leads to pluralism".

Probably the most significant intervention I want to offer is that media play a leading role in the transition in South Africa. While the media did not cause the former regime to break down or trigger the transition to democracy, they did play crucial roles in determining how, when, and to what degree democratisation took shape in both the transition and consolidation period. This prominence of the media coincides with the decline of more direct means of deliberation and the rise of indirect forms of democracy. Mass media emerge as political and social actors in their own right. First, though, I will offer a brief overview of the main contours of the political and economic transition.

From Apartheid to Democracy and Beyond

F.W. de Klerk's decision on 2 February 1990 to begin negotiating the demise of apartheid, followed by South Africa's democratic elections in April 1994, as well as the initial performance of the new democratic state, have provoked numerous attempts at explanation by political scientists and historians especially (Howarth 1998:193; Guelke 1999; Bond 2000). One result has been a pluralisation of the theoretical idioms used to analyse South African politics and society.

When reviewing the events of just more than a decade since 1990, it is easy to understand why many writers and analysts have likened South Africa's transition to a "miracle" or stressed its "lessons" for other "divided societies" (cf. Hain 1996; Sparks 1996; Guelke 1999; Marais 1998). Observers worldwide have often marvelled at the apparent consensus achieved between the major protagonists, and it was indeed a massive undertaking. However, the awe with which the transition is regarded may also tend to obscure some of the continuities in South African society, particularly economic inequality.

The first two years of formal constitutional negotiations after 1990 were unproductive. The initial meetings set the context for a narrow political transition, which de-emphasised transformation of the economy. By December 1991, the negotiating forum, the Convention for a Democratic South Africa (Codesa), had its first formal meeting. In May 1992 Codesa collapsed over disagreements between the National Party (NP) and the African National Congress (ANC) over constitutional-change mechanisms. The ANC wanted the Constitution to be drawn up by an elected Constituent Assembly (CA), made up of the members of the two Houses of the proposed Parliament after democratic elections had been held. In contrast, the NP wanted an interim Constitution to be agreed on by Codesa and passed by the then whites-only Parliament, with the final Constitution passed by the CA (cf. Solomons 1998). A month later all contact between the two main parties was broken off by the ANC leadership furious over the massacre of 48 ANC supporters in the township of Boipatong outside Johannesburg. (A subsequent independent investigation was scathing of police inaction during the attack as well as the quality of the investigation.)

In August 1992, a new mass action campaign by the ANC and its allies targeted homeland governments opposed to the ANC's agenda. The "homelands", known more popularly as bantustans, were created in the early 1960s as a response by the apartheid government to the process of decolonisation sweeping through Africa at the time. In this scheme, franchise rights were extended to the African majority but only within geographically bound and fragmented entities. The logic of this scheme was the eventual denationalisation of the majority of black South Africans and their reconstitution as foreign citizens "exercising full political rights outside of South Africa's [white] constitutional order" (Klug 2000:40). Known to the apartheid government as "separate development", it resulted in the establishment of four "independent" bantustans and aimed to engineer a permanent balkanisation of the country. These bantustans were Transkei,

Bophuthatswana, Venda and Ciskei (the so-called "TBVC-states"). A further set of "self-governing territories" was later added, but not granted "independence". These included KwaZulu-Natal, Gazankulu and KaNgwane. Many of these "governments" colluded openly with the apartheid state, were characterised by repression and were hostile to the ANC or internal resistance movements.[2]

The ANC and its allies (principally the trade union federation Cosatu and the South African Communist Party) specifically targeted the Ciskei homeland situated in the Eastern Cape, and its leader Oupa Gqozo. On September 7, 1992, this campaign went horribly wrong for the ANC when Ciskei armed forces fired at protesters marching on the homeland's capital, killing 28 demonstrators and injuring 200 others.

Despite all this, that same month, the NP and the ANC signed a "Record of Understanding" to restart negotiations; soon after, bilateral deal-making between the two parties commenced again. A key moment came when Joe Slovo, leader of the South African Communist Party (SACP) published his "Strategic Perspectives" document, which contained a number of "sunset clauses". These included that white civil servants (which essentially meant almost *all* civil servants) and members of the largely white security forces would retain their jobs for the initial post-apartheid period (for five years). Despite initial and widespread opposition within ANC circles, the proposals soon gained broad acceptance.[3] They also had the crucial effect of putting white fears at ease: after all, the SACP was viewed with extreme trepidation by most whites and Slovo was considered by many in elite circles in the white community – including the media – to be a hardliner (Sparks 1995:118; Waldmeir 1997:214).

However, on 16 November 1992, Judge Richard Goldstone,[4] who was appointed by De Klerk (under pressure from Mandela) to investigate allegations of violence by security forces, announced the existence of a "directorate of covert collection". This directorate had engaged in "dirty tricks", including "hit squad" killings of apartheid's opponents, and fomented violence in black townships and between black opposition groups after 1990. According to Goldstone's investigations the violations had taken place with the full knowledge of the senior corps of the armed forces. De Klerk claimed he knew nothing of this, suspended some generals, and closed down the unit. However, suspicion remained. It would contribute to Mandela's distrust in the face of De Klerk's palpable failure as state president to do something about the violence in black communities (Mandela 1995).

Despite these setbacks, by early 1993 the NP had come to accept the inevitability of some form of "one person, one vote" democratic majority rule. This paved the way for open elections in April 1994. But setbacks did not cease. On 10 April 1993, Chris Hani, the general secretary of the SACP and a probable successor to Mandela, was murdered in a white right-wing conspiracy. The country erupted in violence, beyond De Klerk's ability to restore order. He was forced to turn to Mandela, who appeared on state television in a national broadcast and successfully calmed his angry supporters. On that day, Mandela appeared as the country's de facto president, lending a sense of inevitability to the transition process, and calming white fears in the process (Waldmeir 1997:276; Krabill 2002).

In another setback, on 25 June 1993, right-wing demonstrators attacked the World Trade Centre outside Johannesburg where formal negotiations were taking place. However, transitional negotiations were back "on schedule" when in July 1993 an election date was set and shortly after the multiparty negotiating forum endorsed the interim Constitution. The whites-only Parliament passed the interim Constitution in November 1993 (the last piece of major legislation it would pass). In December 1993 the Transitional Executive Council, a sort of parallel government, was set up.

Hani's murder and the June demonstrations were not the end of the political violence though. On 25 July 1993, five gunmen of Apla (African People's Liberation Army),[5] the military wing of the Pan Africanist Congress (PAC) which served as the ANC's main rival for the loyalty of the black majority, burst into a Cape Town church, killing 12 people and injuring 56 others. On 30 August 1993, a large number of people were killed in Tembisa township outside Johannesburg when Inkatha Freedom Party (IFP)-aligned hostel dwellers attacked township residents, while the police stood by. On 7 September of that year, 24 people were murdered in Wadeville outside Johannesburg, and a month later on 6 October, a crack squad of the South African army burst into a house in the capital of the Transkei homeland (whose leader at the time was sympathetic to the ANC and the PAC) and "mistakenly" killed five teenagers while ostensibly looking for Apla members. By year-end, 5 706 people had been killed in political violence since 1990.

The early part of 1994 was characterised by last-ditch resistance from two homeland governments (Bophuthatswana and Ciskei), the refusal of the IFP and the white right wing to participate in elections, as well as bombing campaigns by disparate right-wing and extreme black nationalist factions. However, none of this could break the momentum for a settlement; in fact, its effect was to strengthen the tendency towards "pacting" by black and white moderate elites (bringing their supporters along) in the ANC and the NP. In a turnaround, the IFP and the Freedom Front (an Afrikaner group led by a former head of the apartheid army and probably the most prominent and well-organised formation of the white right wing) relented at the eleventh hour and participated in the elections.

On 27 and 28 April 1994, South Africans of all races went to the polls. Voting took place simultaneously for national and provincial assemblies. The process, to the surprise of many, went off peacefully, except in KwaZulu-Natal where a decade of clashes between the ANC and the IFP provided the backdrop to the elections. Results indicated a 62,5% win to the ANC nationally, giving the party majorities in both national Houses of Parliament – the National Assembly and the Senate.[6] The NP finished a distant second with just above 20% of the votes, followed by the IFP, the white "liberal" Democratic Party, the PAC, the African Christian Democratic Party and the Freedom Front. Nelson Mandela, the revered leader of the liberation struggle and international symbol of democracy in South Africa, was voted the first democratic president, with Thabo Mbeki, highly regarded in the exiled wing of the ANC, as his deputy. Special provisions in the interim Constitution guaranteed a deputy presidential berth to the NP (De Klerk took this position) as well as a number of Cabinet seats in a Government of National Unity (GNU). Continuing this consensus-style rule, the IFP was also awarded a number of Cabinet seats. The ANC ruled seven of the nine provinces and entered into provincial coalition governments with the IFP in KwaZulu-Natal and with the NP in the Western Cape. A final Constitution was passed two years later, establishing the Constitutional Court, and setting up of a number of institutions "in support of democracy" such as the Human Rights Commission, the Independent Electoral Commission, the Public Protector, and the Gender Commission. The formal institutions of democracy were thus in place.

Outside the legislative sphere the ANC government, especially Nelson Mandela, worked hard to foster a climate of "reconciliation" to appease the white population. Some of these measures include Mandela's highly publicised visit to the home of the widow of Hendrik Verwoerd, considered the architect of apartheid, controversially suspending earlier talks for a "wealth tax", as well as setting some limits on the Truth and Reconciliation Commission (TRC), that was set up to investigate apartheid human rights abuses.[7]

In mid-1995 and early 1996, South Africa held its first "nonracial" local elections for new, restructured municipal councils, and in June 1999 the country held its second nationwide general elections. Mandela, breaking with trends on the African continent, stood down after one term, making way for Thabo Mbeki. The second set of local elections took place in November 2000. All of these elections went off relatively peacefully and "freely".[8]

The period from the release of Nelson Mandela and the unbanning of the liberation movements, including the constitutional negotiations, and lasting up until the April 1994 first democratic elections, which fundamentally reformed the political system, was also crucial for setting the fundamental rules of the game as far as the media regime and its place in the social order after the end of apartheid was concerned. Media, particularly television, became crucial in creating an "audience of transition", and to establish political capital for the transition (as "smooth transition"), which in its earlier phases was characterised by high levels of violence, murder and instability (cf. Nixon 1995; Bell 2001; Peretti 2001; Krabill 2002).[9]

The political negotiations between the major political players that dominated the period gave rise to and impacted directly on sector-wide negotiations between major players in the media sector and on arts and culture initiatives at the time. The main features of these debates and discussions were that the political players (represented by the ANC, the NP and big capital, both local and international, in the main) had a big stake in how the media sector (and cultural production) would turn out. As a result the divisions between media "stakeholders" largely coincided with the political divisions. For example, the deliberations about the future of broadcast media reflected very much the political stances of the two main political agents: the ANC and the NP (cf. Louw 1993). As television and radio emerged as potentially the most crucial election media, the NP and the ANC fought hard for the control of broadcasting. Secondly, a wedge was driven between the kinds of reforms pursued in the broadcast sector as opposed to print. Broadcasting was subjected to extensive legislative reform that resulted in the SABC's monopoly being broken, while the structural underpinnings of print (meaning: ownership and control and its linking to production, distribution and advertising) continued to be governed exclusively by market principles. This would have important implications for the kind of public sphere that would develop over the long term. One final and decisive characteristic of the "media negotiations" was that the liberal democratic basis of political negotiations permeated the tone, nature and extent of the transition within the media sector as it did in most other sectors of South African society. This, along with the second characteristic of the early 1990s reforms, had the most profound effect on the nature of the post-1994 media sector.

Specifically, the most significant changes to broadcast media were the beginnings of the South African Broadcasting Corporation's transformation from a state propaganda machine to a public broadcaster (a board of directors publicly appointed through Parliament, for example) and the establishment of the Independent Broadcasting Authority (IBA), the first agency independent of the state and the SABC to regulate broadcast licences. The IBA would ultimately be responsible for the introduction of noncommercial "community radio" immediately after the 1994 elections, as well as the simultaneous licensing of a number of new commercial radio stations to challenge the SABC's monopoly. However, the seemingly profound changes masked a series of limitations to the "opening up" of the sector.

On the surface, South Africa's media appear very "democratic" after 1994: the media are protected by the country's Constitution[10] and have the freedom to criticise government, the freedom to print oppositional voices, as well as unprecedented access to state-held information.[11] The media sector also witnessed the diversification of commercial print media with the introduction of new titles and changes in the until-now exclusive racial ownership patterns. Even the Internet, relatively underdeveloped in South Africa up to now, is presenting new possibilities.[12]

Most accounts of these events and the unprecedented changes have emphasized the subsequent proliferation of civil society organisations, including the media, nongovernmental organisations (NGOs) and trade unions, and the flowering of new cultural expressions in literature, television, dance, theatre, poetry and music. Similarly impressive has been the revival of popular protest, mainly by poor people in urban areas around basic rights to electricity, health care and affordable housing, for example. These are seen as signs of a healthy democracy (cf. Bond 2000; Marais 1998; Taylor 2002).

From the above narrative it is easy to understand what has impressed so many observers. It is also not surprising that South Africa's transition has spawned a whole academic literature, including a growing industry of consultants, on conflict resolution and consensus-building based on the South African experience, that have been exported to other "trouble-spots". In fact, applying "lessons" from the TRC elsewhere has become something of a cottage industry, resulting in opportunities for South African intellectuals to land academic posts at universities such as Harvard and the Center for Transitional Justice at New York University, as well as setting up a think tank (the Cape Town-based Institute for Justice and Reconciliation, for example) and securing a number of human rights prizes for the main personalities in that process (cf. Taylor 2002). The same can be said for the constitution-building process and individuals and groups involved in violence monitoring, mediation and conflict resolution. Cyril Ramaphosa, the ANC's chief negotiator between 1991 and 1994 and first chairperson of the Constitutional Assembly (1994-96) which drew up the "final Constitution", joined the former Finnish president Martti Ahtisaari, in overseeing the decommissioning of weapons in the Northern Ireland conflict in 2000. Although he was not included in the final United Nations investigating team following an Israeli army attack on Palestinian refugee camp Jenin in April 2002, Ramaphosa was also mentioned in connection with that mission. F.W. de Klerk, despite his unpopularity at home, is a sought-after speaker on the lucrative "lecture circuit" in North America and Western Europe. South African negotiators have also assisted in African post-war negotiations, most notably in the Democratic Republic of the Congo as well as Rwanda and Burundi (where Mandela personally intervened) as well as constitution-building in Nigeria.[13]

However, the initial euphoria regarding South Africa's democratisation has been replaced with scepticism and in some circles disappointment, as the advancement in formal democratic institutions has not been mirrored in economic and social conditions, which have worsened (cf. Desai 2002). Local protest movements, often clashing with ANC-dominated municipal governments, have sprung up around the country to object to lack of services and price increases in privatised services (Marais 1998; Bond 2001). South Africa is ranked as the third most unequal society in the world – only Brazil and Guatemala are worse. Unemployment is at 40% and the economy has lost half a million jobs since 1995. Approximately 45% of South Africans live in poor households that earn an average of R352,53 (equivalent to US$32 at the time of writing) per month per adult by 2002. In mainly rural provinces the unemployment figure rises above 50%. Sixty-one percent of Africans are poor compared to 1% of whites. The largest proportion of those in the top income quintile are white (65% of households) and Indian (45%). Only 17% of coloureds and 10% of Africans earn incomes sufficient to put them into that category. Since 1994 the size of the African elite has expanded rapidly, pointing to a sharp reduction in the disparity between white and African disposable income. However, there is little to indicate that there has been any substantial reduction in the overall level of inequality between rich and poor since 1993 (Guelke 1999:173). About 3 million people still need housing, 7,5 million lack access to running water and 21 million go without sanitation services. An estimated 3,6 million of the country's 44 million have HIV/Aids. Crime rates are among the highest in the world.

The social, economic and political disquiet in South Africa has been met with little hard-hitting analysis. In most popular or mainstream accounts the problems with democracy and the dissatisfaction of the black masses so soon after 1994 are seen as the fault of the ANC, as merely the effects of bad or inexperienced politicians, or institutional problems with representative democracy. Economic questions are reduced to social issues to be corrected through "development", policy or the market, rather than as structural problems (cf. Fine 2002). Obviously the political leadership *are* to blame for much of the situation, but there seems to be a failure to confront the structural and economic bases of inequality – of race and class – and of the continuities of apartheid to post-apartheid. I will argue later that this is also reflected in the way access problems to democratic institutions, for example in media, are reduced to policy questions to be corrected by laws and state intervention.

Approaches to the Transition

The most common approach to the transition focuses on politicolegal changes and on the make-up of democratic institutions post-1994. As a result, economic and structural inequality is either left out, or attributed to market imperfections to be corrected through social policy (cf. Fine 2002). And indeed, this was how the transition was framed for public consumption and to a large extent in the minds of the protagonists at the time: Codesa was concerned primarily with political power questions and left economic questions outside of its remit. For example, in May 1992 Codesa negotiators agreed on a number of working groups that focused exclusively on politicolegal questions, explicitly confining economic questions to discussion by one body, the National Economic Commission (NEC). The Codesa working groups had the following focus areas: (1) Climate for free political competition; (2) Constitutional principles; (3) Transitional arrangements; (4) Future constitutional position and re-incorporation of homelands; and (5) Implementation of agreements of other groups.

Moreover, the NEC was constrained from the start to working within a narrowly defined framework. In his autobiography F.W. de Klerk (De Klerk 1998), emphasizes that economic "negotiations" were not open-ended. Six "guiding principles" formed the basis of economic restructuring: (1) the generation of sufficient investment in labour to improve skills and promote employment; (2) macroeconomic stability with regard to prices, interest rates and the exchange rate; (3) fiscal discipline; (4) trade liberalisation with a view to strengthening the competitive position of South Africa's producers in both domestic and foreign markets; (5) the promotion of effective competition; and (6) the strengthening of market forces (De Klerk 1998:227-228; see also Waldmeir 1997). My main criticism of the politicolegal approach is that it takes this process at face value, failing to acknowledge that economic negotiations were foreclosed even before they started.

Proponents of this approach also place a lot of emphasis on the personalities of Mandela and De Klerk (Harvey 2001; Guelke 1999:184; Sparks 1996:3, 15; Waldmeir 1997:64, 79). The personal chemistry between the two men is seen as crucial to the successful outcome of negotiations and the initial stability of the post-1994 period (cf. Howarth 1998). Crudely, this view can be summarised as follows: South Africa has been "fortunate" in having political leaders willing "to compromise away the dogmatic convictions of their followers". On the Afrikaner side, the heroes are De Klerk, who is said to have undergone "a spiritual leap" when he became leader of the NP, and Constand Viljoen of the Freedom Front, who was sensible enough to turn to parliamentary opposition after flirting with armed resistance.[14] On the ANC side, the compromisers are seen to be Mandela, whose objective remained no more and no less than majority rule, and Joe Slovo and the SACP, who are given "the lion's share" of the credit for sustaining the ANC's commitment to nonracialism. However, even if it is accepted that personal interaction between key power-holders played a part in overcoming prejudices that remained an obstacle to the initiation of negotiations, it does not explain how the elites were able to overcome prejudice in the white community (Guelke 1999:185) or temper expectations within the black community.

The major exponent of a rational choice approach to the transition is US political scientist Timothy Sisk. In his study *Democratisation in South Africa* (1995), Sisk advanced four interrelated arguments (summarised in Howarth 1998). First, he stressed a shift in perceptions amongst the major political actors in South Africa from a "zero-sum" to a "positive-sum" game. Thus the cost of a winner-takes-all scenario, in terms of which either the ANC or the NP could completely subordinate its adversary, came to be viewed as greater than the cost of co-operating to create a jointly determined set of institutions to govern a common society. This change, he argued, arose from two important factors: the growing awareness of a "shared destiny" and "recognition of interdependence", as well as growing parity among the major parties to the conflict.

Second, Sisk focused on what he called the inevitable period of uncertainty following the initial drive to negotiations, which arose from the need to create and adopt untried sets of institutional rules. He argued that pacts among the major protagonists reduced uncertainty about a possible return to zero-sum politics, and provided minority forces (such as the predominantly Zulu and regionally-based IFP, the white right wing, and the black nationalist PAC) with incentives not to exclude themselves from negotiations, thereby jeopardising the negotiation process as a whole. For Sisk then, once formal negotiations were under way, uncertainty about respective parties' vital interests ceased to be a constraint on negotiation, giving way to indeterminacy about the prospects of winning the game according to new rules. In this way, it performed the positive function of sustaining the democratisation process.

Third, Sisk considered the dynamics of the negotiation process itself, arguing that the strongly divergent interests of the opposed parties were increasingly modified as a result of the search for an agreed outcome. This convergence was focused on the articulation of a new social contract designed to "institutionalise and maximise co-operation among the moderate centre in order to avoid violent conflict". This is made possible by the overall context in which the discussion took place. The new "social contract" for Sisk was more concerned with dealing with conflicting "ethnic politics" than economic interests. So for Sisk the two major causes of conflict in South Africa were the politics of identity and the "unfairness of race discrimination". He called for the establishment of an "inclusive hegemony" that crossed ethnic and race boundaries.

All of this is well and good, but the problem is that Sisk ended by describing what needed to be explained. *Why* did perceptions shift when they did? What were the underlying political dynamics? None of this can be gleaned from within a rational choice model. As Howarth (1998:194) points out, "[Sisk's] analysis is still restricted to a consideration of decontextualised and self-interested agents with an a-historical rationality". Rational choice relies on a structural-determinism in which it does not really matter who the political actors are or what their specific histories are; as long as they are rational, one can replace any set of actors for another. Thus no real effort is made to locate democratisation in relation to the specific historical trajectory of political struggle in South Africa.

The third politicolegal approach is probably the most mainstream and most popular among political scientists (Butler 1995) and has been termed "pactology" elsewhere (Howarth 1998:186). This approach draws heavily on comparative studies of democratisation in Latin America and Southern Europe (cf. O'Donnell et al 1986; Huntington 1991; Karl and Schmitter 1991; Prezworski 1991). Specific to South Africa is the work of Frederik van Zyl Slabbert (1992), and later the work of particularly political scientists Hermann Giliomee (1994; 1996), Vincent Maphai (1996), and R.W. Johnson, for a while director of the "liberal" Helen Suzman Foundation in Johannesburg and a leading columnist on South Africa in British and US media.

These writers base their arguments on the fact that international debates about democracy have witnessed a growing ideological convergence around two fundamental trends. These are the "demonstrable predominance of market economies" and a growing consensus of belief about the meaning of democracy (Howarth 1998). The latter, which is at the core of the argument, centres on two fundamental principles: the idea of contingent consent, in which victors and losers in electoral contests confirm to the established "rules of the game", and the principle of bounded uncertainty, in which the inevitable precariousness of democratic political systems are bounded by clear constitutional principles that guarantee the right of citizenship. Both these principles ensure transparent rules of democratic procedure.

Slabbert, for example, in order to analyse and predict the course of democratic transition in the South African case, rejects approaches which emphasize certain institutional and structural prerequisites for democracy, as advocated by theorists of democratic modernisation, arguing that the supposed preconditions may turn out to be the consequences of democracy. Instead, Slabbert focuses on the critical role of "key political actors and their strategic choices" concerning democracy, democratisation and each other. He locates such choices within the context of opportunities to be exploited and obstacles to overcome, and goes on to plot a probable outcome to the process. In this way "structural factors are seen as interacting with the strategic choices of key actors rather than predetermining them, which provides a more reliable picture of the dynamics of transition".

Slabbert identifies four ideal-typical modes of transition: a pact between leaders within and outside the regime to be democratised, a unilateral imposition by one particular force, reform as a result of mass pressure from below, and revolution. Each mode is an important determinant of the likely outcome of the democratisation process. "Top-down" modes of transition – a leadership pact or imposition – are seen to have a better chance of stabilising into a democratic regime than "bottom-up" modes based on reform or revolution. Slabbert characterises the South African transition as an exemplar of the first type. For him apartheid domination can be classed as colonial (minority settler domination), though not as resoluble by white withdrawal or an imposed and monitored solution by external agencies (like at Zimbabwean independence). He provides a fourfold categorisation of the causes for negotiation in the South African context charted along two sets of axes: planned/unplanned and internal/external pressures for change. In this regard, unplanned internal pressures include the process of black urbanisation, whereas planned internal pressures include the growing black revolt against apartheid during the 1980s. The unplanned external pressures consist of the rapprochement between the Cold War superpowers, while planned external pressures consist of the gathering international campaign (principally through economic and political sanctions) to isolate the apartheid state (see Howarth 1998).

According to Howarth, Slabbert's analysis of democratic transition centred on three problems to be dealt with in corresponding phases of the negotiating process and the post-democratic elections period. These are the problems of normalisation, democratisation and consolidation. The first refers to the process of granting or restoring rights and privileges to those denied them by an existing authoritarian state, thus ensuring an appropriate legal and political context for negotiations. In South Africa the questions of political violence and security were and remain of prime importance. "Democratisation" refers to the involvement of previously excluded groups in various levels of actual policymaking, and centres on four aspects of South Africa's social system. These are the democratisation of the constitution, the state, the budget and the economy. Slabbert's work is more about the first two, largely political dimensions – normalisation and democratisation – than consolidation, which he argues depends on the decisions taken in the early part of the transition process. He suggests that the success of the process ("the conditions for a successful transition") depends on four agreements amongst the main actors:

these include a civil-military pact, an economic contract, an agreement on redistribution and development, and consensus on a new democratic constitution.

Regarding the workings of post-1994 democracy, pactology is predominantly prescriptive and technicist. Some South African scholars and commentators use the pactology model to argue on behalf of certain kinds of moderate politics (see for example Giliomee and Schlemmer 1994; Adam et al. 1997). Pactology places emphasis on "negative" constitutional mechanisms to secure the successful operation of democracy (it assumes that the black majority needs to be prevented or "policed"). These include the type of electoral system, a federal state structure designed to counter drives towards hegemony by any party (but largely fearful of the ANC's electoral majority – unassailable in the near future), and to foster "greater group accommodation" at a national level (a remnant of the consociationalist debates of the 1980s), the restructuring of the armed forces to bring them under civilian control (thereby lessening the possibility of a coup d'etat), and efforts to reduce the extreme dangers of economic inequality between racial and ethnic groups (on these the constitution is, however, vague or subject to multiple interpretations) [cf. Giliomee and Simkins 1997].

This approach contains much of explanatory value. At the same time, however, the emphasis on comparative dynamics tends to obscure elements that are specific to South Africa. By placing South African politics within a larger framework of transitions borrowed from Eastern Europe and Latin America, the "pactologists" risk implying that an almost teleological process is at work. It is as if the forces of liberal democracy and capitalism are playing themselves out in some sort of inexorable historical process. More seriously, it serves a legitimising function within academia of a particular political and economic project – that of elite consensus around liberal democracy and neo-liberalism (Butler 1995, Klug 2000). In this regard, it is notable that a number of leading pactologists became advisors to the ANC regime or close to its leaders, including Van Zyl Slabbert himself, as well as political philosopher Willie Esterhuyse and others.

The other main contender for explaining the transition and its aftermath developed out of Marxist scholarship. Many such scholars, such as historian Neville Alexander, have been highly critical of mainstream takes on the transition. Writing in 1993, he suggested, with reference to pactology, that ". . . the science (or is it science fiction?) of transitology has been used by literally hundreds of South African and foreign scholars and politicians in order to predict the most likely path of development" (1993:3). Alexander concluded that "sadly few, if any, of these helped us to make sense of the inscrutable social reality in our benighted country even if they have led some people to a more nuanced understanding of such values as equality, democracy, the market, etc." (1993:3)[15]

By the 1970s and 1980s, Marxist accounts of South African society dominated much of social science discourse. This scholarship provided the intellectual support to the national liberation movement (collected around the ANC) as well as to the broad left-wing political project in South Africa (cf. Saul 2001, Alexander 1992). It is currently making a comeback in South Africa in a modified form, with an eye on a more nuanced account of events (cf. Marais 1998; Bond 2000). In its early form, it was predicated on a radical-political commitment to a revolutionary socialist transformation of South Africa's "racial capitalist" society, and a rejection of "reformist" and "reactionary" positions. It rightly pointed to the narrow political transition of South Africa (which it does not entirely dismiss). However, it also insists that if the socioeconomic inequalities that have been inherent in South Africa's brand of racial capitalism are not addressed, any new freedoms would quickly be rendered very formal indeed for the vast mass of the black population. It is therefore the first of the approaches outlined here to move beyond the political, and to seriously interrogate the economic and structural basis of the transition.

In this analysis there is a move away from the elite pacting and a concern with the modalities of democratisation (as defined by the pactology scholars), in favour of an analysis of the likely possibilities of structural reform in South Africa. This results in an examination of the political forces engaged in pursuing this objective and the obstacles that such a transitional strategy would have to overcome.

Apartheid is analysed as a mutually reinforcing system of racial capitalism. At the same time, the articulation of racial domination and capitalism was viewed as potentially contradictory. Moreover, during the organic crisis of apartheid in the post-Soweto 1976 period, these two structures were understood to unravel in various critical ways. The result was that it facilitated attempts by business and liberal elites within and around the NP to reform and deracialise South Africa's "racial Fordist accumulation regime" (cf. Marais 1998; Bond 2000). De Klerk's flawed reforms at the end of the 1980s is explained by Marxist scholars as an attempt to break up the growing political stalemate in South Africa, while simultaneously destabilising the ANC, and preparing a favourable ground upon which to negotiate the end of apartheid rule. This double-edged strategy was essentially "top-down", setting the scene for the elitist nature of the negotiations that ensued.

Alexander suggested in 1992 that the transition was characterised by "four pillars of consensus" (1993:4-5) on the nature of change in South Africa. Firstly, the ruling classes in South Africa had to reform the racial capitalist system. In its apartheid form, it had become a counterproductive burden since at least the early 1970s. Secondly, the opposition movement (both inside and outside the country) had not succeeded in overthrowing the apartheid state. He was adamant: "In spite of its increasing vulnerability, the ruling elite has retained its grip firmly on all repressive apparatus of the state." Thirdly, the system of racial capitalism, given the new world order and the hegemonic consolidation of reformist strategies among formerly anti-apartheid social forces, would persist in a changed form in the short to medium term. Class alliances as well as the legitimising discourse of the system would change. In general, the movement would be from race to class, even if for the majority of black people and for some white people the realities of life would either not change at all or would become considerably worse. Fourthly, the potential for social conflict would be enhanced in the short term (Alexander 1992:5-6).

Alexander, like the pactologists, puts emphasis on the impact of unforeseen events at the global level, such as Mikhail Gorbachev's reforms in the Soviet Union. Specific to South Africa, he argues that there is no doubt that economic and political realities made it clear to the South African ruling class that the apartheid option of the racial capitalist system had been exhausted. By the early 1970s already the system had reached its ceilings and become counterproductive in all important aspects. The reform of the system was a deliberately pro-active strategy on the part of the rulers recognising that the 1976 uprising demonstrated the system's total loss of legitimacy. Alexander comments:

> It is important to stress this, not in order to downgrade or trivialise the heroic battles fought on all fronts by our people in the decade between 1976 and 1986, but in order to concentrate our minds on the fact that the "racist Pretoria regime" has not been defeated militarily. This awkward but stubborn fact is usually elided in discussions about the present conjuncture and about our perspectives, even though it is clearly one of the central features of the political landscape. (1993:45)

Crucially for Alexander, the need to state clearly the character of the transition stems from the fact that without doing so, ". . . we shall be aware neither of the limits nor of the possibilities inherent in the present conjuncture" (1993:46). That is, the NP (aided by capital) has restructured the economy and society within certain definite limits. For this argument, he draws on the work of two South African economists, Morris and Padayachee (1988) to isolate three elements in the reform initiatives of the state and capital. These were initiating a limited process of democratisation of ideological and political life, implementing racialisation of social and political life; and instituting a partial and selective "redistribution" – a dual process of "de-/re-racialisation" of social resources towards the black majority (Alexander 1993:47).

A variant of the Marxist or left-wing approach developed from within the national liberation movement by academics close to the ANC as well as the internal resistance movement. It is less sophisticated in its analysis and comes across as very triumphalist (as the direct parallel to the first approach outlined above), confuses tactics with political reality and assumes that the ANC/liberation movement overthrew apartheid. It places enormous emphasis on the role of mass struggle, combined with the effect of sanctions and the armed struggle (cf. Marais 1998). It overstates the role of the armed struggle (cf. Barrell 1990; Alexander 2002) and of the internal resistance movement, as well as the effect of economic and cultural sanctions on the white community (Glaser 2001). It also disguises the ANC leadership's active role in initiating negotiations since the mid-1980s while keeping up a radical stance (cf. Fine and Rustomjee 1996; Alexander 2002). It contains an element of teleology that is not grounded in historical reality, and finally, they have a nationalist understanding of the transition that results in particular in a narrow understanding of the workings of post-1994 democracy (Johnson 2000).

In my view, a shortcoming shared by all these approaches is an overemphasis on the state. Marxist analysis as it developed in South Africa has been most guilty of this, collapsing the political economy of privilege into the apartheid state. This of course was (and is) a more tactical, rather than an analytical approach. But as Marais (1998:2) points out, what is generated is an instrumentalist conception of the state, one that regards it as a site of concentrated power which, once captured, would become the central agent of transformation. It is guilty of the same overemphasis as the first approach on the political institutions of state. They have continued in the same vein in the post-1994 context, excusing the nexus of power that falls outside of the state. As Marais reminds us: "... in capitalist society the circuits through which power and privilege are reproduced course not only through the state, but through civil society, which is dominated by the formation of capital."

What this Means for Mass Media

Like the mainstream of transition scholarship, current research into the political role of the media in post-1994 mainly focuses on politicolegal questions (cf. Duncan 2000; Horwitz 2000). The focus of research includes documentation of the far-reaching changes to the media landscape since the early 1990s, questions around freedom of expression, the nature of state-media relations, and the implications of such changes for the day-to-day operations of the media.

In the bulk of such research, liberal democratic institutions of civil society, including the media, are accorded automatically positive valuation. The media is either a neutral conduit for (beneficial) information or a positive agent in the sense that it contributes to "democratising" public political space. The media is not seen as a political actor in its own right, but rather a cog in the machinery of democracy; hence there is a concern with protecting the media or building its capacity. It implies that now that apartheid has legally been defeated, the institutions of democracy, such as the media, can function properly. It sees the state at best as a neutral body, but more consistently tends to scepticism and wariness towards the state. As a result, much of the focus is on what the state does to impede media freedom. There is limited or mere passing interest in the relationship between the media and capital or the media's overtly political role. Journalism educators, media houses, journalist unions and nongovernmental organisations mainly concerned with monitoring media or "freedom of expression" favour this approach.

A second set of media analyses focuses almost exclusively on the relationship between the media and capital. Largely the work of South African left-wing academics, under apartheid such studies focused mainly on the role of the media as hegemonic agents of apartheid and racial capitalism (cf. Tomaselli et al. 1987; Switzer and Adhikari 2000). In a post-apartheid context this approach to the media maintains its focus on power dynamics, but, in my view, continues to assume a too-easy causality between economic factors and the way the media operates in a democratic context. It continues to view the media as the servant of particular class or economic interests, without interrogating the bases of such relationships. In some cases they also have retreated to do "cultural studies" of media.

Marxists confuse "civil society" and the "public sphere" (the hoped-for locus of positive political change) with the ruling party: the ANC and its allies. In effect, it suggests that the correction of the media sphere would be achieved by having ANC or left-wing media. Others suggest setting up "alternative" media. They reject the mainstream (commercial) media, relying almost exclusively on official or state policy initiatives to change the media set-up. A set of debates before and after the 1994 election about community radio to diversify the broadcast sector (until 1993, the state held a monopoly over the broadcast sector, both radio and television), setting up a regulatory authority, as well as an ongoing debate about state-led "corrective action" in the print media sector have been heavily driven by such a view (Duncan 2000). They place, for example, much hope in institutions such as the Independent Communications Authority (as the IBA is now known) as well as the newly-established Media Development and Diversity Agency (MDDA).

I want to suggest that the approaches to media reviewed above rarely if ever interrogate the political character and effects of mass media in the post-1994 public sphere as well as its interaction with changes to the broader political and social system. The politicolegal approach predictably offers overly optimistic views of the South African media landscape; the Marxist approach is content to deliver unrealistic policy prescriptions that ignore demand for commercial media (cf. Berger 1999; Horwitz 2000; Duncan 2000; Krabill and Boloka 2000). While correct in identifying a close relationship between the media and democracy, both families of approaches reduce that relationship too much: either "democracy leads to free media" or "free media leads to democracy".

As should be clear from the foregoing, these debates are in many ways a mirror of the debates around transition: the politicolegal approach, with its subsets of institutionalism, rational choice and pactology, focusing almost exclusively on the establishment of the "right" institutions and kinds of civil society; and a materialist or Marxist approach focusing overwhelmingly on the role of capital.

In my approach the transition is less a miraculous historical rupture than a yet inconclusive outcome of a concerted and far-reaching attempt to resolve an ensemble of political, ideological and economic contradictions that had accumulated steadily since the 1970s (cf. Marais 1998; Bond 2000, 2001). It therefore differs from the conventional narratives that gauge the transition in predominantly political terms.

The basis for the transition lay in a historical deadlock achieved between the ruling bloc and the (mass) democratic opposition that reached its high point in the late 1980s. The impasse rested on the apartheid state's inability indefinitely to suppress the challenge from the democratic opposition, which in turn had become powerful enough to prevent that bloc from devising and imposing a resolution that could unequivocally favour it. At the same time, the opposition was unable to force the capitulation of the old order.

The situation that presented was straightforward: The old ruling bloc (National Party) had become a liability, both for the political and economic elite; apartheid was no longer compatible with capitalism. At the same time the emergence of a well-organised resistance made things worse. Big capital and white political leaders came to the conclusion that while a negotiated settlement would not resolve the differences or crisis, at least it "could serve as the gateway for an ongoing bid to modernise South African capitalism" (Marais 1998:3). Marais points out that the transition also held some promise for opposition or democratic forces. These groups saw in a settlement an opportunity to usher in a transition that heralded – even if it could not guarantee – far-reaching adjustments aimed at undoing the patterns for the allocation of power, privilege and opportunity. However, the key propellant of the negotiations was the realisation among sections of the ruling bloc that the capitalist system in South Africa had to be modernised – both in political and economic terms. In short, South Africa had to become a "normal" capitalist society. Despite its haphazard reform efforts of the 1980s, the NP had proved unequal to the task.

For capital, two adjustments were required. The first was the abandonment of the exclusionary political framework of apartheid. This meant that the NP would no longer function as the party of the ruling bloc. "That role would befall the ANC, albeit on terms, business hoped, that inhibited its ability to advance the interests of the disadvantaged majority at the expense of the key prerogatives of capital" (Marais 1998:4).

The second area of adjustment was the economic transition. At its core it aimed at revising an economic growth strategy that had become steadily derailed since the 1970s, as reflected in economic indicators. It is important to underline that this latter economic dimension gets overlooked in overly politicised accounts of the transition.

Unlike the Marxists, who see this second transition as complete (and resolved to the benefit of capital), I side with the view that there is a struggle post-1994 over the terms of this transition. South African capitalists had hoped that political democratisation would serve as grounding for structural adjustments that could inaugurate a new cycle of sustained accumulation, a process that would include efforts to cultivate and incorporate a black economic elite as junior partners within the white-run economy. As Marais concludes: "Left unchallenged, the defining trends of the transition seem destined to shape a revised division of society, with the current order stabilised around, at best, 30 percent of the population. For the rest (overwhelmingly young, female and African) the best hope will be some trickled-down from a 'modernised' and 'normalised' new South Africa." However, Marais also adds:

> South Africa also remains invested with a robust array of popular organisations, including the ANC, many of which played decisive roles in bringing about the stale-

mate of the late 1980s. Loosely grouped in a putative popular movement, these formations seem to represent a powerful antidote to the prescriptions advanced by capitalists inside SA and beyond its borders.

Beyond the specifics of the South African case study, I read this transition in the context of two broader interrelated developments that have been identified in democracies (including transitional societies) elsewhere. These relate to how deliberation within democracies is organised and hold important implications for how the above "struggle" plays out within the democratic polity. The first is the decline of traditional forms of political organisation – such as mass political parties – that have served as the means for citizens to access political power. One consequence is that party memberships are demobilised and parties are transformed into professional organisations geared at elections. The second development is the rise of indirect forms of political organisation and narrow, interest-based politics. This is usually the politics that is referred to in the literature as the rise of "civil society". Its main expression is the myriad of well-funded nongovernmental organisations and pressure groups which now take the place of civic and grassroots organisations in lobbying and acting on behalf of groups of citizens (Swanson and Mancini 1996). One consequence is that highly constricted deliberation processes replace more inclusive processes. The new deliberation processes are restricted to policy professionals and already empowered (meanly large "white" and neo-liberal) nongovernmental organisations, business, professional lobby groups, as well as think tanks (Neocosmos 1998; Johnson 2000). As one observer notes, "The irony is that the levels of involvement in political and civic issues were higher under the repressive machinery than under the new democratic dispensation" (Blake 1998:45).

Two other processes provide an eerie backdrop for the rise of mediated democracy. While the developments above have implications for how deliberation takes place, the ones outlined below have more to do with the content of deliberation as well as that which sets the broad parameters for policy debates within the mainstream. The first development is the rise to prominence of a neo-liberal policy grid internationally that dilutes the autonomy of the state. The result is an increase in the power of unelected public agents over policy and the coincidence of the interests of such agents with that of economic elites (Bond 2000). The second related dynamic is that transition to democracy in the early 1990s was part of a tremendous global democratic expansion of liberal democracy. Indeed, liberal democracy has been put forward as the global panacea for securing order, stability and economic growth in fragile and deeply divided societies. However, as some observers have pointed out, this limited form of democracy primarily shows "concern for the sensibilities of capital" by deflating the role of the state in politics (which includes economics) as well as limiting the scope of democratic gains to the political sphere (cf. Saul 1999; Klug 2000). These of course are insights of the pactologist approach. The difference here is that while the pactologists tend to celebrate these developments as preconditions for democratic transition, in this approach they are seen as constraints on the form of that transition (Peet 1998).

Media directly impact political, economic and social processes. Media are no longer viewed as merely conduits for governments, political parties or citizens, but "emerge in modern polyarchies as an autonomous power center in reciprocal competition with other power centers" (Swanson and Mancini 1996:11; see also Sükösd 2000:160). Media are always subject to powerful interests, including those of capital and the state, but neither set of interests is paramount, and even both together are insufficient for understanding how media work.

Notes

1 The writer would like to acknowledge valuable discussions he had at various times in preparation of this chapter with Herman Wasserman, David Styan, Ron Krabill, Tuija Parikka, Suren Pillay, Kalina Kamenova, Jeffrey Goldfarb, and Jessica Blatt.

2 See Switzer, L. 1993. *Power and Resistance in an African Society: The Ciskei and the Making of South Africa* (Madison: University of Wisconson Press); Finnegan, W. 1988. *Dateline Soweto. Travels with Black South African Reporters* (New York: Harper and Row).

3 For references on this debate, see Slovo, J. 1992. Negotiations: What room for compromises? *African Communist* 130; Jordan, J. 1992. Strategic Debate in the ANC: A Response to Joe Slovo. *African Communist* 131; Nzimande, N. 1992. Let us Take the People With Us. *African Communist* 131. See also Mandela (1995) and De Klerk (1998).

4 Later chief prosecutor at the International Court of Justice in The Hague.

5 Azanian People's Liberation Army.

6 The Senate was converted in 1996 to a National Council of Provinces.

7 For more on this debate, see Strelitz and Steenveld (1998); Pillay (2000).

8 For analysis of the June 1999 elections, see Reynolds (1999).

9 Bell (2001) gives an interesting account of how media disposition buried a big story that would have put De Klerk in a very bad light just as he was about to accept the Nobel Prize for Peace – he had ordered the killing of supposed Apla guerrillas in Transkei, but it turned out to be schoolchildren. No news medium used the story, because in the words of the BBC correspondent, 'Who wants to mess up a fairy tale?'

10 According to the Bill of Rights in Chapter 2 of the Constitution (Act 108 of 1996), everyone has the right to freedom of expression, which includes: freedom of the press and other media; freedom to receive and impart information and ideas. Several laws, policies and organisations act to protect and promote press freedom in South Africa (GCIS 2002:121).

11 The Promotion of Access to Information Act, 2000.

12 The Internet has great potential for the speedy dissemination of information by relatively independent organisations or even individuals. Entry into the market is much easier. However, in South Africa access to the Internet is limited to a small group of wealthy (mostly white) people and most of the rest of Internet users have access to the worldwide web from their offices. The majority of the people do not have enough money, equipment and education to access the Internet, so as a result the Internet is not (yet) an important disseminator of information. Since the late 1990s, a number of worldwide web and email-based publications have seen the light of day. Companies have also invested in web-only news portals.

13 For discussion on the continental aspect of this development, see Vale and Maseko (1998).

14 On the eve of the 1994 elections, far-rightwing white groupings invaded the capital of the Bophuthatswana homeland to 'assist' the homeland's leader Lucas Mangope to crush a popular uprising. They were repelled by members of the homeland's army sympathetic to popular forces.

15 He expanded on these ideas in Alexander, N. 2002. *An Ordinary Country: Issues in the Transition from Apartheid to Democracy in South Africa*. Durban: University of Natal Press.

References

Adam, H., Moodley, K., and Slabbert, F. van Z. 1997. *Comrades in Business*. Cape Town: David Philip.

Alexander, N. 1993. *Some More Equal Than Others*. Cape Town: Buchu Books. Barrell, H. 1990. *MK: The ANC's Armed Struggle*. Johannesburg: Penguin Books.

Bell, T. 2001. *Unfinished Business. South Africa, Apartheid and Truth*. Cape Town: Redworks.

Berger, G. 1999. Towards an Analysis of the South African Media and Transformation, 1994-1999. *Transformation*, 38. 84-115.

Blake, M. 1998. Are the Poor Being Heard? In Barberton, C., Kotze, H., and Blake, M. (eds.) *Creating Action Space. The Challenge of Poverty and Democracy in South Africa*. Cape Town: David Philip and Idasa.

Boloka, G. and Krabill, K. 2000. Calling the Glass half full: A Response to Berger's "Towards an analysis of the South African Media and Transformation, 1994-1999. *Transformation*, 43. 74-85.

Bond, P. 2002. Johannesburg Left Prepare to Summit Against the Global Elite. *ZNet Commentary*. July 30, 2002.

Bond, P. 2001. *Against Global Apartheid: South Africa Meets the World Bank, IMF and International Finance.* Cape Town: University of Cape Town Press.

Bond, P. 2000. *Elite Transition. From Apartheid to Neo-Liberalism in South Africa.* Pietermaritzburg: University of Natal Press/Pluto Press.

Bratton, M. and Van der Walle, N. 1997. *Democratic Experiments in Africa: Regime Transitions in Comparative Perspective.* New York: Cambridge University Press.

Butler, A. 1995. *Democracy and Apartheid: Political Theory, Comparative Politics and the Modern South African State.* London: McMillan Press.

Comaroff, J. 2002. Criminal Obsessions: Imagining Order after Apartheid. Paper presented at Afrika Studiecentrum, University of Leiden. 22 November 2002.

De Klerk, F.W. 1998. *The Last Trek. A New Beginning. The Autobiography.* London: MacMillan.

Desai, A. 2002. *We are the Poors. Community Struggles in Post-apartheid South Africa.* New York: Monthly Review Press.

Duncan, J. 1999. Talk Left, Act Right: What Constitutes Transformation in South African Media. *Communication Law in Transition Newsletter*, 1(6), June 10, 1999. http://pcmlp.socleg.ox.ac.uk/transition/issue06/duncan.htm.

Duncan, J. and Seleoane, M. (eds). 1998. *Media and Democracy in South Africa.* Pretoria: Human Sciences Research Council.

Fine, B. and Rustomjee, Z. 1996. *The Political Economy of South Africa: From Minerals-Energy Complex to Industrialisation.* London: Hurst and Company.

Giliomee, H. 1998. South Africa's Emerging Dominant Party Regime, *Journal of Democracy*, 9(4), October. 128-142.

Giliomee, H. and Simkins, C. 1997. *The Awkward Embrace.* Cape Town: Tafelberg.

Giliomee, H. 1996. *Liberal And Populist Democracy In South Africa: Challenges, New Threats To Liberalism.* Johannesburg: SAIRR.

Giliomee, H. and Schlemmer, H. (eds.). 1994. *The Bold Experiment: South Africa's New Democracy.* Johannesburg: Southern Books.

Glaser, D. 2001. *Politics and Society in South Africa. A Critical Introduction.* London: Sage Publications.

Guelke, A. 1999. *South Africa in Transition: The Misunderstood Miracle.* London: IB Taurus.

Hain, P. 1996. *Sing the Beloved Country: The Struggle for the New South Africa.* London: Pluto Press.

Harvey, R. 2001. *The Fall of Apartheid.* London: Palgrave.

Horwitz, R. 2000. *Communication and Democratic Reform in South Africa.* Cambridge: Cambridge University Press.

Howarth, D. 1998. Paradigms Gained? A Critique of Theories and Explanations of Democratic Transition in South Africa. In Howarth, D. and Norval, A. (eds.). *South Africa in Transition. New Theoretical Perspectives.* London: MacMillan Press.

Huntington, S. 1991. *The Third Wave: Democratization in the Late Twentieth Century.* Norman and New York: University of Oklahoma Press.

Jacobs, S. and Calland, R. (eds.). 2002. *Thabo Mbeki's World: The politics and ideology of the South African president*. Pietermaritzburg: University of Natal Press.

Jacobs, S. 2000a. Is the Media Democratic? *Mail and Guardian*. 22 October 2000. 32.

Jacobs, S. 2000b. Mass Media for Minorities. *Mail and Guardian*. 14 January 2000. 26.

Jacobs, S. 1999a. The News Media. In Reynolds, A. *Elections '99: South Africa. The Campaigns, Results and Future Prospects*. Cape Town: David Philip/James Currey.

Jacobs, S. 1999b. Tensions of a Free Press: South Africa After Apartheid. Research Paper. Joan Shorenstein Center for the Press, Politics and Public Policy. Cambridge, MA: Harvard University. June.

Johnson, K. 2000. 'The Trade-offs Between Distributive Equity and Democratic Process: The Case of Child Welfare Reform in South Africa', *African Studies Review*, 43, December. 19-38.

Johnson, R.W. 2000. Stand up and be counted. *The Spectator*, London, June 24, 2000. 18-19.

Karl, T. and Schmitter, P. 1991. Modes of Transition in Latin America and Eastern Europe, *International Social Science Journal*, 128. 269-284.

Klug, H. 2000. *Law, Globalism and South Africa's Political Reconstruction.* New York: Cambridge University Press.

Krabill, R. 2001. Symbiosis: Mass media and the Truth and Reconciliation Commission of South Africa. *Media, Culture and Society*, 23. 585-603.

Louw, P. E. 1996. The New South African Hegemony and the Press. *Media International Australia* 79. 76-82.

Louw, P. E. (ed.). 1993. *South African Media Policy Debates of the 1990s*. Durban: Centre for Cultural and Media Studies.

Mandela, N. 1995. *Long Walk to Freedom – The Autobiography of Nelson of Mandela*. New York: Little Brown and Co.

Maphai, V. 1996. The New South Africa. A Season for Power-Sharing. *Journal for Democracy*, 7(1), January. 67-81.

Marais, H. 1998. *South Africa: Limits to Change: The Political Economy of Transformation*. London/Cape Town: Zed Books and University of Cape Town Press.

Morris, M. and Padayachee, V. 1988. State reform policy in South Africa. *Transformation*, 7. 1-26.

Neocosmos, M. 2002. 'The Construction of a State-Consensus in South Africa: Authoritarian Nationalism, the Depolitisation of Politics and the Exclusion of Popular Democratic Discourse.' Paper presented at the International Conference on 'Reconceptualising Democracy and Liberation in Southern Africa'. 11-13 July 2002. Windhoek, Namibia: Nordic Africa Institute/Namibia Institute for Democracy/Legal Assistance Centre, Windhoek.

Neocosmos, M. 2001. 'The Post-Development State in Southern Africa: Towards Consensus as a Mode of Legitimation.' Paper Presented to Workshop on 'Interrogating the New Political Culture in Southern Africa', 13-15 June 2001, Harare, Zimbabwe: Southern African Regional Institute of Policy Studies / Institute for Development Studies, University of Helsinki.

Nuttall, S. and Michael, C. (eds.). 2000. *Senses of Culture: South African Culture Studies*. Cape Town: Oxford University Press.

O'Donnell, G., Whitehead, L. and Schmitter, P. 1996. *Transitions from Authoritarian Rule: Tentative Conclusions about Uncertain Democracies*. Baltimore: John Hopkins University Press.

Parenti, M. 1993. *Inventing Reality: The Politics of News Media*. New York: St Martin's Press.

Peet, R. 1998. From Socialism to Neo-Liberalism: ANC Development Policy, 1955-1995. Unpublished Paper. Department of Geography, Clark University, Worcester, MA.[16]

Saul, J. 2002. Starting from Scratch: A Reply to Jeremy Cronin. *Monthly Review Online*, 54(7), December. URL: www.monthlyreview.org/1202saul.htm

Saul, J. 2001. Cry for the Beloved Country: The Post-1994 Denouement. *Monthly Review*, 52(8), January. 1-51.

Sisk, T. 1995. *Democratisation in South Africa. The Elusive Social Contract*. Princeton: Princeton University Press.

Slabbert, F. van Z. 1992. *The Quest for Democracy: South Africa in Transition.* London: Penguin.

Solomons, H. 1998. *The Soul of A Nation: Constitution-Making in South Africa*. Cape Town: Oxford University Press.

South African Human Rights Commission (SAHRC). 2000. *Faultlines. Inquiry into Racism in the Media. Report of the South African Human Rights Commission*, August 2000. URL: http://www.sahrc.org.za/main_frameset.htm.

Sparks, A. 1996. *Tomorrow is Another Country. The Inside Story Of South Africa's Road To Change*. Cape Town: David Philip.

Swanson, D. and Mancini, P. (eds.). 1996. *Politics, Media and Modern Democracy: An International Study of Innovations in Electoral Campaigning and Their Consequences*. London: Praeger.

Steenveld, L. and Strelitz, L. 1998. The 1995 Rugby World Cup and the politics of nation-building in South Africa. *Media, Culture and Society*. 20. 609-629.

Switzer, Les, and Adhikari, Mohammed. 2000. 'Introduction' in Switzer and Adhikari (eds.), 2000, *South Africa's Resistance Press: Alternative Voices in the Last Generation under Apartheid.* Athens: Ohio University Press.

Tomaselli, K. 2000. South African Media 1994-7. Globalizing via political economy. In Curran, J. and Park, M. (eds.) *De-Westernizing Media Studies*. London/New York: Routledge.

Vale, P. and Maseko, S. 1998. South Africa and the African Renaissance. *International Affairs* 74(2). 271-287.

Waldmeir, P. 1998. *Anatomy of a Miracle. The End of 1994 and the Birth of a New South Africa*. Cape Town: David Philip.

Note

16 Also published as 2000. Ideology, Discourse, and Geography of Hegemony: From Socialism to Neo-Liberalist Development in South Africa. *Antipode*. 58-90.

CHAPTER THREE

Sampling the Past: Sound, Language and Identity in the New South Africa

Stephanie Marlin-Curiel

Introduction

In one of his most famous speeches to the (white) South African nation, D.F. Malan, the first apartheid-era prime minister, said, "Seek in the past everything that is good and clean and build thereon your future".[1] Malan was quoting Paul Kruger, the legendary founder of Afrikaner nationalism and leader of the Boer struggle against the English at the turn of the 20th century. By evoking Kruger, who believed that the Boers were the "chosen people", Malan legitimised his "purity" campaign, which not only excluded an alliance with the English but also became the core of the apartheid system.

Today, in the "new" South Africa, DJ (disk jockey) Heine du Toit, borrowing the name of Afrikaner poet D.J. Opperman as his stage name, mixes Malan's words with trance music for a young, Afrikaans-speaking crowd. Along with samples of Malan's 1948 speech, he cuts in the voices of a familiar Afrikaans storyteller, a well-known rugby commentator, and several other Afrikaner nationalistic icons of his generation's youth, embarking on a journey at once critical, celebratory, and healing. As the featured act at a party in December 1999, Du Toit/Opperman triggered not only aural memories, but also visual memories. He projected symbols of Afrikanerdom onto huge screens that served as a backdrop for the dancers. The streaming images included mostly monuments, memorabilia, figureheads and logos, but significantly, this "family photo album" also included the tragic image of the dead 13-year-old Hector Peterson being carried in the arms of his classmates. This image of the first student killed in the 1976 uprising against Afrikaans instruction in the black township of Soweto was projected at the point in Malan's speech where he says the goal of his new government is "om billikheid, reg and geregtigheid aan albei die twee blanke taalgroepe te laat geskied, asook teenoor die nie-blanke bevolking van ons land" (*to achieve what is right and fair for both the white language groups and the non-white people of our country*). As the images sped up they fell out of sync with the music. In this dizzying combination of aural and visual stimuli, Du Toit/Opperman succeeded in submerging the revellers in the dream space of their youth, while propping one eye open to a sardonic vision of the past.

I witnessed Du Toit's act at no ordinary party, but one billed as an Afrikaans rave "that will put Afrikaans in a whole new context" (Matthews 1999). Bringing together Afrikaans-speaking musicians from varied racial and cultural backgrounds, the rave effectively repositioned Afrikaans from its place as the "language of the oppressor" to the lingua franca of cutting-edge sound. "The implication is that Afrikaans is now no longer God's holy chosen language, but a versatile, modern, and extremely adaptable communication tool [. . .] uniquely positioned to be symbolic of how achievable unity is in South Africa," said Manie Spamer (1999), my host for the evening. To emphasise this inclusive flexibility, the event combined the hardcore Deejay music, the subversive tone, and the drugs-and-dance aesthetic common to raves, with the mind-bending techno trance music, the rustic outdoor space, and the hippie aesthetic common to trance parties.

The young Afrikaners who organised the rave hoped it would propel a new movement redefining Afrikaner identity in the wake of apartheid's demise. While the nation is distancing itself from its past, these young Afrikaners are embracing it with a post-apartheid sensibility. The Afrikaner nationalism and Afrikaans language that glorified their youth marginalises them today. The rave represents an effort to rehabilitate Afrikaner identity by bonding with black or "Coloured" Afrikaans speakers, through shared genealogy of language and through shared marginalisation of Afrikaans language and culture in the present-day, post-apartheid South Africa. Separated under apartheid by race from the Afrikaners and by language from the "Africans", the "Coloureds"[2] were relegated to an in-between space where they remain today.

Although democracy is theoretically based on an open public sphere accessible and proportionally represented by all language and cultural groups, rarely is this the reality. The South African political transition has been criticised in the media on at least two main counts: firstly, the material legacies of apartheid have left huge disparities of wealth based largely on race and geography that have not been corrected; and secondly, the Truth and Reconciliation Commission, which granted amnesty to so many perpetrators and attempted to deal with the past through national catharsis, amounted to a call to forget, rather than to remember, the past. And yet, not only has the persistence of material disparities forced a questioning of the "post" in "post-apartheid", but I would argue that the past persists in the shaping of social identity in South Africa today. "Coloureds" still suffer political stigma for supporting the National Party in the 1994 election,[3] whereas Afrikaners suffer moral stigma for the crimes of apartheid.[4] The Truth and Reconciliation Commission effectively defined a new hegemonic ideology by which post-apartheid social identities are negotiated, based on moral standing in relationship to the past.

It is this newly instituted ideology based on moral culpability that Afrikaner youth seek to delegitimise. In 1995, as a response to the onset of the Truth and Reconciliation Commission hearings, Gilda Swanepoel opened the Boerebar[5] in Pretoria as a sign of her refusal to be shamed by her Afrikanerness. The bar, a hangout decorated with Afrikaner memorabilia that celebrates local Boer culture and features alternative Afrikaans musicians, including Piet Botha, the son of apartheid-era foreign affairs minister Pik Botha, stands for the idea that "we are not responsible for what our parents did and we do not have to throw away who we are" (2001). Swanepoel was recruited to help organise the rave. Though she was dubious about the response they would get in Cape Town, she agreed. Spamer, an ex-lawyer and the co-organiser of the rave, does not believe that Afrikaners in Cape Town are apathetic. He explained to me that the low publicity budget was partly responsible for the low turnout. The sparseness of the crowd did not worry him as this was only the first of what he hoped would be a series of parties staged in several major cities around the country to spread the message that it was time for Afrikaners to reclaim their personal and cultural identity. The seeds had already been planted; many of the bands and DJs performing that night were already established and were keeping Cape Town on the map of new alternative Afrikaans music.[6] Nevertheless, not only was the budget low for this event, so were the revenues. After being flatly turned down for a government grant, Spamer and his cohorts had to give up organising further parties. Swanepoel now works as a marketing manager for IMAX and Spamer has gone back to law and has opened his own firm. He says the rave "got some of my existential angst exorcised, so I'm ready to face reality again" (2001). The party may not have spawned a movement, but it served its purpose. The rave became a space for Afrikaner youth to cross temporal, cultural and geographic boundaries and forge a subjectivity at once post-apartheid and postcolonial.[7] Using language, sound and dancing bodies, these young people sought to exorcise the demons of Afrikaner nationalism, "purifying" it through post-apartheid critique and transgressive acts of "mixing", and yet refusing to accept the guilt and culpability assigned to them by post-apartheid discourses.

By the time I arrived at the party, which was held at Barn Celos, a converted abandoned barn in Melkbosstrand (located about 40 minutes outside of Cape Town), I had just missed the first act of the evening. It was a short film called *Fobofobie: Die Vrees om Bang te Wees* (Phobophobia: The Fear of Being Afraid) by underground painter and sculptor M.J. Louwrens. Spamer introduced me to Louwrens even though I had missed the film. I gathered that the film was a surrealist montage reflecting Afrikaner lives ruled by Calvinist-instilled fear. As the young filmmaker spoke to me in drug-inflected nonsensical phrases, a jazzy trumpet riffed over drum 'n' bass.[8] After the set, the trumpet player took up the accordion and joined his other band, Gramadoelas. This group juxtaposed specifically Afrikaans genres: goema music from the "Cape Coloured" community with Afrikaner boeremusiek.

By now it was nearly one o'clock in the morning and time to clear the floor for the hip-hop dancers, who spun on their heads and anything else they could use as an axis, while the Cape Flats group, Brasse Vannie Kaap (BVK), rapped in "Gamtaal" (a derogatory, but reclaimed, reference to the Afrikaans spoken by "coloured" working-class people in Cape

Transmissie ravers gyrate before the image of Paul Kruger, the founder of Afrikaner nationalism, during DJ Opperman's multimedia title performance, *Transmissie,* Barn Celos, Melkbosstrand, 17 December 1999. (Photo by Stephanie Marlin-Curiel)

"Mr Phat" (right) of BVK, performs with two hip-hop dancers at *Transmissie,* Barn Celos, Melkbosstrand, 17 December 1999. (Photo by Stephanie Marlin-Curiel)

Town). BVK was followed by DJ Overdose spinning Afrikaans *kwaito*. Kwaito, a home-grown version of American house music,[9] is considered the music of South Africa's black youth. Very few people of colour were in the audience, beyond the immediate friends and family of the performers. By inviting DJ Overdose, the organisers were underlining the fact that most kwaito is chanted in a street slang strongly based in an Afrikaans variant called "Tsotsitaal".[10] Even the name, kwaito, comes from the Afrikaans slang word *kwaai*, meaning "those house tracks were [so] hot, that they were kicking"[11] – in other words, "phat", or "cool".

Including black Afrikaans music tested the possibilities and limits of an Afrikaans, as opposed to Afrikaner, language and consciousness. Could an Afrikaans-speaking community reconcile itself with the past and the deep divisions within it? How could black Afrikaans speakers come to trust white Afrikaners? How will the younger generation of white Afrikaners overcome their parents' crimes and misguided illusions? These questions are too difficult to solve in one night of dancing. As the evening faded into dawn, the remaining party-goers were still lost in Du Toit's intoxicating multimedia memoryscape.

Searching for a New Identity: The Groot (Great) Trek II

The rave evoked the past even as it proposed a new and different future: establishing an identity for Afrikaners that is simultaneously Afrikaans and African. The party acknowledged black speakers of Afrikaans[12] as both possessing the historical roots of Afrikaans and holding the power to guarantee its future as a recognised South African language. Such an alliance potentially benefits black as well as white speakers of Afrikaans.

Feelings of marginalisation, criminalisation and general nervousness about their place in the new South Africa are common among Afrikaners, from the right-wing extremists to the progressives or *verligtes* ("enlightened"). During 1999, the centenary of the Anglo-Boer War, the renegotiation of Afrikaner identity became a highly visible issue. In the Anglo-Boer War, the Afrikaners unsuccessfully defended themselves against the English, losing many men on the battlefield, and many women and children to disease, overcrowding and starvation in English concentration camps. The war was recently renamed the "South African War" in acknowledgement of the many black Africans who died along with Afrikaners in the camps. For some Afrikaners, sharing this memory of martyrdom, which has long been a source of nationalistic pride, means the erosion of Afrikaner culture and history. For others, the re-examination of this central nationalistic myth "put things right" by providing a means of securing Afrikaners a place in the "new South African" history.

In addition to feeling displaced, Afrikaners living under a black-led government have had to contend with the negation of their sense of righteousness. The Anglo-Boer War experience along with Calvinist doctrine had furnished the core of a moral justification that fueled their battles against British colonialism, African "contamination", and the African National Congress's "communism".[13]

The political changes of the second half of the 20th century gradually reshaped the romanticised notion of the Boer agrarian past at the basis of Afrikaner *volk* (people) identity. From the 1950s to the early 1990s, the escalation of a broad-based multiracial resistance campaign compounded growing class and ideological factionalism within Afrikanerdom, finally leading to the demise of apartheid. As pressures built in the 1980s, the National Party began to bend, making concessions to the national and international anti-apartheid movement. The Afrikaner volk became right-wing radicals who branded the leaders of the National Party as traitors. By the end of the 1980s, Afrikanerdom, however defined – as a national destiny, a white supremacist regime, or a path-builder to economic success – had unequivocally failed. When Nelson Mandela and his African National Congress (ANC) at last gained power in South Africa's first democratic elections in 1994, Afrikaner identity was further thrown into question (Verstergaard 2001).

In 1996 the ANC government instituted the Truth and Reconciliation Commission (TRC), whereby perpetrators of gross human rights violations could receive amnesty in exchange for public confessions, further confusing Afrikaner sense of selfhood. Six months prior to the beginning of the amnesty hearings, victims[14] were given the opportunity to tell their stories in public in order for the TRC to perform its function of "rehabilitat[ing] and restor[ing]" their "human and civil dignity" (TRC 1995). This nationally and internationally broadcast performance irrevocably turned the tables on Afrikaner claims to moral righteousness. Despite efforts toward evenhandedness, the TRC, in the eyes of some Afrikaners, staged a moral drama pitting mostly black victims against mostly white Afrikaner perpetrators (Verwoerd 1996:67). Although there were many exceptions to this scenario, the TRC hearings effectively invalidated the cherished Afrikaner martyr role established by the Anglo-Boer War. Afrikaners were instead shown to be the authors of calculated, evil methods used to terrorise and obliterate so-called enemies of the state.

Within a new South African society that allows freedom of speech and freedom of the press, Afrikaner youth are encountering histories that flatly contradict the versions they learned in school and at military training bases where they underwent compulsory military training during the apartheid years. For many young Afrikaners who never took much interest in politics or who were successfully shielded from it by their parents and institutions, this new knowledge has been a harsh awakening.

In this context, the title of the rave, and the potential new movement, *Transmissie*, has special significance. "Transmissie" signifies both communication and an automobile gearshift. This younger generation is not only "shifting gears" away from their parents and the lies with which they grew up, but they are also shifting away from the overtly political *alternatiewe* (alternative) movement of the late 1980s. The "alternatiewe" movement, a dissident group of Afrikaans-speaking writers and musicians, deliberately tried to attack the Afrikaner establishment by using the "holy and pure" Afrikaans language to give voice

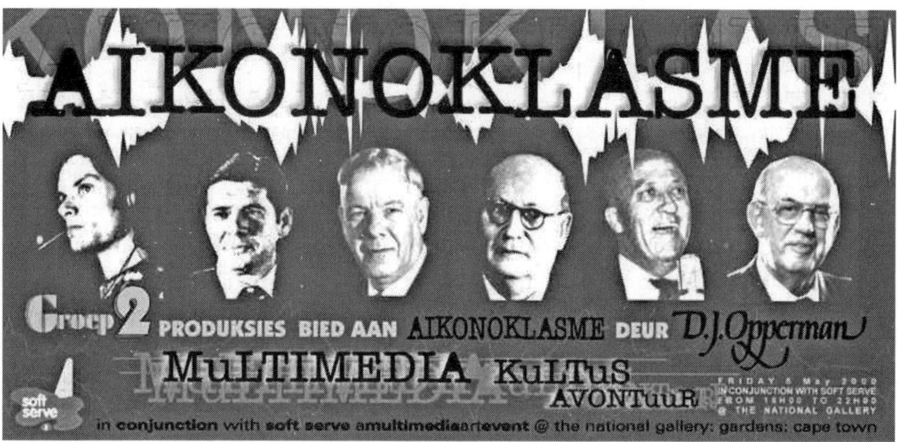

The flyer for the subsequent development of DJ Opperman's *Transmissie* piece *Aikonoklasme* ("iconoclasm") which was performed at *Soft Serve II ("Art at Play")* held at the National Gallery in Cape Town on 5 May 2000. The figures from left to right are: DJ Opperman (Heine du Toit), Gerhard Viviers, Hendrik F. Verwoerd, D.F. Malan, Dana Niehaus, and P. W. Botha. (Courtesy of Stephanie Marlin-Curiel)

to their rebellion. In contrast, *Transmissie* was about freedom and fun, not resistance and rhetoric. According to the rave organisers, the time for politics is over: "Whatever needed to be said has already been said. It is time for people to simply enjoy their freedom" (Spamer 1999). Part of this freedom means freedom from thinking about politics.

While this generation recognises that they were fed lies as part of an indoctrination process, they are reluctant to condemn the pleasant memories of their youth. Their memories of the poems, stories and music they experienced as children are happy ones and "they don't want to have to feel guilty about it" (Spamer 1999). Even the political speeches, which served as a source of inspiration during apartheid, are still a source of strength (Du Toit 2000a). While the TRC was serving up hard-hitting truths and administering high doses of shame directed toward Afrikaners, the *Transmissie* revellers wanted to reconcile themselves with their past in a way that would allow them to salvage their self-esteem. In Du Toit's words:

> The concept really is the Truth Commission. It's about taking truths from the past and making peace with them. That is the whole idea of the Truth Commission. But in this case it was more fun, it was taking politics [...] and dealing with it in a fun, laughing way, in a light way instead of people sitting there and having to ask those questions, "Why did you . . . ?" "Why was the . . . ?" As opposed to, "This is what happened." Take rugby. It reflects on culture then. It brings back good memories instead of bad memories. That's the whole point. Good memories as opposed to bad memories. I hope I didn't contradict myself. (2000a)

Du Toit's search for a positive sense of identity has some parallels with the behaviour of second-generation post-World War II German youth who have also been described as avoiding politics and substituting "object-ties of a more clinging nature" to re-establish their self-esteem (Mitscherlich 1975:221). Du Toit's multimedia piece spun a web of ambiguity around nostalgic objects displaced in time and space. This sense of ambiguity accurately reflects the present historical moment, which finds Afrikaners, young and old, still reeling from the shock of having their world turned upside down.

Now that the contradictory worlds that the Afrikaner system took such great pains to keep separate are coming together, it is possible for Du Toit to consider political speeches such as Malan's as both good and bad memories. The indoctrination process imposed upon Afrikaner youth was more than propaganda. It was a complete artificial environment enforced by a powerful "behind-the-scenes" network called the *Broederbond* (brotherhood). As Peter Lambley discusses in his book, *The Psychology of Apartheid*, the Broederbond made it "possible for the Afrikaners to raise its [*sic*] children as if its views on reality are in exact accordance with reality" (1980:198). The Broederbond ensured that there were Afrikaans versions of every social network and facility for both children and adults. In 1948 when the National Party came to power and gained control of the South African Broadcasting Corporation (set up as a 'public broadcaster'), Afrikaners were subjected to the incessant broadcasting of nationalistic programming on state-sponsored media, and warnings from the Broederbond against the dangers of non-Afrikaans movies, books and music. Together, the Broederbond and the government attempted to ensure that Afrikaners did not encounter any reason to doubt that they were "superior, Godly, [. . .] descendant[s] of brave men and women who fought for their beliefs and values" (Lambley 1980:198).

As Lambley explains, travel, cosmopolitanism, and other experiences outside this closed system were vehemently discouraged and construed by the state as threats (1980:217). Afrikaners therefore had some awareness of other worlds without ever coming into direct contact with them. Such a thorough segregation created the conditions that today result in nostalgia for the "good old days".

This may account for the enduring admiration many Afrikaners have for their childhood heroes, even after becoming aware of their participation in a brutal, totalising machine that programmed every aspect of their lives. Some of these heroes were rugby players; rugby served as a training ground for Afrikaner machismo, discipline, and anti-English sentiment (Nauright 1997:87).[15] Du Toit compares his affection for rugby commentator Gerhard Viviers to the American affection for Howard Cossell (the boxing commentator).

Dana Niehaus, a children's storyteller whose voice is also heard in Du Toit's mix, was for storytelling "what [sportscaster] Gerhard Viviers was for rugby" (Du Toit 2000a). Du Toit muses on Niehaus's voice: "[...] I mean again [it is] instantly recognisable. You hear his voice, you revert back to those days where you sat in front of the record player and he took you away. He took you to la-la-land" (2000a). For Du Toit the memories of his childhood are all "good clean stuff" – or in the words of Malan's immortal speech, the "good and clean from the past to build thereon a future".

On the surface, the Niehaus story included in the mix seems similar to stories I read as a child. A jackal tricked a wolf into going through a hole in a fence, fed him so much he couldn't get back out, and then called the farmer over to kill the wolf. In the context of Afrikaner ideology, Du Toit said, "the stories have a serious edge to them [. . .] they were a way of tricking you into buying into the system" (2000a). Somewhere inside him, Du Toit knows that this is not the "good clean stuff" he wants to believe it is. Asked about the inclusion of Malan's speeches in his piece, Du Toit commented:

> I think essentially it's bad memories but there was a certain nationalism in it. They were protective and the anthem was sung. I still cannot help it, but I get goose bumps because I played in a military band. The thing is forceful. It was driving . . . Marching music is positive, forward, energetic, and I think one thing that those speeches were all about is determination. They were really determined to get the Republic and they got it. If you are determined [. . .] But it was more about recognising the ridiculousness of it all. It was about the ideology that was so blindly followed that in the end it crashed [. . .] (2000a)

Young Afrikaners like Du Toit cannot go along with the present moral narrative that condemns everything they draw strength from, and yet in order to live in a post-apartheid South Africa, they cannot ignore the charges laid by the national reckoning process.

Du Toit includes images of black children in his show as brief reminders, flashbacks of the unsavoury aspects of Afrikaner nationalism. He includes a photo of a group of black secondary school students and comments that these photos, as well as the Hector Peterson photo, were included "as a reflection of the fear that was invoked by the National Party" (Du Toit 2000b). Although the faces of the black students in this latter photograph display no fear, their association with the tragedy of the Soweto revolts characterised them, in Du Toit's mind, as "symbolic" of fear. Burying the image of Peterson's death in the depths of his subconscious, Du Toit verbally acknowledges the oppressiveness of Afrikaner power but not the loss of life. He sees the fear in the black students' eyes, but not their defiance.

Return to Innocence

The carnival atmosphere of the rave presents a natural counterpoint to the rationalising, nationalistic context in which nostalgia historically has been performed in South Africa. As "a purified past, exempt from claims and contradictions of everyday experience" (DaSilva and Faught 1982:55), nostalgia has often been used by Afrikaners to "create a sense of cultural security during a loss of political, and possibly cultural, power" (Nauright 1977:165).

The rave as an "alternative" social setting implies an intention to "critique the dominant social order" (Martin 1999:87). If such a critique was embedded in *Transmissie*, it came in the form of a seemingly incongruous mix of the identification with Afrikanerness and the deconstruction of that Afrikanerness by means of "campy" techniques common to raves (Martin 1999:85). By using icons of Afrikanerdom, Du Toit traces the degree to which social conditioning controlled Afrikaners from birth. His nostalgic longing is not for power, but for innocence. The "good old days" are not so much associated with prosperity as they are with security. Without the burden of responsibility and self-reflection that came with the national ritual of the TRC, Afrikaners had no reason to question the values they had been taught. Those who had travelled abroad when they grew up saw racial hierarchy as a norm wherever they went and regarded the international condemnation of apartheid as outright hypocrisy (Du Toit 2001).

The mocking critique of the Afrikaner icons in Du Toit's visual sequence is more like the jibes of a rebellious adolescent than the protests of a revolutionary. Paul Kruger acquires a hastily drawn cigarette and several shapes of glasses during the course of the loop. Multiple P.W. Botha images and old National Party logos scroll by in rapid succession like the frames at the end of an old-fashioned film, or cover the entire screen, as in a souvenir necktie or tablecloth. Du Toit's nostalgic use of album covers and monuments is as much tongue-in-cheek as it is genuine. Knowing that several of his friends and their parents collected such albums – of rugby games when the South African Springboks were triumphant, of political speeches by Afrikaner national leaders, and of mothers pining for their soldier sons "on the border" – Du Toit asked his friends to lend him their collectables for his piece. The unmediated memories of the sounds came face-to-face with their constructed memories as memorabilia; sound selections were not only meant to be recognisable in and of themselves, but were also meant to refer to their collectability.

With the commemorative album of mothers yearning for their brave sons on the border, however, unmediated memories and constructed memories collided painfully. These maternal praises, which Du Toit underlay with ever-escalating drum rolls, were both an ironic critique and a sincere plea meant to purge the incredible anxiety he associated with his own military experience. The military was not a "good and bad" memory, just a bad memory.

Serving in the South African Defence Force (SADF) was obligatory for young white men under apartheid. Students were refused permission to write their final-year high school exams until they signed up. The military service constituted the first time these young men had ever ventured outside their secure environment. Contrary to their mothers' fantasies, and despite the honours bestowed posthumously upon those who died, the young men on the border did not feel brave or manly. They felt unprepared, frightened and betrayed.

One of their "preparations" for military service was a popular photo comic, *Grensvegter* (Border Fighter), featuring hero Rocco de Wet (Rocco the Law). Stationed on "the border", De Wet protected Afrikaner families on farms from "communist terrorists". Some woman would inevitably fall in love with Rocco, but his duty to his country always came

A scene from the photo comic book, *Grensvegter* (Border Fighter). Translation of caption: "But the Russian is surprised . . . and too slow." (Courtesy of Stephanie Marlin-Curiel)

first. The apartheid era government used Cold War rhetoric to further enhance their moral justification for fighting the ANC and other Southern African independence movements both outside and inside South Africa's borders. Images of blacks never tainted the pages of these comic books. Instead, the Cuban and Soviet troops assisting the independence movements stood in for the black "communist enemy" – Angolan, Namibian, or South African.

A parody of this photo comic and others like it turned up at the rave to challenge the pretences of *Grensvegter*. A new version, *Koertz Kotze en die Vrouekolonie* (Koertz Kotze and the Women's Colony), distributed as a party favour, was far from an unadulterated bit of nostalgia. The parody explicitly emasculated the stereotypical macho characters that filled previous photo comics. Conceived by Gilda Swanepoel as a promotion for her Boerebar, the story is about a detective who must solve the murder of a man who died from having his penis cut off. He discovers the Vrouekolonie where women are drugging men to give them hard-ons and then having their way with them. When the women are tired of one of their captives, they kill him by cutting off his penis. The detective, of course, meets the same end. While Swanepoel denies being a feminist or having been angry when she wrote *Koertz Kotze*, the story confirms that the first step to debunking Afrikanerdom is to castrate Afrikaner masculinity. (It may also bring to light the urges generated by years of repression under Afrikaner patriarchy.)

This photo comic, which wields daggers at Afrikaner masculinity, is not the first of its

Conceived and directed by Gilda Swanepoel, photography by Daniel Erasmus; courtesy of Stephanie Marlin-Curiel.

kind. *Bittercomix* has been shattering the Afrikaner value system since 1992. *Bittercomix*, like *Koertz Kotze*, often uses scenes of sex and violence to break the taboos of Afrikaner Calvinist culture and also attempts to deal with the identity crisis that is the inevitable consequence of this dismantling of traditions. Like Du Toit's parody of rebelliousness, *Koertz Kotze* was also a satire on *Bittercomix*, created for its comedic rather than its shock value. Still, it constituted a more forthright critique of Afrikaner values than Du Toit's séance, which invoked the psychological power of major figures in Afrikaner national history. White bodies gyrating in front of their spiritual ancestors is as exorcistic as it is celebratory. Yet, as Fabio B. DaSilva and Jim Faught note, nostalgia loses its capacity to serve as a critique the more it encourages an audience's "experiential emersion [*sic*] in the data" (1982:51). Raves foster group cohesion rather than individuated experiences conducive to a critical approach to the material. Was the rave nothing more than an escape from the present by means of a reversion to a more stable, familiar Afrikanerness? Or did it represent an intention to face the present by subjecting Afrikanerness to a progressive border crossing that would challenge the negative dialectic from which Afrikanerness was constructed?

Shifting Gears, Edging Forward: The New (?) "Alternatiewe" Movement

It is difficult to know at this stage whether we are witnessing the end of an old *alternatiewe* movement or the beginning of a new one. The effort to destabilise the ideologically limited range of signification possible within Afrikaans began in the late 1980s with an *alternatiewe* literary movement by black Afrikaans writers that solidified in the Western Cape. These were writers who, while labelled "Coloured" under apartheid, identified themselves politically as black. Nevertheless, the desire to write in Afrikaans was a departure from the radical politics of the 1976 Soweto student uprising when black students took to the streets to protest compulsory instruction in Afrikaans (they preferred English). More than an anti-Afrikaans movement, however, the Soweto uprising, inspired by the Black Consciousness Movement, was ultimately a movement of self-determination. It empowered blacks to choose their language of expression; black[16] writers in the Cape chose to reclaim their mother tongue, which was Afrikaans (Gerwel in Willemse 1990:375). Writing in Afrikaans was also a way of identifying with the class struggle, as Afrikaans was the language of the rural black working class. This *alternatiewe* literary movement attracted white Afrikaans writers interested in distancing themselves from the Afrikaner establishment. Most black Afrikaans writers focused less on outright protest than on reflecting their own experiences in their own language. White Afrikaans writers, as much as the censors allowed, used the Afrikaner language as a language of protest to counteract its history of oppression. As a whole, the movement focused on the Afrikaans language as the key to breaking down the racist exclusivity of Afrikaner national identity, which laid claim to a "pure" Afrikaans language (Barnard 1992:80).

The question of whether young, white Afrikaners' recuperation of words and images from the architects of apartheid, even in an altered form, simply provides an escape into an unreal fantasy, or offers a way of acknowledging the wrongs of the past, echoes the debate within the *alternatiewe* literary movement over the use of Afrikaans. The debate centred on whether writing in *Kaaps* (Cape Afrikaans) or *Kombuis* (Kitchen Afrikaans) – which wreaked havoc with standard rules of grammar and spelling – re-entrenched race-class stereotypes (Willemse 1990:393), constituted an opposition to the Afrikaner establishment, or merely endowed Afrikaans with more flexibility and strength (Barnard 1992:87).[17] So the same question may be posed about whether the late-20th-century focus on creating a new Afrikaner identity will spawn a new nationalism that will be counterproductive to the cause of democracy.

Since the old Afrikaner establishment tried to expand its base of support by constructing a cultural identity inscribed within the Afrikaans language, identity and language were natural avenues of subversion for the 1980s *alternatiewe* movement.[18] However, Ian Barnard argues that during the 1980s, efforts to effect change in Afrikaner consciousness through formal experimentation with the language failed (1992:91). *Somer II* (Summer II, 1985) the punk novel by Koos Kombuis (the stage name of Andre Letoit), for example, "mixes genres, confuses chronology, relates incidents from various narrative threads seemingly at random, [and...] gleefully discards the notion of language purity in favour of the Afrikaans that is actually spoken today" (1992:84, 86). Nevertheless, it fails to be truly subversive because it does not manage to create a tension between reality and fiction in its narrative (1992:92). Reminiscent of Du Toit's comment that the presence of the Hector Peterson photo and the photos of other black students in his work represent the "fear instilled by the National Party", Barnard points out that there is "no outrage" (1992:88) in *Somer II* against the apartheid reality, simply acceptance.

A mostly white *alternatiewe* music scene paralleled the '80s *alternatiewe* literary scene and also attacked Afrikaner hegemony by deconstructing its language and identity. While 1980s "mainstream" Afrikaner musicians sang of idealised, romantic landscapes which reinforced a hegemonic false consciousness about the "rural" history of the Boers (Jury 1996:2-3), *alternatiewe* musicians deconstructed those images through plays on words in Afrikaans or English. Many of their stage names, for example, used words that were either sacred or profane in Afrikaner culture, such as Koos Kombuis – the author of *Somer II,* who is also a musician – which translates as Koos "Kitchen". Others include Bernoldus Niemand (or Bernoldus "Nobody"); Valiant Swart ("Black Prince" or Valiant Black); and Johannes Kerkorrel (literally John "Church Organ"). Although some of the musicians' names make reference to nonwhite speakers of Afrikaans, their lyrics overtly protested their own reality – particularly military conscription – but never directly addressed apartheid as experienced by their nonwhite compatriots. In *alternatiewe* music, experiments in sound proved to be even more subversive than experiments in language. The *alternatiewe* Afrikaans music movement culminated in the 1990 *Voëlvry* ("outlaw", or "fugitive") music tour, which was a confrontational attempt to fracture white Afrikaner power politically and culturally. The *Voëlvry* musicians set Afrikaans lyrics protesting apartheid and military conscription to 1950s American style rock and roll. Although by 1990 rock was no longer revolutionary, the *Voëlvryers* knew their music would provoke the wrath of the conservative Afrikaner Nationalist government.

The *Voëlvryers* used the postmodern aesthetic techniques of juxtaposition and montage to deconstruct an inherited tradition, but they did so more in order to generate historical dissonance than to recover from it. Although *Transmissie*'s "new" *alternatiewe* Afrikaans musicians inherited much from the *Voëlvryers*, they refuse to engage in political polemics. Du Toit's iconoclastic multimedia performance using futuristic music parodied both the power these musicians had over young minds as well as his *alternatiewe* predecessors' transgressive rebellion against this power. Twenty-first century *alternatiewe* Afrikaans musicians experiment more with sound than with language. This is an effort to distance themselves from an older generation of alternative Afrikaners, such as the Group of 63,[19] who seek to protect the place of Afrikaans in South African culture by intellectual means.

Some cross-cultural experiments with sound, such as the kind Gramadoelas performs, were already taking place in the 1980s. Boeremusiek had been enjoying a revival since the early '80s. Symphony orchestras were playing "ethnoclassical" music, and popular music artists played "afro-rock" or "afro-jazz" (Byerly 1998:15). Boereqanga emerged from a combination of boeremusiek and mbaqanga, a black township musical style. Gramadoelas, meaning "outback" or "sticks", combines two musical types that share closely related origins and rhythms: Afrikaans boeremusiek, and goema music, which is associated with the annual minstrel-style festival known as the "coon" carnival.[20] While the rhythm of both is the same, the cultural iconographies of the two types of music differ radically. The instrumentation, tempo and dance steps have evolved along separate lines due to apartheid, which kept white Afrikaners apart from those they labelled "Coloured". Named for the *ghummy* drum (and played on drums, sax, trumpet, banjo, guitar and percussion instruments such as rattles and tambourines), goema is a faster, more sprightly version of vastrap, an Afrikaner dance rhythm usually played on concertinas and accordions. The term "vastrap" means "to step firmly", referring to the stamping technique used to create a floor out of cow dung, which the Boers learned from the Khoisan (Van Heerden 1999). Goema and vastrap share a repertoire of melodies, such as the "langarm", a polka-like dance common to both rural Afrikaners and "coloured" Afrikaans-speaking communities. By combining two Afrikaans musical traditions that had most likely begun as one and then split apart, Gramadoelas aims to repair the fissures in Afrikaans culture.

If Du Toit's piece was about revisiting the myths of Afrikanerdom, Gramadoelas "is about telling the truth" (Van Heerden 1999). The music attempts to recuperate the history of cultural exchange between Boers and Africans in order to legitimise Afrikaner cultural citizenship in the new South Africa. As Gramadoelas' leader Van Heerden recounted, "the *real* Afrikaans culture was not white" (1999). The Afrikaans language developed among slaves attempting to learn the Dutch spoken by their European masters. For years, the Dutch Afrikaner settlers regarded Afrikaans as a coarse language spoken only by poor whites and "Coloureds". Not until their defeat in the Boer War did white Afrikaners appropriate and standardise this "coarse" language, making it into their "national language" in an effort to define themselves as a nation separate from Europe, especially from Britain (Barnard 1992:79).

In post-apartheid South Africa, Afrikaner cultural survival depends not only on a repudiation of Afrikaner nationalism, but on an emphasis on historical ties with nonwhite Afrikaans speakers. Articulating these ties only in terms of commonalities and cross-fertilisations of cultures, however, seems to bypass the material injustices perpetrated by the Dutch settlement of the Cape and the Afrikaner-led apartheid government.

Ready or Not: Brothers from the Cape Will Not Stop

The inclusion of the Cape Flats rap group Brasse Vannie Kaap in a rave that self-consciously focused on the post-apartheid reformulation of Afrikaner identity must be looked upon with a mixture of hope and skepticism. BVK's lyrics demonstrate that apartheid is still very much present on the Cape Flats. Here it becomes clear that post-apartheid discourses are determined as much by class as they are determined by personal histories that can be implicated in a national narrative of victimhood. If Du Toit's piece might be seen as a critique of the past on an ideological level despite a clear denial of guilt, BVK's songs blame the apartheid government for the material conditions they face, and yet express their refusal to play the victim.

Beyond playing good dance music, BVK's mission is to empower the Cape Flats community with the knowledge that drugs and gangsterism are not their own creation but part of the plan fomented by the apartheid regime's security police. Ready D, the DJ for BVK, cautioned, however, that this mission is a delicate one:

> . . . having the information so you can have a better understanding of what is going on around you can help you elevate yourself further as an individual. So in one sense it is keeping me enlightened. But in another sense part of that information you have to give to people in reasonable doses. I would say because if you give it to people all in one go, it's too mind-blowing, people won't understand. They will think it's a bunch of bull. They'll think we're smoking some shit. (1999)

He also recognises that politics is "passé" in South Africa:

> We don't want to go out there preaching. That kind of stuff goes over people's head. They don't want to listen to that. They think apartheid is over. They're all happy. We use humor to get the message across. (1999)

The humour lies in the punning and rhyming of Gamtaal. For example, one of their raps describes a teenager who becomes a gangster to be "the man", but ends up being thrown into jail and sodomised. In English, one of the lines of this rap translates as "if you want something, you gotta lay". Using Gamtaal, the rappers invert the words and play on internal rhyme to communicate a serious message in a humorous way.[21] To illustrate how different Gamtaal is from standard Afrikaans, Ready D explained that a white Afrikaner and his Cape Flats compatriots listening to the same sentence will come away with completely different interpretations.

Despite the real possibility that white Afrikaners understand only a fragment of the lyrics, they make up most of BVK's audience. The majority of BVK's performances take place at what are essentially white Afrikaans festivals.[22] Inheriting an attraction for the innovative use of language from the *alternatiewe* movement of the previous decade, white alternative-thinking Afrikaners see in Gamtaal a means of lifting themselves out of their cultural isolation and stagnation. By performing for white Afrikaans audiences, BVK hopes to legitimise Gamtaal and erase the class bias attached to its stereotypical image. In the eyes of their own communities, they are out to prove that "Gamtaal is legal and that you can get a positive message across without slipping into the feel-good 'hêppie coons' trap" (Haupt 1998).[23]

Like Afrikaans, Gamtaal's search for normalisation will end when acceptance replaces stigma. Gamtaal will have to achieve its legitimacy as an oral rather than a written form. Ready D explained that writing a dictionary of Gamtaal would be impossible because the language changes every day. Gangsterism, arising from apartheid divisions even within Cape Town's "Coloured" townships, creates the necessity to continually revise the in-group code language. Gamtaal develops not only on the streets, but also in the prisons. By isolating people from their own communities and throwing them together with people from other areas, the prison system creates new factions that form their own languages. When these people return from prison, they find that the language in their communities has changed and they are forced to learn new meanings for old words. But more important than having a written form, BVK's CDs and tours have stamped Gamtaal with an even more important mark of legitimacy and social leverage, an exchange value in the global hip-hop circuit.

Like the "new" *alternatiewe* Afrikaners who prefer positive self-expression to political protest, BVK avoids the pitfalls of the *alternatiewe* literary movement by avoiding confrontation with the establishment. Aiming for acceptance rather than change, BVK seeks to enable nonwhite Afrikaans speakers to decolonise their minds; in other words, to dispense with the apartheid mentality of conforming to white society by speaking its language.[24]

On the basis of events such as *Transmissie*, Ready D sees the possibility of destigmatising Gamtaal in his own community, as well as "de-othering" Gamtaal among white Afrikaans speakers. In Ready D's words, "Once white people start clicking into it, a lot of people will be much more open to speak and to basically just being themselves" (1999).

Are white Afrikaners really hearing BVK's lyrics as a "reality" that might challenge their nostalgic revisitation of their past, or is BVK's performance at the *Transmissie* rave just another experimentation in form that potentially legitimises Afrikaner citizenship in the new South Africa?

Despite a veneer of progressivism, Afrikaners would prefer that the "African" in President Thabo Mbeki's "African Renaissance" be spelled "Afrikaan". Max du Preez, a progressive Afrikaner journalist, wrote a column in the predominantly liberal *Mail and Guardian* newspaper in which he asked for assurance of the inclusion of Afrikaners in Mbeki's African Renaissance. This piece sparked a heated public debate over whether or not Afrikaners could call themselves Africans.[25]

The heavy media coverage of the proceedings of the TRC and the "rainbow nation" image have too readily linked the politics of memory and identity with the cause of societal transformation, such that the very gesture of revisiting the past can be considered a step toward reconciliation. Protected by the prevailing ANC discourse of reconciliation, unity, and "South Africanness," the collaboration of Afrikaans speakers across colour lines may look like progressive politics.[26] Unfortunately, such intentions are tainted by the tired tactics of the old National Party's enfranchisement strategies of offering advantages to "Coloureds" in order to garner their votes.[27] The TRC modelled an accountability based on confession alone rather than punishment or reparation, such that citizenship in the "new" South Africa is more dependent on reconciliation and forgiveness than the responsibility to improve the quality of life for all the nation's citizens.

Truth: The Road to Reconciliation?

In the throes of their current identity crisis, Afrikaans speakers, black and white, share many of the dilemmas of their brethren of a decade ago. In re-evaluating these dilemmas, it is important to recognise that while the 1980s *alternatiewe* movement fought against the purity of the Afrikaans language as a symbol of Afrikaner power, the current alternative Afrikaans movement is fighting against the stigmatisation of Afrikaans.[28] Granted, we cannot concede that fighting for cultural survival in a nascent democracy carries the same urgency as fighting an oppressive regime. And yet the recognition of diverse groups, including those that share the Afrikaans language, is a cornerstone of democracy. The globalisation-conscious South African government favours English much as Black Consciousness revolutionaries did during the fight against apartheid, as a language of power. Like English, and many other South African languages, Afrikaans is shared by multiple groups defined along the lines of race, class and ethnicity. More so than any other South African language, however, Afrikaans serves as an open battleground for these groups. Now that the Afrikaner extremists have taken up arms, and globalisation continues to wedge a divide between the government and the people, the promotion of an alternative, inclusive, Afrikaans identity may be a matter of physical, as well as cultural, survival. More than this, the struggle to lay claim to an alternative Afrikaans language and identity may be one of the most viable South African sites for democracy in the making. But if democratisation is to occur on material, as well as discursive levels, social identities must be constructed according to moral standing in relationship to the present as well as the past.

Notes

1 This speech from 1948 was included on a commemorative album, *Die argitekte aan die woord* (The Architects Speak), released just prior to the foundation of the Republic of South Africa on 31 May 1961. This translation and the translation of Malan's speech excerpt were provided by Heine du Toit.

2 In this chapter, I use the term "Coloured" with a capital "C" when the reference is during the apartheid period and "coloured" with a lowercase "c" for references in the post-apartheid period. In either case I use quotes around the word in order to recognise its contested status in the past and present. See note 11 for more on the use of these terms and their implications. Most black Afrikaans speakers generally

belong to the group designated "Coloured" in apartheid terminology. They were distinguished from "African" because they were perceived to have lighter skin and straighter hair, the result of mixing between Dutch settlers and the Khoisan peoples in the 1600s.

3 Because whites are a minority in South Africa, the National Party depended on "Coloured" support for survival. Although "Coloureds" were gradually divided politically as opposition to apartheid grew, the National Party managed to hold on to a significant contingent of "Coloured" support. The apartheid regime afforded "Coloureds" a better material existence and greater freedom than "Africans" as part of the construction of a race-class system that equated lighter skin with "civilization". In the first democratic elections in 1994 the National Party successfully secured the majority of the "Coloured" vote by warning them that they would be alienated and made insecure materially by a black majority government. This is a condensed version of an extremely complex and fluctuating history. For a more detailed account, see Giliomee (1995).

4 The terms "Coloured" and "Afrikaner" are used in South Africa today with much more discomfort than the terms "white" and "black". The terms "white" and "black" have become common signifiers to describe the economic and ideological disparities of the historic and current political landscape. However, the lowercase "c" in "coloured", does not succeed in normalising the term in post-apartheid South Africa. The term is not supported by global alliances as are white and black identities, but instead leaves "coloureds" behind in the apartheid past. Some have tried to reappropriate the term to construct a self-determined identity that would prevent them from slipping through the cracks between black and white, but most politically savvy "coloureds" I spoke to feel that the term cannot escape its negative associations. They prefer to identify just the region or neighbourhood they are from: "I am from District Six"; "I am from Manenberg"; "I am from the Cape Flats", etc. When talking about themselves in a politicised context, blacks and whites frequently say they are "black South African" or "white South African". "Coloured South African", however, does not exist in public discourse. "Coloured" still represents the abject past. There is no consistency in post-apartheid terminology but, generally, academic and journalistic discourses use the term "coloured" by itself with or without quotes, or with a regional designation like Cape Coloured in order to recognise a distinct local culture.

In today's political climate, Afrikaners also feel themselves to be a minority that is losing its language, and therefore losing its voice. Increasingly, they are eschewing the term Afrikaner in favour of "Afrikaans", to designate not only the language but also an identity inclusive of "coloured" and even black Afrikaans speakers. However, I have again chosen to use the more historical term, "Afrikaner", without quotes because it is a self-determined national identity. It is also clearer, particularly for non-South African readers, if I use the term Afrikaner to refer to the identity and Afrikaans to refer to the language. Finally, it is more expedient to be able to say Afrikaner, as opposed to white Afrikaans speakers. Race is relevant here for many reasons, not the least of which is that the inclusive term, "Afrikaans", reflects the self-determination of enlightened Afrikaners but not necessarily that of all Afrikaans speakers.

5 Despite its name, iconography and music, the Boerebar is not just for Boers. In one of the many paradoxes of race relations in South Africa, the Boerebar has an all-black staff (one of whom appears in a nonracialised role in the *Koertz Kotze* photocomic discussed later) and many black patrons who drink beer beneath ironically displayed pictures of the architects of apartheid, including Hendrik Verwoerd and D.F. Malan, displayed prominently on the walls.

6 BVK is topping the charts in South Africa and in Europe. Gramadoelas' hybrid boeremusiek has become accepted by the Afrikaner mainstream; they play regularly at Afrikaner establishment functions. The drum 'n' bass band, ELX, has come out with a new CD, and Du Toit continues to develop and personalise the sentiments of Transmissie in different multimedia formats. He is on his way to becoming a cult figure in the underground art scene.

7 By using the term "postcolonial" here I do not mean to equate the structural aspects of apartheid with colonialism, but to acknowledge certain analogous discourses of power and resistance. If "post-apartheid" is taken to signify a temporal period after apartheid, albeit compromised by the persistance of material inequalities, "postcolonial" signifies a discursive movement beyond apartheid as the centrally organising epistemology. (For further discussion see Magubane 2003.)

8 Drum 'n' bass evolved from jungle music, which originated in London ("the concrete jungle") and was named for a specific club called "Jungle". It consists of a looped asynchronous rhythm (otherwise known as breakbeat) consisting of a fast drumbeat and distinct bassline. The overlays can range from jazzy to electronic trance. The form has been in existence since about 1994 and is epitomised by Roni Size. Drum 'n' bass is usually produced electronically, but here it was played acoustically.

9 American house music was born in Chicago around 1985. The DJ dance music consists of spinning soul and disco tunes and overlaying them with a machine-generated 4/4 beat.

10 Tsotsitaal is another hybrid linguistic variant of urban, working-class black South Africans like the Gamtaal that BVK uses, but Tsotsitaal is from the black townships of Gauteng.

11 This quote from well-known kwaito artist, Mdu Masilela, appears on several kwaito websites. See <http://www.megweb.uct.ac.za/www/students/RRKROB001/roots.htm>.

12 The majority of "non-white" Afrikaans speakers are "coloured," but many who supported the African National Congress and not the National Party identify themselves politically as black and would still favour this term over the term "coloured".

The term "non-white" should be avoided because it indicates that white Afrikaans speakers make up the majority while in actuality more than half of Afrikaans speakers in South Africa are black.

13 Many of Paul Kruger's successors promoted strong cultural identity as a tool for economic and political survival in the face of English industrial enterprise in South Africa. By the time the Afrikaner National Party gained power in 1948, industrialisation had prompted a large-scale urban migration of rural Africans that threatened Afrikaner racial purity and economic hegemony. The Afrikaner anti-imperialist platform was redirected with vehemence against nonwhite racial groups. Apartheid was as much an oppressive economic system based on race as it was a means of ensuring white political supremacy.

14 Victims as defined by the TRC meant only victims of gross human rights violations. This did not include victims of forced removals, Bantu education, pass laws, and many of the other abuses of power levied against "nonwhite" South Africans, particularly black Africans.

15 The British brought rugby to South Africa. Afrikaners first participated in it as an expression of Europeanness and, following the Anglo-Boer War, as a space to continue their fight. Nelson Mandela's strategic appearance at the 1995 Rugby World Cup has been interpreted as the moment that "united" South Africa and as a gesture of reconciliation (see Nauright 1997). It can also be seen, however, as an attempt to break down the exclusivity of what had been a playground for Afrikaner nationalism.

16 As mentioned earlier, these people were labelled "Coloured" under the apartheid system, but identified politically as black.

17 These languages were appropriated and "standardised" by the Afrikaners who wanted to abandon Dutch along with their European identity in order to differentiate themselves from the English. In time, however, they came to be viewed within Afrikaner nationalist culture as bastardisations of "pure" Afrikaans.

18 In the years before "democracy", the Afrikaans literary agenda was first defined by the power struggles between the Afrikaners and the English and later between *verligte* (enlightened) and *verkrampte* (conservative) elements within Afrikanerdom. During the intensification of the struggle against apartheid in the 1970s and '80s, dissident Afrikaans writers, white and black, focused their efforts on freeing the language from the control of the National Party (Barnard 1992:83).

19 The Group of 63 is a "bipartisan" coalition assembled in May 2000 and comprised of Afrikaner conservatives and dissidents seeking constitutional protection for the Afrikaans language and cultural rights. Individual rights are protected under the Constitution but these do not necessarily translate into group rights. The Afrikaans-speaking community wants to be assured of their own cultural space within the larger society (see Barrell 2000).

20 For a history and explanation of the cultural influences and politics of the "coon" carnival, see Jeppie (1990).

21 For both his work with BVK and his other band, Prophets of da City, Ready D has extensively researched how apartheid was at the root of the drugs and gangsterism that ravish the Cape Flats today. According to Ready D, it is this perspective that the SABC (South African Broadcasting Corporation) has sought to suppress by banning much of Prophets of da City's music.

22 The Klein Karoo festival is one of these. Supposedly "alternative", it has been judged by critics as falling back on in-group white alternative politics year after year (see Hans Pienaar, "Boerwors turns at Klein Karoo festival", *Independent Online* 1 April 2000, http://www.iol.co.za/index.php?set_id=9&click_id=5&art_id=ct2000040118522313 2K600317, and Zebulon Dread, "Arts festival or Boerfest?", *Weekly Mail and Guardian,* 20 April 2001, www.sn.apc.org/wmail/issues/010420/OTHER5.html, and Loren Shantall, "Festival falls short," *Mail & Guardian,* 2 April 1999, <http://www.sn.apc.org/wmail/issues/990402/ARTS5.html>).

23 Coon refers to the "coon" carnival celebration of urban working-class "coloureds" (see note 21). "Hêppie" mimics the Cape Flats pronunciation of "happy". A "hêppie coon" is the stereotypical happy-go-lucky "Coloured" who is too busy drinking and singing to worry about the fact that he is being oppressed.

24 Fostered by the apartheid system, strong classist sensibilities within the "Coloured" communities led many to try to pass as white.

25 For a summary of this debate see Matshikiza (1999).

26 A report in the US press shamelessly reinforced this party line. A review of the Grahamstown National Arts Festival exaggerated that the combination of Afrikaner Boer music and African mbaqanga being played by a band in the middle of town was "the music of national unity" (Rhagavan 1995).

27 See note 10.

28 English predominates in South Africa despite the fact that there are 11 constitutionally recognised languages. The SABC carries programmes in English and Afrikaans, as well as Zulu, Xhosa, and occasionally Sotho, but other languages are rarely heard in public forums.

References

Barrell, Howard. 2000. 'Fighting For Cultural Space.' *Mail & Guardian*, 24 November 2000, <http://www.sn.apc.org/wmail/issues/001124/OTHER104.html>.

Barnard, Ian. 1992. "The 'Tagtigers'. The (Un)Politics of Language in the 'New' Afrikaans Fiction." *Research in African Literatures*, 23, (Winter). 77-95.

Byerly, Ingrid. 1998. 'Mirror, Mediator, and Prophet: The Music Indaba of Late-Apartheid South Africa.' *Ethnomusicology*, 42, 1 (Winter). 1-44.

Da Silva, Fabio B. and Faught, Jim. 1992. "Nostalgia: A Sphere and Process of Contemporary Ideology." *Qualitative Sociology*, 51,1. 47-61.

Dread, Zebulon. 2001. "Arts festival or Boerfest?" *Weekly Mail and Guardian,* 20 April, <http://www.sn.apc.org/wmail/issues/010420/OTHER5.html>.

Du Toit, Heine. 2000a. Interview with author. Cape Town, 20 January 2000.

2000b E-mail correspondence. 29 May 2000.

2001 E-mail correspondence. 2 February 2001.

Giliomee, Hermann. 1995. 'The Non-Racial Franchise and Afrikaner and Coloured Identities 1910-1994.' *African Affairs* 94. 199-225.

Haupt, Adam. 1998. "Die Brasse Vertaal." *SL*, September. http://oppi.mg.co.za/brasse.html

Jeppie, Shamil. 1990. 'Popular Culture and Carnival in Cape Town: the 1940s and 1950s.' *In The Struggle for District Six: Past and Present*, edited by Jeppie, S. and Soudien, C. 67-87. Cape Town: Buchu Books.

Jury, Brendon. 1996. 'Boys to Men: Afrikaans Alternative Popular Music 1986-1990.' *African Languages and Culture* 9,2.

Kombuis, Koos. 1985. *Somer II: 'n Plakboek*. Cape Town: Perskor.

Lambley, Peter. 1980. *The Psychology of Apartheid*. Athens: University of Georgia.

Magubane, Zine. 2003. "Could the 'post' in Post-Apartheid be the 'post' in Post-Colonial? Language, Ideology, and Class Struggle." In *Postmodernism, Postcoloniality, and African Studies,* ed. Magubane, Z.. Trenton, N.J.: Africa World Press. 135-165.

Malan, Daniel François. 1961[1948]. "Die argitekte aan die woord" Sound recording 1474.fa 1, Johannesburg: Gallo.

Martin, Daniel. 1999. "Power Play and Party Politics: The Significance of Raving." *Journal of Popular Culture* 32, 4. 77-99.

Matshikiza, John. 1999. "Trouble among the natives." *Mail and Guardian*, 16-20 July 1999. 10.

Matthews, Michelle. 1999. "Trance met 'n Missie." *Daily Mail and Guardian*, 17 December 1999, <http://www.mg.co.za/art/music/9912/9912217 - transmissie.html.

Mitscherlich, Alexander and Margarete. 1975. *The Inability to Mourn*. New York: Grove Press, Inc.

Nauright, John. 1997. *Sports, Cultures and Identities in South Africa.* Cape Town and Johannesburg: David Philip.

Pienaar, Hans. 2000. "Boerwors turns at Klein Karoo festival." *Independent Online* 1 April, <http://www.iol.co.za/index.php?set_id=9&click_id=5&art_id=ct20000401185223132K600317>.

ReadyD. 1999. Interview with author. Cape Town, 20 December 1999.

Rhagavan, Sudarsan. 1995. "'Crossover' is New Buzzword in South Africa; From Music to Theater to Painting, the Popular Arts are Becoming a Chorus of Diversity." *Los Angeles Times*, 11 July: World Report. 2.

Roots of Kwaito <http://www.megweb.uct.ac.za/www/students/RRKROB001/roots.htm>.

Shantall, Loren. 1999. "Festival falls short." *Weekly Mail and Guardian,* 2 April 1999, <http://www.sn.apc.org/wmail/issues/990402/ARTS5.html>.

Spamer, Manie.1999. Interview with author. Cape Town, 29 December 1999.
2001 Email correspondence. 25 January 2001.

Swanepoel, Gilda. 2001. Telephone communication, 7 February 2001.

Truth and Reconciliation Commission. 1995. *Promotion of Unity and National Reconciliation Act*, No. 34. <http://www.truth.org.za/legal/act9534.htm>.

Van Heerden, Alex. 1999. Interview with author. Cape Town, 29 December 1999.

Verwoerd, Wilhelm. 1996. "Continuing the Discussion: Reflections from within the Truth and Reconciliation Commission." *Current Writing* 8, 2. 66-85.

Vestergaard, Mads. 2001. "Who's Got the Map? The Negotiation of Afrikaner Identities in Post-Apartheid South Africa." *Daedelus* Winter. 19-44.

Willemse, Hein. 1990. "Die Skrille Sonbesies: Emergent Black Afrikaans Poets in Search of Authority." In *Rendering Things Visible: Essays on South African Literary Culture*, edited by M Trump. 367-401. Athens, OH: Ohio University Press. 367-401.

CHAPTER FOUR

Dial-up Identity: South African Languages in Cyberspace[1]

Herman Wasserman

A recent report by the United Nations Information and Communications Technologies Task Force regarding African Internet usage indicates that more Africans are online than ever before. The report states an increase of 20% in the number of Internet dial-up connections in Africa in the 18 months preceding October 2002, with an ever higher growth rate in corporate or shared network connections. The bad news, however, is that levels of connectivity show great differences between regions and still compare poorly with the developed world (Jensen 2002, BBC News). In another recent statement, delegates to the 6th Highway Africa Conference earlier this year emphasised in their Charter on African Media and the Digital Divide that the digital divides between the developed and developing countries were *widening*, as were the divisions related to political, economic, geographic, gender, race and class factors within countries (http://www.pambazuka.org/newsletter.php?id=10893). Underlying the concern about this divide is an optimistic belief by some in the potential benefits the Internet holds for developing countries. On the level of culture and community, some critics see the Internet as "particularly well adapted" to the practices of self-definition and political mobilisation essential to community building by minorities (Chalaby 2002:5-6), while others fear the Internet might have a negative impact on cultural and linguistic minorities (Nyamnjoh 1999:36-37).

One's view of the role that the Internet could play in Africa seems to depend at least to some extent on whether you prefer to see a glass as half empty or half full. It also depends on where in Africa you are looking from, what you are looking for and why. What data you might find might also vary depending on your source. Contradictions seem to be inevitable when attempting to chart the intersection of information and communication technology (ICT), global forces and local dynamics, cultural flows and material constraints.

This chapter will focus on the relation between the Internet and cultural and linguistic communities in South Africa. However, it does not attempt to provide conclusive or comprehensive quantitative evidence, nor does it purport to deal exhaustively with the topic of language and culture in post-apartheid South Africa. The aim of this chapter is rather to situate the use of the Internet in South African languages within broader debates about globalisation and culture, and to provide some examples to illustrate the potential as well as the problems attendant upon the relationship between the Internet and South African languages. One of the recommendations of the above-mentioned Charter on African Media and the Digital Divide is that African media should "promote the dissemination of African content in a wide range of African languages" (http://www.pambazuka.org/newsletter.php?id=10893).[2] To what extent this is taking place on the Internet and by what material and power relations this dissemination is influenced, will be touched upon in this chapter.

Because the position of South African languages on the Internet is determined by global as well as local processes, these two areas of influence will first be considered separately before going on to a brief exploration of how they relate to the specifics of the South African situation. The technological transformation of global media has fundamentally changed the character of communication. The Internet is at the centre of the information technology industry, and has come to epitomise the "information superhighway" of which the significance in shaping culture can hardly be overestimated (Castells 2000:161, 356-357; Nyamnjoh 1999:32). Because the Internet contributes to the time-space compression of the world and the intensification of the experience of the world as being interconnected and interdependent, it could be seen as one of the most recent developments in the acceleration of globalisation (cf. Barker 1999:34; Tomlinson 1999:2). Because globalisation is seen as a force emanating from the so-called developed world, some critics envisage the destruction of localities and cultural specificities within minority countries and communities. On the other hand, some critics argue that global and local forces interact in the process of globalisation, making it a multidirectional process from which local cultures and languages can benefit and even draw empowerment. Instead of the single global village that Marshall McLuhan forecasted, critics such as Alvin Toffler (quoted in Hachten 1996:93) pointed out that the world media system was more likely to consist of a multiplicity of global villages, all struggling to retain their own individuality. Let us briefly look at the Internet, as a globalising medium, from these two approaches respectively before focusing on the South African situation.

The Internet as an Exponent of Global Cultural Imperialism

Critics of new media technologies contend that the "global village" masks fundamental inequalities and dominance by Western culture and the English language, that it serves capitalist interests and has a homogenising effect on culture and identity (Barker 1999:38). Within the globalised world order, English is at the top of the hierarchy of dominance. It is the most commonly spoken second language and the lingua franca in the international business, media, scientific and academic worlds. While some welcome English as a means of communication with the potential of overcoming the global tower of Babel, others argue that minority languages might become threatened by "language death" (Tomlinson 1999:78-79).

On the Internet specifically, English is also the dominant language. Also in non-English-speaking countries there are many websites that do make use of English, because of the presumption that English provides better access to the international community (Kaschula & De Vries 2000). This dominance of English on the Internet is one of the reasons why cybertechnologies are sometimes seen as "tools of a continuing colonial globalisation" (Wood 1997) that threatens indigenous minority cultures. In South Africa, for instance, globalisation is often referred to in negative terms in the debates about the future of Afrikaans in the post-1994[3] society. The so-called "language struggle" is then seen as part of a global power struggle between those in favour of the domination of the English-oriented North, and those who would rather see a more equal distribution of power between the North and the South (Alexander 2001:9).

However, it is also possible to see the Internet as facilitating a multidirectional flow of information that other critics see as one of the central characteristics of globalisation.

The Internet as a Facilitator of Multidirectionality

Although the Internet has contributed to accelerated globalisation, this does not necessarily entail a one-way traffic from the North to the South, or from the West to the rest. Many commentators are of the opinion that the Internet has radically decentred positions of speech, democratised cultural production and created the opportunity for local and global cultures to interact. Rheingold (2000:170) concludes that the Internet has turned the traditional mass communication model of few-to-many around into a many-to-many environment in which publishing has been democratised. Some have even come to describe the medium as a "virtual democratic utopia" (Arnold and Plymire 2000:188) because of the diversity of ideas being made possible by its accessibility compared to traditional publishing. Because the Internet in this view also provides the opportunity for local communities to access global resources, it can contribute to a postcolonial "writing back" to the global metropoles and serve as a means of survival and dissemination of local languages and cultures.

The argument that the Internet as a mass medium merely subjects indigenous cultures to hegemonic discourses from the West furthermore does not take into account the principle of the "active audience", namely that media users are not merely effects being produced by texts, but are themselves also actively producing meaning. They interact with the texts from within their own contexts and are also able to resist certain meanings and reinterpret them (Barker 1999:110). Although one could argue that active production of meaning can only take place within the range of choices available, the nature of the Internet is such that individuals and groups can themselves provide content with relative ease and in so doing expand the range of choices available to other users. Internet users should therefore also be seen as cultural agents rather than merely docile subjects succumbing to globalising forces. This, Chalaby (2002:4) points out in a different context, is especially true since the Internet, with its "diversity of content and flexibility of use" lends itself towards customisation according to the needs of individuals. This has been described as a shift from "mass media" to "me media" (Naidoo 2001:7). New technologies make it easier for users to gain control over communication to suit their specific needs since they reduce the power that intermediaries used to have over the flow of information to society (Verwey 2002:v). As will be illustrated later, several cultural minorities worldwide have used this medium to obviate communicative restrictions or limitations in order to consolidate cultural identities, and in South Africa this has also started to take place to a certain extent. In order to understand this process within the post-apartheid South African context, one first needs to understand the position of language within the South African sociopolitical history.

Local Determining Factors

As was the case with other African languages and literatures (Gagiano 2000), the centuries of colonial rule in South Africa – of which apartheid, as a form of internal colonialism,[4] was the most recent example – have also detrimentally affected linguistic development. Tomaselli (2000:282) points out that linguistic and cultural diversity was politicised during apartheid, which resulted in antagonistic ethnic consciousnesses. During apartheid the country had two official languages, namely English and Afrikaans. Other languages were not afforded the same opportunities for growth and development, this in spite of the fact that only 25% of all South Africans have English or Afrikaans as their mother tongue (Kaschula and De Vries 2000).

Afrikaans was an empowered language under apartheid – it was assiduously promoted in order to acquire the high-status functions previously belonging exclusively to English (Alexander and Heugh 2001:20). However, Afrikaans had a peculiar double positioning vis-à-vis colonial discourse. It was not only the language of the coloniser, but simultaneously also the language of the colonised. Because Afrikaans was appropriated by the white Afrikanerdom, the black[5] speakers of the language were thereby marginalised (Redelinghuis 1997:17,20), even though these speakers amounted to more than half of the total number of speakers of Afrikaans (Viljoen 1996:163). Afrikaans was also the language in which strong literary criticism against apartheid was offered. As will be shown later, the shift that has occurred in the position of Afrikaans within the South African language dispensation provides an interesting case study for the opportunities the Internet creates.

South African Languages after 1994

The South African language dispensation changed quite radically with the advent of a liberal democratic system in 1994. The new Constitution (agreed to in 1996) accorded equal official status to all eleven languages in South Africa on a national level. While it indicated that indigenous languages would be developed and their limited rights extended, it also stipulated that existing language rights may not be diminished (Van Rensburg et al. 1997; Lubbe 2001). For instrumental purposes, English has become the lingua franca in South African public life (Alidou and Mazrui 1999:106), being seen by some as a universal language and one that is ideologically neutral (Painter 2002). While this means that the use of Afrikaans has been dramatically scaled down to occupy the position of a minority language, the other nine indigenous languages are at an even bigger disadvantage.[6]

The scaling down of Afrikaans on government-sponsored television and the anglicisation of companies and state institutions has led to an outcry amongst a sector of Afrikaans speakers. That this debate about the perceived threat to the continued existence of Afrikaans has raged seemingly unabated since the initiation of the democratic negotiations around 1990, is due to the strong position of Afrikaans media companies, publishing houses and cultural and educational institutions. Not only in media such as newspapers and radio, but also in scholarly articles and journals, and in discussion forums at Afrikaans cultural festivals (which mushroomed in number and popularity), questions regarding the position of Afrikaans as a language and the identity of its speakers have been and still are hotly debated. Although this debate has given rise to conservative groupings receiving criticism for their alleged intent on using Afrikaans as an instrument to obtain political power and thereby adding to further ethnic polarisation,[7] it has also displayed attempts to break away from Afrikaans' association with apartheid and exclusive identities. While previously marginalised speakers of Afrikaans now form an important part of the cultural and aesthetic production in the language, Afrikaans is also increasingly seen by its speakers as an indigenous African language, rather than a language of European origin (Kaschula and De Vries 2000).[8] The Internet has played a part in this repositioning of Afrikaans.

Virtual Communities as Spaces of Minority Empowerment

Castells (2000:390) notes that groups considering themselves oppressed or marginalised in society are more likely to communicate on the Internet, because of the protection this medium affords them. Computer-based communication could create the opportunity to overturn power relations existing in other forms of communication, he argues.

Wood (1997), in referring to the utilisation of new technologies by Hawaiians, has shown that the Internet can also be appropriated by minority cultures as a means of cultural empowerment. The same potential has been illustrated with reference to other minority communities, such as the Indian diaspora in the USA (Mallapragada 2000) and the Cherokee Indians (Arnold and Plymire 2000). The formation of virtual communities in cyberspace makes it possible for groupings such as these to gain social power and consolidate their cultural identities in spite of societal constraints or geographical borders by producing and circulating their own knowledge (Arnold and Plymire 2000:188). The empowering of minorities means the creation of possibilities for indigenous languages to come into their own on the Internet. Kaschula and De Vries (2000) are of the opinion that the Internet "liberates languages from finite communicative resources and provides an economically competitive platform for the dissemination of material".

The use of non-English languages on the Internet has (globally) soared in recent years, even though English is still used in 57,4% of Internet activities (Kaschula and De Vries 2000). A recent report (Pimienta 2002) has indicated that the relative presence of English on the web (in terms of the number of web pages) has declined from 75% in 1998 to 50% today.[9] The number of non-English Internet users was expected to rise, according to another report (EU Business 2002), to 65% by 2002.When seen in this way, the Internet does not necessarily cause the elimination of locality and particularity, but has the potential of setting in motion the interaction of local cultures and languages with global influences. The result of this interaction created by globalisation is the coming into being of a new form between the local and the global, a so-called *glocality* (Tomlinson 1999:9). This means that while the insistence on particularity and diversity is increasingly becoming a global discourse, and traditional and local cultures are being affirmed globally due to the weakening of the nation-state, globalisation is also producing new hybrid identities (Barker 1999:42). Both these tendencies can also be noted regarding the position of South African languages on the Internet. While the Internet has provided a vehicle for the affirmation of minority identities, it can also be seen to create a space for a new hybridity to develop. This development is however subject to several specific local determining conditions.

As far as virtual communities organised around linguistic and cultural issues in South Africa are concerned, Afrikaans has made extensive use of the opportunities that new technologies offer.[10] A plethora of virtual communities in Afrikaans already exists, while the proliferation of websites in Afrikaans or with Afrikaans as subject matter shows no sign of abating. Such is the extent of websites in Afrikaans that some websites have sprung up that serve as portals to link the user exclusively to other Afrikaans sites. One such site, http://www.dieknoop.co.za, claims to have links to more than a 1000 Afrikaans Internet pages, with a new one added every day.

Among these, the website Litnet (http://www.mweb.co.za/litnet or www.litnet.co.za) could serve as an interesting case study. It has shown a significant increase in popularity since it went online in 1999 (Steyn 2001:122) and although its emphasis is on Afrikaans, Xhosa and English also have a presence. The increasing usage of Zulu and Sotho on the website has also been noted (Kaschula and De Vries 2000). Litnet features news and announcements of a cultural nature; contributions of fiction and poetry; book, theatre and film reviews; scholarly and polemic essays, regular columns; a page devoted to the language debate; and a very popular letters page. Not only does a website such as Litnet create the opportunity for an affirmation or reiteration of existing cultural identities, it also sets the platform for the re-imagining of these identities. By serving as a contact zone for different South African languages and literatures, it creates the possibility for transcultural flow, going against the linguistic and literary hierarchy of apartheid which was aimed at preventing social contact between ethnic or racial groups (cf. Alexander and Heugh 2001:19-20; Smit and Van Wyk 2001:139).

In as far as a site such as Litnet has the *potential* of accommodating cultural and linguistic difference in this way, it could serve as a liminal space where the fixity of language and culture imposed through colonial discourses could be undermined. Even though Litnet displays a rare multilingualism, the balance is still tilted in favour of Afrikaans and English. However, by creating a multicultural space where different South African languages co-exist and contribute – albeit in an embryonic form – to the creation of a postcolonial hybridity, Litnet is an exception to the rule (Hall 2000:468) that virtual communities tend to be monolingual and culturally homogenous. However, the site is iconic of the position on the whole of South African languages on the Internet, in that Afrikaans dominates the site even though the potential for interaction is created.

The strong position of Afrikaans on the Internet can at least partly be attributed to economics. Although Afrikaans can be seen as a minority language in post-apartheid South Africa, its speakers still occupy the strongest economic position[11] in the country. While having been relegated to being a linguistic minority, Afrikaans speakers, generally speaking, are still an economic majority.[12] This means that access to the Internet is relatively easy for Afrikaans speakers compared to other language groups. The extent to which economic factors are important in determining the presence of South African languages on the Internet becomes clear when the position of other South African minority languages are brought into focus.

The Presence of South African Languages other than Afrikaans and English on the Internet

To only celebrate the opportunities that the Internet has created for Afrikaans and taking that as representative of the experience of South African languages on the whole, would be presenting an overoptimistic picture of the situation. Examples of (other) indigenous languages[13] on the Internet are hard to find. A recent guide to the Internet in Africa (Young 2001) lists only one Zulu site, (http://www.geocities.com/CapeCanaveral/6570/) run by an English-speaking webmaster from Guildford, England; one Sesotho site (http://www.cyberserv.co.za/users/~jako/sesotho.htm) with an introduction to Sesotho; and two

Xhosa sites (http://mokennon.albion.edu/Xhosa.htm), a translator from English to Xhosa and vice versa, and a site (http://members.tripod.com/Sabelo/isiXhosa.htm) which provides online lessons in Xhosa. These examples are in stark contrast to the ten listed Afrikaans sites, of which one, the already-mentioned Die Knoop, has more than a thousand links. Some government sites have multilingual content (such as the Department of Education (http://education.pwv.gov.za), and the SABC's site (http://www.sabcnews.co.za) carries news in English, Afrikaans, Zulu and Sotho (Kaschula 2000). Some others, such as the Xhosa Virtual Resource Network (http://www.saol.co.za/xhosa/welcome.htm), provide rudimentary Xhosa content, but are presented as translations for English speakers who want to learn Xhosa or are just brief statements in Xhosa relating to missionary work done by Christians (www.greatcom.org/laws/xhosa) or Dianetics (http://xhosa.dianetics.org).

A small discussion forum, the Mzika_kaPhalo forum, was formed in May 2001, aimed at assisting translators who work in the English-Xhosa language pair. Four months after its inception, the forum had only seven members (Makwetu 2001).

Although exact figures about the number of websites in indigenous languages are hard to come by, searches on the Internet lead one to conclude that there is little available in these languages. Where inquiries into these languages do produce results, it is mostly references to sites which provide information *on* these languages (in English) rather than information *in* indigenous languages. This seems to be a problem also concerning indigenous languages from other African countries (Smith 2000).

However, to search for websites that formally use one of the indigenous languages as their basis might be the wrong approach in establishing the extent to which indigenous South African languages are present on the web. Because of the decentralisation of information and communication on the Internet, the targeted audience have more of a choice as to the messages it receives, and the individual relationship between sender and receiver is thereby enhanced (Francoise Sabbah, quoted in Castells 2000:368). Looking at South African websites, these individual relationships often result in languages being used in ways that are aimed at immediate comprehension or as passwords providing access to and acceptance in a specific virtual community. In the process formal linguistic boundaries are overstepped. Bulletin boards or guestbooks may carry messages mixing English (as well as English sociolects such as hip-hop speak) with Afrikaans and African words.[14] The Internet also provides for the celebration of an urban culture that undermines the linguistic or cultural notions which the dominant mainstream considers proper. Websites such as Urbantainment (http://lightning.prohosting.com/~africa99/urbantainment/index.shtml), www.blaconline.co.za, the Johannesburg radio station Y-Fm (http://www.yworld.co.za) and www.rage.co.za, although mainly written in English, provide outlets for the dissemination of information about street culture. Urbantainment, for instance, describes itself as a "first step toward building a black virtual community in South Africa". On these sites art forms such as graffiti, South African jazz and kwaito obtain wider currency. These forms portray a unique South Africanness, partly because of the innovative use of language.[15] These sites would correspond with Wood's (1997) observation that the Internet is best suited for the production of cultural meaning that is not fixed or static, but that comes into being through interconnection and exchange, a dynamic rather than a static conception of culture.

But probably the greatest barrier in the way of indigenous languages gaining a presence on the Internet remains the problem that has come to be known as the digital divide.

The Digital Divide

However optimistic one could be about the possibility of the Internet creating a counter-flow of ideas and culture within the global communications network, access to the Internet is still marred by severe inequalities. A premature celebration of the positive potential the Internet holds for smaller cultural communities might result in a mythologising of virtual communities without acknowledging the extent to which "real" social relations are repeated in "virtual" contexts (Jones 1995:14). One should also guard against technological determinism and bear in mind that many other factors than connectivity alone are at play in the representation of languages on the Internet. The role language choice plays in a culture of aspiration could also for instance have an effect on the use of English rather than indigenous languages on the Internet. As a result of apartheid policies, which afforded languages other than English and Afrikaans inferior positions, many speakers of indigenous languages do not consider indigenous languages adequately equipped for e.g. scientific concepts (Alexander and Heugh 2001:24). The idea that English provides better access to the international community[16] (Kaschula and De Vries 2000) would also play a role in language choice on the web. However, although one should avoid thinking about connectivity in deterministic terms, material factors cannot be ignored, especially considering the extent of inequalities with regard to Internet access. These inequalities are firstly a global problem, seeing as the divide between rich and poor countries is evident from their connectivity or lack of it. Within South Africa itself, this divide is further related to the huge material inequalities still existing as a result of apartheid. When looking at figures indicating Internet access and use in different societies, countries and across gender, racial and social lines, Jones's (1995:23) statement rings true:

> The ability to create, maintain, and control space (whatever we call it – virtual, non-place, networld) links us to notions of power and necessarily to issues of authority, dominance, submission, rebellion, and co-optation [. . .] Just because the spaces with which we are now concerned are electronic it is not the case that they are democratic, egalitarian, or accessible . . .

On the whole, the continent of Africa does not share in the large-scale transformation that new communication technologies have brought about in the developed world. Although South Africa is in some ways an exception (Nyamnjoh 1999:42), the information superhighway is still passing Africa by. Despite the adoption of strategies[17] for information and communication in Africa, implementation in individual countries has been slow, due to economic, infrastructural, political and social constraints (Nyamnjoh 1999:42-44). Although the Internet is continuing to grow in Africa, most recently with 20% within 18 months (Jensen 2001, 2002), Sub-Saharan Africa remains the region in the world with the lowest percentage of Internet users.[18] Some critics have also cautioned that growth figures might mostly represent Internet use in elite institutions (Nyamnjoh 1999:44), at the top end of business, wealthy families or major cities (Jensen 2002), among educated, wealthy males (Robins 2000) or could have been bolstered by growth in a few countries such as Nigeria (Jensen 2002). The comparison between Africa and the rest of the world is stark. The number of dial-up Internet subscribers in Africa is around 1,7 million (Jensen 2002). If each connection supports between three and five users, it can therefore be estimated that Africa has about 5 million to 8 million Internet users in total (Jensen 2002), of which only 1,5 million to 2,5 million users are outside North and South Africa. This translates into one user for every 250 to 400 people – compared to the North American and European average of one user for every two people (Jensen 2002).

Considered against the rest of the continent, South Africa is still relatively well off and could to a certain extent be seen as the exception[19] to the rest of Africa's connectivity backlog (Nyamnjoh 1999:42), having the most Internet subscribers on the continent (Jensen 2002) and the second largest multinational Internet Service Provider (ISP) in Africa, M-Web (Africa Online being the largest) (Jensen 2001). Within South Africa itself, however, there are huge disparities regarding access to the Internet. These disparities, when analysed, might go some way in explaining one aspect – connectivity and the lack of it – linked to the virtual absence of indigenous South African languages on the Internet.

The enormous class differences inherited from apartheid by and large still correlate with the old ethnic divides. In this regard, virtual South Africa still largely reflects actual South Africa (cf. Hall 2000:470), where the polarisations of the past are still far from being erased. Studies done in recent years illustrate these disparities. In 2000, the average South African Internet user earned more than R11 000 (approximately US$1100) a month and was white, while less than 1% of the country's black population had access to the Internet (Smith 2000). Surveys have shown that while there is a measure of growth in overall Internet access, black people are still at a significant disadvantage, while women in general are worse off than their male counterparts. In April 2000, 12,2% of white men had web access at home (an increase from 9% the previous year) and 12,8% had web access at work. The percentage of white women with web access at home was 10,6% (compared to 7,4% the year before) and at work 12,2% (up from 8,2% in 1999). However, in April 2000 only 0,2% of black South African men had access to the Internet at home (no increase from 1999) and 1,8% could access the web at work (an increase from 0,4% in 1999). Black women were worst off: Of 500 black women interviewed in a survey, only one (0,2%) had web access at home and two (0,4%) had web access at work. This figure showed no growth from the previous year (Webchek 2000). Although the number of South Africans using the web is on the increase, these users consist mostly of upper-income earners (Webchek 2001).

Although these figures might vary according to different sources, they give a clear indication of the divisions that exist and that these divisions reflect negatively on the position of African language speakers on the Internet.

The South African government, NGOs and the private sector alike have however gone some way in addressing these problems. Some strategies include the connection of schools to the Internet, where computer facilities are also serving the broader community. The government has already established 73 community-based telecentres, providing access to telephones, fax, email and Internet (Thorne 2001) and the media company Naspers has erected three computer centres, two of which are in the rural towns of Calitzdorp and Carnarvon, where Internet access is provided to school children (see Hall 2000:473 for further examples). A translation project (www.translate.org.za) is under way, which aims to translate email, web and desktop tools into all the South African languages, in an attempt to make it easier for untutored computer users to gain access to digital technology by providing the basic software to them in their mother tongue.

In Africa as a whole, efforts to promote better access to ICTs remain on government agendas, and a framework document entitled the "African Information Society Initiative" has been adopted by all Africa's planning ministers. South Africa is one of 17 African countries that have finalised their strategies for the development of a national information and communication infrastructure. Many of the issues regarding ICT systems in Africa are also being addressed by the African Union and their New Partnership for Africa's Development (Nepad) (Jensen 2002).

Conclusion

The overview of South African Internet usage and the presence of South African languages on the web indicate that globalising media should not only be seen as a negative influence on cultural diversity. The extent to which the Internet has provided a tool for Afrikaans speakers to reposition themselves within a changing linguistic landscape indicates the potential the Internet has to serve as a platform for linguistic minorities. Certain South African websites have also shown that the Internet can serve as a space for the construction of new hybrid identities and the bridging of the imposed cultural borders of the past. However, before the Internet can really promote multilingualism and multiculturalism in South Africa, the severe inequalities that mark access to the medium need to be overcome, maybe through the sharing of resources between minority languages, of which Afrikaans is economically in the strongest position. One way of attaining this could be to create and promote new "virtual communities" that transcend linguistic boundaries and undermine static, closed notions of language and culture. Co-operation to overcome inequalities is the challenge to face if the "new media" are to create something new rather than reinforce old divides.

Notes

1 The author wishes to thank Sean Jacobs, Keyan Tomaselli and Krista Johnson for comments on earlier drafts of this chapter.

2 An interesting – if ironic – development in the role of the Internet in also preserving the languages some critics accuse it of helping to destroy, is the Rosetta Project, which will provide an online archive of 1445 languages. One of the aims of the project is to "record and recover moribund languages that are undocumented and typically spoken only by a few elderly people" (Mayfield 2002).

3 Britz (2002:4), for instance, links the phenomenon of language death to globalisation and quotes statistics estimating that of the current 6000 languages in the world today only 3000 will remain by the year 2100. He then compares Afrikaans speakers with Tolkien's hobbits, a small team of elves and trolls that have to hold forth against the global power of English. The Group of 63, a group of Afrikaans intellectuals promoting minority rights, also mention globalisation in their policy document (2000). One of the group's members, Johann Rossouw (quoted in Steyn 2001:126), reflected this view of globalisation when he labelled it an "undemocratic impulse".

4 Apartheid was called Colonialism of a Special Type by the South African Communist Party (Visser 1997:79). For further discussion of the term "internal colonialism" to describe apartheid, see JanMohamed 1985:72, De Kock 1993:65 and Ashcroft et al. 1994:83.

5 According to the racial differentiation of apartheid, these speakers would predominantly have been classified as "coloured", but the term "black" was used by the signified themselves in order to create solidarity among the oppressed and in order to reject the categorisation of apartheid (Willemse 1987:205, see also Smith et al. 1985) and is therefore also the term used here.

6 English dominates in institutions such as television, education, government, administration, courts of law and the Defence Force (Kamwangamalu quoted in Kaschula and De Vries 2000). In the workplace English, and to a lesser extent Afrikaans, still dominates as the medium of communication, threatening to further marginalise workers, of which 75% are not sufficiently proficient in English (Kajee 2000). Studies quoted by Painter (2002) have indicated that while English is simplistically seen as a "correc-

tive to a history of ethnic and racial fragmentation in South Africa", this portrayal of English as ideologically neutral and a facilitator of societal transformation has had the concomitant effect of constructing other South African languages as remaining bound by racial identities. This means that should speakers of those languages insist on the use of these languages in the public sphere – as guaranteed by the Constitution – they are seen as racist.

7 For some of these conservative arguments, see Lubbe's (2001:86) examples of Afrikaans being used as a instrument in the continuation of an exclusive Afrikaner nationalism. For critical responses highlighting the conservatism in some of the new language movements such as Praag (Pro Afrikaanse Aksiegroep) or criticism related to the role of Afrikaans in the minority politics of the Group of 63, see respectively Kaschula and De Vries (2000) and Steyn (2001:127, 130). For an argument outlining the importance of Afrikaans speakers not to mobilise themselves along ethnic lines but to form an alliance with other non-dominant indigenous languages, see Alexander (2001). The Group of 63 also came under attack during November 2002 for their perceived apologetic stance towards right-wing Afrikaners suspected of being responsible for a series of bombings of railroad tracks in Soweto and at a mosque.

8 Approximately 5,8 million South Africans have Afrikaans as their mother tongue, which makes up 15,7% of the South African population. Afrikaans has the third most first language speakers in South Africa, after Zulu (21,61%) and Xhosa (17,44%). Approximately 9 million South Africans can speak and/or understand Afrikaans. This means that 15 million people in total – 48% of the population – can therefore understand or speak Afrikaans (Van Rensburg et al. 1997:80-82). Only approximately 8,68% of South Africans have English as their mother tongue (Kaschula and De Vries 2000). Less than 25% of black South Africans understand English well enough to function fully in public life, although English is practically the only language used in important public domains (Webb and Kembo-Sure 2000:38).

9 Another recent report (EU Business 2002) puts the number of English websites at 80%.

10 Apart from the Internet, Afrikaans has also made use of new technologies such as CD Roms (e.g. *Verswêreld,* a standard anthology of Afrikaans poetry) and online publishing (at www.contentlot.com).

11 Almost half of the total number of Afrikaans speakers (about 4,3 million in total) are white. Afrikaans speakers contributed R161,497 billion to the domestic spending in South Africa in 2000. That amounts to 32,3% of the total domestic spending (Rossouw 2001), as opposed to 27,9% of spending by English speakers, 22,3% by Nguni (Xhosa, Zulu, Ndebele and Swati) speakers, and 17,6% by Sotho (Sotho, Pedi, Venda, Tswana and Tsonga) speakers (Du Toit 2000).

12 Groups can be seen as minorities although they are numerically a majority, as South African blacks had been under apartheid (Loomba 1998:14). Similarly, one could

speak of a group such as Afrikaans speakers as an economic majority while being a cultural minority – although one should not lose sight of the fact that enormous class differences also exist within the Afrikaans community, also as a result of the inequalities inherited from apartheid. Languages should be considered majority or minority languages not on the basis of their number of speakers, but on the basis of the function and status attached to them (Webb and Kembo-Sure 2000:42).

13 In this section of the chapter, the term "indigenous languages" denotes official South African languages other than Afrikaans and English. Although it is discussed separately, Afrikaans is taken to be an indigenous South African language. In spite of its Dutch roots, Afrikaans is not strictly speaking an ex-colonial language. It arose from African soil at grassroots level, among soldiers, slaves and Khoikhoi herders in the process of acquiring the Dutch of the colonisers. Afrikaans shows several semantic, phonological and grammatical differences with Dutch; its vocabulary, pronunciation and intonation patterns contain a large amount of elements originating in Africa. It is not spoken in any significant way outside Africa, expresses an African frame of reference and could therefore be seen as an African language, even though it was appropriated by its white speakers during apartheid and its European roots emphasised (Webb and Kembo-Sure 2000:39-40). To the extent that the English spoken in South Africa also differs from English spoken in other parts of the world, one would also be able to refer to this English as an Africanised or ex-colonial language. In spite of the fact that English has been indigenised in South Africa, it can only be spoken well by less than a quarter of the black population (Webb and Kembo-Sure 2000:38-40).

14 The guestbook of a South African urban entertainment website (Urbantainment, http://lightning.prohosting.com/~africa99/urbantainment/index.shtml), for example, contains messages that read as follows (random examples):

> "Peace goes out to that phat ass skwatta kamp crew holding it down in SA nahwhumsayin"; "all I can say is this site is 2 damn duidlik peace"; "Awe ouens Kak duidelik en alles maar nou kan 'n man 'n gesignde copy van die nuwe CD kry?"

The site http://watkykjy.co.za also subverts mainstream Afrikaans culture by providing content in a form of Afrikaans littered with English, swearwords and obscenities. It positions itself in competition with more established Afrikaans sites such as M-Web Afrikaans and celebrates a suburban or ironic version of rural, workingclass Afrikaans culture, as indicated by links to sites of amongst others a pawn shop, the farming magazine *Landbouweekblad* and middle-of-the-road singer Patricia Lewis.

15 Kwaito, for instance, contains a mixture of South African languages and slang (cf. the kwaito star Arthur Mafokate's comments on this in www.rage.co.za/issue29/kwaito.htm and also Stephens 2000:256).

16 Also cf. Schlemmer (2001:98) for the findings of a poll conducted into the preference of English as medium of instruction on tertiary level because of the view that it provides better opportunities.

17 Such as the African Information Society Initiative launched by the UN Economic Commission for Africa in collaboration with the International Telecommunications Union, the International Development Research Centre and Unesco, and the policy documents adopted by the SA government (see Hall 2000:465).

18 Sub-Saharan Africa shares this position with South Asia, but South Asian Internet use is growing faster (Jensen 2002).

19 One should guard, however, against a pessimistic homogenisation regarding the development of connectivity in Africa. Progress is being made – Ghana, for instance, was the first country in West Africa to establish local Internet service in 1994 and has since become one of the five "Silicon nations" to watch in terms of the development of "connectivity, information security, human capital, business climate and priority by government to technology", it has been reported (Safo 2001). In Tanzania, the number of Internet cafés has shown "huge growth" and technology there is especially benefiting women (Dickinson 2002). Jensen (2002) also points to several "significant developments" that are not reflected in the somewhat disparaging overall figures.

References

Alexander, Neville and Heugh, Kathleen. 2001. Language policy in the New South Africa. In: Kriger, Robert and Zegeye, Abebe. 2001. *Culture in the New South Africa.* Cape Town and Maroelana: Kwela Books and South African History Online.

Alexander, Neville. 2001. Die noodsaak van universiteite vir die oorlewing van die nie-dominante tale in Suid-Afrika. In: Giliomee, Hermann et al. 2001. *Kruispad – Die toekoms van Afrikaans as openbare taal.* Cape Town: Tafelberg. 8-14.

Alexander, Neville. 2001. Die oorlewing van nie-dominante tale van Suid-Afrika. *Litnet.* www.mweb.co.za/litnet/seminaar/05neville.asp. Viewed 7 September 2001.

Alidou, Ousseina and Alamin, M. Mazrui. 1999. The Language of Africa-Centered Knowledge in South Africa: Universalism, Relativism and Dependency. In: Palmberg, Mai. (ed.) 1999. *National Identity and Democracy in Africa.* Uppsala and Cape Town: The Human Sciences Research Council of South Africa, the Mayibuye Centre at the University of the Western Cape and the Nordic Africa Institute. 101-118.

Arnold, Ellen L. and Plymire, Darcy C. 2000. The Cherokee Indians and the Internet. In: Gauntlett, David (ed). 2000. *Web.studies.* London: Arnold.

Ashcroft, Bill, Griffiths, Gareth and Tiffin, Helen. 1994 (1989). *The Empire Writes Back: Theory and Practice in Post-colonial Literatures.* London & New York: Routledge.

Barker, Chris. 1999. *Television, Globalization and Cultural Identities.* Buckingham and Philadelphia: Open University Press.

BBC News. 2002. Africans embrace mobiles and the net. 2 October 2002. http://news.bbc.co.uk/1/hi/technology/2290486.stm. Viewed 11 November 2002.

Britz, Etienne. 2002. 'Afrikaanses is soos Tolkien se hobbits.' *Die Burger,* 14 Februarie 2002.

Castells, Manuel. 2000. *The Rise of the Network Society*. Oxford: Blackwell.

Chalaby, J. K. 2002. Freedoms of intimacy and the Internet. *Communicare* 21(1). July. 1-16.

Croteau, David and Hoynes, William. 2000. *Media/Society*. Thousand Oaks: Pine Forge Press.

De Kock, Leon. 1993. Postcolonial Analysis and the Question of Critical Disablement. In: *Current Writing*. 5(2). 44-69.

Dickinson, Daniel. 2002. Tanzanian women get online bug. *BBC News World Edition*. http://news.bbc.co.uk/2/hi/technology/2487821.stm. Viewed 18 November 2002.

Du Toit, Johan. 2000. 'Afrikaanses het meeste koopkrag,' sê verslag. *Die Burger*. 10 February 2000. P.S1.

European researchers tackle language barriers on the Internet. EU *Business*. http://www.eubusiness.com.

Gagiano, Annie. 2000. The Asmara Declaration on African Languages and Literatures and its message to multilingual South Africa. *Litnet*. www.mweb.co.za/litnet/seminarroom/asmara.asp. Viewed 23 May 2001.

Groep van 63, 2000. Die vraagstuk van die Afrikaanse minderheid. *Litnet*. www.mweb.co.za/litnet/seminaar/versamel.asp. Viewed 23 May 2001.

Hachten, William A. 1996. *The World News Prism – Changing Media of International Communication.* Ames: Iowa State University Press.

Hall, Martin. 2000. Digital SA. In: Nuttall, Sarah and Michael, Cheryl-Ann. 2000. *Senses of Culture*. Cape Town: Oxford University Press. 460-475.

JanMohamed, Abdul R. 1985. The Economy of Manichean Allegory: The Function of Racial Difference in Colonialist Literature. In: *Critical Inquiry* 12. Autumn. 59-87.

Jensen, Mike. 2001. The African Internet – A Status Report. May. http://demiurge.win.apc.org/africa/afstat.htm. Viewed 5 June 2001.

Jensen, Mike. 2002. Information and Communication Technologies (ICTs) in Africa – A Status Report. Presented to the Third Task Force Meeting, United Nations Headquarters, 30 September – 1 October. http://www.unicttaskforce.org/thirdmeeting/documents/jensen%20v6.doc. Viewed 12 November 2002.

Jones, Steven G. 1995. *Cybersociety – Computer-mediated Communication and Community.* Thousand Oaks, London & New Delhi: Sage Publications.

Kajee, Leila. 2000. Language policy and practice in industry: Ensuring the usage of African languages. *Litnet*. www.mweb.co.za/litnet/taaldebat/05kajee.asp. Viewed 23 May 2001.

Kaschula, Russell H. and De Vries, Izak. 2000. Indigenous Languages and the Internet: With LitNet as a case study. *Litnet*. www.mweb.co.za/litnet/taaldebat/netlan.asp. Viewed 23 May 2001.

Loomba, Ania. 1998. *Colonialism/Postcolonialism*. London and New York: Routledge.

Lubbe, H. J. 2001. Inhoudsontleding van die gespek rondom Afrikaans en die gedrukte media vir die tydperk April 1994 tot 1996. *Tydskrif vir Geesteswetenskappe* 2001, 41(2). 81-117.

Makwetu, Miranda. 2001. Personal communication via email. 10 September 2001.

Mallapragada, Madhavi. 2000. The Indian Diaspora in the USA and Around the Web. In: Gauntlett, David (ed). 2000. *Web.studies.* London: Arnold.

Mayfield, Kendra. 2002. Word Up: Keeping Languages Alive. *Wired News.* 4 November 2002. http://www.wired.com/news/culture/0,1284,54345,00.html. Viewed 5 November 2002.

Naidoo, Trusha A. 2001. The implications of the personalisation of the media www.ubuntu.co.za for democracy. Unpublished M.Phil (Journalism) assignment, University of Stellenbosch.

Nyamnjoh, F.B. 1999. Africa and the information superhighway: The need for mitigated euphoria. *Ecquid Novi* 20 (1). 31-49.

Painter, Desmond. 2002. What's that got to do with language? Perspectives on language and race in South Africa. *The Researcher, Bulletin of the Psychological Society of South Africa.* No.1.

Pimienta, Daniel. 2002. Put Out Your Tongue and Say 'Aaah'. Is the Internet Suffering from Acute 'Englishitis'? Unesco Newsletter on Communication and Information in the Knowledge Society.
http://www.unesco.org/webworld/points_of_views/300102_pimienta.shtml. Viewed 5 March 2002.

Redelinghuis, Aubrey. 1997. Afrikaans en demokratisering. In: Willemse, Hein; Hattingh, Marion; Van Wyk, Steward and Conradie, Pieter (eds.) 1997. *Die Reis na Paternoster.* Bellville: UWC.

Rheingold, Howard. 2000. Community Development in the Cybersociety of the Future. In: Gauntlett, David (ed). 2000. *Web.studies.* London: Arnold.

Robins, Melinda B. 2000. Africa's Women/Africa's Women Journalists: Critical Perspectives on Internet Initiatives. Paper presented at the Spring Meeting of the Southeastern Regional Seminar in African Studies.

Rossouw, Arrie. 2001. Hoe gaan Afrikaans en ander minderheidstale in Suid-Afrika oorleef? *Litnet* www.mweb.co.za/litnet/seminaar/06arrie.asp. Viewed 23 May 2001.

Safo, Amos. 2001. Ghana – from commodities to technology. *Africanews.* December. www.peacelink.it.afrinews/69_issue/p10.html.

Schlemmer, Lawrence. 2001. Taaloorlewing en die glybaan van goeie gesindhede: 'n meningsopname en ontleding. In: Giliomee, Hermann; Schlemmer, Lawrence; Alexander, Neville; Du Plessis, Bertie; Loubser, Max. 2001. *Kruispad – Die toekoms van Afrikaans as openbare taal.* Cape Town: Tafelberg. 94-114.

Smit, Johannes A. and Van Wyk, Johan. 2001. Literary studies in post-apartheid South Africa. In: Kriger, Robert and Zegeye, Abebe. 2001. *Culture in the New South Africa.* Cape Town and Maroelana: Kwela Books and South African History Online.

Smith, Cameron. 2000. Speaking in Tongues? A Shona Language Web Site. Balancing Act News Update 14, www.kabissa.org. Viewed 19 June 2000.

Smith, Julian F., Van Gensen, Alwyn and Willemse, Hein (eds.) 1985. *Swart Afrikaanse Skrywers*. Cape Town: UWC.

Stephens, Simon. 2000. Kwaito. In: Nuttall, Sarah and Michael, Cheryl-Ann. 2000. *Senses of Culture*. Cape Town: Oxford University Press. 256-273.

Steyn, J.C. 2001. Afrikaans 2000: Nuwe suksesverhale en terugslae. *Tydskrif vir Geesteswetenskappe* 41/2. 118-132.

Thorne, Karin. 2001. Community Media and ICTs, quoted on The Communication Initiative, www.comminit.com/pds62001/sld-2161.html. Viewed 26 June 2001.

Tomaselli, K. 2000. South African Media 1994-7. In: Curran, James and Park, Myung-Jin. 2000. *De-Westernizing Media Studies.* London: Routledge.

Tomlinson, John. 1999. *Globalisation and Culture*. Cambridge: Polity Press.

UN Report: African Net Usage Growing, But Still Lags. 2002. Pambazuka newsletter. www.pambazuka.org/newsletter.php?id=10893. Viewed 24 October 2002.

Van Rensburg, Christo (ed.), Achmat Davids, Jeanette Ferreira, Tony Links, Karel Prinsloo. 1997. *Afrikaans in Afrika*. Pretoria: Van Schaik.

Verwey, Sonja. 2002. Editorial. *Communicare*. 21(1) July. v-vi.

Viljoen, Louise. 1996. Postkolonialisme en die Afrikaanse letterkunde: 'n verkenning van die rol van enkele gemarginaliseerde diskoerse. *Tydskrif vir Nederlands en Afrikaans* 3(2). 158-175.

Visser, Nicholas. 1997. Postcoloniality of a Special Type: Theory and Its Appropriations in South Africa. In: Gurr, Andrew (ed.). 1997. *The Politics of Postcolonial Criticism, Yearbook of English Studies* vol. 27. 79-94.

Webb, Vic and Kembo-Sure. 2000. *African Voices.* Cape Town: Oxford University Press.

Webchek Newsbrief. 2001. May. www.webchek.co.za. Viewed 1 June 2001.

Webchek Newsbriefs. 2000. May and July. www.webchek.co.za. Viewed Webchek 1 June 2001.

Willemse, Hein. 1987. "Maa' die manne waver nog": Jonger swart Afrikaanse skrywers. In: Malan, Charles (ed.) 1987. *Ras en Literatuur/ Race and Literature*. Pinetown: Owen Burgess. 197-205.

Wood, Houston. 1997. Hawaiians in Cyberspace. First Online Conference on Postcolonial Theory. www.fas.nus.edu.sg/staff/conf/poco/paper2.html. Viewed 21 March 2001.

Young, Libby. 2001. *The All-Africa Internet Guide*. Millpark: M&G Books.

CHAPTER FIVE

Cultural Studies and the Transformation of the Music Industry: Some Reflections on Kwaito

Gibson Boloka

Introduction

Today one can find any type of music anywhere in the world. One does not have to be in Brazil or ever visit the country to buy or listen to samba. Neither is it necessary to be in South Africa to purchase a kwaito compact disk. Distance no longer matters. Ours is a world characterised by interconnected spaces, which are in continual dialogue with each other. Consequently, the sharp distinction between local and foreign is completely blurred. What was once termed authentic and original "local music" has somehow evaporated, leaving behind only fragments and hybrids. This can be attributed to influences by other genres across the globe and consumption witnessed also in foreign spaces. This does not mean, however, that the foreign (global) has totally replaced the local. In fact, the local has become a path through which the global has to travel. Therefore, cultural spaces have become, as Doreen Massey (1994) posits, "sites of power-geometries" where different cultures struggle for dominance. In essence, the global brings about the re-mooring of traditions characterising the local, wherein fixity is replaced by mobility.

Furthermore, as understood within cultural studies paradigms, music like any cultural product is capable of generating multiple meanings. It is this capability that enables it to travel even beyond the spaces of its origin. Meaning, cultural studies points out, is the source of struggle because it is continually contested. In fact, contestation, as this chapter demonstrates, results from different uses and approaches employed in understanding and interpreting music as cultural texts. Cultural studies does not only celebrate the politicisation of culture, its production and consumption within social relations; it further requires us to understand culture and power within the networks of transformation. Again, cultural studies' interest in contemporary issues links us to the spaces we occupy and thus provides a good framework for understanding culture.

Popular music in South Africa has over the years undergone tremendous changes, with one genre seeming to dominate at one point, only to be replaced by another whose dominance is also short-lived. This trend has undoubtedly intensified since the 1970s, presumably due to the increase in consumers and demand, and by them identifying with different musical genres in given periods. However, as the cycle continues, it is often permeated and eventually shaped by certain cultural contacts and influences, economic pressures and globalisation that affect not only the content, but the rhythms of these music genres as well.

This chapter explores the genealogy of kwaito music, tracing its origin both to processes of globalisation as well as to its particular local political, social and economic context. Through its study of kwaito, this chapter aims to demonstrate how culture has changed from being just a nucleus of society to an instrument of change through which social relations are transformed. The chapter uses a cultural studies approach to examine the changing patterns in the production, distribution and consumption of kwaito and how that impacted on social relations. The aim is to provide an overview of the historical development of kwaito as a manifestation of a changing society. The periods described here do not necessarily imply the nonexistence of other genres. The overview is also not exhaustive, for it is used here to illustrate primarily how this musical evolution represents the changing society and how it has transformed the industry over the years.

The relevance of cultural studies is seen not only in terms of the centrality that is given to culture, nor looking at music as reflective of cultural transition occurring in the country. The emergence of kwaito is also driven by questions of power relating to consumption, globalisation and cultural integration. Since globalisation is broad, the term is used here to explain the intensification of the world as a single system whereby culture, as seen through music, travels from one space to the next. The definition is largely influenced by the manner in which music, despite strict regulation, is capable of crossing borders. It is a process promoted by high technology, improved transportation systems and increased human and capital mobility. As it evidenced by the production and consumption of music: everywhere is the same as everywhere (cf. Giddens 1981).

A Genealogy of Kwaito

Despite South Africa's rich history of popular music, and the tendency of some kwaito artists to sample the work of artists from the 1950s and 1960s such as Miriam Makeba, Sophie Gcina and Hugh Masekela,[1] the origins of kwaito can probably be traced more directly to the early 1970s. Mbaqanga or jive, a music deeply rooted in the African townships around Johannesburg, played a major part in kwaito's genealogy. Mbaqanga originated from marabi dance, a genre influenced by traditional songs and played in the shebeens (illegal drinking houses). Musicians used every instrument at their disposal, from old guitars to pianos, concertinas and homemade percussion instruments (cf. Bergman 1985). Unlike their earlier counterparts, these musicians primarily made music for enjoyment. Like with marabi, shebeens became arenas of mbaqanga. In contrast to marabi, for mbaqanga, the meaning of music was deeply embedded in the message it conveyed. While entertainment was the primary function of music, it was in this regard relegated to other functions such as education, cultural expression and identity construction. The success of mbaqanga can largely be attributed to a number of factors: the pivotal role of the shebeens serving as public spheres, the separate radio stations broadcasting regionally for South Africa's different "ethnic" groups, the popularity of radio as a communication medium and the migrant labour system. Ironically, on a larger scale the apartheid struggle created a certain kind of common culture and sympathy, and contributed to the popularity of mbaqanga, not only locally amongst musicians and listeners, but also internationally (cf. Bergman 1985).

Mbaqanga gave birth to "bubblegum" in the 1980s. As the name itself suggests, bubblegum music's popularity was often short-lived. Though still attached to meaning as embodied in lyrics, bubblegum marked the beginning of a shift or a cultural turn in the content and form of South African popular music. Changes in the media landscape also contributed to its popularity. With the introduction of separate state television channels for different "ethnic" groups in the early 1980s, the growth of this music was guaranteed as television programmes targeting black audiences played this music. Musicians such as Brenda Fassie with her debut album *Weekend Special*, and Yvonne Chaka Chaka with *I am Burning Up* emerged as the leading exponents of this genre. Another notable bubblegum artist was Chicco Twala, who survived the death of one of South Africa's legendary groups, Harari, and went on to form Image and Chimora respectively. From Harari also emerged the individualism of Sipho "Hotstix" Mabuse, Alec Khaoli and the band Umoja, Condry Ziqubu, Stimela and CJB, among others.

Kwaito developed out of these musical roots but also in response to the political, social and economic transition South Africa undertook since 1990. Kwaito represented the coming together of a number of South African music genres (bubblegum, mbaqanga, township jazz, Afro-pop, among others) and Western genres (e.g. rhythm and blues, house, hip-hop, jungle, and drum 'n' bass). The word "kwaito" was Afrikaans slang derived from the word "kwaai", meaning wild. For kwaito music this meant, as described by the artists themselves, that the music was hot or "jamming". Simon Stephens suggests that:

> . . . many saw a positive change occurring in popular music where they could enjoy dancing without having to engage with any sociopolitical discourse in the verbal text. Considering the political element that has motivated a large selection of South African popular music for so long, kwaito is breaking from the tradition. In this respect it reflects post-apartheid society by freeing the African body – at least for men – from political consciousness, and repositioning it in spaces of new physical freedoms (Stephens 2000:263).

Three characteristics of kwaito are worth re-emphasising: one, kwaito as a disengagement with sociopolitical discourse; two, kwaito as a break from the tradition; and three, kwaito as a reflection of post-apartheid society. Kwaito further demonstrates how mass media influences the creation of a "new" society by implanting a new "common" culture based on consumption. It is through this culture that new identities are forged. Stephens' observation on the nature of kwaito is further confirmed by Neal Ullestad (1992:37) who comments on global trends:

> An exciting tension surrounds popular music in the 1990s: invention facing tradition, creativity confronting stagnation, tolerance versus intolerance, rebellion against authority, commercialism versus authenticity. This tension is not a simple struggle of positive and negative, "good" or "bad" [. . .] it is much more than a struggle to decide what music we hear, when we hear it, where and how.

It is within the context of these tensions that kwaito exists and defines itself. The history of kwaito is the history of rebellion, commercialism, creative tolerance and, above all, democracy. The tension is primarily between culture, change and tradition, which, as Stephens asserts, kwaito wants to break away from. Though it started entirely as a youthful black invention, kwaito has gained broad appeal across racial boundaries. Not only is it played on SABC radio stations targeted primarily at a white audience, such as 5FM, it has become a symbol of South African "unity".

The compression of spaces has impacted heavily on the production, distribution and consumption of music in general. Contrary to the past where music was understood in terms of identifiable genres, formats and localism, today it resembles spaghetti or pasta. And above all, it is consumed in different physical spaces. In other words, not only is it a mixture of various genres, it is also influenced by traditions traceable from various continents and regions, designations attesting to the argument posited earlier that the distinction local/foreign music is blurred.

As elsewhere, South African popular music is no longer purely local, but interacting with kwasa-kwasa (Central Africa), South American salsa and North American pop, and rhythm and blues. Caribbean reggae, ragga and ska also demonstrate their influences. In contrast to its South African predecessors, kwaito is produced mainly with the help of technology, in particular digital audiotapes (DAT), to combine various continental sounds from some of the genres above and adding new versions to them. Thus, kwaito is not only a hybrid, it also indigenised. By indigenisation, I am simply referring to the adoption of foreign products or technology which are changed to suit local settings (see also Thompson 1996). The indigenisation process is seen in the way in which different sounds and genres are blended in the production of kwaito music. Like other genres of popular music, the meaning of kwaito is largely subordinated to dance.

Inasmuch as kwaito has overwhelmingly conquered South Africa's musical centre stage, it has not been free from criticism. Criticisms include that, as a cultural text, it is unable to connect to the daily lives and experiences of the larger society, as well as that the lyrics are meaningless and the language vulgar. Interestingly, kwaito artists have dismissed some of the criticisms, citing that the genre is a breakaway from the seriousness of life and that it captures the lives of youths in South Africa.

Such criticism confirms the tensions described by Ullestad, namely that tradition, stagnation, authority and authenticity are used as benchmarks for the understanding of popular music in general. In my view, the criticisms are presumably based on the expectation that music should perform certain functions within a society. The criticisms, however, fail to account for the fact that, like any other cultural text, kwaito is used by different consumers in different contexts for different purposes, hence its consumption remains heavily contested. Thus, while some use it for locating meaning, others use it for pleasure and ideological aims respectively. According to Storey (1996:4), meaning is a social production. A text or practice or event is not the issuing source of meaning, but a site where the articulation of variable meaning can take place. Therefore, the problem confronting kwaito stems from the fact that critics perceive it as issued and complete with meaning.

Cultural Studies and Kwaito

How do we use cultural studies to make sense of these processes? As a set of approaches or methods attempting to understand the relationship between culture and power in society, cultural studies requires us to look at popular music as cultural texts capable of generating multiple meanings (Grossberg 1993). Perhaps it would be appropriate to delineate the major issues captured by the historical analysis above. These issues, I presume, will also foreground the relevance of cultural studies to this chapter and understanding kwaito in particular. The following issues emerged from the scenario.

Firstly, music is a product of a particular historical tradition confronted by certain problems. As indicated in the section on genealogy, various issues confronting different periods could be detected, therefore enabling us to measure the relevance of popular music to their paradigms. As an example, though kwaito can be considered a post-apartheid genre, it emerged during the threshold of transition when racism prevailed. As a result, songs such as Arthur Mafokate's "Don't Call Me Kaffir" capture this experience.

Secondly, popular music is part and parcel of culture, and therefore subject to contestation. Culture is nothing more than the way of doing things and thinking about them, which differs from one society to the next. In a multicultural society such as South Africa, the difference is embodied in popular music. As an example, kwaito is known for its use of the multiple languages spoken in the country, an element presumably taken from the adoption of eleven official languages in South Africa. This is contrary to mbaqanga whose songs were largely monolingual, a factor attributable to the cultural separation policy of apartheid. The attachment of kwaito to its culture can also be seen in its tendency to adopt repetition and what Bergman (1985) refers to as call-and-response technique. Apart from providing easy memorisation, these elements strengthen the interaction between the singer and the listeners. The following lyrics from Arthur Mafokate's hit, "Mnike" (2000) illustrate this. As the singer, Arthur will say: "Hey, Queen! Hau Mnike!" Together with the backing vocalist, the listeners will respond: "Mnike!" The repetition and call-and-response continue until the end of the song without more complex words added to it.

Albeit an expression of certain communities, music travels and therefore transcends geographical borders. It is therefore transnational, because it is capable of going beyond its geographical borders. Today kwaito artists are often invited to perform in various shows around the world.

Thirdly, music is intertextual. By intertextuality I simply refer to the inevitable influence on a musical text by other existing ones. Intertextuality occurs both in content and form as exemplified by the influence of mbaqanga and bubblegum on kwaito. When analysing these genres, one can see clearly how other genres such as jazz, marabi, hip-hop and soul impacted on them. In this century, the process is further enhanced by the technological advancement through computers. Kwaito, for instance, relies on cut and paste through which sounds are blended.

In a capitalist world, consumption is the power behind the production of music. In other words, the rapid change in music demonstrates how the music fulfils the commercial demand driven by consumer interest (see also Stephens 2000). "Consumption", argues Storey (1996:98), "is an active, creative and productive process concerned with pleasure, identity and production of meaning." Storey's statement evokes one important element in the production and consumption of kwaito, namely consumers. Their importance lies not only in the consumption of these artefacts, but also in the production of the meaning embodied in them. This means that inasmuch as consumption is a critical force driving music, other important questions relating to their appropriation and use should be considered. Based on Adorno's claims on popular music, John Storey (1996) describes it as standardisation and evoking a sense of passivity by confirming the world as it is. These claims describe popular music as consumer-oriented, and as Storey argues, driven by the power of commercialism. Given this fact, one should therefore not only examine kwaito from a cultural perspective, but also from the perspective of the power of capitalism driving and shaping it. Within this framework, consumerism reigns. Although kwaito, like any popular music, carries ideology as embodied in class, social groups, gender, race and ethnicity, Terry Lovell (1983:60) points out that people do not purchase these cultural artefacts in order to expose themselves to this ideology, "but to satisfy a variety of different wants".

Kwaito, Change and Resistance

Popular music, as James Lull (1987) contends, originates and resides in the social and cultural worlds of people. Since popular music is a product of culture, it is a vehicle for identity construction. This is evidenced by the languages it uses, the issues it addresses, the social classes it represents and the cultural spaces it symbolises. These elements contribute towards identity formation. If carefully considered, they present identity as a complex process, for it answers questions not only relating to who we are, but also about difference (see also Hall 1991).

Since its invention, kwaito has not just changed the consumption of popular music in South Africa as earlier indicated. It has, above all, transformed the society by strengthening social integration, thus confirming that culture as an instrument of change transforms society. As mentioned earlier, when kwaito started, it was described as "youthful" and "black". Over the years, all these perceptions shifted to a certain degree as kwaito became played in "national" public spheres such as political rallies and sports matches involving national teams, in particular soccer and cricket. The breaking point was reached during the 1998 Soccer World Cup in France where the group TKZee's hit *Shibobo* (literally referring to the action of placing the football between the opponent's feet to demonstrate one's skill) became the slogan for the South African national soccer team. Benni McCarthy, a young South African striker who was featured in the video, later in the tournament managed to do just that when he put the ball between the feet of the Danish national goalkeeper, Peter Schmeickel, adding to the popularity of the song.

The Soweto artist Mandoza's hits, "Godoba" and "Nkalankatha" were played at the matches of the overwhelmingly white South African cricket team and its mainly white followers in the Trinations Cricket Tournament in Australia in 2002. Apart from being played on historically white radio stations, young white artists such as Tamara Day and Lekgowa have made their mark in this genre through individual and collaborative projects.

Taken together, these events obviously enact the changes made by kwaito in South African society in political, cultural, economic and social spheres. James Lull (1987) explains this aptly by outlining the role that music plays in a society as an agent of socialisation. It functions in any culture integrated into the fundamental social operations of its people and these circumstances vary from culture to culture. Finally, music is a unique form of symbolic expression that can exist alone as cultural event or product (concert, street performance), serve as the content focus for another medium, or contribute to the overall aesthetics and meaning of another content display (say the background for television and film, accompaniment for rituals such as church services, weddings, funerals, ceremonies, sporting events and so on).

As a further manifestation of kwaito's penetration of South African society, today the following phrases are used to identify with this music: it is local, it is our own thing, it is African and so forth. The phrases have since been strengthened by the promotion of the phrase "local is lekker" (local music is good), a slogan which does not only demonstrate protectionism, but further reflects a new identity forged through culture, and also differs from the usual cultural inferiority that white South African cultural expression felt towards Britain, both under apartheid and continuing in the post-1994 period. The slogan advocates the importance of "the local". These sentiments can also be interpreted as desperate attempts to construct new identities and resistance to globalisation. Factors such as language play an important role in the construction of identities, for it is a carrier of norms, values and ideologies which give a sense of unity to society. Unity is maintained by ideology as an instrument of representation. Ideology, as Althussser (1971:241) contends, represents "the imaginary relationship of individuals to their conditions of existence". In other words, it is a means through which people make sense of the world in which they live.

Globalisation is an inevitable process, manifesting itself in different forms. The spaghetti format referred to earlier is just another example. The format has undoubtedly proved that the confinement of popular music to territorial spaces is no longer adequate. As it transgresses borders, popular music constructs new identities reflecting these transgressions. However, it is important to note that identities forged out of musical traditions, especially popular music, are never real nor permanent, but imaginary, multiple and temporal. Since music constructs identities based on consumption, it has to be viewed as an attempt to create collective representation, an instrument of fighting the "other" which is in this instance represented by globalisation. As much as identity gives people a sense of belonging, it has proved to be used, as evidenced in the phrases mentioned earlier, as a means of exclusion. Thus everything considered not "ours" or "un-African" is excluded. This exclusive tendency has further penetrated forums where cultural policies are formulated. In South Africa, this penetration is seen in the 20% of local music that is supposed to be played by radio stations and the annual South African music week. This, in my view, reflects attempts to apply protectionism or to protect what is ours from foreign infiltration. Based on this, one can see that the identity construction process can sometimes be used as an instrument of resistance. Taking the genealogy of South African music as an example and the development of kwaito in particular, one is compelled to probe into the necessity of collective representation. The uncompromising attachment to the local proves therefore that although globalisation seems to be an inevitable process, it is sometimes met with resistance. Apart from the imposition of quotas, in music resistance is manifested by the continuation or recycling of certain local musical traditions. This attests to John Storey's (1996) idea that popular music can be empowering and resistant at times. The above scenario demonstrates the importance and the centrality of culture in modern societies. Not only does culture "creep into every nook and crevice of contemporary social life" wherein it mediates everything; it has further become a vehicle where meaning is located (Hall 1997). According to Paul Du Gay (1997:6), culture is crucial because "it structures the way people think, feel and act in organisations" (cf. Thompson 1997).

Kwaito and the Transformation of Cultural Industries

Musical artists and their products are the outputs of a particular society that shapes their identity and understanding of the world. This is reflected in the music that is produced and the issues artists raise and engage with critically. These processes render the musicians and producers as located within a particular space.

The emergence of globalisation symbolises how music travels, how spaces shrink and become more complex. The complexity stems from the integrative process carried by globalisation. Thus, instead of being discrete, spaces have become arenas of social integration. As explained earlier, different cultures are consumed within one single space, changing their character and social relations to a certain extent. The description about the consumption of different musical genres within South Africa attests to this point. We have entered an era in which culture and economics share common boundaries because, as Paul Du Gay (1997:5) argues, the production of cultural artefacts cannot be divorced from economic processes and forms of organisations. Economics as a cultural phenomenon depends on meaning for its effects and has particular discursive conditions of existence, and also points to the growing importance of culture to doing business in the contemporary world.

A small number of North American and Western European companies dominates the global music industry – Bertelmann, Philips Recording, BMG, Sony Music Entertainment, Teal, Gallo Recording and Electrical Music Instrument (EMI) amongst others (cf. Herman and McChesney 1997). All these companies own manufacturing facilities and distribution systems in South Africa (Alexander et al. 1998).

In South Africa, a number of established "big" media companies with music business interests, such as Primedia Music, CCP Records and RPM, dominates the kwaito market. However, a number of independent labels or studios also exists. These include labels started by kwaito musicians and producers themselves, such as Kalawa Jazzmee, Mdu Music (the artist Mdu Masilela), Wicked Sounds, Ghetto Ruff (initially the pioneers of hip-hop in South Africa) and Triple 9 Studio. Specialising in kwaito, both Kalawa and Triple 9 Studio represent a new form of ownership within the South African music industry. These are usually independent production houses owned by kwaito artists who brought together a number of artists. Contrary to their global counterparts, the South African firms are relatively small. Most of these firms sign the artists and are responsible for the recording and production of tracks and albums, but other activities such as manufacturing, promotion, packaging and distribution of the products are still largely done elsewhere. The global links are also quite obvious. The distribution and marketing of the music are also still largely confined within South African borders. When sending the products abroad, they use the services of Sony, EMI and so on. Though competition for artists' signatures started domestically between kwaito labels, it has since become internationalised as artists seek international exposure and the interest in "world music" grows in the lucrative First World markets. This is manifested in the large exodus of artists from emerging independent studios to those with international connections such as Primedia Music. The latter's holding company, Primedia, is internationally integrated. Apart from owning Primedia Music, it has within its stable Ster Century (the European- and Middle-East-based film distributor). The company's other assets include radio stations.

Conclusion

Locating the texts and practices within the field of their economic determinants is clearly important, but it is insufficient to do this and think one has also analysed important questions of audience appropriation and use (Storey 1996:96). Contestation is part and parcel of cultural consumption. Therefore, it is inadequate to think of them only in economic terms. The contestation can be attributed to various ideologies shaping the production and the consumption of cultural texts, of which kwaito is but one part. The cultural studies method employed in this chapter demonstrated, firstly, that culture is a means through which societies reflect and make sense of their experiences. Since these experiences vary as shaped by different classes, gender, ethnicity, race and so forth, they will inevitably be contested. Secondly, the essay pointed to the significance of the political transition in shaping the development of kwaito in South Africa, which in turn created new identities based on consumption. The evolution of kwaito marks the dawn of a democratic era bringing with it freedom of expression. When musicians blend and borrow tradition and lyrics, they do that on their own, without fear of incarceration. So various sounds of popular music consumed in South Africa have to be interpreted within the freedom of expression paradigm. Thirdly, "no element of commercial culture and communication changes as much and constantly as popular music" (Alexander et al. 1998:207). Consumer taste shifts, thus making the consumption of popular music unpredictable. It is this shift in taste that drives the (un)popularity of this music, as manifested in the transformations of South African music. Recording companies move between countries in pursuit of "the popular", the determinant of their survival. With the different roles performed by kwaito in the new South Africa, the future looks brighter both for the industry and the society as well.

Notes

1 The group Bongomuffin has sampled tracks by both Makeba and Masekela, while Mafikizolo, produced by Oscar wa Rhona, has sampled Gcina.

References

Albarran, A.B. 1996. *Media economics: Understanding the markets, industries and concepts.* Iowa: University Press.

Alexander, A., Owers, J. and Carveth, R. 1998. *Media economics: Theory and practice.* New Jersey: Lawrence Erlbaum Associates.

Althusser, L. 1971. *Lenin and philosophy and other essays.* London: New Left Books.

Anderson, B. 1983. *Imagined Communities: Reflections on the origin and spread of nationalism.* London: Verso.

Bergman, B. 1985. *African pop: Goodtime Kings.* Poole: Blandford.

Du Gay, P. (ed.). 1997. *Production of culture/cultures of production.* London: Sage.

Ullestad, N. 1992. "Diverse rock rebellions subvert mass media hegemony". In: Garofalo, R. *Rocking the boat: mass music and mass movements.* Boston: Southend Press.

Giddens, A. 1981. "A contemporary critique of historical materialism", Vol 1: *Power, property and the state.* London: Macmillan.

Grossberg, L. 1993. "Can cultural studies find true happiness in communication?", *Journal of Communication* 43(4). 89-97.

Hall, S. 1997. "Introduction". In: Hall, S (ed.). *Representation: Cultural representations and signifying practices.* London: Sage Publication.

Hall, S. 1991. "The local and the global: Globalisation and ethnicity". In: King, A. (ed.). *Culture, globalisation and the world-system.* London: Macmillan.

Herman, E.S. and McChesney, R. 1997. *The global media: The new missionaries of corporate capitalism.* London: Cassell.

Lovell, T. 1983. *Pictures of reality.* London: British Film Institute.

Lull, J. 1987. *Popular music and communication.* London: Sage.

Massey, D. 1994. *Space, place and gender.* Cambridge: Polity Press.

Sowetan, 2001. "Local is better in all media", 23 October 2001. 19.

Stephens, S. 2000. "Kwaito". In: Nuttall, S. and Michael, C. *Senses of culture. South African Culture Studies* Oxford: Oxford University Press.

Storey, J. 1996. *Cultural studies and the study of popular culture: Theories and practice.* Athens: The University of Georgia Press.

Thompson, K. 1997. *Media and cultural regulation.* London: Sage.

CHAPTER SIX

"Sometimes it feels like I'm not Black enough": Recast(e)ing Coloured[1] through South African Hip-hop as a Postcolonial Text

Jane Battersby

Postcolonialism and Popular Culture

South African hip-hop as a genre is a form of postcolonial text and as such offers opportunities for new identities for the South African Coloured community. Postcolonialism is read as a process that "critically scrutinises the colonial relationship" (Boehmer 1995:3). Colonial rule depends on the belief of the subordinate nature of the colonised people and the belief of superiority by the colonist. Postcolonial texts "challenge the dominant culture on its own grounds and in its own terms" (Boehmer 1995:172), through the use of Western genres and styles to subvert colonial power and to obtain a voice.

Postcolonial literature is a largely retroactive art. Bhabha has addressed this retroaction as follows: "The importance of retroaction lies in its ability to re-inscribe the past, reactivate it, relocate it, *resignify it*. More significantly, it commits our understanding of the past, and our interpretation of the future to an ethics of 'survival' that allows us to *work through the present*" (Bhabha 1996:59).

Postcolonial literature has been limited in its power since many postcolonial authors have been drawn from elites (often exiled), and are the product of the colonial education systems. While these elites were taught in the colonists' languages and traditions, the general population remained illiterate to much of the colonial means of representation. This problematises postcolonial literature, as although its aim is often to challenge colonialism and to encourage colonial subjects to overcome the ideologies forced upon them, their expression in high art and in the empire's language has limited their transmission to the general population. The majority appears still to be denied a voice.

The term "postcolonial" implies a similar experience in terms of colonial oppression and resistance (McClintock 1994:298). This simplification of the colonial and postcolonial experiences opens postcolonialism to co-option by more dominant colonised groups. This problem of co-option is one that has been a constant issue for postcolonialism.

Despite these limitations postcolonialism is still a powerful tool of analysis. As Taylor (1995) has asserted, it still has relevance since the legacies of colonialism continue to haunt the globe. The new era of global capitalism has renewed sensitivity to the struggles of new nations (Taylor 1995:17). Global capitalism in its current phase "projects a process which separates, compartmentalises, specialises, and dispenses: a force which operates uniformly and makes of heterogeneity a homogenous and standardising power" (Jameson 1988 in Wise 1995:41). This increasing dominance of one particular ideology and means of asserting it globally to all groups may yet provide greater opportunities for postcolonial alliances (JanMohamed and Lloyd 1990 in Wise 1995:41). Postcolonialism may yet find new opportunities to express a counter-dominant experience as the apparent power of global capitalism becomes ossified. By providing an increasingly common experience of oppression, today's "colonists" may have provided their subjects with the tools to develop a powerful and common language of resistance.

One such tool can be popular music. There is a body of literature that asserts that mass culture, and more specifically popular music, has no intrinsic value as a tool for understanding social processes. Adorno's argument against the value of popular music was that "modern capital is burdened by the problem of overproduction. Markets can only be stimulated by *creating* needs . . . needs which are the result of capital rather than human logic and therefore, inevitably, false" (Frith 1983:44-5). This is reflected in Hebdige's argument that due to the burgeoning capitalism and relative affluence of the 1950s, the economy was forced to seek out new markets in order to continue the growth that assures its survival. The new market created was the teenager (Hebdige 1988 in Valentine, Skelton and Chambers 1988:4). This notion has been furthered by Ritzer's "McDonaldization of Society" (1993). In this it is asserted that society and its cultural artefacts are based on efficiency, calculability, predictability and control (Longhurst 1995:15). Through this it is implied that mass culture is inherently commodified, that it offers limited choice, that it is a part of a global homogenisation (and is unfulfilling, satisfying for only a short time until the latest product is purchased).

Although there is a considerable bulk of literature denying the value of popular music as a tool of social research, there is a larger body of research to refute this view. Fiske challenges the view expressed above: "Their [capitalist industry's] skills in sugar coating the pill is not so great that the people are not aware of the ideological practice in which they are engaging as they consume and enjoy the cultural commodity. I do not believe that 'the people' are 'cultural dopes'. They are not a passive, helpless mass incapable of discrimination and thus at the economic, cultural and political mercy of the barons of the industry" (Fisk 1989:309). Instead of turning "the people" into a passive, helpless mass, the industrialisation of music has provided a new means of self-expression and of challenging systems (Frith 1992 in Longhurst 1995:19). It appears that capitalism creates everything, including its enemies, in its own image. Popular music is recognised as "a culture of conflict" acting through the forms of resistance and evasion (Fiske 1989:2). Rap is particularly rooted in this conflictual ideology. bell hooks (1990) termed rap a form of "testimony" for the underclass. She asserted, "it has enabled underclass black youth to develop a critical voice" or "a common literacy".

Having recognised popular culture as a potential tool for the expression of views counter to those with power in society, it is vital to recognise that this apparent challenge to power is not unproblematic. Wallis and Malm (1990) located four different relationships that situate popular music in the neo-colonialism debate. They assert that transmission occurs in four ways: cultural exchange, cultural dominance, cultural imperialism and transculturalisation. Cultural exchange is the process by which "cultures and subcultures interact and exchange features under fairly loose forms and more or less equal terms" (Wallis and Malm 1990:173). In terms of colonial rule the means of cultural transference could be seen to be that of cultural dominance, where a powerful group imposes its culture on a weaker one (Longhurst 1995:50).

The form of cultural transmission that is most commonly recognised today is that of cultural imperialism. Under this "cultural dominance is augmented by the transfer of money and/or resources from dominated to dominating culture group" (Wallis and Malm 1990:175). This analysis may however be too simplistic and can be answered in the same way that the notion that popular culture simply represented the will of the market was answered. This understanding of cultural transference again underestimates the resistance to cultural domination. As a result, the fourth kind of relationship has been put forward. Transculturalisation can be understood simply as the creation of a transcultural or global culture, a global culture that is however usually dominated by one culture or group. As such the notion of transculturalisation as a process recognises both the power of domination of a group and the powers of resistance of others. Through this investigation of the nature of popular music it is possible to establish music as a site of understanding complex social processes of domination and resistance, and therefore individual and corporate identity issues.

Hip hop developed from the innercity streets, where it is claimed that individuals began experimenting with recorded sound as they could not afford instruments (Rose 1994:34). The poverty surrounding the early hip-hop movement is illustrated by the explanation that hip-hop artists used to use "electricity . . . pirated from city light poles, cheap turntables, makeshift amps and used records" (Potter 1995:110).

In South Africa the issue of being an underground movement is compounded by the dominance of American products in the market place. Just as all other commodities, imported (particularly American) products are favoured over the local in the market. This issue represents the full working out of theories of cultural imperialism and transculturalisation discussed earlier. It has been asserted by several of the Cape Town-based hip-hoppers that local artists' CDs are often even held under the counter and only offered on request.

In the American case successful artists are frequently accused of "selling out" and therefore losing authenticity and representativeness. This form of accusation has been levelled particularly at gangsta rap artists, who have moved into affluent areas such as Hollywood Hills while still producing music that promotes gang warfare in order to attempt to maintain their "street roots".

This accusation has never been made in South Africa, for two reasons. Firstly, since the market is smaller, artists do not get rich from hip-hop and therefore can't sell out in the same way. At the same time many of the hip-hop crews in South Africa follow the notion that they have a responsibility to their communities (often as a result of their allegiance to some of the Black Consciousness ideals).

Rap as a Language of Resistance

The adoption of rap music as a means of expression by South Africa's Coloured population is part of a powerful local and worldwide culture of resistance. Rap and its broader art form hip-hop can be seen as a continuation of the process of postcolonial production. Hip-hop has been perceived as uninformed street art, but research into the lyrical content and musical production reveals that the sources drawn upon and the philosophies incorporated are far wider than many have assumed. Berman (1996) has noted that in the mid-1980s rappers were drawing on sources such as Foucault. In the Cape hip-hop scene, lyrics draw on both Western and African sources, incorporating and challenging them, thereby questioning Western logic. Postcolonial texts seek to challenge and subvert the accepted relationship between the colonial subject and the colonist. The text must therefore first illustrate to the broader audience the impact of colonialism on the colonial subject.

In this chapter I have focused on the work of Prophets of da City (POC), Black Noise and Brasse Vannie Kaap (BVK). These groups represent what Badsha (2003) has referred to as the "Old Skool" of South African hip-hop. POC consists of a core group of artists who have been a part of the hip-hop scene since the early '80s. They have perceived themselves as artists and political commentators. BVK is a newer group with POC's Ready D a key member. They have a much more local focus and rap mainly in Gamtaal[2] as a counter-discursive act, as discussed by Haupt (2001). Black Noise was formed in 1990 by a group of hip-hoppers who were also a part of the scene since the early '80s. They are led by Emile YX, a former school teacher, who has established Black Noise as artists on a social mission (Black Noise interview 2001). The texts created by the Old Skool hip-hoppers have been instrumental in illustrating the impacts of colonialism/apartheid upon their audience, as discussed above.

One of the clearest and most striking expressions of this is to be found in the inlay art of POC's 1993 album "Age of Truth".

Inlay art from "Age of Truth" (Prophets of da City, 1993)

The background image demonstrates the social reality created by South Africa's history. The photograph shows a bleak image of the violence in South African society. Overlaid is a street art picture that attempts to explain the origin of this reality. The image portrays a strong individual wrapped in the old South African flag (representing the apartheid system) dying by shooting himself in the head. The individual is killing himself with his own arm, but this arm is mechanised. The mechanised nature of his arm is only evident through the burning flag. This arm could be seen as a representation of the loss of control of colonial subjects over their own destiny and the resultant destruction of self. This revelation is the result of the destruction of the apartheid state, as illustrated by the burning flag. Skulls symbolising the extent and history of the relationship portrayed surround the individual.

By demonstrating the colonial relationship, hip-hop seeks to challenge and subvert it. Hip-hop achieves this by various means. Many of the techniques adopted are not dissimilar to those portrayed in Scott's analysis of everyday resistance (1985). Essentialised relationships are used as a position of subversion. The first element of this is the representation of racial groups by music. In America and in South Africa, one of the accepted roles for the black population was that of musician. As such the perception of the Coloured population in South Africa came to be that of the joyful, singing servant of the white people (Gordimer 1986). Hip-hop artists play on their essentialised identities as a base of power. This is perhaps most evident in POC's "Blast from the Past" (POC 1993) in which Prophets of da City incorporate a sample of "Daar kom die Alabama"[3] [translation: "There comes the Alabama"] at the start of a vitriolic attack on white power. "Daar kom die Alabama" is a song long associated with the image of Coloureds as the "hêppie coon" [Translation: "happy coon".] "Coon" is a derogatory term for Coloured and by juxtaposing it with the Gamtaal version of "happy" it becomes a statement of South African power relations. The incorporation of this song in a piece of resistance music provides a powerful tool of opposition.

Within this use of music other essentialised elements of Coloured identity are subtly subverted. One area where this is prevalent is through the use of the vernacular, Gamtaal. The term "Gamtaal" derived from the Afrikaans word "taal", meaning language, and "Gam". "Gam" is the Afrikaans for "Ham", the cursed son of Noah (Western 1981:147). This reference to the language of the Coloured population as the language of a cursed man and his descendants therefore labels gamtaal as a language of shame by whites. The standardisation of Afrikaans by whites played a decisive role in the discourse of power during apartheid, through its exclusion of the variants of Afrikaans spoken by black/Coloured speakers.

The use of the vernacular subverts the impacts of colonialism. The use of the colonial language can be seen to embody the colonial vision, therefore to use the vernacular is to oppose that colonial vision (Boehmer 1995:210). The use of the vernacular creates a unifying force among the colonised and a site of intercultural conflict. Invariably in South African hip-hop the vernacular is used in such a manner as to challenge the logic presented by power structures.

These postcolonial texts also challenge hegemonic power in a much more overt manner developed in American rap. There has been a move to playing to the hegemonic group's fears. The American group Public Enemy's album *Fear of a Black Planet* is a key example of this. Through creating postcolonial texts as overt spaces of resistance many rap artists have asserted black dominance and challenged the confidence of the white populations. This has been reflected in the work of graffiti artists whose tags can be seen as reclaiming areas of the city (Rose 1994:42). Texts that are being created are no longer simply about bringing the oppressed into a place of pride, but also about creating the kind of unease that they have felt in the hegemonic group. Lyrically, this attempt at dis-ease is exemplified in the POC song "Understand where I'm coming from":

> But no justice, no peace. Tell your police they can go kiss the tip of my Bazooka. And I am the shooter and the prosecutor, and you are found guilty of murder, rape and larceny (POC "Understand where I'm coming from" 1993).

Through highlighting the crimes of the dominant and attempting a reversal of the established power relations, a powerful challenge is expressed.

South African hip-hop offers further resistance through its efforts at community empowerment and education. As POC sing in "Understand where I'm coming from" (1993):

> A new South Africa, I don't believe them. I see them with a new scheme, a scam to set up the black man. How can I preach, preach, preach, teach, teach. Teach, is what I wanna do, I gotto do. They wouldn't teach it to me in school.

As individuals educated by a system that encouraged unquestioning compliance with the apartheid mentality, many of the local hip-hop artists have attempted to re-educate their communities in resistance. Black Noise, for example, has established or played a key role in a number of community projects. Hip-hop as a genre, and through its lyrics and projects associated with it, offers a vital site of resistance and a means to express new identities. The following section investigates what form these identities take.

Forms of Oppositional Identity

No identity is static and the expression of one form of identity does not negate the expression of another. Different elements of identity will be adopted and adapted as both exogenous and endogenous elements of society develop. Through the reading of South African rap music as a text it has been possible to locate four main identities relating to the issue of racial identity that have been asserted. These four identities have been spatially grounded as they have in the music. By locating the identities spatially they represent a further challenge to the remnants of colonialism. By claiming places and naming them, the imperial powers denied ownership and belonging to its inhabitants. Through claiming these places as the source of the identity, hip-hop artists are reclaiming space as they reclaim their minds.

The four identities located in their spatiality are: America, "the ghetto", Azania, and District Six. These four interlinking identities need to be analysed individually in both their representation in the music and their meaning for Coloured hip-hop artists. The first element of identity to be discussed, by virtue of its vast influence and the subsequent issues of identity that it raises, is that of "America".

America

A key identity portrayed in Coloured hip-hop is that of "African American". The adoption of an American notion (America as shorthand for the United States) of blackness is one that is considered as being both constructive and destructive to the emergent Coloured identity in South Africa, often with these constructive and destructive elements blending in some form of Faustian pact.

The adoption of African American blackness by the Coloured hip-hop community is a product of the genre itself and also a continuation of previous cultural linkages. From colonial times onward there have been similarities in the experiences of and expectations placed upon the African American and Coloured communities. One key area of this is the stereotypical image created of each. One historical role of the urban Coloured population was that of house servant in white homes; as such many took on the role of musician. The "slave orchestra" was documented by European visitors to the Cape, such as Lichtenstein (1800) and Teenstra (1825) (Constant 1999:58-9). This role and its trappings (such as dress and demeanour) were similar to the role of slaves as musicians in America. The cultural association between African American experiences and Coloureds became evident and was developed with the visit of African American minstrel groups, specifically the Virginia Jubilee Singers, to Cape Town towards the end of the nineteenth century (Constant 1999:87).

The American influence has been evident in other aspects of Coloured life, perhaps the best known being gangsterism. Manuel and Hatfield (1967:85) have noted that since the 1920s there has been an American-influenced gang culture among Cape Town's Coloured population. The most dominant gang on the Cape Flats even goes so far as to call themselves "The Americans" (Kinnes 2000:20).

It would therefore be possible to assert that Cape hip-hop is simply a further step in the general americanisation of Coloured identity. However, it must be noted that hip-hop as a genre can be seen as an expression of a particular facet of African American culture. This blackness is a radical urban identity, relating to ghetto life. The overtly political messages of early US hip-hop and the links with the US Black Power movement struck a chord with many highly politicised Coloured youths in the early 1980s. At this time the youth, dissatisfied with apartheid education, were taking to the streets for their education. Shamiel X, a producer and DJ in Cape Town, said that the reason he got involved in the hip-hop scene was this: "When I was a kid in the early eighties, this music was the first I'd heard that I could relate to. You know, 'Fuck da Police', and all that shit, that's what I was feeling" (Shamiel X interview 1999).

At the same time as being attracted by the anger of the message delivered, many were also drawn to the philosophy of the hip-hop scene in America that was being developed by individuals such as Afrika Bambaattaa and KRS-ONE, which in turn was influenced by the Black Power movement. Afrika Bambaattaa developed the Universal Zulu Nation that has a clear programme of black empowerment through a pseudo-religious philosophy. This combination of music and black empowerment was hugely influential. Local producer Patrick "Caramel" Hickey explained the appeal as follows:

> During the '80s I attended a school which was heavily involved in the anti-apartheid struggle. At the same time I began my life as a B-Boy. The combination of a black-conscious school and the influence of black urban youth culture made me and many other hip-hoppers see ourselves as black (Hickey interview 1999).

The link between American blackness and Coloured youth identity is clear through music, lyrics and names chosen by artists. It is particularly clear in the sampling of US civil rights leaders in "Who taught you". Black Noise repeated the quotes "It's much more criminal than teaching him to hate someone else", "Who taught you to hate yourself" and "This blue-eyed man" (Black Noise 1995). In sampling American civil rights speeches and interspersing them with a South African Black Consciousness speech, the recognition of a similar struggle is made. At this point it is important to note that POC and Black Noise appear to engage more with American civil rights activists than with black South African leaders in their earlier work. This can be interpreted as an outcome of the nature of apartheid constructions of Colouredness. Not only did the apartheid state attempt to create difference in terms of identity and identifications between South Africa's Coloured and black African population groups, but the urbanised nature of Cape Town's Coloured population promoted an apparent link with African American experiences over the experiences of black Africans.

The alignment with the American civil rights movement can be seen as strategic. It enabled alignment with a group who had achieved some form of victory against oppression. By adopting American culture and then adding their own influences, South African rap artists are able to tap into an already powerful oppositional voice. By associating with this American voice South Africa's rappers can already claim some form of victory. This process subverts the argument by McClintock (1994) that the term "postcolonial" is restrictive as it fails to recognise different stages in postcolonial experience. Here, however, this limitation has been a source of power as it uses another people's victory to claim hope. The black American identity adopted is not a carbon copy of the American original, but adapted to meet local conditions.

The desire of the South Africa hip-hop community to maintain only the positive elements of hip-hop is problematic. South African hip-hop has had to come face to face with the negative elements of American blackness evident in hip-hop. The anger that first attracted Coloured artists to hip-hop has in part developed into gangsta rap in America. This form of rap has become a part of the Cape scene, as demonstrated by Blunt's "NBK", which stands for Natural Born Killer (Blunt 1998). This song, with its chorus of "I'm a natural born killer" and claims of being a "nigger", incorporates what are generally seen as negative elements of American black identity. At the same time, by referring to themselves as "niggers", the group proves themselves to be inauthentic and not representative of the South African Coloured experience.

The negative impact of gangsta rap has not been ignored by the established crews such as BVK (Brasse Vannie Kaap). In "Laat dit rik" they rap:

> Yo, man, wassup, kid. Let's do it for the honeys. / That's not the way we praat in the Kaap./ Jy moet wys raak of waai want jou valse accent don't make you kwaai"/ ("That's not the way we talk in the Cape. You've got to get with it or scram because your false accents don't make you tough.")

In their song "Life ain't what it used to be" Black Noise makes a strong case against the wholesale buying into americanism, claiming that negative rap music is being sold in order to bring down the people:

> American media tentacles now affects the world mentality/ acting like you're not in drive-bys or that reality. /They playing up gangsta rap promoting genocide induce,/ fuelling gang violence and tightening the noose around the neck of the black man globally/ using negative rap music to kill the black family. (Black Noise 1995)

This claim of authentic rap being bought out corporately in order to use it for their own purposes in part reflects the argument advanced by Adorno and referred to earlier.

A further problem of the unquestioning acceptance of American culture is that despite the b(l)ack-to-Africa calls of a number of American artists, their insincerity proves them to be as exploitative as the rest of American culture. A telling example is recounted by Ray of Black Noise (Black Noise interview 2001) when explaining why they work under the philosophy of Afrika Bambaattaa's Zulu Nation, but do not use its name:

> It became evident through party clashes between Zulu and Xhosa people, it wouldn't be wise of us to use the name Zulu Nation, because it would be looked upon as choosing a side politically, or even looked upon as, I don't know, a form of assimilation. But then, obviously, Afrika Bambaattaa did not understand . . . I don't know if he didn't understand or didn't want to understand the situation that we were coming from. I think also a lot of them couldn't appreciate the situation because they had never lived here.

It appears that Americans, including African Americans, carry images of Africa which have not only been constructed outside of Africa, but which they also attempt to impress upon Africans. Nixon cites a telling example of this in his discussion of Mandela's visit to the US in 1990. Mandela was portrayed as an almost messianic character for African Americans, yet at the time was questioned on South Africa's debt to the freedom struggle of African Americans (Nixon 1994:176-192). Cultural appropriation and purported debt to the US are key elements evident throughout African American representations of South Africa. This is not widely divergent from general American representations and in some cases is more accentuated through assumptions that their marginalisation negates claims of cultural imperialism.

Although it can be concluded that the claim of American cultural imperialism is too strong an accusation to level at the negative elements of American hip-hop culture, it may be possible to view this as a form of transculturation. The adoption of hip-hop and its adaptation to the needs of the Coloured community represent the extent to which a form of global culture is being created. However, at the same time it must be recognised that this global culture is controlled and determined to a large degree from the United States. In South African hip-hop it has therefore been accepted that American culture will have some influence. It is further recognised by those involved in the scene that although many elements of this American influence may be seen as positive, artists need to be aware of negative aspects that may be adopted.

Ghetto

In South African hip-hop there are constant references to the "ghetto", such as the naming of record companies (Ghetto Ruff) and albums (Ghetto Code). The notion of ghetto identity develops from urban African American identities and locates South African hip-hoppers and their political struggles and opposition to hegemonic power within a broader context. Therefore, when POC sings that "the world is a ghetto, it doesn't matter if you're in New York or Soweto" in the song "Ghetto World" (POC 1994), they are claiming some form of unity in oppression.

The invocation of the ghetto acts as a protest against those who created the ghetto. "Ghetto World" re-inscribes the ghetto as a space of pride and authenticity by the repetition of the lyrics, "Everybody loves their soul, everybody loves their roots" and "We've got to restore ourselves to the kings and queens we were". At the same time it creates a unity by locating the common oppressor with lyrics such as "The West turns around and labels us Third World" and then indicating what the West's common crimes are: hunger, poverty, "dead bodies everywhere".

Ghetto dwellers are portrayed as black, raising the question of what blackness is being claimed. Hip-hop is seen as a black ghetto form of music, yet as a global phenomenon it claims strongholds in Arab communities in France, Maori communities in New Zealand and among white youths in Germany, all claiming some form of blackness. As Shamiel X states: "I've been to London, Sweden, Germany, all over the place. And everywhere, where people felt fucked by the establishment, kids were into hip-hop' (Shamiel X interview 1999). This blackness is not bound by race, but on conditions of exclusion and oppression. Ghettos represent the physical oppression of one by another. The voice from the ghetto is by its very nature a voice that comes out in anger to challenge the status quo.

Through the ghetto identity South African hip-hop can claim to be seeking the same unity as sought by a number of postcolonial authors. A true global ghetto can begin to be imagined through using this readily transferable medium of popular culture. The ghetto as a source of unity and support is evident in POC's 1995 version of the song "Neva Again" where they call out to offer thanks to the global ghetto with these lyrics:

> So I dedicate those who were down with the revolution all over the world and never lose it./ I dedicate this to those who were down with struggle, G, even when things

> got ugly./ 'Cos the black race always had a slapped face/'cos freedom moves at a whack pace./ It sometimes takes a miracle to see my people free/ 'cos it's not done easily/ So I dedicate this to those who don't turn the other cheek,/ to those who would rather speak/ against colonialism, imperialism and racism./ So I'm bringing it back to the basics/ and I know that those who supported the struggle locally,/ I support your struggle globally (POC "Neva Again '95", 1995).

In 1993 POC used the global ghetto as a call to arms with the following lyrics:

> Let me unveil the mystery, like Agatha Christie, about South Africa, yes, we are dissed by the history and the bullshit that they teach you to a school kid, about what some fool did and how he discovered Africa, how he was spectacular. But all he did was suck us dry like Dracula. He also exploited the natives of Australia, America, India. Fuck 'em (POC 1993).

After the end of apartheid, South African hip-hop was able to use this victory to encourage other ghetto-ised people. The implication of this is the same as that of the alignment of the South African hip-hop community with America. That is, the victory has been achieved at least partially by one part of the global ghetto, and this should offer hope to those still facing oppression.

A final element of the global-ghetto-blackness is that it attempts to unite Coloured and blacks in South Africa. By using this simple tool of association through a global struggle many South African hip-hoppers seek to create some unity out of the difference enforced under apartheid.

Azania

The theme of Azania is another that is recurrent in early South African hip-hop. This theme narrows the notion of a ghetto identity to an African and specifically South African black identity. This is of great importance since the ghetto identity can be seen as being linked more to the African American experience than to the African one. Black South Africans tend not to speak of the ghetto, but of the township or "loxion" (location). This is evident in much kwaito music and in the naming of companies run by young black South Africans, such as Loxion Kulcha. The adoption of the ghetto by the Coloured population could be seen as partially resulting from the unwillingness of certain parts of the Coloured population to identify with black South Africans. The theme of Azania developed to challenge this construct.

The Azanian identity has two key elements. Firstly, it engages in the act of African history as a means of reclaiming identity. The second and specifically South African form seeks to create an understanding that the suffering of the Coloured community under apartheid was essentially the same as that of the African community. The symbol of this African renaissance in South African hip-hop is that of Azania.

The name "Azania" as a term for Africa is charged with resistance and pride. Azania symbolises a positive pre-colonial history of Africa and is a term of opposition and post-colonial hope in many parts of Africa. This was particularly prevalent in South Africa's Black Consciousness movement (BC). BC asserted that African history was hidden in order to create political disunity among blacks and thus secure the power of the white population in Africa. By educating people about their history, BC enabled people to empower themselves (Halisi 1991:101).

Although BC has strong links with the term Azania, there is a question why POC and Black Noise should adopt the term. They use the notion of Azania to attempt to forge an association of blackness amongst Coloured listeners, but the majority of black South Africans do not often use the term. The origin of the term is certainly not South African, but has links to the East African coast as a derivation of the Persian "Zanj-bar", meaning "land of the blacks" (Bute and Harmer 1997:118). This adoption therefore links to the adoption of non-South African sources and ideologies discussed before. In addition, a number of the slaves at the Cape who form part of the ancestry of the Coloured population were brought from this area (Bradlow 1978:92).

A further, and more political rather than cultural, reason for the adoption of Azania is the impact of the Non-European Unity Movement (NEUM). This Trotskyite organisation formed in 1943 was open to individuals from all population groups, but consisted largely of Coloured and black intellectuals in the Cape. It was particularly popular among the Coloured middle classes and particularly influential amongst teaching unions in the mid to late 1980s (Simon and Simon 1983:543). This was the time when the core of the Old Skool were at high school and developing their political ideologies.[4] The notion of Azania holds together the theme common to South African hip-hop of getting black pride through knowledge of self and black history. An effort is made to encourage Coloureds to recognise a common past with South Africa's black population. This is demonstrated in Black Noise's "Nobody Knows":

> I come from the Plain not far from Gug's and Nyanga,[5] but still Coloureds and blacks don't mix with one another. If you can do your thing then I can do my thing, we work against each other, we both come out with nothing. Trainlines separate and divide my people and still white Jesuses pollute church steeples. If you can interact and I can interact, then we will both realise that we are both black. And my past is not much different from yours, and we both been fighting the exact same wars. Each one, teach one, we all can recognise a plan was set up for us to trivialise the existence of the other 'cos our shades of skin colour, preventing us from calling each other "Brother" (Black Noise 1998).

In "Da Struggle Kontinues" (POC 1997), POC also calls for Coloureds to continue to align themselves with black South Africans. Colonial and apartheid governments set people apart by physical (spatial) and mental (educational) means to protect their power. "Nobody Knows" proposes that once the truth of the nature of the antagonism between Coloured and blacks is recognised, people will react against the past, a postcolonial resistance. A clear effort to re-educate (or "Afrocate") the Coloured population is that of the sleeve art of POC's Universal Souljaz (1995).

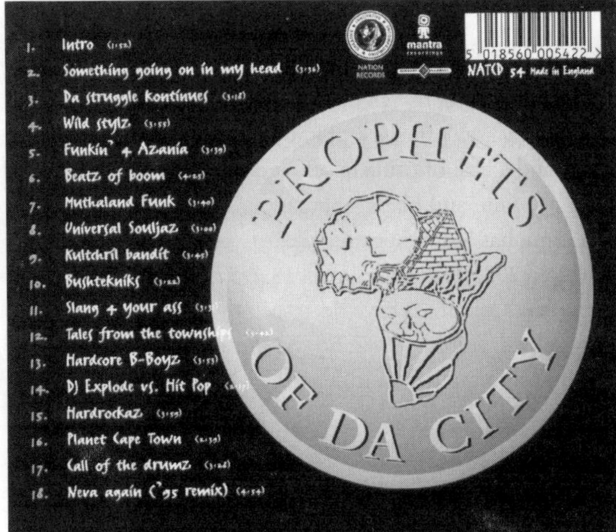

Sleeve art from "Universal Souljaz" (Prophets of da City, 1995)

This image is one that tells a Black Consciousness (BC) understanding of African history, developing the theme of Azania, comprising of four separate images that make up Africa's past and its future. The first image is of the heart of Africa acting as a womb, representing the assertion that Africa is the birthplace of humankind.

The second image is that of Egypt as a base of civilisation, following both Zulu Nation and BC teachings. In "Black Facts" Black Noise raps:

> The cradle of civilisation can be attributed to the black man. A race of no greater intelligence can be found than the Egyptians, who were mistaken for gods because of the great knowledge they had. You can bet the Ancient Greeks never saw the colour black as bad (Black Noise 1995).

The next image is that of the skull, alluding to the people stolen into slavery. This provides a powerful critique of colonialism and the Western claims to civilise. The skull represents the destruction of Africa's history of culture, and not just the physical death of slaves.

A potential Azanian future is the final image portrayed. The image is of South Africa shining a light into the rest of Africa giving hope of overcoming the remnants of colonialism. Artists in South Africa recognise that this future is not yet the present and many write about how to achieve this state. The call for an alignment with the black population both creates a sense of unity in the struggle against apartheid and in overcoming post-apartheid problems, and provides the Coloured population with an alternative identity option to that of the cultural alignment with the white population.

District Six [6]

The last words of POC's album "Age of Truth" are a sample of a white woman saying "Happiness is knowing who you really are." The lack of knowledge of self is said to have led to Coloured-on-black racism and a lack of pride in self and community by Coloured people. The lack of acceptance by white and black populations, coupled with the lack of positive historical representation, has led to negative identity constructions amongst many Coloured communities (Field 2001:112, and Rasool 1996:57).

Since the earliest days of the Cape, Coloureds have been seen by the white population as not quite white enough (Marks and Trapido 1987:29). At the same time, due mainly to their comparatively privileged position under apartheid, the Coloured population has found itself often disliked and untrusted by the black population (Murphy 1998:544-5). Following apartheid, the deeply-felt racial tensions between blacks and Coloureds have remained largely intact, despite educational integration and a number of community projects.[7] I interviewed Coloured pupils who complained about having to sit near black pupils in the class and relied on grotesque stereotypes. I also interviewed black pupils in the same school who had equally negative constructions of Coloureds. They had all been in integrated schools and had attended workshops, but were still primarily influenced by historical constructions. Apartheid created a mindset in all people of all races that will not be changed simply by changing the law. In "Power 2 da People", POC has expressed this in the following lyric: "They saying and they playing like apartheid is scrapped. You can scrap it from the books, but what about the mind, the time, the soul?" (POC 1993).

Emile of Black Noise has attempted to explain the problem that Coloured youth are facing today in terms of identity:

> Being so-called Coloured is the most confusing and mind-boggling thing there is. Although people brush it aside, the sense of belonging is important – especially now in this country. Kids wonder where they fit in. Before, when people spoke of "black", it included us – now it doesn't. A gang can give you a sense of family and security and finance – possibly many of the things a group identity would give. That is what makes it a bit easier for kids living in Khayelitsha and Gugulethu – their sense of family heritage and ancestry (Emile in Visser 1998).

This problem of marginalisation by both whites and blacks which limits pride in identity is further complicated by the problem of "stolen history", as recognised by a number of postcolonial texts. Black Noise claims in "So-called Coloured Folks" that lack of a positive history has resulted in mental slavery: "Mandela can't set the Coloured man free, 'cos the Coloured don't know who the hell he wanna be."

This insecurity through negative representations has led to disunity in the Coloured population as status is often drawn from denying blackness and playing white. BVK's "Jy Smaak My" (BVK 1999), a stilted serenade and social commentary, provides a good example of this mindset. In this a darker-skinned, curly-haired, Afrikaans-speaking male is rejected by a clearly higher-status female. Her actions demonstrate the colour snobbery in some sectors of the Coloured population, based largely on the fear of losing the status they have achieved through close relationships with the white population. The male rapper responds that her statements are destroying the emergent Coloured pride. The song concludes with a history lesson, calling on identity to be based on this and not on pleasing whites. This song calls for a movement towards Coloured unity through a recognition of history.

Just as Negritude based the means of forming a resistance mentality on the rediscovery of a positive past, South African hip-hoppers have focused on the celebration of a Coloured past. Whereas in most popular and mainstream accounts the black population can trace a pre-colonial past, the very existence of the Coloured population has been represented as a source of shame and their past has been hidden (Western 1981, Bradlow 1978:81). The very conditions that led to the formation of the population were made illegal in apartheid South Africa. The Prohibition of Mixed Marriages Act (1949) and Immorality Amendment Act (1950) made sexual contact between whites and all other population groups illegal, thereby making more shameful Coloured history (De Villiers 1988:316). Due to this negative construction of Coloured history, the past that is being invoked is therefore a much more recent past and involves the celebration of District Six.

Although POC has released a number of tracks on this theme, the best example of this is "I remember District Six" (POC 1997). This song is an attempt to remind the Coloured people of their past before they were forced onto the Cape Flats by the Group Areas Act. It attempts to create a kind of corporate memory through personal history. The negative issues of life in "Die Ses" (literally "The Six") are not denied, the poverty and the troubles are present, but are overpowered by claims of community. By showing a common history and making this a source of pride, the memory of District Six provides a means of uniting the Coloured population and provides a site of self-esteem. The song's repetition of "I remember District Six" encourages the audience to attempt to remember and to learn from their shared past. This evocation of memories of District Six reflects the ideal of resignifying the past. In the same way as Azania's mythological status has been invoked on the national and continental scale, District Six is mythologised to provide the community with a sense of self. This notion is perhaps best expressed in the chorus of the song: "This is the heart and soul of the young and old, without District Six we're in the cold" (POC 1997).

The hope of the hip-hop community is that once the Coloured community comes to recognise their history, they will develop enough self-esteem to overcome the petty racism that dominates their relationships with the black population. This may prove to be a faint hope as the transforming of identities is based on considerably more than resignified histories. In South Africa at present the racial tensions between Coloureds and blacks are not being reduced to any great degree. This is the result of a number of factors, including the view that the new education system is marginalising the Coloured population, mass unemployment and positive discrimination towards black men and the continued accusations levelled at the Coloured population of "selling out". (Cross and Mkwanazi-Twala 1997, Murphy 1998, James 1996 et al.). The extent of these continuing racial tensions is evident in the continued Coloured rejection of the predominantly black ANC. Although the hip-hop scene can be seen to represent the population from which its artists are drawn, it must be seen that its attempts to encourage the formation of positive postcolonial identities do not yet represent the reality on the Cape Flats.

Conclusion

This research has uncovered four major forms of blackness that have been adopted by Cape Town-based Coloured hip-hoppers. There are a number of other oppositional identities, including gender and class, which have not been discussed here, but are underplayed in the work of POC and Black Noise. It is, however, the identities described above that are dominant. Adoption of one form of identity is often enabled by the adoption of another, such as the progression from the notion of a global ghetto to that of Azania. The formation of one identity may be the result of limitations experienced in other forms of identity. The main example of this is the expression of a particularly Coloured experience of blackness to overcome the problems of adopting African blackness. These identities are not mutually exclusive and can complement each other. Coloured youth are not restricted to one of these four identity options, as identities are fluid and multi-vocal. Coloured youth identities are rooted in local historical experiences of the population from the constructed shame associated with miscegenation, their gradual political disenfranchisement, the Group Areas Act and the current experiences of marginalisation. These and other factors unique to Cape Town's Coloured population have had implications for identity that are now being expressed through hip-hop.

Bearing these particular local experiences in mind, it is possible to draw conclusions as to why the four forms of blackness have been adopted. For example, throughout the history of the Coloured population the forms of expression, linguistically and stylistically, have been those allowed by the white population. The languages of their ancestors have been lost and therefore the forms of expression open to them have been those borrowed from the dominant group. In an attempt to claim a voice of opposition, the population has adopted the voice used by the American black population. Likewise, the attempts at forming a black African identity relate to an attempt to overthrow the power relations that have dominated Coloured history and an attempt to create a united voice. The identities adopted are fundamentally linked to the unique experiences of the Coloured population in South Africa. These various different forms of blackness have implications for the social and political situations in South Africa, with the focus being on the development of a positive mindset that will encourage peace and progress in South Africa.

Notes

1 This chapter uses the term "Coloured" to refer to those who have "lived through the coloured experience" (Martin 1999:4). It recognises that the Coloured population has been defined and its identities shaped by colonial and apartheid constructions as neither black African nor white. However, this chapter also recognises that Coloured identities are hybrid and constantly made and re-made. This chapter is therefore an attempt to examine some of the transgressive forms of self-representation made available through hip-hop.

2 Gamtaal is a Cape Flats dialect of Afrikaans. Its use in South African hip-hop is discussed later in this chapter.

3 This song is traditionally sung by choirs at the annual "Coon Carnival" in Cape Town. The Alabama was a confederate raider ship that visited Cape Town in 1863-4 (Martin 1999:83). The song's origin has been much debated; what remains certain is that the song is considered emblematic of the slave culture at the Cape.

4 In fieldwork conducted in high schools in Cape Town in 2001-2 I interviewed a number of teachers who were still profoundly influenced by the ideals of the NEUM.

5 Black townships of Cape Town.

6 District Six was the predominantly Coloured area of Cape Town declared a white area in 1966 under the Group Areas Act. Approximately 66 000 people were subject to forced removals from the area (Venter 1974:56). As such District Six has come to be seen as South Africa's pre-eminent site of forced urban removals (Soudien 2001:115).

7 This was particularly evident when conducting fieldwork in high schools in Cape Town in 2001-2.

References

Badsha, F. 2003. "Old Skool Rules/New Skool Breaks: Negotiating identities in the Cape Town Hip-hop Scene", Chapter in this volume.

Berman, M. 1996. "Shouts in the street". In Merrifield, A. and Swyngedouw, E. (eds.) *The Urbanization of Injustice*. London: Lawrence and Wishart.

Bhabha, H. 1994. "Remembering Fanon: Self, psyche and the colonial condition." In Williams, P. & Chisholm, L. (eds.) *Colonial discourse and post-colonial theory: A reader.* New York: Columbia University Press. 112-123.

Boehmer, E. 1995. *Colonial & Postcolonial Literature: Migrant Metaphors*. Oxford: Oxford University Press.

Bradlow, F.R. 1978. "The origins of the early Cape muslims." In Bradlow, F.R. and Cairns, M. (eds.). *The Early Cape Muslims*. Cape Town: AA Balkema Press. 80-106.

Bute, E.L. and Harmer, H.J.P. 1997. *The Black Handbook: The People, History and Politics of Africa and the African diaspora*. London: Cassell.

Cross, M. and Mkwanazi-Twala, Z. 1997. "The dialectic of unity and diversity in education: Its implications for a national curriculum is South Africa." In Cross, M., Mkwanazi-Twala, Z. and Klein, G. (eds.). *Dealing with Diversity in South African Education: A Debate on the Politics of a National Curriculum*. Kenwyn: Juta. 3-35.

De Villiers, M. 1988. *White Tribe Dreaming: Apartheid's Bitter Roots as Witnessed by Eight Generations of an Afrikaner Family*. London: Penguin.

Eyal, D. 1999. *Cape Town's Hip-hop Scene*. Rage online: http://www.rage.co.za/hiphopct.html downloaded 04/08/99.

Fanon, F. 1994. "On national culture." In Williams, P. and Chisholm, L. (eds.). *Colonial Discourse and Post-colonial Theory: A Reader.* New York: Columbia University Press. 36-52.

Field, S. 2001. "Fragile identities: Memory, emotions and Coloured residents of Windermere." In Erasmus, Z. (ed.). *Coloured by History, Shaped by Place: New Perspectives on Coloured Identities in Cape Town.* Social Identities in South Africa Series. Cape Town: Kwela Books and SA History Online. 97-113.

Fiske, J. 1987. "TV: re-situating the popular in the people" In *Continuum: Australian Journal of Media and Culture* Vol.1 No. 2. http://wwwmcc.murdoch.edu.au/ReadingRoom/1.2/Fiske.html.

Frith, S. 1983. *Sound Effects: Youth, Leisure and the Politics of Rock 'n Roll.* New York: Pan Press.

Gordimer, N. 1986. "What were you dreaming?" In Kaplan, D. (ed.). *Sax Appeal.* 1986. University of Cape Town Rag Magazine. 58-61.

Halisi, C.R.D. 1991. "Biko and Black Consciousness philosophy: An interpretation." In Pityana, A., Ramphele, M., Mpumlwana, M. and Wilson, L. (eds.). *Bounds of Possibility: The Legacy of Steve Biko and Black Consciousness.* Cape Town: David Philip. 100-110.

Haupt, A. 2001. "Black Thing: Hip-hop Nationalism, 'Race' and gender." In Erasmus, Z. (ed.). *Coloured by History, Shaped by Place: New Perspectives on Coloured Identities in Cape Town.* Social Identities in South Africa Series. Cape Town: Kwela Books and SA History Online. 173-191.

hooks, b. 1990. "Postmodern Blackness" in *Postmodern Culture* Vol. 1 No. 1. http://muse.jhu.edu/journals/postmodern_culture/v001/1.1hooks.html.

James, W. 1996. "The devil who keeps promises." In James, W., Caliguire, D. and Cullinan, K. (eds.). *Now That We Are Free: Coloured Communities In a Democratic South Africa.* Boulder, CO: L. Reiner. 39-45.

Kinnes, I. 2000. *From Urban Street Gangs to Criminal Empires: The Changing Face of Gangs in the Western Cape*. ISS Monograph Series No. 49 June 2000. Pretoria: Institute for Security Services.

Longhurst, B. 1995. *Popular Music & Society*. Cambridge: Polity Press.

Manuel, G. and Hatfield, D. 1967. *District Six*. Cape Town: Longmans.

Marks, S. and Trapido, S. 1987. *The Politics of Race, Class and Nationalism in Twentieth Century South Africa.* Harlow: Longman.

Martin, D.C. *Coon Carnival: New Year in Cape Town, Past to Present.* Cape Town: David Philip Publishers.

McClintock, A. 1994. "The angel of progress: Pitfalls of the term 'Post-colonialism'." In Williams, P. and Chisholm, L. (eds.). *Colonial Discourse and Post-colonial theory: A Reader.* New York: Columbia University Press. 291-304.

Murphy, D. 1998. *South from the Limpopo: Travels through South Africa*. London: Flamingo Press.

Nixon, R. 1994. *Homelands, Harlem and Hollywood: South African Culture and the World Beyond*. New York: Routledge.

Potter, R.A. 1995. *Spectacular Vernaculars: Hip-hop and the Politics of Postmodernism*. Albany: State University of New York.

Rasool, E. 1996. "Unveiling the heart of fear." In James, W., Caliguire, D. and Cullinan, K. (eds.). *Now that We Are Free: Coloured Communities in a Democratic South Africa.* 54-58.

Ritzer, G. 1993. *The McDonaldisation of Society: An Investigation in the Changing Character of Contemporary Social Life*. Thousand Oaks, CA: Pine Forge Press.

Rose, T. 1994. *Black Noise: Rap Music and Black Culture in Contemporary America*. Hanover, NH: University Press of New England.

Scott, J.C. 1985. *Weapons of the Weak: Everyday Forms of Resistance*. London: Yale University Press.

Simons, J. and Simons, R. 1983. *Class & Colour in South Africa 1850-1950*. London: International Defence and Aid Fund for Southern Africa.

Soudien, C. 2001. "District Six and its uses in the discussion about non-racialism." In Erasmus, Z. (ed.). *Coloured by History, Shaped by Place: New Perspectives on Coloured Identities in Cape Town.* Social Identities in South Africa Series. Cape Town: Kwela Books and SA History Online. 114-130.

Taylor, P. 1995. "Rereading Fanon, rewriting Caribbean history." In Rajan, G. and Mohanram, R. (eds.). *Postcolonial Discourse and Changing Cultural Contexts: Theory and Criticism.* Westport, CT: Greenwood Press. 17-31.

Venter, A.L.J. 1974. *Coloured: A Profile of Two Million South Africans.* Cape Town: Human & Rousseau.

Visser, M. 1998. The Real Crack Pack in SA Give Life a Chance. *Sunday Times* 16/8/1998. http://www.suntimes.co.za/suntimesarchive/1998/08/16/cape/anec02.htm.

Wallis, R. and Malm, K. 1990. "Patterns of change" in Frith, S. and Goodwin, A. (eds.). *On Record: Rock, Pop and the Written Word.* New York: Pantheon Books. 160-180.

Western, J. 1981. *Outcast Cape Town.* Minneapolis: University of Minnesota Press.

Wise, C. 1995. "The dialectics of Négritude: Or, the (post)colonial subject in contemporary African-American literature." In Rajan, G. and Mohanram, R. (eds.). *Postcolonial Discourse and Changing Cultural Contexts: Theory and Criticism.* Westport, CT: Greenwood Press. 33-45.

Interviews:

Shamiel X - 15/06/1999
Patrick 'Caramel' Hickey - 6/08/1999
Black Noise - 26/01/01

Discography:

Black Noise. 1995. *Rebirth*. Cape Town: Making Music Productions.
Black Noise. 1997. *Questions.* Stockholm, Sweden: Polar Studios.
Black Noise. 1998. *Hip Hop won't stop.* Cape Town: Nebula Records.
Black Noise. 2001. *Circles of Fire.* Cape Town: Gimba Music.
Blunt. 1998. *The Banned; The Kutz.* Cape Town: Southside Productions.
Brasse Vannie Kaap. 1999. *BVK.* Johannesburg: Polygram South Africa.
Brasse Vannie Kaap. 2000. *Yskoud.* Cape Town: Ghetto Ruff South Africa.
Prophets of da City. 1993. *Age of Truth*. Cape Town: Tusk Music Co.
Prophets of da City. 1995. *Universal Souljaz.* Johannesburg: Warner Chappell.
Prophets of da City. 1994. *Phunk Phlow* Cape Town: Teal Trutone Music.
Prophets of da City. 1997. *Ghetto Code.* Johannesburg: Gallo.

CHAPTER SEVEN

Old Skool Rules/New Skool Breaks: Negotiating Identities in the Cape Town Hip-hop Scene

Farzanah Badsha

Introduction

In both the popular and academic imagination post-apartheid South Africa is a radically different place. Indeed, the changes that have assaulted the society since the process of democratisation began in the early 1990s have been so dramatic and traumatic it has made putting them into historical context difficult, let alone trying to interrogate the manifold ways that they have transformed the environment. In many ways South Africa was rudely thrust back into the world, and into a world of hypermodernity in which the processes of change and flows of information are sped up incredibly rapidly, but where there is the simultaneous presence of elements of modernity. The use of a term such as "post-modern" is not useful, as it implies a break with the modern and the creation of a new identity, way of living and thinking. The particular juxtapositioning of the modern and the hypermodern in South Africa brings with it many innovations but also stresses involved with dealing with the contradictions of living with elements of society still mired in apartheid, alongside the changes which have occurred since the first democratic elections in 1994. People are still struggling to understand and deal with the effects of this rapid transformation and to understand how and to what extent it has changed people's identities and ways of living, as well as struggling with the very real economic and political changes that they are experiencing.

As part of this deluge of new options and ideas that have become more accessible to South Africans, there has been a concerted effort to use the tools of enquiry already in use around the world to help re-view and re-understand our society. This process has in particular focused on reworking our understanding of South African culture and identity, both under apartheid as well as in its more contemporary shapes. Within academia this has meant that areas of study such as youth culture and identity, which may not have been given as much attention in the past, became more popular topics of interest. Academics have begun to look beyond what Sarah Nuttall and Cheryl-Ann Michael have called the "over-determination of the political, the inflation of resistance, and the inflections given to race as a determinant of identity" in cultural theorising (2000:10).

This essay is a part of this new tendency and trend in the popular and academic imaginings, but also an attempt to argue that we should not throw out the trusted categories of race and resistance in trying to make sense of the new. I will use the case study of the hip-hop scene in Cape Town to show the many and vibrant negotiations of identity that have been facilitated by South Africa's headlong rush into hypermodernity. At the same time, I would also like to use this opportunity to suggest that in our rush to rethink things, we should not forget that change is never a simple process and that it never occurs in a logical order with the old being replaced by the new. Instead, as Allan Pred argues:

> In each capitalist commodity society industrial modernity, high modernity and hypermodernity have had their place-specific manifestations, their array of (geographical hi)stories in which the local has intersected with the extralocal and the "global", in which new forms of domestic and foreign capital – new forms of production and consumption – have intersected with already existing – more or less deeply sedimented – everyday practices, power relations and sets of local and wider taken-for-granted meanings (1995: 21).

Although Pred is making particular reference to Europe[1] in this text, the idea that different phases of modernity can overlap and interact as well as potentially come into conflict with each other in the same space at the same time is a particularly relevant one for a country such as South Africa, where because of the policies of apartheid there are such vast differences in the levels of development that people experience each day in close proximity or even in the same spaces, and where different moments of modernity co-exist with one another.

For this reason it would be problematic to ignore or dramatically downplay "the political", "resistance" and especially the notions of race and class while uncritically embracing the concepts of multiculturalism, hybridity or creolisation. Instead, as I hope to show in the essay, we need to be flexible and open enough to be able to see how the past and the present are in constant negotiation and that it is within this negotiation that many of the most exciting and creative innovations often occur.

In light of this, my title "Old Skool Rules/ New Skool Breaks" might seem contradictory because it seems to imply a polarisation of the old versus the new, rather than a negotiation. However, I feel that this piece of hip-hop slang can be usefully manipulated to show that while this scene in South African youth culture provides a fascinating and hopeful example of some of the ways that youth are negotiating identities that cross many of the rigid racial and class boundaries that kept them apart under apartheid, there is also a need to remember that the power structures and relationships of apartheid have not disappeared and still have real effects in people's everyday lives and the way they negotiate their identities.[2] What I am trying to sketch is a nuanced and sometimes ambivalent picture of this part of South African youth culture.

The exciting thing about change and innovation, particularly in youth culture, is that it forces one to think in more complex terms than a simple black/white contrast and to read the rich layers of meaning from seemingly simple but always complex interactions and performances. As a result, there are many ways to read my title "Old Skool Rules/New Skool Breaks".

Generally, the old skool and the new skool are used to refer to the past and the present, or more specifically stages in the development of hip-hop music and the other subcultural elements associated with it, including graffiti, breakdancing, rapping or MC-ing and DJ-ing. This division is often used to denote nostalgia for some sort of authentic era when hip-hop was imagined to be untainted by commercialisation and motivated by a strong sense of community and social awareness. This is contrasted with the new skool which is considered to have "sold out", losing some of the essence of the culture, and having been contaminated by money, as well as a preoccupation with sex and violence. In this context it is seen as positive for the old skool to "rule", in the sense of it supposedly being superior to the new skool. On the other hand, the idea of "rule" could refer to laws and restrictions, which could be seen as negatively restricting innovation and policing the culture, which would be a quality that would not appeal to the youth. And in this context a break would be seen as more positive than negative, in the sense of having the freedom to break with the past and create new meanings and practices rather than a break being a fault, and old would be characterised as old-fashioned.

In South Africa this deconstruction is further complicated because the old skool is often used to refer to the apartheid era, while the new skool is used to denote post-apartheid society. In this case the rules of the old skool could be associated with the apartheid legislation that stunted the development of youth culture and placed so many restrictions on what was possible, so that the new skool was a break with these rules that allowed innovation and interaction that would not have been possible in the past, and in particular the breaking down of global/local divisions imposed by the country's isolation from the global stage by sanctions. However, the old skool is also sometimes used to describe the first generation of hip-hop producers in South Africa who were almost exclusively coloured youth living in the working-class townships of Cape Town popularly known as the Cape Flats.[3] These pioneers of hip-hop culture from the mid 1980s are respected for having adopted the culture early on in its history, and for having developed the skills needed to be producers of hip-hop music and culture, despite having limited access to resources and information. In the post-apartheid scene many of these pioneers are the people organising the parties and acting as teachers and mentors to the new skool hip-hop followers. The new skool is largely made up of younger white youth from middle- and upper-middle-class backgrounds. The new skool-ers are sometimes characterised as merely being consumers of hip-hop culture rather than participating in its creation and local reworking, but this is not a totally accurate assertion, as many of these youth are becoming more actively involved in the hip-hop scene all the time.[4]

Yet another and slightly ironic spin on this old skool/new skool concept is that one of the main elements that has managed to bring together youth from across racial and class boundaries has been a shared appreciation of the genre of music referred to as "break-beat" music. This genre includes jungle, drum 'n' bass and hip-hop, and their related subcultural elements such as graffiti, skateboarding and manga.[5] So it could be said that it is the breaks that have brought youth together rather than being divisive.

In the same vein I would like to describe and briefly consider a moment of spontaneous performance that I witnessed between the members of the TVA[6] graffiti crew. I have repeatedly returned to this moment as a way of helping to illustrate that although strong links are being created between youth from different racial and class backgrounds, they are still aware, even hyper-aware, of the history and burden of older identities and social roles, and that they might be involved in reworking or breaking down these traditional roles and identities but cannot escape them completely.

In mid-1998 I was "hanging out"[7] with the members of the TVA graffiti crew: Falko, Mac1 and Mantis. This crew is one of the oldest and most established in Cape Town and Falko in particular is respected as one of the pioneers of graffiti in the city and for his skills with a spray can. Falko has been an active graffiti artist since the 1980s while Mantis and Mac1 are newer members of the crew. Falko and Mac1 are both coloured men from the working-class area of Mitchells Plain on the Cape Flats, while Mantis is a white man from the upper-middle-class area of Constantia. At this time Mantis and Mac1 were sharing a house in the suburb of Woodstock along with some other graffiti artists, and Falko was a de facto housemate although he officially still lived with his parents in Mitchells Plain.

On this afternoon the crew was preparing to paint a wall along the railway line in Woodstock and had bought a tin of paint to use to prime the wall before they graffitied over it. The paint was not the right colour and Falko and Mac1 were trying to stir in pigment so that it met their requirements. In the process they spilt paint onto the floor of the courtyard of their house and were rather unsuccessfully trying to clean it up. Mantis, who had been playing video games until this stage, then noticed that they were making more of a mess in the process of cleaning up and took over. Falko and Mac1, as fairly typical coloured men, had little experience of domestic work, as this burden would have fallen on the women in their family. (At this point it would be important to note my position as observer and as a woman because at one point they all, half jokingly, tried to get me to do the cleaning up because I was the only woman present. I was however able to avoid doing this because of my position of relative power within the group. I was seen as not having to perform traditional gender roles because I was an educated woman with access to resources, in particular I had a car which they needed to use. This would not have been the case if I had been a coloured woman or one of their sisters or girlfriends who would not have been exempted from performing traditional gendered roles.)

Mantis, as he later told me, had however been in the South African Navy (like most white men of his generation, he underwent compulsory military service) and so had had to learn to scrub the decks and was much more efficient with a mop and broom. As Mantis cleaned up the mess, Falko and to a lesser extent Mac1 began to take on the exaggerated voices of cowering employees bowing and scraping to a "baas".[8] They feigned asking for forgiveness from their "baas" for messing up and were re-enacting the kind of employer-employee relationship and interaction which would have historically been enacted between middle-class white men and working-class coloured men.

This performance was self-consciously ironic as they were all aware that Mantis was the one who was more domesticated and landed up doing much of the manual work and was at the time in a position of apprenticeship to the more experienced Falko when it came to graffiti skills. It was also ironic because their relationships were far from the historical norm – here were three men from different class and racial groups sharing a home and working together within the intimate and trusting setting of a graffiti crew where the other members become your surrogate family. This did not however mean that they were unaware that this was an unusual set-up even in post-apartheid South Africa and that many of the historical power relationships were still at play. Mantis, for example, still had a certain level of power in the relationship because his identity as a white man afforded him easier access to financial resources and business networks which they often drew on to get work doing graffiti art.

Again, this illustrates the fact that youth identities are not created by breaks with the old and then suddenly new ones appear instantly. They instead overlap and are negotiated constantly, both in a spirit of playfulness and sometimes of conflict, making it difficult to make strict or clear divisions between old and new skool.

"Keeping it Real": The Struggle over Authenticity in Hip-hop

There is in fact much conflict and contestation in the Cape Town hip-hop scene with much of it playing itself out as disagreements around authenticity, or in the jargon of hip-hop around who is "keeping it real". Some of the older coloured hip-hop heads are still thinking in terms of the old skool, and feel that the hip-hop scene and the parties in particular are too commercialised and have sold out, especially since they think that much of the emphasis on youth development and raising social consciousness through involvement in hip-hop has been lost. This refrain is not a new one or particular to the South African hip-hop scene, but takes on a particular edge of racial and class tension here, as the old/new division here is usually understood in terms of race, with the inclusion of large numbers of middle-class white youth into the scene being thought of in terms of the commercialisation and commodification of the culture at the expense of its countercultural or radical edge.

However, here it becomes evident that this sort of discourse is not about rigid boundaries between old and new or the commodified and uncommodifed, but is instead a negotiation of the changes that South African youth culture has had to adapt to since the early 1990s. These transformations have been facilitated by the breaking down of the apartheid legislation and the way that this has also facilitated the ending of the isolation that was imposed on South Africa by the international community. Here it is useful to return to the quote that was cited at the beginning of this essay from Allan Pred and to realise that much of the accusations of the new skool of hip-hop "selling out" are actually about the hip-hop scene being thrust into the reality of hyper-globalisation and commodification. Rather than it being about a break between old and new, it is about having to renegotiate identities in the context of much more rapid change and easier flows of information and meanings. Or as Allan Pred puts it:

> Unavoidably then, as pivotal spectacular spaces of consumption have appeared in different capitalist commodity societies, they have produced different confrontations between the new and the already existing, they have generated different symbolic ruptures, have resulted in singular cultural reworkings of the spectacularly marketed goods and (would-be) hegemonic discourses associated with industrial modernity, high modernity and hypermodernity (1995:21).

Before 1990, youth culture was constrained by the limitations imposed on it by the apartheid state, and it was much harder for youth to plug into the global youth scene and the commodities of youth culture were much harder to procure. You had to go to great lengths to get hold of hip-hop tapes and videos, as well as the other commodities that are so important to developing youth identities such as clothes and drugs. This in a way helped to maintain the exclusivity of some youth subcultures such as hip-hop because it was only the really dedicated that could gain access to the material and intellectual markers of this subculture, as they were not widely distributed. For example, hip-hop was not played on South African radio stations, and in the case of hip-hop this was largely confined to youth within the coloured community of Cape Town. It was these young people who managed to link into international hip-hop networks and get access to tapes of the music and videos, which were then illegally copied and distributed through informal networks in the townships. It was from listening to and watching these tapes and videos that they were able to learn the skills of breakdancing, rapping, DJ-ing and graffiti art.

As South Africa opened its borders and trade sanctions were lifted, the commodities of youth culture became much more accessible to more people. Seemingly overnight South African youth had far greater and easier access to information and influences from international youth culture. MTV was no longer just this mythical TV station that only the privileged few who had travelled overseas had seen or that had been experienced through grainy and highly copied video tapes that somehow started circulating in a neighbourhood, and more and more international companies returned to South Africa, feeding the consumption demands of youth culture. The country became a stop on the global youth travel circuit and along with the backpackers came graffiti artists and DJs eager to find the hip-hop on the southern tip of Africa that they had heard about. South African youth were also more able to travel abroad and the almost obligatory trip to the UK or Europe that so many white South Africans took after finishing school became more and more popular. With all this travel, exchange of information and growing access to trends in youth culture across the globe, young people in South Africa were more connected to world youth trends than ever before.

The first few cohorts of young people that had been able to take advantage of the 1990 desegregation of government schools were also coming of age and looking for social spaces that gave them the freedom to continue socialising with their friends across racial boundaries. They were also looking for places that were playing music that was trendy and spoke to them, and many of them discovered drum 'n' bass, jungle and hip-hop.

At this time many of the old skool coloured youth, although some of them were no longer so young, were also discovering that their hard-earned skills and street credibility were being sought by a whole new group of people. Now there were middle-class white kids who wanted to learn to do graffiti or to have a hip-hop DJ play at their party and they had to turn to those pioneers of hip-hop on the Cape Flats if they wanted to learn.

With the commodities of youth culture easily available to so many more youth and with the almost exclusive hold that coloured youth had over the production of hip-hop culture being challenged, they were having to refine the ways in which their identities were differentiated and the way they defined themselves.

So when the old skool claims that the new skool is vastly different, this claim needs to be interrogated at many levels. On the one hand, this kind of assertion by pioneers of youth culture that the people that adopt the culture later, once it has become more commodified and popularised, are less authentic is a common one in all youth cultures.[9] But in the case of South Africa in the 1990s this kind of process of the "recuperation" of a subculture into the mainstream occurred at the same time that the country was experiencing a shock of modernity. Because South African society was having to cope with the effects, both positive and negative, of the rapid globalisation and commodification of society that had previously been buffered from the full strength of these forces by apartheid isolation, it was easy to blame many things on these processes. However, this obscures the fact that the old skool was also part of global networks and the culture was then also commodified – it is just that these things had become heightened, less controllable and less easy to understand at this time of hypermodernity. So the new skool should be thought of as a continuing negotiation of the old skool rather than a break with the past.

Tension and Interaction

In my continuing attempt to try to destabilise the idea that there can be fixed notions of what it is to be old or new skool, I would like to sketch another situation in which these categories seem to be fixed but are in actual fact in tension and interaction rather than part of any linear progression. One of the main claims asserted by the old skool is that the new skool has lost its critical edge, that it has been consumed by the mainstream and does not provide any resistance to the status quo. There is nostalgia for the era of the anti-apartheid struggle when the hip-hop music made in South Africa was highly politicised and radical, to the extent that many of the albums made by groups such as the very influential Prophets of da City were banned by the apartheid government because of the political content of the lyrics. Other members of the old skool also claim greater authenticity in the present moment because they are still actively engaged in "community work". The best example of this would be the Black Noise crew who organise anti-drug and HIV awareness workshops that use hip-hop to get their message across.

This claim to greater authenticity by the old skool is countered by some members of the new skool who turn the argument around. They claim that it is actually the members of the old skool who are transforming their cultural capital into financial capital by organising parties and working as DJs and graffiti artists who have sold out and are no longer maintaining their countercultural edge. Sandra Klopper has made the interesting suggestion that the young white men who took up graffiti in the 1990s are experiencing a similar sense of alienation as the black youth who were first attracted to hip-hop. This is because they are now finding themselves in an environment where they have lost much of their political and social power, and are no longer guaranteed jobs, and are feeling the burden, real or imagined, of affirmative action. Many of these young people are expressing this alienation through the adoption of the hip-hop culture, so the walls of the city and of the middle-class white suburbs were soon daubed in the tags of hip-hop graffiti. The people doing this were not outsiders from the townships expressing their alienation from the wealth and privilege of the suburbs, but the youth living in the comfortable houses and going to the good schools (Klopper 2000:185-186).

There is also a sense in which the very definition of resistance has been reworked by South African youth. While they may not be actively involved in politics as they were during the anti-apartheid struggle, it is in their everyday lives and in small negotiations that they are able to create transformations of the status quo. In this way, the TVA crew, just by sharing a house together and managing to create a relationship in which they feel comfortable enough to send up the traditionally racially-based hierarchies of South African society, are in their own way being revolutionary.

Often it is through the tension between old and new that the most radical changes and most innovative creations are wrought; however, it is also easy to be highly critical of these creations because they often involve a compromise as part of their creative negotiations.

This is particularly evident in the creation of hip-hop music, where there have been many interesting collaborations between old skool coloured hip-hop artists and white artists from a variety of genres of music. One of the most successful of these groups is called Moodphase5. This band incorporates elements of hip-hop with funk, jazz and reggae elements. The band is comprised of two coloured youth who are the vocalists and four white instrumentalists. One of their most popular tracks is called "Geto @ Sunset", which was written by Denver Turner who is the rapper and main songwriter in the group. While searching the Internet I found the lyrics of this song on a website devoted to South African hip-hop[10] and realised that in the recorded version of the song on Moodphase5's debut album parts of the earlier lyrics had been left out. I have included the lyrics, as I found them, below with the parts that were left out highlighted:

Darkness falls over the place where I live in
a public zoo, Friday nights about to begin
end of the month people getting on & off trains
where they going straight home if they got brains
the gangsters on the corner with the shiny blade
he's waiting for you to come cuz he knows you just got paid
the kids waiting for moms to bring clothes
while dads drunk in the yard, playing dominoes
money scarce, so the eldest had to drop out
to pay for the rent, the M-net & help momma out
the others rush home for opentime's loving
to see the rich & the bitch & the daily huggin
while on the otherside of this beautiful mountain
CD, Porshe and a pool with a fountain
the rugged & rich, what they want they gonna eat
while we sitting empty freezer, broken fridge & no meat
well does it matter, yes it does but we dont cry
becuz tommorow somehow we gonna get by
the yuppies checkin out a club he hasnt been to yet
but me , i love the geto @ sunset

chorus
cape town city is the city I claim, but I love the geto@sunset
cape town city is the city I claim, but I love the geto, the geto

the smell of smoke in the alleys, fill the air
the shebeens fulla people with blank stares
a door slams, a baby cries, the parents fight

while the rich get ready for a cool night
boys & girls in the geto getting drunk & laid
and in the morning dont know what the fuck they made
the youth rots in the hood cuz they don't know better
they ambition, a gangster with a Berreta
and as I refer to the otherside
a kid with a TV and a phone in his own ride
and it don't mean a damn thing to me
cause they the ones doin coke and LSD
and then they try to blame it on a black kid
Man . . . don't have the money to waste o that shit
but as i go on fridaynight the weekends warm
pass the bottle get drunk & watch your friends perform
have a party pump the music & lets begin
becuz tommorow its the same thing ove again
I'm not trying to kill the good vibes
I'm telling it like it is cuz I live in the same tribe
so brother if you lovin this moe is what you gonna get
yo, I love the geto @ sunset

chorus
roll of the dice, flick of the knife, shot of a gun
as the gangs get ready for some action
theres the congregation, organisation nagotiation...huh
they need no persuation
theres the running, the shoutin & then the sparks flying
swords dragging on the ground and many dying
the gunshots 1,2,3,4
no its not the cops cuz thy'll just kill more
we dont need em,cuz they always so fuckin late
and in the geto thet the ones that people love to hate
cuz they too busy protecting they're own kind
or beating up on drunks, strollers or who-ever they find
and if you think I'm making up a pack of lies
take a train to a township, we'll see who survives
cuz no ones got problems like brothers in the hood
acting like its cool when they do no good
yo, all it was supposed to be was nuthin but a party
now ya mommas at the bed to identify the body
this goes out to my brothers who be lying dead
rest in peace, I love the geto @ sunset

It seems quite telling that the parts of the song that have been left out of the recorded version are those that make strong commentary against white youth and that challenge them to "take a train to the township". This challenge is a provocative one because the majority of white people have never ventured into the black townships that are on their doorsteps, largely out of fear and ignorance. It would be easy to argue that by taking out much of the criticism of police and gangster violence, and the direct challenge to white youth in the song, much of its power and credibility have been lost. But I would instead like to argue that although there has clearly been a negotiation in the tone of the lyrics and the song as a whole, this does not mean that it can be ignored or dismissed. For one thing, the critique has not altogether been removed although it has been muted by the foregrounding of the softer woman's voice repeatedly singing the chorus and accompanied by the melodic sound of a jazz saxophone and a gentle drum rhythm. The critique is now directed towards coloured township culture with its problems of gangsterism and poverty. So perhaps there has been a change of focus so as not to alienate the new target (and importantly, paying) audience of white youth. On the other hand it could be said that the new focus was chosen to try to educate these youths about conditions in the townships which they would not otherwise be aware of because they don't usually "take train[s] to [the] township[s]". It should be pointed out that many white youth have begun to venture into the townships precisely because of their interest in hip-hop, as much of the best graffiti in Cape Town can be seen in the coloured townships of the Cape Flats, and as guests of their friends and mentors in the hip-hop community.

Moreover, Klopper points out in relation to graffiti, but equally relevant to other art forms, that there is often a double standard regarding the art of black people. It is valued and celebrated as long as it remains on the margins of society and it is criticised if it breaks into the mainstream, and particularly if the artists manage to make a financial success of their art (2000:186). There seems to be an element of this in a potential critique of Denver Turner for having "sold out" by mediating his message so that he could get his music recorded. A similar critique would not be made of the white musicians in the band for adopting elements of hip-hop into their music when they have a classical or jazz background. Again, it seems most important that one does not try to direct blame or judge from a rigid viewpoint. Instead, categories such as old skool and new skool, or race and class need to be contextualised and understood in terms of tension and negotiation, rather than as being in direct conflict with one another.

To reiterate: it is imperative when reconsidering South African culture, and its youth culture in particular, to broaden the field of inquiry beyond the narrow and restrictive tools of politics, resistance, race and class. At the same time though, these tools for helping to understand the society cannot be totally discarded, because what is needed is an approach that can take into account the many levels of complexity and meaning which people are negotiating every day to navigate through their identities as well as their everyday activities. There has to be enough space to accommodate ambiguity and sometimes confusing complexity because it is in these uncertain and volatile spaces that many of the most exciting and significant ideas and practices develop.

Notes

1 Stuart Hall made a similar and useful point in relation to the way we should think about race and ethnicity when he wrote in his essay "New ethnicities" (in Morley and Chen 1996) that: "I have a distinct sense that . . . we are entering a new phase. But we need to be absolutely clear what we mean by a 'new' phase because, as soon as you talk of a new phase, people instantly imagine that what is entailed is the *substitution* of one kind of politics for another. I am quite distinctly not talking about a shift in those terms. Politics does not necessarily proceed by way of a set of oppositions and reversals of this kind . . . There is no sense in which a new phase in black cultural politics could replace the earlier one. Nevertheless it is true that as the struggle moves forward and assumes new forms, it does to some degree *displace*, re-organize and reposition the different cultural strategies in relation to one another" (1996:442).

2 See Tricia Rose (1994) for a comprehensive look at the history and development of hip-hop in the USA. Rose's description of what she calls the "postindustrial" environment of New York in which hip-hop developed in the 1970s is very reminiscent of the environment of the Cape Flats during the 1980s when hip-hop first took root in the coloured community, and suggests that even this early stage of hip-hop development can be read in the context of globalisation despite South Africa's isolation in the 1980s.

3 It could even be theoretically useful to trace the old skool back even further to other moments in South African history where there was a borrowing, and blending of musical influences from the USA occurred. For example, Hannerz (1996:161) suggests that Sophiatown of the 1950s was part of "continuous cultural exchange and blending within a global ecumene" and could usefully be compared to Harlem of the 1920s.

4 For a very useful look at this dynamic in particular relation to Cape Town graffiti artists, see Klopper (2000).

5 Japanese animated movies.

6 TVA stands for The Villainous Animatorz and is the tag or pseudonym which this graffiti crew uses.

7 Much of the material that I have drawn on for this article has been gathered through participant observation research which was largely conducted between 1999 and mid-2001. During this time I was able to interview both formally and informally many members of the Cape Town hip-hop scene and I would in particular like to thank Hamma and the TVA crew for their time and insights, as well as my friends Quanita

Adams, Jools Jonker, Zen Marie and Candice Borzechowski and the many others who came to lots of hip hop parties with me and contributed to my understanding of the scene. I would also like to thank Jonathan Faull for his support and forwarding me all those articles on hip-hop.

8 In South Africa the Afrikaans word "baas" (translated: boss, master) has strong connotations of authority and employees, usually black, have historically used the term with deference and a subservient tone but sometimes with much bitterness.

9 See for example the early and influential discussion of the "recuperation" of subcultural style into mainstream culture by Dick Hebdige.

10 http://www.africaserver.nl/geto3000/content/index.html.

References

Hannertz. 1996. *Transnational Connection: Culture, people, places*. London: Routledge.

Hebdige, D. 1979. *Subculture the Meaning of Style*. London: Routledge.

Klopper, S. 2000. Hip Hop Graffiti Art. In: Nuttall, S. and Michael, C. (eds.). 2000. *Senses of Culture: South African Cultural Studies.* Cape Town: Oxford University Press.

Morley, D. and Chen, Kuan-Hsing. 1996. *Stuart Hall: Critical Dialogues in Cultural Studies*. London: Routledge.

Nuttall, S. and Michael, C. (eds.). 2000. *Senses of Culture: South African Cultural Studies*. Cape Town: Oxford University Press.

Pred, A. 1995. *Recognizing European Modernities, A Montage of the Present*. London: Routledge.

Rose, T. 1994. *Black Noise: Rap Music and Black Culture in Contemporary America*. Connecticut: Wesleyan University Press.

CHAPTER EIGHT

Hypertheatrical Performance on the Post-apartheid Stage

Keith Bain

The performing arts sector has undergone radical changes in South Africa since the demise of apartheid. Many of these changes are not simply related to the new sociopolitical environment, however, but find their roots in global developments as well as revitalised thinking with regards to what constitutes "theatre" or "performance". Some of the more interesting developments relate to a rediscovery of indigenous cultural traditions which have infused contemporary performance approaches, resulting in products that are unique, fresh and potentially appealing to both local and international markets. To discuss in a few pages the many faces of South African theatre would be an impossible task; this is therefore not an overview of the entire performing arts scene, but a brief investigation tracing some of the effects of the post-apartheid climate on the way in which South African theatre is being created for local audiences, looking at certain developments in the nature of local theatrical performance and at the emergence of identifiable trends in post-apartheid performance.[1]

Under discussion is a subject whose ephemeral nature is increasingly highlighted by the shift in thinking about theatre from the strict formal eurocentric paradigm to a range of performance forms that encompass ritual song and dance, as well as classical Western well-made plays. Indeed, the concept of "theatre" has undergone radical change in recent decades, and it is often more appropriate to speak of "performance" – particularly within the neo-African context – rather than referring to the somewhat limiting "theatre". The notion of theatre within Western societies is traditionally an elitist one dominated by observations of canonised (written) texts and performances staged in "proper" theatre spaces (Hauptfleisch 1997:27). The Western emphasis on literary culture which has been dominant in colonial South Africa has effectively erased at least 8000 years of indigenous history and given rise to distorted perceptions of the region's sociocultural traditions. More specifically, indigenous theatre (or performance) – which existed as a structured and formal system before the arrival of European colonisers – has largely been forgotten because it has never been reduced to the written word.

In recent years, the development of a form of theatre that is uniquely South African, that blends and integrates the performance styles of two distinct traditions – those of Africa and those brought to the subcontinent from the Western world – has emerged as an area of significant interest. "Syncretic" theatre (Coplan 1985) or "hybrid" and "crossover" theatre (Hauptfleisch 1997) are terms given to manifestations of performance which make use of thematic and formal elements from a range of traditional as well as imported forms, giving rise to something that is original and potentially unique.[2] According to Hauptfleisch (1997:60), the categorisation of "hybrid" theatre does not imply that a "single, uniform and clearly defined theatrical form" is under discussion, but rather that we are dealing with "a specific, yet eclectic, attitude towards playmaking, at a much expanded concept of (South African) performance". To this concept of a hybridised theatrical form, I would like to add the notion of "total theatre", and more radically, "hypertheatricality",[3] or the idea of performance that surpasses the framework of any theatrical forebear. Such "theatre" is necessarily eclectic, drawing on diverse and even disparate styles in order to produce work that traces its roots to the dawn of cultural activity by the earliest inhabitants of the region, but might well be termed postmodern. It represents, as will be discussed, a merger between old and new, Western and African, ritual and commercial performance cultures.

It is within this "expanded" framework of theatre and performance that I wish to look at a number of issues regarding the development of the local "theatre industry". Ours is a uniquely heterogeneous society, and on top of the already diverse range of influences on our creative cultures, external factors continue to exert considerable impact and make certain demands. From within, a diversity of expectations with regards to what constitutes art or entertainment obviously exerts influence over the work that is created. Somewhere betwixt the demand to satisfy audiences, a desire to communicate a distinct message, and the need to compete internationally, theatre practitioners are having to deal with a unique set of circumstances and the result is a complex array of creative possibilities and opportunities that must ultimately compete at the box office.

The Myth of Cultural (R)evolution

"Performance" in South Africa can be traced back at least as far as the shamanic dance rites of the San[4] whose earliest rock painting recordings date back at least 25 000 years (Hauptfleisch 1997:73). Various African groups that subsequently settled on the subcontinent also brought with them performative practices which were embedded in their ritual and cultural traditions and intimately woven into their way of life. Mime, storytelling, dance and ritual were, for various pre-colonial African societies, more than mere entertainment. These forms of ritual, ceremony and performance were powerful events that linked daily life with the spiritual realm and highlighted issues and themes designed to maintain social unity, order and harmony. "Performance" – as a live, interactive experience – supported and fed into a certain type of social reality, making it something more ethereal than "theatre" in the Western sense.

"Theatre" in the traditional Western sense is relatively new to the region, however, and finds its roots in the arrival of various European traditions during the seventeenth and eighteenth centuries. Of course, with the influx and intervention of white colonists, much of the ritual and performance that once served an essential social function within indigenous communities was lost or forgotten. As Western sociocultural paradigms were adopted and enforced, traditional performance cultures were forced to adapt and evolve into something new – something increasingly divorced from traditional practices.

Whereas indigenous "performance" practices focused on sustaining a particular way of life through the ritual enactment of culturally significant memories, Western colonisation brought with it the notion of *theatrical* performance. European colonialism, and the eventual institutionalisation of apartheid, resulted in the widespread decimation of traditional indigenous cultural practices. Existing social institutions were marginalised and sidelined, ridiculed as inferior or "primitive", while the tenets of Western cultural authority – foreign languages and religious beliefs – were imposed as "official", dominant and superior. A performance culture which had once been central to the way of life of indigenous societies was largely forced into the shadows by oppressive and prohibitive laws. In black communities such cultural activity evolved and adapted itself to emerge as an area of entertainment separate from that typically enjoyed by white audiences.

Until the 1950s, the "Western" theatre form which had been established in South Africa played a distinct role in preserving colonial life and served to heighten an affiliation with European roots. Classical and popular theatre productions were performed for privileged (white) South Africans in theatre buildings modelled on European theatres. New written work in English and Afrikaans was influenced by the style and tradition of European texts. Black playwrights who emerged during the apartheid years also conformed to the principles and dynamics of a distinctly European dramatic form, which – in contrast with indigenous ritual and storytelling traditions – revolved around drama based on written texts.

During the apartheid era, white cultural domination was "as real as it was perceived" and racist practices were observable throughout the arts and culture domain (Van Graan 2001).[5] The infusion of apartheid into every aspect of daily life extended to the administration and functioning of all performing arts institutions, which included the legal and hegemonic exclusion of black people from participation in any type of state sponsored theatre. In the cold, austere urban theatre buildings constructed by the white Nationalists, traditional European performance forms (dramas, operas, ballets and orchestral recitations) served the interests of a privileged minority and essentially served as an escape from the "reality" of African life. Playing to whites in the service of white interests, the monuments to colonial oppression were a link with European traditions, European heritage, European culture.[6]

In the black townships, theatrical events took place in clandestine spaces, in community halls or whatever makeshift performance area could be conjured up. Accordingly, much black South African theatre and performance developed as a form of "alternative theatre", the majority of which was committed to raising community consciousness, promoting political ideologies, addressing social aspirations, and in some cases (usually in collaboration with whites interested in theatre and change), making the world aware of what was happening within the borders of a culturally isolated and hegemonic country.[7] It was within this context that hybrid forms such as the "township musical"[8] emerged.

Non-state-funded theatres such as the world-famous Market became venues where people of all backgrounds could make the stage a place not only for political protest, but also where the social restrictions of apartheid could – in a metaphorical sense – be left at the door. These were essentially havens for believers in a theatrical practice founded on nonracial principles and established out of the urgent need for an independent, revolutionary performing arts collective. The Market, from humble beginnings in 1976, developed an international reputation, not only as a multiracial theatre facility, but also as a stage for telling human stories, advocating for change, criticising the regime and pointing the way towards a time when a truly integrated performance tradition might emerge. It was also here that the innovative *Woza Albert!* (literally "*Rise Albert!*") was devised and first staged by director Barney Simon and performers Percy Mtwa and Mbongeni Ngema during the early 1980s. The production's amalgamation of elements that are strongly associated with various aspects of both Western and African performance traditions (European *commedia dell'arte* and Nguni praise-singing, for example), is indicative of the evolving hybrid form which is, according to Hauptfleisch (1997:61), "a complex fusion of a variety of traditions, conventions and performance techniques drawn from various times and cultures" to the extent that "the new hybrid work truly constitutes a gestalt of its own".

Indeed, since the mid-1980s political transformation has steadily altered the landscape of theatre and performance in South Africa, and collaborative works that have experimented with cross-cultural performance elements have enjoyed increasing popularity. As apartheid laws were relaxed, nonracial theatre groups were increasingly able to explore and experiment, enabling the exchange of ideas and the emergence of new work that is often seen as indicative of a uniquely South African theatrical style.

While transformation has enabled the emergence of a distinctive cross-cultural performance paradigm, it can also be seen to have impacted on the theatre industry in other ways. Firstly, the disappearance of apartheid has meant that one of the principle themes of pre-1994 critical theatre has also expired.[9] Accordingly, a period of creative confusion, relaxation or inhibition (depending on one's point of view) has tended to refocus a great deal of energy within an ever-expanding market of theatrical entertainment. Secondly, a much-changed infrastructure has dramatically altered the funding of the arts, forcing theatre practitioners to refigure the way in which they do business.[10] These two issues, which are intimately linked, are the focus of the next part of this discussion.

"Show(biz) me the Money!" The Culture of an Entertainment Economy

One of the biggest challenges facing theatre in South Africa (and worldwide) is the overwhelming competition for audiences, particularly from the juggernaut of mass-produced entertainment synergies (dominated by television) which increasingly focus on transforming "reality" into banal spectacle.[11] The focus of the arts and culture industries (worldwide) has shifted tremendously in recent years, edging towards intensive commercialisation which favours market forces and consumer demands over "socially valuable" or "culturally significant" products that are supported by public funding. We exist in an age in which the distinction between artistic and commercial practices is blurred, in which all art is necessarily influenced (or "corrupted") by economic interests; theatre is not untouched. Ours is a "design economy", which confuses material wealth and technological advancement with culture and marketing (Gibney Jr. and Luscombe 2000:44) – often to the detriment of older forms such as live theatre. Priority in the performing arts industry has thus tended to focus increasingly on marketing strategies which must compete with an expanding platform of entertainment synergies.[12] Accordingly, many artists have also had to capitulate or adapt to the intrusion of commercial practices into the theatrical arena.[13]

Within this cycle of rapidly changing social and economic pressures, theatre has not only had to reposition itself, but also relocate itself within the consciousness of theatregoers. Everywhere, the obituaries of new and serious writing are being written, while musicals and more commercially viable cabarets, revues and stand-up comedy shows remain the major theatre drawcards. Worldwide, the theatre zeitgeist smacks of faddishness, trend-spotting and political somnolence. Caught in the overspill of Hollywood plasticity, live theatre is increasingly pressurised to redefine itself in terms of an expanding global entertainment industry. In a volatile socioeconomic climate such as that of South Africa, the relevance of live theatre is understandably questioned; no longer associated with social ritual or tribal cohesion, performance is easily thought to be an elitist luxury.

Is theatre therefore in danger of disappearing beneath a simulacrum of entertainment delights that privilege the commercial temptations of globalised culture? In a world where theatricality and performance play themselves out in the arena of sensationalist political broadcasts or the banal antics of "reality" television, it is little wonder that those with a stake in live performance industries fear the demise of serious theatre. Ironically, drama is everywhere – on our sidewalks, in our prisons, at our nightclubs, around our Constitution – and yet perceptions prevail that theatre is increasingly devoid of drama; spectacle and spectacular entertainment are the main forces which now inspire our stages and attempt to fill our auditoria. Theatrical tragedy is tragically forgotten and thought-provoking parody has descended into "penis, pussy and '*pomp*'[14]" jokes. Where audiences do exist, they flock to frequently prosaic drink-and-view send-ups of popular music and stand-up soliloquies flaunting the cheapest in debased humour and try-hard political-incorrectness. Everywhere the bums-on-seats machine is ensuring that entertainment is prioritised over serious theatre. Thankfully, such dark analyses of the current situation suggest only part of the picture and ignore many of the positive developments (in terms of both audience interests and artistic innovation) that have manifest themselves.

Indeed, the unprecedented box-office success of the Bobby Heaney-directed production of Arthur Miller's *Death of a Salesman* (2000/2001), is a potent reminder that "meaningful" drama is still yearned for by the small percentage of South Africans who do attend theatre. It is perhaps significant that *Salesman* – itself a theatrical indictment of consumptive capitalism – managed to draw full houses despite its highbrow, noncommercial aesthetic.

An interesting irony is suggested, however, if one draws comparisons between the relatively enormous success of this production of the sophisticated *Salesman*, and the mass appeal of the unapologetically lowbrow South African e-tv television chat programme, *The Toasty Show*. Produced and co-hosted by white celebrity actor-comedian Bill Flynn (who played Willy Loman in *Salesman*), the television show stood in direct contrast to Miller's capitalist cautionary drama. *The Toasty Show* sold itself to a mass consumer audience with a hodge-podge of mostly young presenters who were joined by various celebrities, wannabes and nobodies during the early hours of the morning. Self-effacing and to some extent parodying the high-minded civility of other breakfast shows, *The Toasty Show* was (barely) held together by recurrent product announcements and competitions which essentially bought into a culture of consumerism and infotainment. In an ironic conflagration of roles, Flynn became representative of two very different despairing souls: the performer as artist attempting to sustain good-quality, traditional (Western) theatre, and the artist as businessman tackling the commercial entertainment desires of a nation with fairly moderate tastes and expectations.[15]

Our fascination with the spectacular has, in turn, altered the way in which we are able to experience more "serious" endeavours. The global turn in popular culture has dramatically transformed the way in which the world experiences classical narratives and paradigms, and it is no longer necessary to obstinately distinguish between serious art and entertainment. In most areas of cultural development, distinctions between critical and commercial work are becoming irrelevant as all manner of marginalia are absorbed into the mainstream of an expanding global culture. It is also within this area of distinctly postmodern reinvention that the borders of traditional paradigms of Western performance are seen to be softening. One thinks, in this regard, of the cultural brouhaha which spilled out into popular consciousness in an attempt to categorise the controversial American rap-crossover "artist" Eminem, or the MTV-generation recycling of Shakespeare in Baz Luhrmann's popular cinematic coup *Romeo+Juliet*.

Classical works from the Western paradigm are now revamped, reworked and recycled with all manner of accents and affectations, within any range of settings, focusing on any number of contemporary agendas. Shakespeare is but one of numerous Western/European canonised icons who is today regularly transformed not only for reasons of commercial expedience, but in order to make classical messages and narratives more accessible and meaningful. In South Africa, the Bard has for years assumed local flavours, the most famous example being Welcome Msomi's *Umabatha*, a Zulu translation of *Macbeth*. The show even found its way to London's recreated Globe Theatre in 2001. In the same year, *Julius Caesar* received a local political spin in Yael Farber's *SeZaR*, which cleverly alluded to President Thabo Mbeki. Clearly reverberating the "plot" against Mbeki which punctuated media headlines for countless weeks during the early part of the year, the production also zoned in on the president's stance on HIV/Aids as well as his inclination to favour international affairs above those closer to home. These are, in many respects, popularisations of classical Western dramas, designed not only to imbue new meaning to old texts, but to enhance the accessibility of traditionally "highbrow" works. Such manifestations of the classical and traditional mixing and merging with the contemporary and the colloquial indicate that there is some value in the appropriation of global cultural phenomena by local artists.

One should also not forswear the positive impact of foreign productions and texts which are staged locally – even where box-office returns constitute the bottom line. Just as local artists compete to get their work performed abroad, so exposure to foreign products and narrative paradigms is essential to the ongoing development of high-quality, professional local work. There is some danger in looking down one's nose at the manifestations of Andrew Lloyd Webber and imported Irish line-dancing (*Lord of the Dance*) that have graced our performance spaces, since these "irrelevant" and expensive productions ultimately feed into a growing spirit of tolerance and cross-cultural sensitivity that is essential to local performance culture. There is, perhaps, an equal danger that our moderate tastes will be consumed by an infatuation with the inventive homogenising wizardry of the West, encouraging us to abandon local and colloquial traditions as we are irresistibly seduced by more "sophisticated" sensibilities. In this respect, it is necessary to maintain a balance between the needs, concerns and interests of local audiences and the overreaching ambitions of producers and showbiz entrepreneurs.

There is a proven need to guard against the rapacious tendencies of certain forms of "entertainment theatre". In 2001, for example, R20 million was wasted on what was to have been the biggest production of *Grease* ever staged – *Grease the Stadium Spectacular*. Staged at a Johannesburg sports stadium, the production was seen by many as little less than an unadulterated disaster, with plans for a later Cape Town run being abandoned and the production company involved forced into bankruptcy. The problem is not so much that R20 million was wasted on the production (this was, after all, a business *misad*venture), but that it is a show that wholeheartedly misses the pulse of South African culture. Clearly, it is a show that attempted to exploit mainstream or mass tastes. But whose tastes? How can the public not be suspicious of "theatre" when R20 million is devoured by a poorly-conceived disaster that inappropriately recasts a massive piece of grossly irrelevant kitsch Americana while millions of South Africans do not have homes, are starving, jobless, or dying of Aids?

There are serious social ramifications connected to the expenditure of exorbitant sums of money[16] in the interests of a foreign cultural product which extols the virtues of simplistic teenage romance within a nostalgic era that predates Aids and appears ignorant of many contemporary youth issues (such as drug abuse). South Africa had, after all, already witnessed a public expenditure scandal when the new government spent millions on the ill-fated Mbongeni Ngema musical *Sarafina 2* in 1996.

Despite the large-scale *Grease* disaster, interest in the Western commercial aesthetic continues to flourish. Cabaret and revue, stand-up comedy and light musicals are the order of the day, while moneyed audiences are regularly wined and dined and entertained at exclusive venues such as Stellenbosch's splendidly colonial Spier Estate.

Of course, marketing does play some part in establishing a pattern of self-loathing with regards to local product. The international popularity of perennial stage musicals such as *Grease*, *Evita*, *Jesus Christ Superstar*, "*Les Mis*", and *Cats* attests to the power of successfully branded cultural products. Such branding for foreign fare offering decidedly Western theatrical motifs and narrative structures carries the weight of worldwide exposure and popularity, which greatly enhances their performance when staged for salivating audiences in once-ignored regions such as South Africa.

While "branded" foreign productions have always attracted sizeable white audiences eager to revel in the perceived quality associated with overseas inventiveness, the threat of cultural commercialisation has been exacerbated by the depoliticisation of South African drama. This factor has filtered into the experience of performance by urban black South Africans. Edward Tsumele (2001:10) cites that during apartheid, township people went to live productions because "theatre" played a vital role as part of the political discourse; it served to conscientise audiences, was relevant and impactful. Today, this catalytic function no longer exists, and – for "ordinary" people, at least – other entertainments are prioritised. Sowetan playwright Peter Ngwenya notes that in the new South Africa, "potential audiences still shy away [from township theatre], preferring instead to watch television or drink at the nearest shebeen[18]" (Tsumele 2001:10).

Black consumers are being dutifully targeted by television and radio channels offering local programming that is relevant, accessible and certainly cheaper than live theatre. Broadcasters not only market local content to black audiences, but also provide viewers with stars and celebrities whose connection with vernacular cultures is intimate and affirming. Television has become a popular tool for addressing members of communities for whom theatre and live performance might once have played a central role. While the enduring popularity of live musical and sporting events is indisputable, it is unfortunate to note that theatre has failed to sustain credible impact.

Ngwenya (in Tsumele 2001:10) notes that some black people prefer to drive to the Market or Civic theatres which are located in the city (Johannesburg). Whereas for black audiences Western theatre staged in lavish (if vulgar) city venues was once associated with the apartheid regime, it was also ironically associated with a degree of "quality" that was legally inaccessible. Now that these expensive white products from the outside world are available for general consumption, the lure of commercial productions staged in previously-white areas are treated as markers of economic and class status – a symptom of the power of cultural and entertainment "branding".

Another manifestation of theatre as a potentially viable commercial form has been the recent emergence of a burgeoning "arts festival circuit". As formula copycats of the 27-year-old National Arts Festival[19] held in the economically sedate Eastern Cape university hamlet of Grahamstown each year, there are now numerous similar (if smaller) festivals held around the country at various times of the year.[20] The Grahamstown experience retains an international image and reputation as the paragon of South African theatre activity, however, summed up by Bulgarian theatre critic and academic Kalina Stefanova (2000:191), who claims that "One is baptised into the South African theatre religion only in Grahamstown". While there is room to doubt the existence of any "theatre religion" in the country at present, it is apparent that Grahamstown remains a popular gathering of souls and, increasingly, attracts foreign audiences and producers looking for products that can be marketed abroad. Primarily an English "African Edinburgh Festival", the midyear arts platform is steadily broadening its base to ensure that it becomes more representative of indigenous culture and increasingly relevant to previously disadvantaged audiences, for example. While these "events" typically host a number of major works, they echo the Edinburgh formula by fielding numerous "fringe" productions which run the gamut of theatrical possibilities, from serious dramas to comics of the scatological persuasion.

While the festivals represent culturally significant showcasing opportunities for new works and are often the *only* places where individuals with different theatrical backgrounds, experiences and expectations can meet, their allure for potential audiences is equally connected to the experience of such events as carnival – the appropriation of both serious and popular culture within a climate of participatory entertainment.[21] While potential audiences gather to experience culture and theatre, they are equally attracted by the event – for young people in particular, the festival experience signifies a type of neo-cool. Here music, dancing, drinking, partying, raving and the proverbial "hanging out" combine with more high-minded cultural pursuits. The festival is an escape from everyday life, while being an opportunity for people of all walks of life to celebrate their collective exuberance. Of course, as with any luxury, such events remain costly and therefore out of reach for the majority of South Africans.

While the festivals inevitably represent an opportunity for numerous independent companies to lay claim to heftier box-office receipts, the burgeoning "festival circuit" is an admirable alternative to the arguably more commercial aspirations of city theatres which must compete with the daily rigours and less daunting entertainment options offered by city life. The festival circuit at least encourages the touring concept – the notion of theatre as a democratising and purposeful agent.

Ultimately, the gravest danger in fostering a theatre industry fuelled by financial instincts is that future audiences – the youth – will have limited experience of, or exposure to, dramatists who engage the emotions in the interests of something more than sensory gratification or quick-fix entertainment. However, the future of theatre will be determined by the many masks that it wears today, and it is gratifying to note that – in addition to the onslaught of purely commercial, Western-copycat ventures – there are numerous successful and enterprising developments in the arena of provocative, uniquely South African, performance. These developments, which represent a synthesis of African and Western, inherited and new performance paradigms, suggest a move towards what I refer to as "hypertheatrical" performance.

Total Theatre: Hypertheatricality and the Enigma of the Cultural Clash

As suggested above, there are genuine concerns that South African theatre – as something unique and recognisable – will dissipate into the thin air of "global culture". Despite the promise that "globalisation" has the potential to draw once-disparate cultures together, real "multiculturalism" is often invisible, prevented from developing by the overwhelming power of better-marketed Americana to absorb and redefine local traditions and cultures. I would argue, however, that "genuine South African theatre/performance" is distinctively – necessarily – global, for the true roots of contemporary local performance lie in the hybridisation (or crossover or syncretisation) of a variety of indigenous and imported performance forms.

To a large extent, it is the manner in which existing and emerging cultural phenomena are packaged and sold to various publics, that will determine the fate of industries such as theatre. Television critic Darryl Accone (2001c) has argued that South Africa is already "some way down the slippery slope towards blandness and committed in its obeisance to neo-liberalism" and has frequently warned of the danger of caving in to the homogenising effects of American imperialist culture ("*à la* Hollywood").[22] Somehow, while efforts must be taken to preserve existing local artefacts, and nurture the creation of new work, global influences cannot be ignored. Ignoring the tastes of tourists, for example, would be folly in a country that must necessarily prioritise marketable enterprises in its bid to remain internationally visible and attractive. Accone (2001c) nevertheless argues that there exists the very real "danger of exotic, endangered and precious locales in the so-called Third World having their essences diluted, cutesified and – worst case scenario this – theme-parked". He argues that while the arts and culture sectors of the tourism industry are valuable in accessing foreign revenue, selling these industries to foreign markets may come at a cost to local concerns. The danger exists that local arts and culture industries will become entirely obsessed with the tourist-related phenomenon of "display" which is concerned purely with an image – often prettified or theme-parked – that is projected to the outside world.

R.L. Rutsky (1999) argues that the notion of "tourism", in whatever form, "implies that a colonisation has already taken place" and that tourism is necessarily plagued by a type of Disney-fying theme-park effect. In this model, tourism conveys a sense of new and imaginative experiences within environments that are "almost totally controlled". Hauptfleisch (1997:73) notes that "[t]oday much of the original [indigenous performance] tradition is being artificially preserved, resurrected, or even exploited", usually in the interests of milking "native culture" for commercial or tourism purposes. One has only to think of the decontextualised showcasing of Zulu dances at ethnic villages or gumboot dancing at various tourist venues. Rather than representing a hybrid of forms, such performances are effectively examples of "local culture" that have been removed from their ritual context and transformed into commercially rewarding theatrical events – in the Western sense. Such "theatricalisation" not only devalues experiences that once served a ritual function and thus constituted a form of performative magic, but also results in a loss of historical and cultural "authenticity".

Local history, for example, is packaged (and fiercely marketed) to foreigners as a three-and-a-half-hour tour to Robben Island, the prison made famous by political superstar Nelson Mandela. A veritable "living" memory of apartheid evils, the island attraction is at once a striking tribute to florid racial guilt and a museum of CNN-styled histories. One of the biggest drawcards for tourists seeking the "Out of Africa" experience is the ultra-kitsch casino-hotel complex, The Lost City, which is a veritable concrete wonderland of westernised African myths and motifs. Tourists congregate around sites that far from typify the genuine experience of South African life. Attractions such as Robben Island and Cape Town's Waterfront development, far from stressing interactions and communication, contact and affinity between various spectra of South African society, emphasise and reiterate separation and segregation, highlighting the links between wealth and culture, European heritage and white economic hegemony. The "rainbow nation", in this sense, remains somewhat elusive.

This is not necessarily a problem which can be blamed solely on globalisation, however. There is a tremendous lack of homegrown familiarity with local strengths and opportunities for cultural growth. A social nervousness still prevails which suggests that "reality is elsewhere", that the "real world" exists beyond our borders, and, worst of all, that true creative genius exists overseas. An understandably white psychological tick, this phenomenon often prevents an acceptance of the diversity and brilliance that awaits discovery within our own country.

Coming to terms with the past and establishing a positive self-image which is not measured solely in terms of our reflection in the mirror of foreign (Western) culture, is an essential component of positive nation-building.

At the heart of all theatrical activity lies communication, and it is therefore essential that local performance cultures maintain open dialogue with the international community, and that the potentially catastrophic effects of any backlash against cultural globalisation are avoided. While the preservation of indigenous art is important, "the great danger is cultural xenophobia: the feeling that in order to protect national and local cultures, the invading, colonising culture has to be uprooted and destroyed" (Accone 2001c).

Ironically, while there is a tendency for South Africans to look down their noses at "local" theatre, the international view is somewhat different. Bulgarian critic and academic Kalina Stefanova claims that her recent visits to the country have exposed her to what she regards as a style of performance achieved with only limited success by international theatre practitioners. She argues that "what theatre-makers in other countries have to resuscitate from remnants of folklore and rites and then patch together, in South Africa is simply alive and bursting with energy" (Stefanova 2000:193).

This recognition of the inherent theatricality of the performance style which has evolved out of traditional indigenous practices apparently gives local theatre an advantage over developments in "the recent and present history of world theatre" (Stefanova 2000:192). It is a theatricality which exists in a natural form in South Africa and therefore does not require "excavation and resuscitation", needing only to "be drawn from the environment and put on stage" (Stefanova 2000:193).

Stefanova (2000:193) finds that the storytelling and ritual qualities evident in black theatre have – to a great extent – survived in a "natural, not yet commercialised" state. The beauty of current black theatre, she argues, is that it has not yet been transformed into a purely tourist-oriented practice.

Of course, local culture can be "packaged" for the tourist industry without undermining its inherent "purity". One example is a remarkable enterprise undertaken by actor/singer/director André-Jacques van der Merwe. At the behest of an Oudtshoorn ostrich farmer, Van der Merwe worked with unemployed members of the local community in order to produce a show that was initially targeted solely at foreign tourists. A lively musical telling the story of the heyday of the ostrich farming industry, *Struisvogelstories!* (literally "*Ostrich Stories*") was initially conceived as a "cultural cabaret" performed on the Cango Ostrich Farm as part of the tourist season attractions.

From these roots as a marketing and social-enrichment tool, the production went on to be performed at Oudtshoorn's annual Klein Karoo Nasionale Kunstefees (Little Karoo National Arts Festival), earning the award for best cabaret/musical theatre. Told from the perspective of the coloured people who perform in the show, it highlights – using dance, text, wit, energy and the music of a West Coast local, Pieter van der Westhuizen – the story of the disenfranchised people who never really shared in the wealth of an era during which ostrich feathers were big business.

Such success has spawned various touring opportunities for the company, including city and festival engagements. The show's success also indicates that there is room for the tourism and culture industries to co-exist comfortably without threat of diminishment to local heritage.[23]

Suip![24] is another local musical that has grown from humble roots to enjoy widespread recognition. Written by Oscar Petersen and Heinrich Reisenhofer, the show has gained national and international recognition, having already toured London and Australia. The much-travelled show uses vibrant humour to candidly look at the socio-historic circumstances of a particular South African community. *Suip!* focuses on a community that was not only disenfranchised during apartheid, but continues to exist outside the parameters of "normal" society. The ancestors of Cape Town's "*bergies*"[25] lived on the slopes of Table Mountain before the arrival of various colonisers, and today they live in the shadows of the landscape that was once their own. Often perceived as drunkards, foul-mouthed homeless layabouts and miscreants, these people are observed with genuine humanity in a show that imaginatively brings to life the horrors of their history under the white man. The text uses a lively storytelling format to equate the physical effects of alcohol with the cultural fermentation of a people decimated by a collective addiction to the ruinous substance, and the role of the Europeans in that process of decimation. The production combines various theatrical traditions, including storytelling, vaudeville, *commedia dell'arte* and musical theatre. Like much of the theatre that might be described as "total", *Suip!* has a Brechtian quality that frequently forces audience members to look back at themselves from outside the production.

Although Stefanova's observations are concerned primarily with what she refers to as "black South African theatre",[26] there are increasing examples of collaborative productions that meld the qualities of indigenous performance with aesthetic principles that are strongly associated with European theatre (*Struisvogelstories* and *Suip!* are two such examples). Significantly, much of the theatre that is emerging strays from the linear and literary narrative tradition that for so long distinguished it from indigenous performance culture and ritual. The evolving "total theatre" can be understood as a performance style that eclectically borrows from a range of cultural paradigms and mixes dance, song, live music and text in an effort to treat "all human senses" (Stefanova 2000:192).

With equal footing in the ritual traditions of pre-colonial South Africa, such performance implies a rediscovery of performative spirituality, with reduced emphasis on materiality. In this sense, priority is given to the actors, the story and the audience imagination to create a stage reality, rather than emphasis being placed on physical objects on stage. Such theatre necessarily involves a direct bond with the audience, frequently incorporating direct address and a breaking of the fourth wall. The performance is about relating a story to a group of friends rather than staging a show in front of an audience. The performance is framed by unexpected and incredible humour which is used to weld together seemingly incongruous narrative threads or pieces of stage reality. A sense of authenticity is generated by the coupling of unbridled energy and emotion with a documentary style that is inherent to the storytelling quality of the performances, which are also rooted in the mythical and the ritual. Thus, "total theatre" is recognisable as a rediscovery of the organic function of the indigenous performance culture.

Are there ways of "packaging" a uniquely South African variant of total theatre that is both firmly rooted in the traditions of our indigenous cultures, and somehow attractive – not only to foreigners, but to theatre lovers from diverse theatre backgrounds? While many in the theatre industry may attempt to emulate the literary genius of Athol Fugard or walk in the footsteps of the latest hotshot American or European director weaned on postmodern self-consciousness, it is vital to identify a mode of theatrical activity that will be capable of sustaining itself and attracting audiences from the full spectrum of South African society, without necessitating a return to the selective arts paternalism of the apartheid era.

The inherent theatricality of African culture finds resonance in the work of Brett Bailey and his Third World Bunfight Theatre Company. Bailey, arguably South African theatre's *enfant terrible* of the moment, practises a type of "packaging" which some might argue is "theme-parking". An eclectic provocateur who draws on diverse elements strewn together in performances that resemble either ritual enactments or hodge-podge cultural stews, Bailey's remarkable talent is for concocting overwhelmingly visual and visceral theatrical experiences that draw the audience into an almost trance-like immediacy with the performance. His first plays (or rather "hypertheatrical events") – *iMumbo Jumbo*, *Ipi Zombi* and *The Prophet* – filter the genuine ritualism of indigenous performance cultures through a postmodern design aesthetic which emphasises surrealistic theatricality, spectacle and dramatic surface. These productions have been inspired by documented South African stories – real life myths and tragedies – and have managed to engage a universal consciousness that is somehow uniquely South African.

Bailey conceives bizarre and triumphantly theatrical blends of myth, history and media culture, tapping into dance and music, tribal rituals and contemporary theatre techniques to tell African stories. His plays fetishise vivid, yet surreal, imagery and emphasise a style of performance that evokes the spirit of genuine ritual.

Singing and dancing merge with text and emotionally charged performances by casts of black actors who ultimately blur the boundaries of Stefanova's definition of "predominantly black theatre" which she refers to as "uniquely authentic". In some quarters, Bailey's plays have been criticised for their "exploitative" nature, for tapping into a traditional cultural resource to satisfy his own aesthetic interests. However, what Bailey has seized upon is a commercially viable appendage to the "natural" style of "theatre" that existed before colonisation; a white man's aestheticisation of "multiculturalism" or "total theatre". He is not so much dealing in cultural clashes as discovering a local aesthetic and inflecting it with an eclectic theatrical resonance, including the advantages of contemporary technologies.

Bailey, then, creates acts of dramatic spectacle which bring myth, magic and ritual to life through the medium of pronounced theatrical excess. Bailey's is a South African vision of Wagner's *Gesamtkunstwerk*, combining sound and vision and dramatic action in a magnificently disconcerting maelstrom of spectator delights designed to erode the viewer's resistance.

Big Dada (which premiered in 2001) represents something of a departure from Bailey's earlier productions. Having previously explored the "ritual as framework" performance context, he finds in this grotesque cabaret which lampoons and caricatures the Ugandan dictator Idi Amin (the show is subtitled *The Rise and Fall of Idi Amin Dada*) an opportunity for the play-within-a-play paradigm to be more boldly, more garishly highlighted. Here, Bailey deals less in the Wagnerian ideal than in a distinct theatrical iconoclasm.

A sneering, yet somehow jovial, caveat to the horrors of postcolonial tyranny, Bailey nevertheless satirises the flirtatious relationship between overarching power and the showbiz excesses of celebrity (exemplified in Amin's rendition of Sinatra's "My Way" during the final scene). This is a teasing invitation to laugh at perverse injustices and genocidal atrocities committed at the hands of a political showman – the statesman as *homme fatale*, if you will, who brings a nation to its knees. In a manner not unlike that of playwrights such as Pieter-Dirk Uys who use humour to highlight tragedy, Bailey's production illuminates certain horrors through fierce comic manipulation.

Theatre critic Robert Greig has argued that *Big Dada* "doesn't think about Idi but seems to use him as a provocation to spectacle" and that because it misses "the hard vertebrae of fact" it is ultimately "a hectic response to what seemed like an idea of Idi Amin" (Greig in Accone 2001a). Such an observation hints at Bailey's postmodernist concern with the failure of "History" to enlighten or provide insight into "Truth". His snapshot vignettes, glitzy cartoon cut-out characters and "ham-fisted iconography" (Accone 2001a) are visually sublime antidotes for the trivialisation of "History" that is so apparent in other areas of mediated culture. And yet, despite the apparent "trivialisation" of its subject matter through stylistic and aesthetic innovation, *Big Dada* (like *SeZaR*) responds not only to the legacy of colonialism in Africa, but also to the dangers of postcolonial despotism – inevitably it is a show that sends out "warnings about the possibility of that supreme form of one-upmanship developing [in South Africa]" (Accone 2001b).

Sharp criticism could be levelled against *Big Dada* for its "shapeless" cartooning of its subject matter through "a procession of journalistic snap-shots and media-aping cheap tricks" that might be comparable with an "*Idi Amin for Beginners*, filled with the sort of invidious biographical impressions that Oliver Stone is so good at" (Accone 2001a). Comparisons with Stone are pertinent, however, particularly with regards to the directors' shared visual bravura and proclivity for reassembling history through the demythologising kaleidoscope of the artistic inventor. Robert Greig (in Accone 2001a) refers to *Big Dada* as a "design work" that "gets its momentum through a series of visual shocks" that, while cheap, "work most of the time". In this respect, Bailey may be offering little more than a "guilty pleasure", but he satisfies and engages audiences with his riffs on Stone's undeniable ability to capture both imagination and intellect using the kind of "theatrical" bravado that has overwhelmed a generation of MTV addicts.

Bailey's is a style far removed from the structured narratives, introspective poetry and character-driven interactions of a playwright such as Fugard, yet his work points the way to a theatrical style that is capable of activating suppressed memories and speaking to the makers of history to come.

This is a theatricality that escapes the eurocentric, linear, literarily text-based and effectively highbrow traditions of mainstream theatre as it developed under apartheid, placing emphasis instead on something that is highly visual, visceral, physical and ultimately "theatrical".

Stefanova insists that the examples that she has observed in South Africa represent the type of performance that has the ability "to bring the art of theatre back to its roots, to restore its ritual nature and its festive character, or in other words to create theatrical authenticity on stage" (2000:193). In this sense, Stefanova notes that she has observed only limited success by theatre practitioners in the international scene, while (black) South African performances offer the "real thing". This understanding of authentic performance is a theatre of the imagination, of the emotions, and involves a genuine sense of communication between performers and audience members. It is a theatre drawn from the real world and transformed into an event which is immediate in its magical ability to "release the human energy both of the people on stage and in the theatre hall" (Stefanova 2000:193).

Multicultural collaborations leading to shows such as *Big Dada* and *Suip!* certainly represent the sort of theatrical magic described by Stefanova. These "products" have been anything but "cutesified"; rather, they present uncompromising reflections of various cultural "realities" within a framework that integrates existing paradigms. That these evolve as highly marketable and highly entertaining productions is a sociocultural phenomenon not to be frowned at, but rather to be celebrated.

Once Upon a Time . . . in the Immediate Future

Much of the value of live performance lies in its im*media*cy, its ability to connect and communicate with audiences in the instant. While this suggests something of the ethereal, magical and transient nature of theatre, it is also indicative of the need for theatre to evolve with the times and to respond to changes in the sociocultural environment.

Change in South Africa has been radical in recent years. Accordingly, theatre practitioners and practices have developed in various directions as they respond to global influences, local expectations and a somewhat altered set of social and infrastructural circumstances. Much of the theatre that has emerged in the so-called post-apartheid years has failed, but there have also been many success stories. Within a contemporary quick-fix market, it is the relationship between commercial viability and theatrical engagement that requires sustained attention. In this regard, it is the experimental and challenging innovations of creative chance-takers such as Brett Bailey that may well have the edge on securing the future of a uniquely South African performance culture.

The real challenge for South African "theatre" practitioners lies in the rediscovery of a tradition in which "performance" is a part of everyday life, and not merely a part of marginal or fringe culture. This may smack of the postmodern concept of the erasure of the distinction between "art" and "reality", but it is equally a call to make theatre both accessible (or "entertaining") and enriching. It is this fine line between commercial and critical cultural principles that must be negotiated if our children are to be exposed to *our* stories in the performance platforms of the future.

Notes

1 Such an endeavour immediately calls into question a number of issues: Does a post-apartheid climate exist? Is there such a thing as a uniquely South African theatre form? Is there such a thing as a local audience? This last question in particular is complicated not only by issues of socioeconomic diversity, but also by the impact of taste (whether cultural, intellectual, aesthetic, or other), which has enormous political implications. The enormous success of the 2001-2002 staging of Andrew Lloyd Webber's *Cats* in Cape Town and Pretoria, for example, speaks directly to this issue, but also demonstrates that South African audiences (or perhaps a certain portion of the population) simply share in the global love of big, lavish, well-branded, brilliantly-marketed international success stories.

2 According to Hauptfleisch (1997:60), it is within this category of performance "that all the varied strands of convention, tradition and experimentation somehow seem to get tied together in a hybrid form of performance which is uniquely South African".

3 Literally, "more theatrical than theatrical".

4 Commonly referred to as "Bushmen".

5 From the administration of museums to the training of performers, the system was wholly devoted to the concerns, tastes, standards, values, bank balances and experiences of white people. Even in those spheres of the arts industry where racism could not be inherently identified, there existed a certain degree of guilt because apartheid helped finance them and prevented black people from participating in them.

6 Cultural taste imported from Europe played a valuable role in the edification of the minority and its attendant interests, and against these "tastes", an aesthetic order and standard of civilisation was measured. The classical theatre (as well as opera, ballet and orchestral music) which was associated with "civilised culture" was not only irrelevant to the majority of people in South Africa, but was largely inaccessible thanks to apartheid law as well as more basic deterrents such as distance and economics.

7 Many white writers and other interested parties forged valuable allegiances with artists

from black communities to create collaborative works that excoriated the horrors of apartheid and looked forward to a day of triumph over the regime. At a time when government sponsored the tastes of a white elitist minority, while a handful of activists collaborated to produce some of the most valuable dramas highlighting the plight of the majority, theatre – by its very existence – was "political". For serious wordsmiths living in South Africa, there was little else to write about; apartheid was a complex but easily definable enemy. Much of the so-called "protest theatre" which emerged during the dark years of apartheid is the theatre for which South Africa is known, and its authors are the names that are remembered and cherished in the annals of local theatre history. Even the most celebrated South African playwrights were banned, arrested, imprisoned. Apartheid essentially represented an era when theatre developed with a sense of radical and meaningful urgency.

8 A theatrical style made popular by Gibson Kente and Sam Mhanghwane. These creative entrepreneurs were heavily influenced by Harold Bloom and Todd Matshikiza's famous "African musical", *King Kong* (1959) – essentially a musical in the American tradition, but involving black creative personalities and a distinctly South African theme.

9 Although there continue to be many works which critically deal with both the memory and the after-effects of apartheid.

10 The status of theatre – and the arts in general – is much-changed in the context of a Third World economy struggling to heal from the wounds inflicted by apartheid. There is, in fact, a general feeling of despair regarding the cultural sector: "Five or six years after 'transformation' began in earnest, there is a general feeling that the cultural milieu is a sorry state of affairs. The performing arts infrastructure is in decline; museums are riddled with uncertainty; budgets continue their downward spiral; performing arts companies struggle to survive; government arts and culture departments generally are ineffectual, as are their 'arm's length' funding bodies. This sorry state of affairs – mothballing of theatres, closure of orchestras, downsizing of playhouses, emigration of practitioners, collapse of cultural NGOs – is associated with 'transformation' i.e. with the coming into being of a largely black government, and more particularly, with the demographic transformation of government departments . . . responsible for arts and culture, and of the governance and management of subsidised performing arts and heritage infrastructure" (Van Graan 2001). Van Graan, who serves as interim chairperson of the fledgling Performing Arts Network of South Africa (PANSA) argues that the major problem with the performing arts in South Africa is not a lack of activity or creativity, but a weakness in the country's infrastructure. He notes numerous brilliant productions and various initiatives and writing programmes that encourage productivity. Examples include writing programmes run by Artscape and the Baxter, new work generated by Kultcha Klub and even a financial incentive from the National Arts Council promoting new work by playwrights

and theatre companies. Frequently, however, infrastructural problems inhibit the sustained success of new works which, despite even brilliant critical and audience response, seldom survive to become financially viable.

11 Programmes such as *Big Brother* and *Survivor*, which are marketed as examples of "reality television", emphasise the seduction of the banal and the pre-eminence of human voyeurism.

12 South Africa is certainly not alone in this regard. The world is a much-transformed and rapidly evolving place in which cultural exchange and evolution occur at breakneck pace and with whiplash consequences. Social, political and cultural change are pre-empted by radical innovations in every sphere of human existence; global revolutions transform communication, culture, media and art at every turn. Generally, these evolutions are linked to the economies of the West (or "North"), and are flogged wholesale to the nations of the South, the East, and the developing world. South Africa has, for example, along with social freedom, gained (legalised) pornography, liberal broadcasting policies, and increased exposure to various forms of Western culture.

13 There is fair argument for the legitimacy of "lowbrow" (or "popular" or "mass") entertainment forms, which is based on the democratisation and liberalisation of aesthetic "taste". Serious theatre, for example, is often viewed suspiciously – as a sociocultural pariah, perhaps – since many consider it a marginal and fairly obsolete entertainment form which appeals to the highbrow curiosities of an intellectual elite, is expensive and drains public funds, and which prioritises didactic highmindedness over entertainment. For many, works of serious theatre communicate in ways that are peculiar to a particular segment of society and, even worse, convey some form of class-based contempt.

14 "*Pomp*" is a vulgar slang term meaning "fuck"; literally translated, it means "pump".

15 Of course, the notion of "theatre" as popular entertainment event is no contemporary phenomenon. Roman gladiators were amongst the biggest theatrical stars and just as their "performances" drew fantastic crowds to drool as humans and beasts were slaughtered in furious mock battles that twisted the margins of realism, so today's most illustrious shows tend to be those requiring little more than the ability to hum along or clap in rhythm as recognisable musical numbers, precision dance routines, sparkling costumes and smoke machines embody contemporary eye-candy tastes. We are, and always have been, consumed by a love of spectacle.

16 Nearly seven times the state's contribution to the Market Theatre.

17 A township pub or community speakeasy.

18 Officially known as the Standard Bank National Arts Festival until the close of the 2001 festival. Options for the future funding of this event remain uncertain, although festival chairperson Mannie Manim has assured that the annual midyear celebration of the arts will continue.

19 Grahamstown now finds stiff competition from the chiefly Afrikaans nine-year-old

Little Karoo National Arts Festival which is held in April in the small town of Oudtshoorn which is known for its ostrich farming. Still other festivals that cohere around the performing arts have sprung up around the country, drawing audiences to moderately-sized towns as well as smaller communities.

20 Major theatre player writer-director-producer-trainer Deon Opperman (in Farber 2000:16) has summed up the significance of the festival circuit, claiming that "We go to all the festivals, [because] that's where the audiences are!" – a claim which is supported by the fact that he was responsible in various capacities for 14 plays presented in Grahamstown in 2000.

21 Accone melodramatically argues that despite the positive context in which "globalisation" is sold to the world, its consequences for local cultures are threateningly negative: "What a comfortable, rounded sound the word 'globalisation' has. But as a concept of uniform, worldwide practice, it's not quite so cocooning. It is not only in the economic sphere that globalisation threatens South Africa. Its effects do not so much trickle down into the rest of human society as become an engulfing wave, a tsunami that obliterates local cultures, traditions, beliefs and knowledge" (Accone 2001c).

22 There have also been a number of examples of collaborative works involving established artists and inexperienced performers or nonperformers from an array of poor communities, suggesting a determination to make theatre function in the interests of social enrichment. At the 2001 Little Karoo National Arts Festival (KKNK), popular singer and personality David Kramer staged *Karoo Kitaar Blues* (*Karoo Guitar Blues*), a musical show featuring various "performers" discovered by himself and a documentary filmmaker in some of the country's "most oppressed communities" (Schoonakker 2001:13). The previously disenfranchised, largely destitute nonperformers who were brought together for the remarkably spontaneous and entertaining show received an enthusiastic response from the largely wealthy white audiences. This show has also since been performed in various city centres.

23 Meaning "to drink in excess" or, more appropriately, "to get drunk".

24 Literally "little mountains", the term "*bergies*" loosely translates as "little mountain people" and refers to the homeless inhabitants of the streets of Cape Town who are descended from the original San people who once lived on the slopes of Table Mountain.

25 Or, "predominantly black South African theatre".

References

Accone, Daryl. 2001a. Dada Dada is all I want to say to you. In: ArtRap, 6 July 2001.

Accone, Daryl. 2001b. Bogeyman stalks festival drama. In: ArtRap, 9 July 2001.

Accone, Daryl. 2001c. Threats that globalisation poses to SA culture. In: ArtRap, 17 July 2001.

Coplan, David B. 1985. *In township tonight! South Africa's black city music and theatre.* Johannesburg: Ravan Press.

Farber, Tanya. 2000. A barrow-load from Opperman. In: *Cue*, 2 July 2000. 16.

Gibney Frank Jr. and Luscombe, Belinda. 2000. Design: The Redesign of America. In: *Time*, 26 June 2000. 42-49.

Hauptfleisch, Temple. 1997. *Theatre and Society in South Africa: Reflections in a Fractured Mirror*. Pretoria: J.L. van Schaik.

Rutsky, R. L. 1999. Techno-Cultural Interaction and the Fear of Information. In: *Style*, Summer, 1999, website article.

Schoonakker, Bonny. 2001. Haunted by the past, in search of a future. In: *Sunday Times*, 15 April 2001. 13.

Stefanova, Kalina. 2000. Falling in love with South African theatre (a true story). In: *South African Theatre Journal* 14, September. 184-198.

Tsumele, Edward. 2001. Playing to empty houses in the townships. In: *The Sunday Independent*, 15 April 2001. 10.

Van Graan, Mike. 2001. Is transformation for or against racism? In: ArtRap, 29 August 2001.

CHAPTER NINE

The Birth of the 'New Woman': Antjie Krog and Gynogenesis as a Discourse of Power

Marthinus Beukes

Introduction

Antjie Krog can be seen a poet of renewal in Afrikaans literature, and not only regarding the image of the woman. In her poetry we find a recording of the woman who has reconquered her body, but who has also recovered the text as metaphor of the body. It can indeed be said that her poetry becomes a narrative of that woman who has undergone a new birth, a rebirth in body and text. To define this rebirth, the concept of gynogenesis can be used, as Gouws (1992:106-107) contextualised it in his review of *Die wond en ander verhale*: "More attention should be given to the discourse of power on a personal level, gender level, social level, and not only on political and ideological levels. In this connection gynogenesis – the birth of the New Woman – is especially conspicuous."

In this framework gynogenesis as discourse of power is a corrective on the patriarchal discourse of power, but also on the militancy of extreme feminism. Krog's poetry becomes a report of this changing content of consciousness whereby gynogenesis as a transforming situation is written in ink and blood. In this way she formulates an ideolectic style characteristic of the woman who discovers herself in writing and proclaims herself as human being, therefore more than woman.

For the purpose of this chapter the concept of gynogenesis should be viewed against the background of a worldwide paradigm shift within ideological and political activity, as well as the spheres of human activity where renewal or change is at present emphasised. With regard to this new world spirit the Greek meaning of *geneze* as "origin" or "genesis" is especially important, because the human being as seeker after meaning is hereby centralised again. This reconstructing process of a world spirit will have definite social implications in particular. In this process of origin or of becoming, the human being will therefore be emphasised.

According to the Latin origin of the word, *gigno* stands for "procreate", "generate" and "cause" (Postma 1967:130), but also for "woman". Word combinations with "gyn", "gyno" and "gyne" – according to the Greek – further indicate a connection with women (Brink 1991:176). These etymological explanations of the concept gynogenesis indicate a special link between becoming and being a woman. Gouws et al. (1979:100) furthermore explain *genese* as the origin of something or the beginning of a process of development. In the scope of this chapter the development process of the woman is emphasised and examined in her alteration, renewal and transformation into the New Woman. This leads to the connection between "gyno" and "geneze" which, for the purpose of this chapter, will be joined to describe the birth of the New Woman.

The impact of gynogenesis as a social condition can be related to the changing contents of social consciousness. Change has therefore also taken place in the field of literature where the dehumanising patriarchal ideology of power was dealt with by feminism. The foundation of feminism was a political discourse that declared a dispute with patriarchalism and sexism (Moi 1989:182). A process of change and renewal originated because feminism took the initial steps toward the formation of a new image for women. Gynogenesis as a discourse of power expands feminist views and affirms a new image for the woman in literature: that of the New Woman.[1]

As a new discourse of power, gynogenesis assumes the maintenance of sexual differences, but it is not defined by ideological and political domination. The New Woman's sexuality as such is accentuated. Gynogenetical power is effected, inter alia, when the woman recolonises her body by means of issues that were previously regarded as taboo in literature and in society. A biological reassessment of the female body therefore offers a gynogenetic grasp of a more complete state of being. Rich (1976: 62) explains: "In order to live a full human life we require not only control of our bodies . . . we must touch the unity and resonance of our physicality, the corporeal ground of our intelligence." This liberation denotes, according to Trask (1986:28), the breaking free from the chains of patriarchalism which confined the woman. A new discourse of power is effected with gynogenesis, because the woman establishes herself as human being next to the man. In this process a recolonisation of the female body as an overarching gynogenetic matrix takes place.

Trask (1986:29) argues that the woman is a colonised object because her history, values and culture were taken away from her. The assault was completed by the seizure of the female body as a conquered land: "Our bodies have been taken from us, mined for their natural resources (sex and children), and deliberately mystified."

Feminism aimed at breaking the bondage of partriarchalism and reclaiming the captured "land". This led to reconciliation. The need for further action exists, however, namely the confirmation of this reconciliation and the utilising of the recolonised territory. Gynogenesis as discourse of power essentially also includes colonisation. Marin's (1989:90) viewpoint on the transfer of power is especially important in this regard: "taking one's own turn to use the discourse of might [because] there is a change of master, but there is still a master". In the context of gynogenesis the transfer of power does not signify the ruling of another's territory, but the territory of the *self*. The wielder of power in this case is exclusively active in his or her own territory. Power in such a context therefore remains the sole discourse of force. The New Woman's territory of governance is her own body. With her important poem "man ek lus 'n twakkie" ("man, I crave a smoke"), Krog provides a significant description of the way in which the woman demands her body back and rules her own domain.

The Nature of Gynogenetic Power in the Poetry of Antjie Krog

Viljoen (1991b:20) has pointed out that Antjie Krog's *Lady Anne* was one of the first volumes of poetry in Afrikaans markedly to push through the familiar poetic barriers by including texts which would not ordinarily be considered poetry. In this way Krog inter alia brought about gynogenesis, as traditional and familiar convictions and barriers regarding reality phenomena, literary forms and contents were shattered. By means of this process the code of language becomes chiefly a way of expressing gynogenesis as discourse of power.

Viewed metaphorically, the body in this discourse of power is also the body of the text in which language has an accentuated position. The text as body assists in bringing about gynogenesis. In this way the New Woman confirms herself, because text, which in the Latin is *texere*, i.e. weaving, is a typical female activity. Rowe (1986:64) commented justifiably that the action of weaving is "the female craft par excellence". It is more than this, however, for in mythology the woven cloth is the product of the Life/Death/Life pattern (Estes 1992:95), from which may be deduced that woman possesses power over life and death. By returning to the body, by weaving text, the woman renews herself. In short: from the woman, by the woman and to the woman. It is against this background that Antjie Krog employs language and text as vehicles for a new discourse.

Gouws (1995:559) explains that a linguistic journey is also present in *Jerusalemgangers,* one of Krog's previous collections of poetry. In this volume even the rules of spelling have to be reformulated to adapt to a new era in *Afrika*ans (author's italics). The transforming language code used by Krog acts as signification of this transforming embodiment. In this context language becomes a marker of gynogenesis.

In her significant article "The thieves of language", Ostriker (1986:315) postulated that the language traditionally spoken and written by women was an encoding of male privilege. When the woman uses the language of the man she does so to confirm that she has the power to harness language and to say what she means. The construction of a gynogenetic discourse of power is therefore also reflected in the form, structure and style of the woman's writing. In Krog's poem discussed here as an example of gynogenesis, slang becomes an icon, the reappropriation of language, especially because of the aggressive male sexual undertones.

The reappropriation of language is also accompanied by compositional adjustments. Krog started this process in *Lady Anne* by "bending linguistic boundaries" (p. 108); even the boundaries of genre were overwritten. In this respect some critics remarked on the epic nature of the volume *Lady Anne*. Brink (1989:13) describes it as a novel of verse (also a travel novel), a characterisation which indicates a specific genre transgression. Kannemeyer (1989:41) sees *Lady Anne* as a modern epic and Viljoen (1989:8) regards it as a contemporary epic. When Gouws (1989:43) declares the volume to be an epic of a new epoch, he indicates the perimeters of the development of gynogenesis. Here it is also the epoch of a New Woman in Afrikaans literature.

Cloete's (1986:10) reading of *Jerusamlemgangers* in the framework of "the desire for liberation, liberation also from damage" (my translation), indicates the issues around freedom and liberation which become apparent at different levels, for example in relation to the country, history and personal life. According to Cloete this thematic "damage" is iconically embodied in the damage to language. Supplementing Cloete's view of linguistic damage is Brink's (1986:16) appreciation of the "violence" at different levels in the volume. The indication of structural violence is important for the syntax, regarded even more broadly: the language reflects violence "specifically in the violence done to the language; in the violence *afflicted* here by the language itself where a frightening violence exists, a fire from hell burns itself out (author's italics)".

Language, especially in light of the above, is the womb of this transformation. Krog confirms with *Lady Anne* (and the poem discussed in this chapter) the reformulation of language rules which leads to the embodiment of renewal. Together with divesting herself of her historical alliance, Krog also discards stereotypical language and archaisms in order to create another language register. Malan (1989:103) states that a comprehensive register of obsolete or uncommon words appears in the "historical" text (for example, "bard, livrei [livery], manick [manioc], parasol [parasol] and skattedoor"), but that this is trumped by various neologisms and casual amalgamations such as "macho-mans [macho men], creeps, jog and gym and joga [yoga]".

Discontinuity and fragmentation (Viljoen 1991a:62) in the text confirm the renewing embodiment of a transformed text. In this respect Gouws (1986:125) explains that a broad variety is included and interwoven in both the experience of reality and the writing of poetry. For a new political discourse of power, language therefore necessarily adjusts, because in this way "everything is webbed together" as the poet puts it in a poem from another collection, *Otters in bronslaai* (p. 52).

It is against this background that Krog's poem "slot" [conclusion] (*Lady Anne*, p. 107) ushers in the beginning of the process of gynogenesis. As Krog gradually realises that Lady Anne is "fôkol werd" ["fucking useless"] (p. 40) and she haplographs[2] her from the text, she affirms it by simultaneously offering a new and syntactic language code. It is especially important that Krog abolishes continuity with this first final poem and, therefore, by implication leaves room for the conclusion, which becomes the key to a new style of text and thus also to the New Woman:

This is composed from diaries
and letters: not all the truth –
I had to lie and abbreviate, but
in this way it fits in better among other texts
that will themselves speak or reject in *the web*[3]

The transformation process of the New Woman is a struggle for survival where she herself stands in the centre of events. In this process language is inter alia decisive, as it becomes a mighty means of transformation. Krog's quote from Lady Anne's travel journal is of importance in this regard: "Every page is a page of struggle, I write to destroy the border of unbearable pain" (p. 51). Moreover, it is the *hand* that becomes the mover of boundaries and marker of transformation: "my palm on the *woven* page perspires bloodily its knowing" (p. 13).[4] By writing the poet thus becomes renewed, because the ink is like the blood in the "tampon" (compare the poem "buite perke II" ["out of bounds II"]), a marker of renewal. The new identity of the woman follows in the embodiment cast for her in *Lady Anne*: the image of the New Woman. For the woman, recolonisation of the body is an important way of experiencing a new identity. Out of this recolonised domain follows the exercising of the mandateship: *naming* the new territory. With "man, I crave a smoke" Krog not only names the new mandate, but it also serves as directive gynogenetic text.

5 "man, I crave a smoke"[5] as directive gynogenetic text

Within the changed boundaries of a new time spirit, the following poem supplies a clear demonstration of the image of the New Woman:

"man, I crave a smoke"
she says and digs in the sideboard for more Craven A
she pulls up her legs on the sofa
pulls deeply
blows with a haughty jaw the smoke towards the window

"I looked at him last night
while he was undressing
oh, man, and I thought: that bloody prick
just look at it: prude and selfish and clean cut
the old people, you see
neatly in its place between the balls it hangs
ostensibly wounded

and I turned around and thought of its many years of frolicking
night after fucking night pissed or not
through pregnancies babies abortions
mind you even when I had my period
from all sides that blade cut
the cod actually hissed the way it lifted
until the balls were rock-hard

let me tell you: such a prick
does more than frolic
only it says how generous the mood is
only it says who is thrashed
when it gets up it is time for bend or open
and you'd better be impressed my baby
not just *kierts* or lecherous
but in awe hey

everything, you hear me, every thing fucking turns on the maintainance of cock

and the thing it hasn't got brains, you know
or soul and for that matter also no heart
it's everything. it always shows off
a Man's man
your clit eventually wants to seize up man

my god and now?
now that prick refuses to
with pouted mouth the tip lies
whether it dangles and limply moves this or that way
the balls' straps have sagged
sometimes uncle lifts half mast
but comes right there
it boils over like a pot of jam
frrritters away like a balloon
it still springs condensed milk
but not all like before

and it can't take it, you know
its eyes are quite dull he buys high rise
and his attention is just there, just there all the time

his hands, were he to smoke now, are feverish
his legs quite loamy
if I take him in bed
all the plush and the worry even discharges in his beard
please pass me the lighter . . .

now my mother said last night when I went down there
rumours have it that for generations already
our mothers, grandmothers and aunts have castrated their husbands
and when they then hover like that
we become lustful, hey, really poisonous
like released snakes would disappear into grass
jesus! and then we take crap from nothing."

she gets up
legs slim in multicoloured leggings
corners of the mouth chiselled towards the throat

"my whole fucking body, hey! groans with juices
my tits and fanny chat their own chat
for the first time my baby
I feel, how I, myself, ever so slowly, is coming in tune."

This is very different from the speaker in "die skryfproses, as sonnet" ["the process of writing, as sonnet"] (*Otters in bronslaai*, p. 35), who confessed:

how frightened I've become to think poetically boisterously,
to let my beloved trail out without rhyme or form
how shy I've become to call in shoots of unprejudiced verse
his penis irresponsibly iron-clear by its name[6]

The poem "man, I crave a smoke" no longer demonstrates shyness or anxiety. The initial careful reference to "penis" has been replaced by the slang "prick" and "cock". This poem becomes the report of a woman's experience of her husband's sexual history, as stated in the core line 27: "everything, you hear me, every thing fucking turns on the maintainance of cock".[7] But Krog's poem is essentially an ironic deconstruction of male sexuality and the construction of an own female image. At the end of the poem the woman says:

"for the first time my baby
I feel, how I, myself, ever so slowly, is coming in tune."

Gynogenesis is summarised in these words, because the woman draws her new image in sharply-etched lines. With this she accepts responsibility for her own sexuality without any sign of dependence on the male. In this way she maps as settler[8] her domain in the territory of her own human and female being.

In an ingenious way Krog halves the poem so that the disparity regarding the man's and the woman's sexuality is also compositionally embodied. Lines 1-32 focus on the maintenance of the man's initial sexual power, but lines 33-65 portray the woman's new virility as pendant to the man's *coro.*[9] Krog developed with her poetry, and in particular the last four volumes, the code of the New Woman. Minnie (1992:118) says that Krog initiated the female code in *Lady Anne* by means of the reproduction of a menstruation chart that was included in the volume. She posits (p. 118): "It does not so much deal with femininity; rather, it is an icon of femininity." With "man, I crave a smoke" Krog joins this changed femininity and calls sexuality per se clearly by its name. Gouws (1989:43) correctly explains that this menstruation chart also indicates the birth of a new era – therefore also the birth of the New Woman. Such a changing openness is the birthplace of gynogenesis. For this reason the structural bisection of the poem is semantically charged. The woman brought the two ideologies of power under one structure, as it were. Where the man normally dominated sexual interaction, his sexual power is, in a manner of speaking, cut; just as "our mothers, grandmothers and aunts have castrated their husbands" (line 54). Krog does this textually in an almost iconic way.

In line 63, where the speaker calls her own sexual organs explicitly by name, she conducts a new conversation: "my tits and fanny chat their own chat".[10] The word "chat" here is used as a synonym for discourse. In short: gynogenesis implies the "chat" about the woman's body in a distinctive discourse.

The change in the virility of the man, described in lines 1-32 (part I), is conspicuous in light of the contrast in lines 33-65 (part II) – it follows after the woman's "castrating action". The two profiles can also be described compositionally as a prephase and a postphase. The characteristics of the man's sexual image in part can be categorised as follows:

7 that bloody prick
8 just look at it: prude and selfish and clean cut
. . .
10 neatly in its place between the balls it hangs
. . .
16 from all sides that blade cut
17 the cod actually hissed the way it lifted
18 until the balls were rock-hard
19 let me tell you: such a prick
20 does more than frolic
21 only it says how generous the mood is

22 only it says who is thrashed
23 when it gets up it is time for bend or open

. . .

27 everything, you hear me, every thing fucking turns on the maintainance of cock
28 and the thing it hasn't got brains, you know
29 or soul and for that matter also no heart

30 it's everything. it always shows off

. . .

33 a Man's man

This macho image of the man corresponds with the poem in *Lady Anne* (p. 67) where an entry for the penis from the standard Afrikaans dictionary, the *HAT*, is given in defined constrained language:

penis: male *rod*
stick, switch, cane, with which corporal punishment
is inflicted[11] (author's italics)

In the first part of the poem phallocratism[12] is portrayed: the power of the penis. It is the old discourse about the woman against which feminism revolted. The submissiveness of the woman to this power is particularly obvious. A semantic paradigm of the might of the penis can be as follows:

16 that blade
18 the balls were rock-hard
22 it says who is thrashed
26 in awe
28 hasn't got brains
29 or soul and for that matter also no heart

From the above the earlier male power play over the woman is clear. These words not only denote the sexual dominance of the man, but also the sexual submissiveness of the woman. The man reigns here with the rod and the blade in the hand. In this way he confirms his grasp on the woman. Her image in this sexual play is as follows:

12 and I turned around and thought of its many years of frolicking
13 night after fucking night pissed or not
14 through pregnancies babies abortions
15 mind you even when I had my period
16 from all sides that blade cut

. . .

24 and you'd better be impressed my baby
25 not just *kierts* or lecherous
26 but in awe hey
. . .
32 your clit eventually wants to seize up man

Line 32 also presents the woman metaphorically as a car. When a car "seizes up", the vehicle was driven too hard (without care). In this way the speaker maintains that she was misused by the man as an object of daily use. Lexical information from lines 1-32, especially the slang concerning sexual organs and sexual intercourse, emphasises the earlier phallocratic discourse of power. It is, however, the language code in which the presentation is made that is gynogenetic. By the specific ideolectic language code the woman confirms her new discourse of power, because by moving within the domain of a new female being, she names things and in this way practises her new mandateship. In this light the question posed in line 33 is so much more conspicuous: "my god and *now*?"

The word "now" should be read in the gynogenetic discourse as the profile of the phallocratic man versus the New Woman. In answer to the woman's question she offers a demystifying of his power play, because: "now that prick refuses to" (line 34). This section is the *capado* (disempowerment) of the man. Against this background the discourse of power of the New Woman is lustful and "poisonous" (line 56). A profile of the castrated man, as drawn in lines 33-65, appears as follows:

34 now that prick refuses to
35 *with pouted mouth the tip lies*
36 whether it dangles and limply moves this or that way
37 the balls' straps have *sagged*
38 sometimes uncle lifts *half mast*
39 but comes right there
40 it boils over like a pot of jam
41 *frrritters away like a balloon*
42 it still springs condensed milk
43 but not all like before

The words in italics provide a catalogue of the man's castrated status. This portrays all contrasts with his original sexual aggression. This disparity in his profile also makes the woman's new image more relevant. It is as if in this section she does not need to react in "awe" to the man's power play. She is now the active figure: "if I take him in bed" (line 49). This gynogenetic figure also goes hand in hand with aggression, hence the picture of the snake:[13]

we become lustful, hey, really poisonous
like released snakes would disappear into grass
jesus! and then we take crap from nothing

Through the metaphors the woman's power is spelled out and no longer that of the man. Considering the use of language in this poem, especially the naming of the female and male sexual organs, the woman's power is valid to name gyno-ideolectically, in other words, with the power of New Womanhood.

It is important that the woman, as was the case in the Biblical Paradise after creation, is connected with the snake again, but now *on her terms*. In light of gyno-*genesis*, as the beginning or origin of the New Woman, the snake metaphor is semantically charged. Referring back to the Garden of Eden at the beginning of creation, this poem therefore intends to emphasise the woman's new beginning as equal to the man with her own power resources. Earlier sexuality of the woman is therefore deconstructed, because she, woman, no longer needs to be hunted by the snake (the phallus[14]). She now has the power which the snake formerly possessed: she is lustful and poisonous. Couffignal (1992:394) states justly that the snake could be viewed in a different light: "After all, this 'hostile' creature offered human beings *knowledge* and *power* (author's italics), and actually presented itself in the role of the Benefactor. Moreover, it gave Man the opportunity to occupy that same position, and become master of the system."

Conclusion

In this poem linguistic aspects become the poet's confirmation of gynogenesis. The poem proceeds further with the construction, destruction and deconstruction of language and grammar that already characterised *Lady Anne* as one of the most difficult volumes in Afrikaans (Brink 1989:13). The degree of difficulty becomes iconic of a gyno-ideolectical focus. Krog does not only break through the normal syntactic patterns (compare Cloete 1989:15) in her poetry, but also deconstructs lexical conventions. In this way Krog affirms once again that she is the most important settler poet of gynogenesis, for the idiom is that of the New Woman. By writing in this way, Krog emphasises that the New Woman in Afrikaans literature takes "stront van niks" ("crap from nothing") (line 58). Not only does she emphasise the woman's need for a self-directed sexual expectation, but also the use of language to reinforce her new image. It is indeed a bodily conversation with the self and fellow women: "my tits and fanny chat their own chat" ["my tieties en koekoesnaai chat hulle se eie chat" (line 63)]. The words, as well as the suprasegmental highlighting in line 65, emphasise the woman's occupation of her own body and sexuality: "I feel, how I, myself, ever so slowly, is coming in tune". With this poem Krog ingenuously demonstrates the woman's living in a new guise – the image of a recolonised figure. By exposing the disparity of sexuality in this poem, Krog confirms gynogenesis as textual discourse of power.

Notes

1 Feminism led to the man being forced to reconcile, to a large extent. This resulted in the birth of the New Woman which is indicated by the concept *gynogenesis.*

2 Haplography can be defined in this context as the deliberate omission or imposition of silence.

3 Original Afrikaans: Dié is saamgestel uit wat dagboeke
en briewe rep: nie alles waar nie –
ek moes baie jok en verkort, maar
so pas dit beter tussen ander tekste
wat self sal praat of verwerp in *die web.*

4 Original Afrikaans: "my palm op die *geweefde bladsy* sweet bloederig sy weet".

5 This poem is one of three poems by Krog that were published in the gossip column of the alternative Afrikaans weekly newspaper *Vrye Weekblad* (31 July – 6 August 1992), and appeared in her *Gedigte 1989-1995.* Amendments appearing in the latter have been ignored.

6 hoe bang het ek geword om poëties baldadig te dink,
om my geliefde rymloos en vormloos te laat uitrank
hoe sku het ek geword om in lote onbevange vers
sy penis onverantwoordelik ysterklaar by die naam te noem

7 Original Afrikaans: "alles, hoor jy my, alles fokken draai om die maintáínance van piel".

8 In this framework she functions as new coloniser.

9 In this poem a parallel is drawn with Marita van der Vyver's *coro*-syndrome, in which the man's sexual power is deconstructed. In Van der Vyver's novel *Griet skryf 'n sprokie* (p. 181) Griet tells Jans the following about the *coro*: "'It is the Malay word for a tortoise head – and the poetic term for Penile Shrinkage Syndrome.' But she thought it was a condition that only existed in her imagination. Something caused by castrating witches. *That shrinking feeling.*"

10 Original Afrikaans: "my tieties en koekoesnaai chat hulle se eie chat".

11 penis: manlike *roede*
stok, lat, rottang, waarmee lyfstraf
toegedien word

12 Etymologically the concept of *phallocratism* can be traced as follows: *Kratos* (Greek) means "power", therefore the phallocratic approach would refer to the power of the phallus in society.

13 The metaphor of the snake brings to mind associations with the Biblical creation myth. In gynogenesis the woman is also, as in Paradise, equal to the man.

14 Couffignal (1992:390) says: "the serpent – the monster . . . represents the phallic Father".

References

Brink, A.J. 1991. *Woordeboek van Afrikaanse geneeskundeterme*. Cape Town: Nasou.

Brink, A.P. 1986. Antjie Krog bring merkwaardigste poësie van 1985. *Rapport*: 19 Januarie 1986. 16.

Brink, A.P. 1989. Antjie Krog se '*Lady Anne*': 'n roman van 'n bundel. *Vrye Weekblad*: 18 Augustus 1989. 13.

Cloete, T.T. 1986. Bundel van gemengde waarde. *Die Volksblad*: 22 February 1986. 10.

Cloete, T.T. 1989. 'Te veel boek en te min menslikheid'. *Die Volksblad*: 9 September 1989. 15.

Couffignal, R. 1992. 'Eden'. In: Brunel, P. (eds.). *Companion to Literary Myths, Heroes and Archetypes*. London: Routledge. 389-406.

Estes, C.P. 1992. *Women who run with the wolves*. New York: Ballantine.

Gouws, L.A., Louw, D.A., Meyer, W.F. and Plug, C. (eds.). 1979. *Psigologiewoordeboek*. Johannesburg: McGraw-Hill.

Gouws, T. 1986. *Die komposisionele spel in die poësie – 'n verkenning van Antjie Krog se Otters in bronslaai*. Unpublished MA thesis. Potchefstroom: PU vir CHO.

Gouws, T. 1989. Krog se '*Lady Anne*' gelyke van *Tristia*. *Insig*: 31 October 1989. 43.

Gouws, T. 1992. Soos ons ons skuldenaars vergewe. *De Kat*: November.

Gouws, T. 1998. Antjie Krog (gebore 1952). In: Nienaber, P.J. and Van Coller, H.P. (eds.). *Perspektief en profiel*. Pretoria: Van Schaik.

Kannemeyer, J.C. 1989. Die horries van A.E. Samuel (gebore Krog). *Tydskrif vir Letterkunde*, 27(3). 33-42.

Krog, A. 1981. *Otters in bronslaai*. Cape Town: Human & Rousseau.

Krog, A. 1989. *Lady Anne*. Emmarentia: Taurus.

Krog, A. 1992. Vir dié week se geselsrubriek het Antjie Krog 'n paar gedigte geskryf. *Vrye Weekblad*: 31 July-6 August 1992.

Krog, A. 1995. *Gedigte 1989-1995*. Groenkloof: Hond.

Malan, L. 1989. Ou tyd en eie tyd. *De Kat*, October.

Marin, L. 1989. The narrative trap: the conquest of power. In: Gane, M. (ed.). *Ideological representation and power in social relations: literary and social theory*. London: Routledge. 89-109.

Minnie, T.J. 1992. *Teks en gemeenskap: 'n skryfmatige lesing van Lady Anne van Antjie Krog*. Unpublished MA thesis. Potchefstroom: PU vir CHO.

Moi, T. 1989. Men against patriarchy. In: Kauffman, L.S. (ed.). *Gender and theory: dialogues on feminist criticism*. New York: Basil Blackwell. 180-188.

Odendal, F.F., Schoonees, P.C., Swanepoel, C.J., Du Toit, S.J. and Booysen, C.M. 1983. *HAT: Verklarende handwoordeboek van die Afrikaanse taal*. Johannesburg: Perskor.

Ostriker, A. 1986. The Thieves of Language: Women Poets and Revisionist Mythmaking. In: Showalter, E. (ed.). *The new feminist criticism: essays on women, literature and theory*. London: Virago. 314-338.

Postma, F. 1967. *Beknopte woordeboek: Latyn - Afrikaans*. Pretoria: HAUM.

Rich, A. 1976. *Of woman born: motherhood as experience and institution*. London: Virago.

Rowe, K.E. 1986. To spin a yarn: the female voice in folklore and fairy tale. In: Bottigheimer, R. (ed.). *Fairy tales and society: illusion, allusion, and paradigm*. Philadelphia: University of Pennsylvania. 53-94.

Trask, H-K. 1986. *Eros and power: the promise of feminist theory*. Philadelphia: University of Pennsylvania.

Van der Vyver, M. 1992. *Griet skryf 'n sprokie*. Cape Town: Tafelberg.

Viljoen, L. 1989. Krog se virtuose kompleksiteit. *Die Burger*: Desember.

Viljoen, L. 1991a. Susanna Smit en Lady Anne Barnard – enkele aspekte van Antjie Krog se historiese poësie as tagtiger-verskynsel. *Stilet*, 3(1). 57-79.

Viljoen, L. 1991b. Die teks as transparant: Antjie Krog se 'Lady Anne' binne die Suid-Afrikaanse werklikheid. *Stilet*, 3(2). 19-31.

CHAPTER TEN

'Our Missing Store of Memories': City, Literature and Representation[1]

Phaswane Mpe

Introduction

Bleak House, like *Hard Times* and some other Charles Dickens novels, deals with what its writer saw as a cruel city. Dickens seems to have had a great deal of compassion for London's children in particular, and for its working classes, exploited, as he points out numerous times, by industrialisation, social snobbery and the English legal system in the 1800s. In *Bleak House* Dickens also casts critical strokes at misplaced philanthropy which claims to provide relief in Africa while ignoring suffering in London itself, let alone the whole of England. Dickens's concern with what he regarded as the cruelty of the city is not unique. In the poem "London", for example, William Blake's persona wanders "through each charter'd street, / Near where the charter'd Thames does flow, / And mark in every face I meet / Marks of weakness, marks of woe" (Blake 1988:130).

In South Africa, at least 150 years later, we also have harrowing depictions of cities such as Johannesburg. For example, Mongane Serote's "Alexandra" portrays this city's black township, about twelve kilometres to the north of the city centre, as a "rubble" (1984:385-86), with dongas full of the blood of its children. Mbuyiseni Mtshali's "An Abandoned Bundle" tells of another township, White City Jabavu, full of air pollution, like "pus oozing / from a gigantic sore" (1971:68). Whether it is Dickens or Blake, Serote or Mtshali, what comes through in the writings is that the apparent structural decay and environmental pollution associated with the city is reflective of a decline in its moral fibre, as well as a general sense of social, political and cultural responsibility.

This is not to suggest that all portrayals of the city in literature are absolutely and simply condemnatory or gloomy. Indeed, the four writers I have referred to above suggest that human beings, if made or forced to see and understand the problems associated with their cities, can in fact do something about the problems. While Serote and Mtshali's poems here seem to reflect a sense of resignation, elsewhere this sense is undermined. Serote, for example, calls on blacks to reject discriminatory practices and their own subjugation by their administrators and would-be white employers. A failure to do this, an acceptance of discrimination and subjugation in other words, is "What's in this 'black' shit" of the title of the poem in question. Mtshali, for his part, in "The Master of the House" (1971:61), portrays a black man continuing to visit his lover in the white suburbs where he is not welcome by the white owners. The black man also appears to be excited by the fact that he triumphs somewhat against the prejudice, as long as he remains cunning and exercises caution and excellent timing.

Whether one laments or celebrates the city, one thing is clear. Change often catches the imagination of writers, and provides impetus for their writing. In many instances, change – whether social, political, economic or cultural – is accompanied by dramatic acts of violence and acute feelings of dislocation, insecurity and anxieties. Of course, these feelings can simultaneously be accompanied by a sense of hope in the future, while a successful management of change can lead to much joy and happiness. Because of the dynamic and complex nature of change, trying to understand it, and to unravel its implications for the present and the future, is an equally slippery affair. Commenting on the dynamic and complex nature of problems – which often occasion the need for change – M. Scott Peck writes:

> What makes life difficult is that the process of confronting and solving problems is a painful one. Problems, depending upon their nature, evoke in us frustration or grief or sadness or loneliness or guilt or regret or anger or fear or anxiety or anguish or despair. These are uncomfortable feelings, often very uncomfortable, often as painful as any kind of physical pain, sometimes equalling the very worst kind of physical pain. Indeed, it is *because* of the pain that events or conflicts engender in us that we call them problems. And since life poses an endless series of problems, life is always difficult and is full of pain as well as joy (1990[1983]:14).

While Scott Peck's observations are directed at personal and domestic changes – What, for example, lead people to seek psychotherapists' assistance? How can psychotherapy help them to understand themselves and their families and friends better, and to conduct themselves in ways that would benefit their relationships? – I would argue that they nevertheless apply to social, political, economic and cultural changes as well. How writers engage with the nature of change, and the intensity of the feelings it engenders in them and their respective communities, depends on how individual writers perceive the change, on what they see as its most compelling challenges and possible prospects.

Generally, though, as Pike has noted, the "idea of the city seems to trigger conflicting impulses, positive and negative, conscious and unconscious. At a very deep level, the city seems to express our culture's restless dream about its inner conflicts and inability to resolve them. On a more conscious level, this ambivalence expresses itself in mixed feelings of pride, guilt, love, fear, and hate toward the city" (1981:8). The ambivalence often articulated in literature, as he explains, results from a deeply held ambivalence towards human civilisation and culture. One can imagine, for example, the pride with which America would have held up the World Trade Centre as its symbol of civilisation. Contrast this with the fact that, come 11 September 2001, the World Trade Centre gets hit by aeroplanes in what is, even now, often referred to as the most spectacular terrorist attack on any civilisation. What was a symbol of advancement, a source of pride, now comes to represent fear in the hearts of many, even as it simultaneously serves as a rallying point for American patriotism in the fight against this perceived terrorism. What kinds of literature would the attacks on the World Trade Centre influence?

Or one may like to take a different example, namely Johannesburg. Johannesburg's central business district has, throughout the 1990s, seen a steady decline in its status as the centre of business in South Africa. Major businesses have moved from the inner city to its north, especially to Sandton and, to some extent, Midrand. This change has been accompanied by an equally steady increase in the number of hawkers in the inner city. These days the inner city is generally perceived as a centre of crime and filth rather than the centre of business and affluence, although there is, at the same time, attempts by the Gauteng provincial government to reposition it as the hub of cultural activity; indeed, Newtown, where the famous Market Theatre is located, has been singled out for development and rejuvenation for this purpose. In terms of population, Johannesburg has seen many blacks – both local and from other African countries – come to settle in the inner city and its neighbouring suburbs of Hillbrow, Berea and Doornfontein, which initially were reserved for whites (I will return to Hillbrow later in the discussion). Here, then, one again sees a set of complex developments and attitudes to the city, developments and attitudes that are bound to find their way into literature on the city of Johannesburg.

Pike's discussion, and the examples of the World Trade Centre and Johannesburg above, highlight one of the most important aspects of the city: its capacity to always change, both in its physical structure and social fabric. Physically, as the city becomes "more complex", "the ways of seeing it [also] become more difficult" (Lehan 1998:8), a complexity that is not made any easier to articulate by the fact that, as the city changes physically, its buildings, streets, monuments and other artefacts come to represent and symbolise different things to different observers and inhabitants. This complexity simultaneously applies to how one sees the city as its social fabric diversifies and becomes more complex. This general difficulty is then reflected in the ambivalence of its discourses. Indeed, as Stephen Ross (1991), Pike and Lehan argue, the city itself could be viewed as a text that begs to be deciphered; as a text, different analysts and observers come to it with different experiences, different expectations, and various ways of reading it.

The city, in this sense, could be viewed as a form of discourse with which another form of discourse, namely literature, engages. The dialectic between the city and literature, then, becomes a complex one in that both require to be analysed; in such analyses, we discover "the dangerousness of discourse, not merely that we cannot entirely control it, but that in it we find the voids and negativities that inhabit our own being" (Ross

1991:29). Literature comes to reflect on these voids and negativities; similarly, it also simultaneously reflects on what is to be found in the city, including positive finds. Reading the city against literature and vice versa, then, would point to the positive and negative aspects, the limitations, as well as the possibilities of both forms of texts.

The points raised by Ross, Pike and Lehan make it clear why cities are of such interest to creative writers. Cities – or pockets of them – are often focused on in literature mainly because they are an embodiment of a major change, one or some of its aspects, or provide some radically significant exception to general social rules or expectations. In a similar vein, these changes result in new rules of life – what we sometimes call social disorder or chaos, before we become confortable with it – and new sets of expectations. Cities are spaces where diversities of changes and expectations are apparently at their most remarkable – although this does not necessarily mean that, blow by blow, city life is either better or worse than country life – which explains why they captivate the imagination and occasion much intellectual engagement and emotional excitement.

One of the reasons for Sophiatown looming large in South African literature, for example, has been the fact that it was one of the *mixed* areas in a country in which, during the apartheid days, places were defined as white, Indian, Coloured or black only. This is to say that Sophiatown was something of a glaring *anomaly*. There was, of course, also the fact of the influence of journalistic reporting, writing informed by careful investigation and the acute familiarity of many *Drum* magazine journalists with Sophiatown. The journalists also contributed short stories and poems about the township. Further, as Michael Chapman observes, "The stories in *Drum* of the 1950s mark the *substantial* beginning, in South Africa, of the modern black short story: Prior to the appearance between 1951 and 1958 of over 90 stories, only a few by black South Africans existed in the 'anonymous' oral tradition of folk-tale" (2001:183, my emphasis).

Another reason for the attention focused on Sophiatown might have been that "urbanisation has often seemed '*spectacular*' in its violence and crime, as well as in its political mobilisation" (2001: 226, my emphasis). John Matshikiza's introduction to *The Drum Decade* draws the reader's attention to "the high life and bitter end of the gangster; the blunt, *zol*-fired world of the tsotsi, not so many years older than me, but light years ahead in his swaggering confidence, and as fast as a bullet in the black and white sneakers on his feet – glamour I could only dream about" (2001[1989]:ix). A very good instance of political drama is perhaps the forced removals of the people of Sophiatown to Meadowlands, a section of what came to be widely known as the South Western Townships or Soweto. Indeed, this sense of the spectacular has been mediated extremely well in various writings, including Can Themba's requiem for the township (1972), as well as in the workshopped play, *Sophiatown* (1988).

This forced removal of people from Sophiatown to Soweto in turn put the latter in the spotlight as a place of much political activity. For example, another spectacular form of violence, the 1976 Soweto uprisings, led to other literary works, such as Sipho Sepamla's novel, *A Ride in the Whirlwind* (1981). If for Dickens and Blake, London was an embodiment of industrialisation, Sophiatown and Soweto – and, for similar reasons, District Six in Cape Town and Marabastad in Pretoria (see Es'kia Mphahlele's *Down Second Avenue* [1959] for an unsparing depiction of this Pretoria slum, with its night curfews that kept its black inhabitants running, its shebeens, its emergent jazz and bioscope culture at the Columbia Dance Hall and so on) – in the imagination of many South African writers, have been microcosms of the struggle in which the apartheid state apparatus and its opponents played out their political drama. The two are also often presented as sites of pain, alienation and frustration, while simultaneously serving as anchors of hope in the possibilities of the future.

The ambivalence of representations of the city, or pockets of them, could be explained, according to Pike, by the fact that they are an illustration of what humanity is capable of – as demonstrated by its past and present physical structures and social practices – while this engagement with the past and the present is also in part an attempt to engage with the future. The best and the worst of the past, and what lies between the two extremes, blend into the present, and both are then marshalled to reflect on the possibilities and likely challenges of the future. Indeed, Pike talks of the cities as the meeting points of heaven, hell and earth in the minds of many of their inhabitants and observers (1981:6-7).

Despite the attractions – whether positive or negative – of change in the city, change in some pockets of certain cities is not always recorded as carefully or comprehensively as one might expect. One of the striking examples, for me, is Hillbrow, which shares a boundary with the inner city of Johannesburg. Comprehending, and accounting for, the scarcity of literary books on Hillbrow, given its reputation, is difficult. Despite the scarcity of Hillbrow literature, the neighbourhood has always provided shelter to highly literate people who could have addressed themselves to it in critical and sustained writing. Further, I must point out that Hillbrow has a spectacular history, too, or at least a history that is sufficiently interesting and colourful to merit a number of major literary works. As Alan Morris points out, "Hillbrow is one of the *very few* neighbourhoods in South Africa that, despite the Group Areas Act of 1950, *moved from being an all-white neighbourhood (in terms of flat-dwellers) to being predominantly black*" (1999:3, my emphasis)[2] – a remarkable historical change. Even if this was not the case, the neighbourhood seems to have had advantages, or disadvantages, that could have attracted significant literary attention. Its establishment itself, or at least some advertisements of it, are dramatic. Take this one for example: "On 24 July 1895 a full-page advertisement in a Johannesburg newspaper announced the sale by auction of 466 stands in the new 'residential estate', Hillbrow, 'the healthiest and most fashionable suburb of Johannesburg . . . within two minutes of Hospital Hill'" (cited in Morris 1999: 6).

Apparently the sale of the stands went remarkably fast, and, since it was initially not intended as a commercial or entertainment space, stand-alone residential houses were soon erected in the neighbourhood. Blocks of flats were introduced in the area in the

1920s. Even then, the blocks were few and not very high because there were restrictions on the height of buildings one could erect in the vicinity of Johannesburg. The Johannesburg City Council only lifted the restrictions in 1946. This led to an increase in the blocks of flats being built. Two decades – the 1950s and 1960s – were enough time to ensure, by the early 1970s, the virtual disappearance of private houses from Hillbrow, which would no doubt have led to an increase in the number of people coming to live in the area, as well as to a stronger sense of social change (more diversity, more sense of action, more drama concentrated in this small suburb). A former resident of Hillbrow told me, when we launched *Welcome To Our Hillbrow* in Grahamstown, in July 2001, that he remembered the suburb, in the 1950s and 1960s, as a "humble village". The 1970s would have seen a change in this identity of Hillbrow as a humble village, and of Hillbrowers as fellow villagers.

By 1970, Indians and Coloureds, seeking land because of shortage in the Indian- and Coloured-designated areas, were moving into Hillbrow, initially tentatively, and later in droves. Morris cites the 1970 census which estimates that the inhabitants of Hillbrow at the time comprised 10 517 whites, 17 Coloureds, 8 Indians and 1 095 Africans (blacks). Blacks were housed in the rooms on the rooftops of the blocks of flats. They were not, per se, inhabitants in the sense that they were welcome: they were there simply because they were employed by the owners or tenants of some of these flats. Indeed, the white inhabitants did not welcome even Indians and Coloureds, except that they were supposedly more tolerable than blacks. In some localities, even Indians and Coloureds preferred that Africans be removed, forcibly if need be (Nieftagodien 1995:51).

At any rate, a telling story of the generally negative treatment of the Indians and Coloureds is to be found in that they sometimes had to resort to legal defences against their eviction from Hillbrow. In one case, Judge Goldstone provided a particularly far-reaching court judgement: "The integration of the Johannesburg inner city was dramatically hastened in December 1982 when, in a landmark court case, *State versus Govender*, Judge Goldstone concluded that the notion that a person convicted under the Group Areas Act [of 1950] was compelled to vacate his dwelling was unjust and that this practice had to be halted." Goldstone was concerned that people were evicted despite the fact that no alternative arrangements had been made for their accommodation. Only if it could be proven that satisfactory arrangements had been or could be made, Goldstone argued, was it reasonable to evict illegal inhabitants. If the government had sought through the Group Areas Act to make "segregation . . . compulsory and comprehensive" (Nieftagodien 1995:51), the likes of Goldstone proved to be stumbling blocks in the way of this government objective.

The implications of Goldstone's judgement have to be understood in the context that, from the time it was passed in 1950 – it took at least seven years for the government to implement it – the Group Areas Act, as Nieftagodien argues, had always had opposition from various sectors of the population. For example, throughout the 1950s and 1960s, the South African Indian Congress has used loopholes in the Act to delay its full implementation in various localities. Even some municipalities objected to the Act, especially those municipalities that were dominated by more liberal parties such as the United Party in Uitenhage. This party had some sympathy for Chinese and Indian businesses, and since the implementation of the Act would dislocate them, and thus lead to problems in their municipalities, they had to raise objections to the central government. On the part of the government, it took a while before it decided the number of racial groups that would suffice for the active implementation of the Act. The Population Registration Act of 1950, which identified three racial groups – white, coloured and natives – was deemed inadequate; subsequently, the "coloured" category was subdivided into Coloured, Indian and Chinese for the purpose of the Group Areas Act. Such administrative complexities on the part of the central government, as well as the political and commercial considerations on the part of the municipalities, coupled with the legal loopholes in the Act, led to a constant refinement of the Group Areas Act, through amendments, over a period of about two decades. Where its implementation succeeded, as it finally did nationally through the removal of "black spots" – that is, areas in which people of different racial groups could live together – such as Sophiatown, and the establishment of various "group areas" such as Soweto, the Act had a devastating effect, as many people "were forcibly removed from their homes and herded into segregated areas" (Nieftagodien 1995:59).

The government succeeded in this move in part because the opposition movements, such as the African National Congress, did not have a well-organised mechanism or plan of countering it. In addition, some members of the population, blacks included, saw the opportunity to own houses that the government had built in newly established townships – no matter how small and unsuitable for good living standards – as an improvement on their position as squatters or tenants who were financially abused by their landlords. The result of all this was that many group areas were finally successfully formed, but subsequently became overcrowded and "residents were subjected to a much higher cost of living than they were accustomed to" (Nieftagodien 1995:157). If only for this reason, people would wish to have more land, at affordable costs, for their occupation.

Complicating matters further was that from the mid-1960s onwards the government invested more in the development of the homeland policies than in the development of the urban group areas. This inevitably led to further decline in the standards of living for many blacks in the townships. As further deterioration took place and civil opposition to both the homelands system and the urban group areas became more organised in the late 1960s and throughout the 1970s, and as the National Party came under increasing pressure to accommodate Indians and Coloureds, the Group Areas Act was bound to be undermined. It is in this context – rather oversimplified here – that the significance of Goldstone's judgement must be understood; it provided some of the prohibited inhabitants of Hillbrow with some sound legal ground on which they could defend themselves against the government.

Goldstone's judgement set a tone: it became increasingly difficult to evict inhabitants on the grounds of the Group Areas Act. Some people and organisations, as the judgement shows, were at any rate willing, prepared and able to defend themselves in a court of law. Also, in terms of the general politics, the National Party sought broader support from the limited representations that Indians and Coloureds had in parliament. The National Party was aware that the Conservative Party was increasingly becoming its serious competitor, and that it would no longer suffice to totally disregard, or even ill-treat, Indians and Coloureds who held some potential base for wider National Party support. The National Party was thus caught in a terrible dilemma: having to persuade the white electorate that it would deal severely with law-breakers such as Indians and Coloureds in Hillbrow and elsewhere who were disregarding one of the greatest cornerstones of the apartheid system, the Group Areas Act, and simultaneously having to seek some semblance of friendship with these law-breakers. The Goldstone judgement also meant that blacks who moved into Hillbrow could no longer be evicted easily.

Another complicating factor was that one of the most important companies owning and letting blocks of flats in Hillbrow and its adjoining suburbs, Anglo American Property Services, a subsidiary of Anglo American Corporation, used its economic position to question and challenge the state on the logic of continuing to discriminate against Indians, Coloureds and blacks even if they could afford to pay their rent. Anglo American Property Services finally decided to allow people of all races who could pay to rent flats in its biggest block, Highpoint, and in other blocks. The mid-1980s saw a remarkable movement of blacks into Hillbrow. It took just under a decade and, in 1993, 62% of the Hillbrow population was estimated to be black. In addition to the Goldstone judgement, this movement was further given dramatic impetus by the lifting of influx control in June 1986, which meant that blacks would no longer be arrested under the pass laws. With the unbanning of political organisations in 1990, the idea of racial discrimination became so discredited that, in August of the same year, blacks were allowed to buy and own flats in Hillbrow. By that time, white flight from the apparently encroaching black danger of Hillbrow was high. A 1996 census shows the population of Hillbrow, Joubert Park, Berea and the central business district to be about 95% black (including Indian and Coloured) and only about 5% white, a statistic that has probably changed fairly significantly by now.

But what did Hillbrow represent for some of its most recent inhabitants (in the 1980s and 1990s), and for the general population of South Africa? Alan Morris found that most South African respondents in his research emphasised that they came to Hillbrow because they fled violence in the black Johannesburg townships such as Soweto and Alexandra. There were also political activists avoiding police harassment in these townships. Further, people living in shacks and garages in the townships sought better accommodation. And, of course, there were employers who were keen on assisting their employees to find better accommodation despite the state's restrictions. In addition, Hillbrow was for many people close to their workplace, being within walking distances of the central business district and Braamfontein. Finally, for some, with the lifting of the Group Areas Act and influx control, Hillbrow is believed to have become the meeting point for black prostitutes, in search of richer clients across the racial divide. It is possible that by the end of 1994 Hillbrow accommodated at least 1 000 prostitutes.

"The Hillbrow mosaic", as Morris aptly calls it, shows that throughout its long history Hillbrow was never, and is not now, the homogenous suburb that people sometimes seem to suggest it is. Its heterogeneity extended to its complex, and what sometimes appeared to be its contradictory, social values. As more people moved into Hillbrow, they found occasions to open up commercial and entertainment outlets. Because of the way it was established, it has always invited diverse social groups: some of these people, because their families were not living with them, could afford to be free of moral, cultural and other social restrictions and restraints. They were free in their style of dress and conduct. New outlets facilitated further activities, and therefore more diversity, in the neighbourhood.

The social diversity of Hillbrow provided opportunities for a new consciousness. New consciousness of the type I am referring to, Du Bois shows in his discussion of race relations in America, becomes noticeable once one becomes aware of "double consciousness, this sense of always looking at one's self through the eyes of others, of measuring one's soul by the tape of a world that looks on in amused contempt and pity" (1969 [1903]:45). Du Bois's context is what he regards as America's racism as he wrote his book at the dawn of the twentieth century. A more generous view of new consciousness need not be as negative, although, for some inhabitants of Hillbrow, his sentiment would seem to ring painfully true. The involvement of Indians, Coloureds and blacks would only have contributed to making the Hillbrow mosaic much more diversified and, perhaps, less understood, since new consciousness may or may not mean enhanced understanding that goes with critical analysis and general engagement.

But Hillbrow has been a neighbourhood of professionals, students, academics and other social categories, including working-class people. In such a social milieu, perhaps the notion of double consciousness does not really capture the true sense of the far more multilayered consciousness, with each social group serving as a mirror for itself and the other groups. With the increasing diversity and new consciousness, crime appears to have become increasingly obvious, although some of the stories of crime are exaggerated by sentiment. The Johannesburg police are not innocent in spreading this negative and overstated sentiment, as we will see later. If, for many whites of Hillbrow, the diversity became scary, a lowering of standards of living, then it has generally become something else now. The 1990s saw the coming in large numbers of what Alan Morris refers to as "the new victims" of discrimination: black Africans from other African countries.

Kadima and Kalombo (1995) estimated that in mid-1995 there were about 23 000 Congolese in the Johannesburg area, most of them living in Johannesburg's innercity neighbourhoods. Hillbrow was a primary location. There are no official figures for Nigerian immigrants except the statistic that between 1 January 1994 and 30 April 1997 a total of

2 862 Nigerians had applied for political asylum (information supplied by the Department of Home Affairs, April 1997). From discussions with informants, and taking this figure into consideration, it can be concluded that by the beginning of 1997 there were probably in the region of 3 000 Nigerians living in Johannesburg's innercity. Almost all lived in Hillbrow or neighbouring Berea.

There were, of course, other Africans besides the Congolese and the Nigerians. As Morris points out, reliable figures on illegal migrants are impossible to know, but there are many.

For over a century, Hillbrow has been a neighbourhood of immigrants (from other urban and rural parts of South Africa and even from Europe, and now increasingly from other parts of Africa), people renting flats, in addition to those who could afford to buy. Once settled in Hillbrow, the immigrants of the neighbourhood – of all social classes and racial groups – tended to regard new, subsequent immigration as a lowering of standards of living. Even landlords, as Morris persuasively argues, have tended increasingly to neglect the condition of their blocks of flats. Now, with banks having redlined Hillbrow, many people cannot buy flats there due to a lack of adequate financial resources. Those who can afford would mostly hesitate anyway, given that they are unlikely to view buying as an investment. Besides the lost interest of financial institutions, government does not seem to show much interest in the place either, except when it is time for occasional "visible policing", when there will be a big show of uniformed police officers erecting road blocks and making their raids, arresting many people, an unknown number of whom do not, in fact, even stay in Hillbrow, but nevertheless contribute substantially toward the darkening of the image of the neighbourhood. Hence the general physical degeneration of the neighbourhood continues.

Because Hillbrow is accommodating more and more people as time goes on, it is likely that the degeneration will not stop unless some planned intervention happens. Perceived as a suburb whose inhabitants are in transit – people from rural and other urban areas seeking education and jobs, and subsequently better suburbs; or foreigners seeking refuge or education in the city, or here illegally and involved in drug-trafficking and other unlawful businesses – the Johannesburg Metropolitan government has, to my knowledge, no specific, carefully-considered medium-to-long-term plans for Hillbrow, this at a time when its population is now estimated at over 100 000 (and possibly over 200 000 over weekends), according to Tintswalo Hlungwani, Director of the Hillbrow Community Project and the Co-ordinator of Public Health / Centre for Health Science Education of the University of the Witwatersrand.

I have already indicated that literary works on Hillbrow are scarce, and that this scarcity is difficult to account for, given the factors that have led many South African writers to explore other pockets of Johannesburg in their works, and the compelling history of Hillbrow that merits such attention. There is thus much that interested writers still have to do with regard to the suburb. But what, exactly, are the challenges that writers wishing to explore Hillbrow may face? To answer this question, I suggest, is partly to understand the role of literature in a changing society. As already indicated, problems and pain lead to various feelings and responses in people. The variety of feelings and responses extend to the way individual writers deal with the challenges of change in their communities. Whether a literary artefact appears to betray a strong sense of resignation, to inspire hope and encouragement, or to celebrate, entertain, criticise and so on, the daunting process that writers have to confront lies in raising critical awareness of, or raising a serious debate on, social, cultural, political, economic and other issues that they deem to be relevant to themselves, their communities and their prospective reading publics. This task is difficult because writers constantly have to confront stereotypes and melodramas, and raise the general awareness or debate in such a way that the stereotypes and melodramas can be recognised for what they are, while simultaneously aiming to raise the awareness or debate to a higher level that transcends the stereotypes and melodramas. This should go beyond providing new information, or reporting on recent events or incidents – a role addressed skilfully and often sufficiently quickly by the media.

Stereotypes and melodramas are a result of many converging factors. Perhaps one of the persistent factors in the development and promotion of stereotypes and melodramas is incidental experience or observation, which is then generalised without any rigorous attempt to research and assess the extent to which it may or may not be representative. As we shall see later in the chapter, this has been particularly true in the case of Hillbrow, which many people know, although not as many have actually experienced first-hand. Incidental experiences or observations, especially if appealing to a sense of the dramatic, tend to easily find all kinds of outlets, conduits that take them into the general public imagination. This, then, leads me to the second factor in the development and promotion of stereotypes and melodramas, namely the various media of their transmission and, inextricably linked to this, the people who use the media – as transmitters or recipients – as well as how they get transmitted and received. Indeed, it is through the media, mainly print journalism, and radio and television broadcasts that nearly everyone in South Africa knows about Hillbrow. Oral history and gossip are, of course, also very active agents of this spreading of knowledge about the place and its associations, as migrants and sojourners make their input.

Generally, well-researched academic and critical literary books on Hillbrow are scarce – in comparison to Sophiatown and Soweto, for example. It is my impression that this scarcity of *well-researched* or sustained *critical engagement* with Hillbrow has contributed substantially to the general idea of Hillbrow as a monster – with crime, drug-dealing, prostitution and other attributes that are generally seen as social vices – as its biological components. My emphasis on *well-researched* and *critical engagement* stems from my awareness that what one knows, and how one represents what one knows, are two separate things. I suggest, in other words, that the negative stereotypes about Hillbrow, while no doubt having some solid basis in people's experiences of the neighbourhood, also have a lot to do with how they have been spread. The media or people who, on average, would not have done much research on the neighbourhood have mainly contributed substantially to its general public imagination. Partly for this reason, and partly because of the media and people's tendency toward dramatisation, the negative aspects of Hillbrow have seldom been subjected to critical engagement; equally, some of the neighbourhood's positive aspects have not been noted with due appreciation.

Just as, during the Niger expedition of the early 1800s, Victorian explorers and writers, and their British society generally, tended to "darken" Africa, and subsequently turned the darkened continent into "a mirror, on one level reflecting what the Victorians wanted to see – a heroic and saintly self-image" (Brantlinger 1986 [1985]: 217), many stories of Hillbrow, fabricated or otherwise, are coloured by the desire of the narrators to implicitly suggest that, as morally upright, social critics, the narrators are better than the actors in that perceived theatre of grime, crime, vice and shame. The narrators in question comprise, among many others, journalists, some members of the South African Police Service, politicians, and members of the general South African public. It is to these narrators that literary responses (I am not even making a value judgement on the moral or literary qualities here) have, as already suggested, been scarce. This scarcity is difficult to comprehend, especially since a closer look at their narratives in relation to evidence should also, to borrow Brantlinger's apt words on the Victorians, cast "the ghostly shadows of guilt and regression" on the part of the narrators, who are often energetic actors in elevating the sensational at the expense of proper understanding.

Yet it seems to me that creative writers are developing deep interest in the ever-changing Hillbrow as worthy of critical engagement. (I exclude films and documentaries, such as *Hillbrow Kids*, from my discussion.) In poetry, for example, Siphiwe ka Ngwenya portrays a Hillbrow of "tricksters & pimps", "thighs & bums / Of your heartless angels", "Your sagging breasts heaving to bank notes" (1999:36). A subtle note of the complexity of Hillbrow's identity is glimpsed in Ka Ngwenya's concession that Hillbrow "hide[s] the poor, the criminal & *forsaken*" (1999: 37, my emphasis), which, in my reading, need not suggest that they are destructive and, therefore, necessarily dangerous. While the poem does not say who the forsaken are, who has forsaken them, and under what circumstances, it is clear that Hillbrow, in its own way, provides some sanctuary, and that people who do not live or stay in Hillbrow bear some responsibility for the neglect of their fellow human beings, a responsibility that leads them to discover Hillbrow's sanctuary.

Kgafela oa Magogodi (2000) broadens this critical look at Hillbrow, teasing us with a broader poetic canvass. In the poem, "thy condom come", we read:

> "if / god was the mother / fell pregnant / on joseph's extramarital / semen / would mankind / dismiss her for a prostitute / . . . / if the creator dressed the bible / in red lipstick & black pantyhose / would the patriarch / on the pulpit / be led into temptation & pray / thy condom come to our hillbrow" (2000:55).

Apart from demanding that we re-examine the way in which we view prostitution and sexuality generally, Oa Magogodi, interestingly, opts to implicate us (through our interpretations of the Bible) in the reinforcement of the unquestioning, negative perceptions of prostitution, and to suggest, implicitly, that we tend to turn a blind eye to sexual misdemeanours taking place in areas other than those that we choose to stigmatise. Oa Magogodi expands his focus further in another poem, "varara" (a street name for HIV/Aids), in which he brings issues of rape, child abuse, xenophobia and HIV/Aids, and the society's contribution toward developing and promoting stereotypes, into the picture:

> "some say varara ke lekwerekwere / came galloping down the hillbrow / to eat our women. / . . . / some rape babies / to cheat varara . . . / they say varara / is a prostitute with an artytude / . . ./ some say varara is the wrath of badimo. / . . . / some say horizons are so viagra varara / will not stop til thy condom come" (2000:56-57).

Clearly, if "varara / is a prostitute with an artytude", it is because people, and not varara itself, use the art of spreading both varara and this general attitude of denial, accusation and counter-accusation, rather than of honestly accepting responsibility for their own involvement in the spreading of viruses and diseases as well as sterotypes. Oa Magogodi's overview of some of the issues that go into identity formation and construction of stereotypes is made especially interesting, for me, by his obvious fascination with topical issues – issues such as the general talk about the significance of condoms in curbing the speedy spreading of HIV/Aids, although some people would still claim that varara is "more slippery than chauke"; the rape of babies (less reported about when "varara" was published in 2000); and xenophobia (note the negative references to *Makwerekwere* in the poem).

In fiction, the publication of K. Sello Duiker's second novel, *The Quiet Violence of Dreams*, introduces to us one of its characters, Tshepo, who at the end of the book lives in Hillbrow, "with all its decay" (2001:452). Tshepo claims to be at home with the children, as well as both legal and illegal foreigners he finds in Hillbrow – "so fragile, so cultured and beautiful, our foreign guests" (2001:454), a sentiment many South Africans are unlikely to entertain, especially those represented in "varara" by the voice that associates them with HIV/Aids. Indeed, Tshepo, looking at the whole wide and fascinating spectrum of the Hillbrow society, especially the children he works with, "sense[s] that God can't be one story. He is a series of narratives" (2001:546).

Ivan Vladislavič's *The Restless Supermarket* (2001), offers an exploration of Hillbrow when apartheid was collapsing and, in the view of its ageing main character and narrator, Aubrey Tearle, social standards in Hillbrow – and everywhere in the country – were collapsing, a social decline partly reflected, in his opinion, in the way in which people increasingly made mistakes in their writing, with spelling errors in *The Star* providing a particularly interesting example. Tearle, true to his egocentric personality, goes as far as to imagine that he is the only "gentleman" left in Hillbrow, and he spends much time reading newspapers and other documents to spot and record grammatical or spelling errors, and writing letters to *The Star* to lament the poor social standards, not just in Hillbrow, but generally. *The Star* itself is not immune to his criticism, especially the "rot" that found its way into the "death notices": "The rot reached such unnatural proportions that it began to subvert the purpose of the service itself, and the whole enterprise acquired the tone of a macabre joke" (2001:65).

In his pompous way, Tearle comes to acknowledge that the media, if not checked in its own tracks when it goes wrong, can bear bitter fruit in society, like the "unhappy surprise of those left behind when they came to clip their remembrances" (2001:65). These are errors that can come to sadden individuals, but when the media deal in misinformation, or merely "[n]ew information, fresh news reported, streamed from the [television] set at specified times each day, gathering and subsiding in the official channels to a rhythm as pacific as an ocean" (2001:145), the result is often a general misleading of the public, and the development and promotion of ignorance and stereotypes. Tearle is recording change, "[a]n era [of apartheid] ending" (2001:127), a change that he claims to have seen coming "before anyone else in the Café Europa, and possibly in the whole of Hillbrow (although I wouldn't lay claim to more territory than that)" (2001:127). Aubrey Tearle records, among many things: the president (P W Botha) announcing his resignation, although, on television, he does not tell the public that he has had a stroke; the headquarters of important companies leaving Johannesburg's central business district in favour of Rosebank and Sandton; new suburbs rising unexpectedly while old ones decay; and some old suburbs being resurrected in the form of restaurants and antique shops (2001:128).

But Tearle's sharp eye, and a sustained sense of dry humour, cannot fail also to observe and analyse social movements. Here are a few examples: Germans, English and other Europeans (a group he refers to as Bogeymen, Bohemians, Philistines); the influx of Moodleys and Naidoos (representative of Indians) into Mayfair, returning to the city after spending time in their racially designated areas such as Lenasia (they would have been in Fordsburg, Pageview and the like, much closer to the city, before going to Lenasia); a "growing number of Hi's, Ho's and Fats [representative of Chinese and Japanese] in the Bedfordview area, and influx of -ic's and -wiczs and -ova's [representative of Polish, Hungarians and others] into all areas"; and, in his opinion, "that most striking of all [which] seemed less of a trend than an *aberration* . . . a Merope [representing black South Africans] with a Hillbrow [rather than a Soweto] address" (2001:129, my emphasis). Where sex is concerned, in Café Europa itself, "[a]lways women, in the beginning, on the arms of sallow-skinned men wearing gold jewellery and open-neck shirts . . . [Continental and Slav] men with overstuffed wallets and easy habits" (2001:136). As he summarises the situation, there "an historical migration was afoot, comparable to the great scattering of tribes before Chaka, the King of the Zulus" (2001:129), and he sees in all these movements some of the major causes of overcrowding and littering in the city, especially in Hillbrow. Ironically, while proclaiming himself a proponent of freedom of movement, he also acknowledges his resentment of these movements in the world that, he says, is not ideal.

What is fascinating about Tearle is how he acknowledges that he draws, for some of his information, on newspapers, television and radio, and his love, telephone directories; yet he constantly calls attention to the need for scrutiny and analysis, rather than mere information. Subtly, Ivan Vladislavič, offers readers Tearle not just as a sharp observer, but also, ironically, as a prejudiced and highly opinionated character. The reader is thus able to see through Tearle, to appreciate his keen sense of observation while remaining critical of his many, often racist biases, as well as linguistic conservatism, as reflected in his persistent urge and endeavours to keep both written and spoken English free from the perceived falling standards. Despite his criticism of apartheid, Tearle seems to mourn its demise, as this, to his mind, intensifies racial and ethnic mixing – often accompanied by a decline in moral and linguistic standards – which encourages and leads to overcrowding and littering in what he appears to regard as the territory of "respectable" people, people with "standards", like himself. Interestingly, Tearle is both an observer and a ruthless critic of other people's prejudices, too.

Overall, I read *The Restless Supermarket* as an extremely accomplished novel that is more than a record of social and political change; it is also a document that eschews an easy embrace of some commonly held ideas or stereotypes. Change, Vladislavič shows, is far more complex than most people are willing to see, understand or admit. Indeed, when, toward the end of the novel, Tearle finds himself in trouble, he finds it difficult to comprehend his situation because it is what he thinks of as his former friends, the white, former regulars to Café Europa – this café in which the regulars and newcomers are so mixed as to be almost indistinguishable – that prove to be his utmost enemies. They make it clear to him that he has treated them with arrogance and condescension – which his "proofreading", to borrow his own phrasing, of their styles of dress, speech and manners basically amounted to – for a long time. *The Restless Supermarket* is constantly asking questions, forcing the reader to wonder at, to reflect on, to confront and challenge their own deeply-held values, stereotypes and prejudices. Given an opportunity to write another novel – or any other literary text – there is a possibility that Vladislavič may come to wonder about and question afresh, or even to contradict, some of the issues and questions that he raises and discusses so critically, bravely and satisfyingly in this novel. Equally, certain ideas that he only glanced at could be afforded more space, more analysis, and even be reinforced in a subsequent work. For example, Vladislavič's character, Tearle, makes some brief references to blacks from other African countries – such as Mozambique – which, given the temporal scope of the novel, he tends to marginalise in the novel. (In an engaging, unpublished story on Hillbrow, Ernest Pineth, a black international student at the University of the Witwatersrand, has highlighted that foreigners are not just abused by locals; they also inflict pain on their fellow foreigners. This line of writing by an insider to their circles could yield another major piece of writing on Hillbrow and its neighbours such as Berea, Yeoville, Braamfontein or the city centre itself.)

This, in my view, is the role of literature in a changing society: to ask questions, to probe, to wonder, to challenge and, when appropriate, to contradict (including contradicting one's own earlier opinions and sentiments), to reinforce, to celebrate and entertain. In the end, it comes to the admission that, as Chinua Achebe would put it, life is so complex that one constantly has to resist dogma (1986). Günter Grass has also had occasion to reflect on this. Provocative and funny as usual, Grass wonders "What makes books – and with them writers – so dangerous that church and state, politburos and the mass media feel the need to oppose them?" And he answers:

> Silencing and worse are seldom the result of direct attacks on the reigning ideology. Often all it takes is a literary allusion to the idea that truth exists only in the plural – that there is no such thing as a single truth but only a multitude of truths – to make the defenders of one or another truth sense danger, mortal danger. Then there is the problem that writers are by denifition unable to leave the past in peace: they are quick to open closed wounds, peer behind closed doors, find skeletons in the cupboard, consume sacred cows or, as in the case of Jonathan Swift, offer up Irish children, "stewed, roasted, baked, or boiled", to the kitchens of the English nobility. In other words, nothing is sacred to them, not even capitalism, and that makes them offensive, even criminal. But worst of all they refuse to make common cause with the victors of history: they take pleasure milling about the fringes of the historical process with the losers, who have plenty to say but no platform to say it on. By giving them a voice, they call the victory into question, by associating with them, they join ranks with them (Grass 1999:5).

It is implicit in the overall thrust of Grass's argument that writers cannot give voice to the voiceless, to those apparently on the fringes of historical processes, unless they have a deep understanding of the historical processes themselves. From this angle, it also follows that, having a broad understanding of historical processes, the writer, even when supposedly speaking on behalf of the marginalised, cannot quite speak the same tongue with them. The attempt to resist various forms of dogma is all-pervasive and uncompromising. With regard to Hillbrow, a most dangerous dogma is inherent in the popular stereotype of the neighbourhood as nothing but evil and dangerous, as if there are not many good people inhabiting its space. There is also dogma of a different kind, I suggest, embedded in a blissful complacency that fails to recognise other places, other people, other identities for what they are: *complex. The Restless Supermarket* captures this sense of complexity quite well. In this sense, Vladislavič does not sacrifice subtlety of thought in favour of melodramatic representation.

For better or for worse, societies themselves are always changing. These changes complicate their already complex identities. I suppose, though, that when we talk about changing societies, what we actually refer to are not the changes in themselves, but certain types of changes; dramatic and/or far-reaching changes, perhaps, that lead to heightened individual and social awareness of themselves. For the mere reason that there are always social changes, no matter how seemingly small and subtle, I feel that literature has a responsibility to remain sensitive to the importance of details – of psychological, emotional, social, cultural, political and other natures – and to continually reflect on and articulate these subtleties. This is an open agenda, if you like. The exact details of how participants handle this agenda will differ from one individual writer's text to another, from one writer to another, from one social context to another, and from one time framework to another. In Mphahlele's words, "a writer must continually ask himself what his role is in relation to what his society is going through . . . [T]he writer seldom, to the best of my knowledge, thinks of abandoning his art because it is powerless against forces that destroy human life . . . [H]e feels that if writing is what he can do best, even when he is not necessarily producing literature of direct protest, he has to obey the inner compulsion to give words to what he feels and thinks" (1984:220). Mphahlele's mild phrasing here, written during the apartheid period, might give a false impression that he regards literature as a weak form of social and political engagement. However, having borne the brunt of censorship and political intimidation in South Africa, he knows how demanding, risky and painful the devotion and commitment to writing can be. But, equally importantly, he also knows its joys and pleasures, and its capacity to free the mind and feelings from the cruel claws of various forms of dogma. It is this freedom, and the vision of a future that it might help to shape, that I think is of utmost importance to realise in a changing society.

Notes

1 The quotation is borrowed from John Matshikiza's "Introduction" to *The Drum Decade*.
2 Morris's *Bleakness & Light: Inner-city Transition in Hillbrow, Johannesburg*, is the most comprehensive study of its kind, concentrating on the racial integration, as well as the subsequent flight of white residents from, and the influx of blacks from other African countries into, Hillbrow.

References

Achebe, Chinua. 1986. *Writers in Conversation: Chinua Achebe With Nuruddin Farah* (a video cassette). London: Institute of Contemporary Arts.

Blake, William. 1988. *Selected Poetry and Prose*. David Punter (ed.). London: Routledge.

Brantlinger, Patrick.1986 [1985]. "Victorians and Africans: The Genealogy of the Myth of the Dark Continent." In: Henry L Gates, Jr. (ed.). *"Race", Writing, and Difference*. Chicago & London: University of Chicago Press.

Chapman, Michael. 2001 [1989]. "More Than Telling a Story: *Drum* and its Significance in Black South African Writing." Michael Chapman (ed.). *The Drum Decade: Stories From the 1950s*, 2nd edition. Pietermaritzburg: University of Natal Press.

Dickens, Charles. 1971 [1853]. *Bleak House*. London: Penguin Books.

Du Bois, William E. B. 1969 [1903]. *The Souls of Black Folk*. New York: Signet Classics.

Duiker, K. Sello. 2001. *The Quiet Violence of Dreams*. Cape Town: Kwela Books.

Grass, Günter. 1999. "To Be Continued . . ." *Nobel Lecture – Literature 1999*, http://www.nobel.se/literature//aureates/1999/lecture-e.html.

Junction Avenue Theatre Company. 1988. *Sophiatown*. Cape Town, Johannesburg: David Philip, in association with Junction Avenue Press.

Ka Ngwenya, Siphiwe. 1999. "Hillbrow." In: Siphiwe ka Ngwenya et al., *Dirty Washing: Collective & Individual Poems*. Johannesburg: Botsotso Publishing.

Lehan, Richard. 1998. *The City in Literature: An Intellectual and Cultural History*. Berkeley, Los Angeles, London: University of California Press.

Matshikiza, John. 2001 [1989]. "Introduction." In: Michael Chapman (ed.). *The Drum Decade: Stories From the 1950s*, 2nd edition. Pietermaritzburg: University of Natal Press.

Morris, Alan. 1999. *Bleakness and Light: Inner-city Transition in Hillbrow, Johannesburg*. Johannesburg: Witwatersrand University Press.

Mphahlele, Es'kia. 1959. *Down Second Avenue*. London: Faber & Faber.

Mphahlele, Es'kia. 1984. *The Wanderers: An Autobiography 1957 – 1983*. Johannesburg: Ravan Press.

Mtshali, Mbuyiseni. 1971. *Sounds of a Cowhide Drum*. Johannesburg: Renoster Books.

Nieftagodien, Mohamed N. 1995. *The Making of Apartheid in Springs: Group Areas and Forced Removals*. Unpublished MA dissertation, University of the Witwatersrand.

Oa Magogodi, Kgafela. 2000. *Thy Condom Come*. Amsterdam: New Leaf.

Peck, M. Scott. 1990 [1983]. *The Road Less Travelled: The New Psychology of Love, Traditional Values and Spiritual Growth*. London: Arrow Books.

Pike, Burton. 1981. *The Image of the City in Modern Literature*. Princeton: Princeton University Press.

Ross, Stephen D. 1991. "Discourse, Polis, Finiteness, Perfection." In: Mar Ann Caws (ed.), *City Images: Perspectives From Literature, Philosophy, and Film*. New York: Gordon & Breach.

Serote, Mongane. 1984. "Alexandra." Beeton, D. R. et al. (eds.), *A University Anthology of English Poetry*. Cape Town: Oxford University Press.

Serote, Mongane. 1981. "What's in This 'Black' Shit." In: Michael Chapman (ed.). *A Century of South African Literature*. Johannesburg: Ad Donker.

Sepamla, Sipho. 1981. *A Ride in the Whirlwind*. Johannesburg: Ad Donker.

Themba, Can. 1972. *The Will to Die*. Selected by Roya Harrold and Donald Stuart. London: Heinemann.

Vladislavič, I. 2001. *The Restless Supermarket*. Cape Town: David Philip Publishers.

CHAPTER ELEVEN

Own/Other: Negotiating Cultural Ownership and Social Identity in the Postcolonial State

Julian David Jonker[1]

Miscast

On April 14, 1996, not quite two years after South Africa's first democratic elections, the South African National Gallery hosted the opening of an exhibition by artist and fine art lecturer Pippa Skotnes. The exhibition was titled *Miscast: Negotiating Khoisan History and Material Culture*, and was an attempt by Skotnes to portray, not Khoisan history and material culture, but the representations of the Khoisan that were constructed during the encounters between Khoisan and colonist, and what these representations tell about both European and Khoisan. Skotnes herself described the exhibition as "a critical and visual exploration of the term 'Bushman' and the various relationships that gave rise to it" (Skotnes 1996:18).

The *Mail & Guardian* reported at the time, "Artist Pippa Skotnes launched an exhibition about the oppression of Khoisan people – and found herself under attack for the same thing" (Rossouw 1996), as controversy quickly enveloped the event. Carmel Schrire noted shortly afterwards that the exhibition had "been the talk of the town, if not the country, ever since. It has attracted more interest, outrage, and passion than any other exhibit in the gallery's history, as well as in the history of the people it portrays" (1996).

Miscast brought together various representations of the Khoisan, from photographs taken by colonial settlers in the nineteenth century to more recent representations such as the photographs of Paul Weinberg and copies of rock art made by recent scholars. There were also the more horrific exhibits: portrayals of how the Khoisan body had become an object for scientific study, including live casts that had been made of Khoisan individuals and recovered for the exhibition by Skotnes. The exhibition was accompanied by a book of a similar title – *Miscast. Negotiating the Presence of Bushmen*[2] – an interdisciplinary anthology that brought together academic work interspersed with a "parallel text" containing historical documents, photographs and excerpts from the notebooks of Lucy Lloyd.[3]

A public forum was held just before the opening of the exhibition, and eleven groups representing Khoisan from across South Africa were invited. Some groups praised Skotnes for exposing their continuing plight, but she earned only scorn from the !Griqua National Conference of South Africa, as well as the !Hurikamma Cultural Movement, who said that they were:

> . . . sick and tired of naked brown people being exposed to the curious glances of rich whites in search of dinner-table conversation. At the exhibition we were exposed to yet another attempt to treat brown people as objects (Rossouw 1996).

One Khoisan representative voiced his opinion quite unequivocally at the conference:

> To show these things here is just as the people who did these things long ago. It is continuing the bad thing (cited in Davison 1998:159).

Rustum Kozain, writing in the *Southern African Review of Books*, came away profoundly unsettled by the effects of the exhibition, noting especially how the self-reflexivity and high postmodern self-consciousness of the exhibition rang false. "How do these quotations of quotations necessarily invent a new mode of representation?" demanded Kozain (1996).

The fiercest opposition to the exhibition was voiced by Yvette Abrahams, at the time in the History department of UCT and a member of the !Hurikamma Cultural Movement. Abrahams entered into a debate with Skotnes in the pages of the *Southern African Review of Books*,[4] and it is this debate which will serve as my starting point here. The debate concerned representations of the Khoisan people, and by whom and for what purposes these representations were deployed. Looking at the debate closely, the arguments can be seen to pivot around two focal issues: ownership and identity. *Miscast* will then serve here as a springboard for a meditation on the relationship between ownership and identity. Questions of identity flow naturally from the *Miscast* debate; in order to highlight how ownership figures in such arguments, it is helpful to turn to the related context of the debates around the legal protection of indigenous knowledge.

The Protection of Indigenous Knowledge Bill

The exploitation of indigenous "folklore" or culture has been one of the concerns of legal reform in postcolonial African states, and has recently been receiving attention at an international level by the United Nations Educational, Scientific and Cultural Organization (Unesco) and the World International Property Organization (WIPO). The issue is the use of "traditional" cultural expressions in contexts outside of their customary use, and by persons who do not belong to the originating communities. This use is generally for monetary gain; typical problems are that the original communities have not had any say in the use to which the expressions or derivatives of them have been put, or that compensation for their use has not been paid.

As Atencio López, president of the Napguana Association of Panama says, "indigenous designs are gradually gaining a foothold in fashion and on the runways, but with alien labels or marks that have nothing to do with our peoples . . . Finally, persons who have no connection with our peoples write, record and sell songs, legends and tales for commercial purposes with no concern for the copyright of the peoples affected" (López 1998:2).

A good example of such so-called "*ex situ* use" in South Africa is the domestic and international exploitation of Khoisan rock art. Rock art has been used in contexts ranging from international adverts to the walls of a coffee shop in Germany. Within South Africa, rock art has been used to decorate all kinds of objects: "T-shirts, postcards, writing paper, coffee mugs, table mats, fridge mats, key rings, stamps and telephone cards" (Dowson 1996:315). The ancient art form has even been used as part of the design scheme of the Lost City resort in the North West Province, where some walls have been "adorned by relatively carefully reproduced images of rock paintings that have been taken from a wide variety of popular books". These paintings are also present in the form of signs for public facilities; "[d]espite an unequivocal rock art 'feel', none of these is a re-production of a real rock painting; they are composites" (Dowson 1996:316).

Such activities, seen as an exploitation of indigenous forms of *cultural expression*, mirror the exploitation that has been taking place of indigenous *knowledge*[5] more broadly, especially with regard to medicinal knowledge. Questions about how to protect indigenous knowledge raise broader questions about the impact of modernity on societies that have most often been seen as pre-modern. Posey (1990) shows how there are fewer effective legal mechanisms to ensure the protection and compensation of outsider use of Amazonian Amerindian indigenous knowledge systems; the lack of economic benefits for these resources also leads to disregard by the younger generations of these knowledge systems and a turning to more economically secure but often ecologically destructive ways of life.

In South Africa, the protection of indigenous culture and technology, or "indigenous knowledge systems", has been a topic of discussion by Parliament since 1995, when Dr Mongane Wally Serote, chairperson of the parliamentary Committee on Arts, Culture, Science and Technology, introduced indigenous knowledge systems as an integral element of science and technology policy in South Africa. Amongst measures taken by this committee is draft legislation in the form of the Protection of Indigenous Knowledge Bill,[6] which has the purpose of recognising and protecting indigenous knowledge (and by implication indigenous forms of cultural expression) in South Africa. I have seen a draft of the Protection of Indigenous Knowledge Bill that has since been scrapped (although attempts to draft legislation continue). However, what I am concerned with is not any specific draft or provision of the Bill, but its general approach and the approach that Parliament seems likely to take in future attempts at drafting the legislation.

The definition of "indigenous knowledge" was given a wide ambit by the draft Bill, and included creative expression such as music and art, technologies, and entire "knowledge systems". This latter phrase indicates that the legislature will recognise indigenous activities as having a holistic nature. "Folklore" has been a term used to refer to the issue in debates held under the auspices of Unesco and WIPO, until some began pointing out that the term carried with it negative connotations of being "associated with the creations of lower or superseded civilisations". (Blakeney 1999:2) More recent discussions held by Unesco have used the term "traditional knowledge", which also recognises that folklore is a narrow element of indigenous culture and knowledge, which it is inappropriate to subdivide. WIPO discovered from fact-finding missions in various regions of the world that "in many cases TK holders do not separate 'artistic' from 'useful' aspects of their intellectual creations and innovations; rather, both emanate from a single belief system which is expressed in daily life and ritual" (International Bureau 1999:3).

The use of the term "indigenous knowledges" reflects a respect for the holism of these knowledge systems. It also reflects acceptance of the proposition that knowledge and culture in indigenous circumstances are similar in that the characteristics of both "query . . . the basic concept of human intellectual activity that underpins modern intellectual property rights" (WIPO 2001:3). In indigenous knowledge systems, according to this belief, there is no differentiation between science and art similar to that recognised by Western intellectual property law's separate mechanisms of protection.

But the most important and often-cited of the characteristics that distinguish indigenous culture from the subject matter of intellectual property law is the alleged collective or communal nature of the act of creativity that underlies cultural expression in indigenous communities. In other words, it is believed that "the resource reproduces and transforms itself in a logic that lies beyond, and is independent of, the individualised creativity and innovation from which existing intellectual property rights result" (WIPO 2001:4). On the other hand, modern Western intellectual property law, manifested in specific legal concepts such as copyright, patent and trademark, conceptualises cultural expression as an act of individual creativity (for criticism of this, see Jaszi and Woodmansee 1994). This mirrors a more general dichotomy that sees Western society as individualistic and opposed to the more communitarian nature of indigenous society (Wiessner 2001:272).

How accurate is this dichotomy in relation to creative expression? At least in the field of music it has been disputed that African or other indigenous music is created by communal "quasi-mystical acts of creation" (Ballantine 2000, citing John Blacking). Nevertheless, because of this perceived distinction between individual Western cultural expression and collective indigenous cultural expression, all of the academic commentators have remarked on the need for *sui generis*[7] legislation to protect indigenous culture (see for example Jabbour 1983). Their proposals for legislative intervention to protect indigenous culture have, in keeping with this dichotomy of the individualism of Western cultures and the collectivism of indigenous cultures, relied conceptually on collective or communal forms of ownership and control.

This emphasis on a conceptual system founded on communal or collective rights has been supported by activists for indigenous peoples' rights (e.g. López 1998; Jacanimijoy 1998). The discussions about the protection of indigenous culture held by Unesco and WIPO have also accepted that protection must be based conceptually in collective rights. This is the attitude taken in the most recent deliberations by WIPO (see WIPO 2001), and it is also the approach adopted by the most concrete international document on the subject, the 1982 Unesco/WIPO Model Provisions for National Laws on the Protection of Expressions of Folklore Against Illicit Exploitation and Other Prejudicial Actions, which protects only cultural expressions developed and maintained by communities. Many African states promulgated legislation protecting indigenous culture after independence; these statutes have generally implied the need for protection based conceptually in collective rights, although in practice they have generally relied on regulation of access by a state organ, with ownership accruing to the state instead of the originating community (for a brief survey, see Kuruk 1999:799-806).

South African steps towards reform in the area also adopt this paradigm of indigenous culture requiring collective or communal forms of ownership, while Western intellectual property law concepts only cater for individual creativity and is thus inappropriate for protecting indigenous culture. An executive summary of indigenous knowledge systems presented before the Education and Recreation Select Committee[8] stated that "Western jurisprudence on intellectual property is predicated on individual ownership. The individual may either be a natural person or a *juristic persona.*[9] It therefore has no provision for collective or communal ownership" (Education and Recreation Select Committee, 12 April 2000). Thus the formulation of *sui generis* protection is thought to be required, as was affirmed by Professor Visser of the University of South Africa at the Unesco/WIPO African Regional Consultation on the Protection of Expressions of Folklore (Pretoria, 23-25 March 1999).

Similarly, Nomazwi Siyotula, who participated in drafting the Bill, has stated that ownership of indigenous property inheres in communities (Arts, Culture, Science and Technology Portfolio Committee, 9 February 2000), and Dr Serote of the Department of Arts, Culture, Science and Technology stated before WIPO that indigenous culture "is understood as a communal intellectual creation" and that "[t]his is an important factor, particularly when considerations of restitution or compensation arise" (Serote 1998:5).

Section 1(xv) of the draft Indigenous Knowledge Systems Bill that was made available to me somewhat vaguely defines "indigenous knowledges" as "productions consisting of characteristic elements of the traditional artistic heritage developed and maintained by a community of South Africa or individuals reflecting the traditional artistic expectations of such a community". It goes on to list specific instances of practices that would fall within the definition. The broad definition, however, is clearly premised on the assumption that communities can be identified and their works protected as communal property.

Section 3 provides that the Bill will apply to protect indigenous knowledges "developed and maintained in South Africa ... against illicit use and other prejudicial actions as defined in the Act". The use of "maintained" means that an indigenous knowledge need not have been developed in South Africa, avoiding the thorny issue of when and where a form of cultural expression develops; yet it does not explicitly contemplate the possibility of protecting indigenous practices that are "maintained" by communities other than the indigenous community which developed them (a possibility which would negate the effectiveness of communal protection).

As noted, the Bill that was available at the time of writing is to be revised, perhaps substantially, and was ultimately too incomplete and contradictory in this form to make any specific predictions as to how draft legislation might look when it finally does come before Parliament. However, the features of the Bill described here as well as the minutes of the portfolio committee meetings indicate quite strongly that the approach eventually taken will be conceptually based on collective or communal ownership.

Beyond Law

Behind all the parliamentary committees and international intiatives there lies a fundamental and to some extent unanswered question – to what extent *should* protection be afforded to indigenous cultural forms? One view is that cultural expressions have become part of a world heritage and should be available to all. Another, reflected in the tone of the South African Parliament's discussion, is more concerned with protecting authenticity and ownership; in other words, with "how these images are being reproduced and how their appropriation in these various contexts is affecting perceptions about the art and its creators (Dowson 2000:315). Most legal commentators have concerned themselves with the issue of protecting indigenous knowledge as a narrow question of legal technicality, and altogether ignored the normative question of whether, and to what extent, indigenous knowledge should be protected by legal mechanisms in the first place.

Yet reservations have been expressed about the consequences of extending intellectual property rights regimes to indigenous knowledge systems: for example Posey (1990) notes that this may draw indigenous communities into materialism or, especially in the context of knowledge about ecological systems, that the commercial success and consequent exploitation of one element of a knowledge system may result in the upsetting of the balance of their holistic lifestyles. Wiessner also notes that "[i]ndividual intellectual property regimes of the Western kind . . . [are] geared toward commercial exploitation rather than toward shielding and keeping secrets inherent in the sacred" (Wiessner 2001:273).

By discussing questions around the ownership of cultural expression, I wish to relate these issues to debates around identity; the normative question will therefore also be ignored here, yet in favour of the related task of gaining a broader understanding of the social implications of particular forms of ownership.

Of course, ownership in the indigenous context exists and is claimed outside of the confines of state and international law. For example, there are the normative beliefs of communities and individuals, which may be based in various sources of perceived legitimacy. In addition, communities may follow internal rules of customary law or patterns of behaviour whose function or effect amount to the establishment of forms of ownership, even though these rules and patterns don't "look" like ownership (for example the "internal rules" described by Kuruk 1999:780-786).[10]

It is uncertain whether such nonlegal forms of ownership tend towards individualistic or communal structures. Some argue that certain practices can be interpreted as establishing individual property rights in knowledge and intellectual activity; Suchman (1989) describes how practices viewed from Western perspectives as "magic" may be interpreted as functioning in similar ways to individual rights of ownership. Others argue that "ownership" is not even an appropriate concept (e.g. Blakeney 1999:5-6), given its existence within such communities as a communal sense of belonging or sanctity which cannot be negotiated or alienated. This has been argued in the context of ownership of land by Maddock (1991: 9-10), and can be also applied to cultural expressions. Nevertheless, practices may be likened in their effect or form to what will generally pass amongst readers for ownership; I use the concept of ownership because it is a fundamental conceptual foundation of a modern worldview, from which we cannot escape as much as we recognise its inadequacy.

In the light of all these various meanings and existences of ownership – the legal, the nonlegal, the noncommensurable, the communal, the individual – which permeate and ground cultural practices, how is one to make sense of state intervention when it takes the form of legal reform? How does legal reform affect cultural practice, and what are the implications of different types of reform, in particular the cultural and political as opposed to legal implications, and the mechanisms through which accompanying cultural change is implicated? Discussion about these effects, especially where they extend beyond the legal, has been mute because of the forums in which these discussions have taken place and the restrictions that the languages appropriate to these forums have imposed. So far the discussions surrounding the issue have generally taken place in the language of legal scholarship, in forums such as law journals or the meetings of international law-making bodies.

Yet legal discourse is often overly positivist, rendering it short-sighted. A major contemporary critique of legal discourse is that it offers a stylisation of law as an autonomous sphere, with its own internal logic and separate from other social practices as well as other social meanings. It takes law at face value, and so many legal scholars assume that the law is best perceived in the way that it presents itself. There is no doubt some value in this kind of positivist analysis for legal practitioners, yet it also restricts how others might understand the wider social existence of law and the circulation of "legal" meanings. For example, legal analysis of something called "cultural ownership" might restrict itself to how the legal concepts and rules applicable to cultural production – such as those current in the body of law called "intellectual property" – fit technical definitions of "ownership", while ignoring that "ownership" has a life outside of the discourse of law. Or legal analysis might limit itself to the problems which certain formulations of legal concepts and certain arrangements of rules would encounter when tested in court, while ignoring that formulations of concepts and arrangements of rules have lives outside the courts.

These limitations of legal scholarship prompted this essay and my attempt here to see how ownership in the context of cultural expression (and not only in the context of the protection of indigenous culture, but generally) might have an existence beyond its "legal" or normative existence. What I am concerned with then is what I would like to call discursive intersections – where and how discourses of law (particularly discourses of "ownership" or "intellectual property") and discourses of social identity meet.

Recently there have been movements to set out in fresh directions and approach the relationship between law and society with the freedom to go beyond taking at face value the law's self-presentation, in favour of deeper and less obvious structural features of the relationship. This is an attempt to transcend the "lawyer's perspective", a perspective which understands law simply as the factual existence of legal doctrine and state institutions, and so confines the field of legal enquiry to the domain described by that doctrine and those institutions. Clifford Geertz makes headway in transcending this perspective when he describes law as "part of a *distinctive manner of imagining the real*" (1983:173).

Geertz shows that law and legal concepts are not a reflection of already existing social realities, but active in constituting them. In terms of this approach law can be understood to be "a diffuse and pervasive force shaping social consciousness and behaviour", (Coombe 1998:22). In the words of another critic of orthodox legal thought, law is a force that "regulates not only by coercing those who create disorder and by empowering those who sustain and reproduce order, but also by helping to fix and maintain 'common sense' understandings of the nature of society and social relationships in general" (Cotterrell 1995:8). This approach understands how law might have wider implications for social and cultural epistemologies, and thus suggests a different way of understanding the function and existence of specific legal forms and concepts.

Such an understanding centres on meaning; "[f]ocusing on the production, interpretation, consumption and circulation of legal meaning suggests that law is inseparable from the interests, goals, and understandings that deeply shape or comprise social life". (Coombe

1998:6). From this point of view, it is less important for legal theory to provide the means for working out the finer points of legal doctrine than for it to understand the role of law in creating social meaning and how law works to constitute social common sense. "Legal thought and legal relations influence self-understanding and understanding of one's relations to others. Legal forms provide ways of knowing, and seeing. And so powerful is their presence in our cultural life that their distinctly legal attributes become almost imperceptible"(Coombe 1998:7).

Alan Hunt captures this active and structuring capacity of legal forms by calling for a concept of law that is able to "[embrace] the idea that the 'presence of law' within social relations is not just to be guaged by institutional intervention but also by the presence of legal concepts and ideas within types of social relations that appear to be free of law" (1987:17).

This way of understanding law as controlling the production and circulation of legal meaning is related to a second important approach, that of legal pluralism, which envisions a legal scholarship that no longer confines itself to the state-sanctioned legal system, but looks at law as the co-existence and interrelatedness of various normative systems in society. A key implication of such an approach is that a "legal form" such as ownership can then be understood to have multiple existences, in co-present normative orders; pluralism denies the "predisposition to think of all legal ordering as rooted in state law – and suggests attention to other forms of ordering and their interaction with state law" (Merry 1988:889).

Legal pluralism is an inherently critical approach, since it complicates and destabilises meanings which are stable elements of orthodox legal thought. It is at base a way of understanding law as not existing positively as the state or the legal institutions decree, but rather circulating in multiplicitous forms and discourses whose shifting validity depends on the sometimes partial or contradictory perspectives of individuals and communities co-existing in a society. The prospect of pluralist thinking has therefore been called "an edifying knowledge that, by enlarging and deepening our legal vistas, will contribute towards a radical democratisation of social and personal life" (Santos 1987:299). It appears to be so in that it at least allows the idea that law is constructive of social realities to come to life, by making "law" visible in contexts where it does not immediately appear to be present from the lawyer's point of view.

These two schools of thought form the basis for a meeting-place for legal thought and cultural studies, for they imply a strong relationship between knowledges of law and of culture, those knowledges which are both ways by which societies understand their realities. This is an appropriate intellectual framework then within which to discuss cultural ownership and social identity in the context of indigenous knowledge systems. This framework provides a way of thinking beyond the current literature on the subject, which for the most part focuses on the technicalities of effectively protecting indigenous knowledge. Firstly, from the perspective of legal pluralism, it seems clear that there are senses of ownership other than those which circulate within the law's internal discourse. Secondly, stemming from a commitment to the belief that law is "a diffuse and pervasive force shaping social consciousness and behaviour" (Coombe 1998:22), it seems clear that not only can legislating ownership have wide effects on the way people come to think of the subject matter of ownership, but that there are forms of ownership, whether legal or not, which are already present and which already influence consciousness in this way.

The Relationship between Ownership and Identity

Legal formations have more subtle but structurally fundamental effects than those normally attributed to them by orthodox legal scholarship. By abandoning the strictures of legal thinking, it is possible to think about the effect that legal structures of ownership have upon the forms that cultural expressions of identity take. To begin with, state intervention in the form of conferring communal rights of ownership on a community would have to be preceded by state delimitation of the boundaries of those communities. In other words, the state might, in legislating ownership, also be legislating identity. This may even be an express purpose of the state in legislating.[11] By this I don't mean that there would be a direct determination of identity imposed by state intervention, but rather that such intervention would somehow shape the discourses of identity available to those subject or even peripheral to such intervention. The link between ownership and identity would not be absent where the state does not intervene in cultural practice. Starting from my premise that forms of ownership pervade cultural practice even in the absence of state law, it is possible to imagine a correlation between these "nonlegal" forms of ownership and identity.

The relationship between ownership and identity is also highlighted by the notion of the collectivity of indigenous culture. Collective forms of ownership are often ascribed to indigenous peoples – how do these contribute to the imagining of fixed, primordial identities for indigenous people, as opposed to the individual forms of ownership and corresponding fluid identities which circulate in the Western world?

It may seem self-evident in one sense to say that there is a correlation between ownership and identity, in that claims of identity are often based on contested claims of ownership. But discourses of identity do not merely rely on claims to ownership for their effect, whether they do so rhetorically or otherwise. In addition, the way in which these claims to ownership are structured shapes the way in which identity is felt. Ownership can be structured in a multitude of ways, especially when seen not as an exclusively legal phenomenon but as a feature occurring in multiple normative dimensions. The law can structure ownership in the context of cultural practice in various conceptually distinct ways, as evidenced by the conceptually different forms of intellectual property – copyright, patent, trademark, and other legal formations that effectively structure ownership of intellectual property such as the regulation of unfair business practices or the regulation of specific cultural industries. Nonlegal norms of ownership also vary in form and structure, arising perhaps from rules of customary law, "rites" of ownership or senses of individual or communal entitlement. It seems simplistic then to say that ownership simply grounds or evidences claims of identity, when owership can be structured in these myriad forms.

Structures of ownership, whether legal or nonlegal in manifestation, always permeate spaces of cultural practice. How then do these structures of ownership, in their form and incidence, shape the discourses of identity which accompany cultural expression? Is there any relationship at all? Does the backdrop of rights and norms of ownership, against which cultural practice is played out, also shape contours of those discourses of identity, the possibilities and impossibilities for the identity available to one? If so, how?

Miscast, Again

The *Miscast* debate is not a ready object for conventional legal study as the Indigenous Knowledge Systems Bill might be. It would be hard to extract from the controversy overtly "legal" issues of ownership for which a conventional work of legal scholarship might search. However, the debate does serve as a convenient metaphorical entry point into understanding the relationship between forms of ownership and discourses of identity that I have now outlined. The *Miscast* debate is related to more recent concerns around the protection of indigenous culture. It is even more directly related to my propositions about cultural ownership and identity, for the irreconcilable difference between Skotnes and Abrahams is underwritten by different understandings of identity, as well as by different senses of ownership.

Skotnes, a white South African, appropriated the representations of the Khoisan to express something of her own individual identity, an identity that is capable of recognising its own hybridity and fluidity, and thus negotiating an existence in the "new" South Africa. Her sense of identity is one which is not defined by an unchanging sense of rootedness, but rather expressed in terms of fluidity, in the belief that "[p]ractices of displacement might emerge as *constitutive* of cultural meaning rather than as their simple transfer or extension" (Clifford 1997:3). Skotnes's correspondent is Yvette Abrahams, a "brown" woman (her own appellation) asserting a communal right, on behalf of the community that she claims, to veto representations of the Khoisan. Her claim to this community expresses an identity based in essences and resisting negotiation. In fact, Abrahams lays her essentialist convictions down like a gauntlet: "Now", she writes, "I have little time for the epistemological school which argues that all representations of reality are equally valid. My historical experience tells me otherwise" (Abrahams 1996a).[12]

I don't wish to take a position on the validity of either set of identity politics – it is much better to take both seriously, that is, ambivalently. For example, one might view Skotnes's position more cynically as being amongst those "fascinated observers who are so ready to claim the 'brave new world' of cut 'n' mix culture in which all difference is of the same order, like the difference between Coke and Pepsi" (Friedman 2002:33). The point here is not to take up a position on this, but rather to see how these different discourses are related to and in a sense made possible by underlying sociolegal norms. To do so, it is important to note that these different discourses of identity are shaped by the different sources from which Skotnes and Abrahams seek legitimacy for their claims, and in the negotiability of those claims to ultimate authority over the use of the representations. It is these dimensions of *legitimacy* and *negotiability* that can also be understood as the dimensions along which ownership varies in its effect on discourses of identity.

Skotnes, in the book which accompanies the exhibition, describes how she was allowed and denied access by various institutions in collecting the materials from which she constructed her exhibition. She tells us that:

> All institutions I approached for photographic material (with the exception of the Natural History Museum in London) gave me unqualified access to their material and permission to reproduce images. In the end, and despite the horrors of some of the images, I decided to include examples of the full range of the material I have collected . . . One exception, was the decision not to feature any of the many photographs of women's genitals (1996:19).

Skotnes also explains that she was not allowed to draw or photograph any of the collection of dried human heads (most likely trophy heads collected by settlers after executions or battle) held by the Natural History Museum, even though they would have been prepared to allow access under different circumstances – specifically, for certain scientific purposes. In her words:

> In suggesting that images of the heads may cause offence, the Natural History Museum is not suggesting that the heads should not be "used". On the contrary, it asserts the rights of science to use them. What is denied, however, is the value of any other context in which the heads might provoke insight or stimulate understanding (1996:20).

Here it can be seen how claims to ownership provide a background upon which cultural expression is practised. Skotnes's positioning of her work in the realms of culture is a reaction to the museum's dictation of a divide between culture and science, a divide which the museum enacts through a power of ownership over the objects Skotnes wishes to use. Yet while she questions the museum's decision, she doesn't question the source from which the museum backs up its decision, that source being the state legal system and the accompanying notions of individual property and Lockean "original acquisition" that back up its claims to exercise ownership. This same source of legitimacy underlies the creation of the exhibition, in that Skotnes's never questions her right to use materials where she is given access to them by their owners *in law*. Even her decision not to use the photographs of women's genitals is one made *in spite of* a legal right to do so. Skotnes works against a backdrop of individual, state-enforced rights to ownership.

Skotnes relies on a similar source of legitimacy by defending her work and her authority in terms that emphasise the creative freedom of the author. Although Skotnes states that she consulted with other groups and made changes to her initial plans where necessary (see Skotnes 1996a), it is always clear that she works in the mode of author, as the "original genius" behind her work – a conceptual individualism that is directly related historically and philosophically to the origins of Western intellectual property law (see e.g. Rose 1993). This capacity of author or creator becomes an absolute capacity to negotiate identity with the materials available to her individual creative endeavour:

> So who has the right to represent or interpret that evidence? All of us, surely, or none of us. But each of us must be judged on the merits of our own work and its ability to acknowledge and address the traditions, with all their gross inequalities, within which it functions. Yvette Ahrahams has judged mine, it remains to be seen how her work will meet the challenge of her own arguments (Skotnes 1996a).

Skotnes' account of how she negotiates her identity relies strongly upon an ideology of the creative individual's power of authorship, to create and recreate cultural meaning and affinities. This understanding of herself as creative individual and the sense of negotiability that accompanies this understanding is related to the forum in which the *Miscast* exhibition was held, a gallery and not a museum. Davison says that "[a]lthough museum presentations are always subjectively shaped, they are widely associated with authenticity and objectivity. Consequently, museums have become privileged institutions that validate certain forms of cultural expression and affirm particular interpretations of the past" (Davison 1998:146). Skotnes deliberately avoided hosting her exhibition in a museum, perhaps because she sees herself as a creative author, capable of negotiating validated forms of cultural expressions and affirmed interpretations of the past.

In contrast to Skotnes's reliance on these claims of individual author-ity, Abrahams's argument reflects a constant reliance on the claims of community, and thus a legitimacy based on a sense of shared belonging in essence. It is these differing sources of legitimacy which are in some sense congruent with the distinct contours of the discourses of identity available to Skotnes and Abrahams.

Negotiability

Abrahams's reliance on community also points to another dimension of her discourse of identity, that of negotiability. Her first response to Skotnes begins with a powerful personal narrative, which I repeat in full so as not to do it any injustice:

> When my mother was a girl, the nearest high school (and later university) for African children was 1700 km away in Cape Town. Always, she remembers, on the last day of the vacation it seemed as if the entire extended family and half of the old location came to take tea with my grandmother, oversee the packing and give the departing children the benefit of their advice. When the uncle or aunt would rise to depart, they would call my mother, she being the eldest daughter, and would take out a coin or two for the children to buy themselves something on the long journey south. My mother, as in honour bound, would protest, for sometimes the coins would be a cent or two, and she knew that the giver could ill afford it. To suggest this would have been a grievous offence, of course, and so her protests were silenced and the giver would press into her hand a token of goodwill and their stake in my mother's success. As the coins passed from hand to hand, they became invested with a powerful symbolism of encouragement and obligation. "Do well," they said, "*not for yourself but for your people.*" As I sit here and write, those coins are part of who I am. It has taken us two generations to get to a point where I can be heard in academic journals. Here, I must speak, not just for myself but for my people. The solipsist will object that I cannot "really" speak "for" another. Of course I cannot, and yet I must, until we are all equal (Abrahams 1996, emphasis added).

The "we" that Abrahams feels so much a part of her, returns again and again in her text. When she talks about the casts, a point of focus of the *Miscast* exhibition and the most denigrating feature in Abrahams's eyes because of the sexual objectification they evidence, she says that "those highlighted genitals got on *our* nerves and are there still". Who does she speak for in such phrases, herself or "her people"? The distinction is useless for understanding how identity figures in her text.

When Abrahams refers to the conference held before the exhibition, she describes the meeting of Khoisan representatives, however accurately or inaccurately, as a moment of "brown unity". Skotnes, on the other hand, focuses on the disunity of Khoisan voices at that event, pointing out disagreements between the various groups. It is this attention to disunity, the blurring of lines of identity and uncertainties about ethnicity, that is also a prominent feature of the scholarly work collected in the book edited by Skotnes and accompanying the exhibition. For example, Jolly's essay denies the purity and exclusivity of Khoisan cultural forms and ideological beliefs, and gives examples of "cross-fertilisation between the ideological systems of San-speakers and others" (Jolly 1996:206). In the same volume Prins (1996) shows how concepts from the extinct southern San have become integrated into the worldviews of the southern Nguni and other indigenous groups. Jolly also questions the accuracy of contemporary claims to a "Bushman" identity, questioning whether such an identity "can ever be clearly defined" (Jolly 1996:209).

Alan Morris, in his contribution to *Miscast* discussing the dilemma of the trophy skulls held by some institutions, sums up this fluidity of ethnic identity and its accompanying political complexity:

> No living South African can attest a cultural affinity with these people as their beliefs and way of life are long gone, but a few have a shared genetic origin. But does sharing a portion of genetic make-up mean one that living people can claim the full heritage of the past? These are difficult questions because the bones are symbols as well as specimens, and symbols have different meanings to different people. Certainly the Khoisan never saw themselves as a single people and unifying them into a single "race" was a European, not a native, concept (1996:79).

It is against this background that Skotnes also relies on an idea of identity that is malleable and negotiable. Skotnes is negotiating a new South African identity that goes beyond old oppositions, and her starting point then is the statement by Edwin Wilmsen, in his contribution to *Miscast*, that "all three minds – that of the colonised, of the coloniser, and of the would-be post-colonial – must be treated together before a non-colonial future may be enabled" (1996:186). This is why Skotnes tells Abrahams that "[c]olonial history in this context is about more than just Brown history. Colonial history is about interaction, and the relationships that were established between different groups of people as a result of that interaction" (Skotnes 1996a).

This is also why Skotnes quoted Greg Dening in large red letters which could immediately be seen on entering her exhibition, and again in her book:

> There is no Native past without the Stranger. No Stranger without the Native. No one can hope to be mediator or interlocutor in that opposition of Native and Stranger, because no one is gazing at it untouched by the power that is in it. Nor can anyone speak just for the one, just for the other. There is no escape from the politics of our knowledge, but that politics is not in the past. That politics is in the present (Dening 1992:178).

Abrahams, on the other hand, deals in essences. This is in keeping with the discourse that generally accompanies claims to Khoisan identity, a discourse that is situated in what has been called an "essentialist ethnic-nationalist politics of temporal priority" (Robins 1988:130). She cannot negotiate identity in the way that Skotnes does – the discourse of identity in which she is situated does not allow her to. Hence Khoisan history, in Abrahams's understanding, is not available for Skotnes's self-reflexive uses:

> Fashions change and if the elite today enjoy a spice of guilt, a dash of naked bodies and some charity with their art it really could not matter less to us. But Skotnes' insistence that she in some sense is doing something "for" the Khoisan remains an irritant. . . . How can you speak "for" a people you know so little about? How can you speak "for" a people you do not respect? (Abrahams 1996)

The Indigenous Knowledges Systems Bill: A Second Look

It is time now to apply these insights to understanding the relationship between forms of ownership and discourse of identity – specifically in considering the South African legislature's discussions about the protection of indigenous culture, although I believe that the ideas discussed here might also be applicable to cultural expressions of other kinds.

Miscast was not about ownership in any technically legal sense of the word, but it did concern the power to represent, who may exercise that power and in what fashion, its legitimacy and its negotiability. Ownership can be seen as possessing these two dimensions as well, and when seen in this way, it becomes apparent just how the relationship I have been describing might operate. Ownership is a power over a subject matter, a power both to authorise and deny use of or access to the object. Perhaps this is not a definition that would pass the strictures of a legal definition, but it does approach an effective description of how ownership exists in the social imagination, in both its legal and nonlegal forms. There are different dimensions to this power. An owner may allow access to an object freely, or on her terms, or not at all. So it circumscribes a domain of power, the terms of access to which are controlled by the owner.

Legal and nonlegal forms of ownership may in various ways restrict or entrench access and use by people other than the owner: this is an example of how different forms of ownership are often structured quite differently. This varying ease of use by non-owners is what I have called a dimension of *negotiability*. At the same time the power of ownership is conferred. If ownership is a legal form of ownership, it is conferred by the state; in other forms it may be conferred by community norms or religious principles or in various other ways. I refer to this dimension of ownership as a dimension of *legitimacy*.

These two dimensions are complementary. Negotiability refers to the owner's authority to negotiate the bounds of her ownership; legitimacy relates to the source to which authority is sought in claiming ownership. They refer respectively to the way in which ownership circumscribes the domain of an owner's authority, and how the domain of ownership is in turn circumscribed by a conferring authority.

These dimensions of legitimacy and negotiability in turn correlate with similar dimensions present in discourses of identity. It becomes apparent that the structures of ownership in the presence of which cultural expression is formulated shape the possible forms which the discourse of identity may take. In the *Miscast* debate, Abrahams's reliance on nonlegal, communal claims to a power to represent implied a nonstate and perhaps marginalised source of legitimacy and a negotiability that operates in absolutes, and these in turn shape the way in which identity figures in her argument, in terms of resistance and essence. Skotnes's assumption of the role of individual creator led her to work with legal (that is, state-conferred) patterns of ownership. This allowed her a more malleable sense of identity, and a source of legitimacy that need not look away from the state, so that she works within a discourse of identity founded not on resistance but on notions such as reconciliation and reconstruction, notions which were circulated by the state at that time.

I believe that a similar analysis can be made of the steps planned to protect indigenous knowledge. Communal rights of ownership as envisaged will enforce communal feelings of affinity where they are strongly felt, and perhaps entrench them where they are more fragile. This might result in less flexibility for the negotiation of identity by outsiders, or marginal participants in the culture (such as urbanised members of rural communities or members of communities with mixed heritage). Individual rights, on the other hand, would allow more fluidity of claims of identity. This analysis should keep in mind not only the strong convictions of shared roots, whether biological or cultural, felt by some communities, albeit that others wish to think about contemporary South African culture "as a creolised space" (Nuttall and Michael 2000:7); yet neither should the construction of ethnicity during colonisation be forgotten too quickly (see e.g. Skolnik 1988:74ff). The role of sociolegal order in this sort of project has not ended in the transition to a post-colonial state.

Another way to understand negotiability as a dimension of ownership is to observe the current critique of copyright – one form of legal ownership in cultural expression – that analogises it to censorship. Copyright in fact originated in the English crown's power to license the printing of literary texts (Rose 1993). This power had evolved as a means of regulating the types of texts printed – in other words, as a means of censorship by the crown. Ownership in a text could be withheld where the content of the text was disagreeable.[13]

A key proposition of the discourse of copyright law is that the primary purpose of copyright is not the conferring of rights of ownership but rather the attainment of a proper balance between absolute ownership and public access. Yet, while copyright has strived to balance an owner's power with public access to the "protected" work, this historical narrative provides a metaphor for the way in which copyright *can* function when the balance tilts in favour of absolute ownership. The growing critique of current tendencies in copyright law then is that it increasingly amounts to a privately-held power of censorship wielded by large corporations, especially where new technologies or media advance ahead of the law and allow copyright to become a power of absolute ownership held by such entities (e.g. Boyle 1997). This is one critique which, whether applicable or not, has not surfaced in the current discussions of the protection of indigenous knowledge. It should be borne in mind, especially given current misgivings about state-supported structures of traditional leadership.

The dimension of legitimacy is also important in understanding how ownership relates to identity. The legitimacy invoked by claims of ownership can provide authority boundaries of communities that are otherwise problematic, or that source of legitimacy can provide a site of resistance. So where legal rights in indigenous knowledges are promulgated by the state, it seems likely that the holders of those rights will express their identity in discourses of state legitimacy. Outsiders or marginalised "members" might also come to perceive their struggles in terms of such discourses.

One example of how identity might be formulated in terms of state and legitimacy can be seen in Cape Town's post-1994 hip-hop culture. Klopper describes how Captour and Metrorail have tried to accept hip-hop spray-can art and use it for their own purposes. Parallel to this is a change in the philosophy of the culture's original participants, from one of resistance against the state to one of seeking to "develop a new sense of belonging for those who question the racist values and beliefs of the large number of older-generation Coloureds" and "participate in the political mainstream controlled by blacks" (2000:193). Legitimisation of the culture by state agents corresponds with a shift that sees these participants negotiating their "coloured" identity, a traditionally contested one, in terms of adopting rather than resisting a particular narrative of nation-building that is now proposed by the new government.

In a society such as South Africa, a state subject to the ambiguous condition of post-colonialism, and a state in transition, a plurality of normative and sociolegal orders exists. Many ways of understanding authority, identity and property circulate amongst communities, and it is negotiating these plural understandings that makes living in such a society simultaneously difficult and exciting. What I hope to have pointed out here is that discourses do intersect, and that under the condition of plurality these intersections become more complex. Where there are many ways of understanding ownership, this can have an effect on the ways of understanding identity.

In addition, this might show a way out of the interminable haggling about essentialism and hybridity. While identity is constructed, the way in which communities and individuals conceive of their identity is social fact. One must take cognisance of the fact that some see their identity in essentialist terms. Some would decry the dangers of essentialist rhetoric at play in much identity politics; others take offence at the perceived obfuscation of notions such as hybridity and creolisation. To live in a plural society is to live with these very different conceptions of the human self; to take such plurality seriously, as a theorist, is to take these different conceptions seriously, yet try to understand how and why these meanings come to circulate in the way that they do.

Notes

1 I am indebted to valuable discussions I had with Samantha Cooke, Desmoreen Carolus, Herman Wasserman and Sean Jacobs. Their views are not necessarily reflected here.

2 Skotnes had been prevented from using the word 'Bushmen' in the title of the exhibition by the National Gallery (Skotnes 1996a).

3 Lucy Lloyd was an ethnographer who, working together with philologist Wilhelm Bleek, had transcribed 138 notebooks of Khoisan folklore; these stories have been presented in poetic form by Stephen Watson; see for example Watson (1991).

4 The correspondence can be found in the online *Southern African Review of Books*

archive; see www.uni-ulm.de/~rturrell/antho4html/miscast.htm and www.uni-ulm.de/~rturrell/antho4html/Skotnes.html (last visited 20 November 2001).

5 It is difficult to draw a distinction between indigenous cultural expression or "folklore" and indigenous knowledge, however, especially given the holistic nature of indigenous societies.

6 NACI/99/26.

7 *Sui generis* because it is incomparable in form to existing legal conceptual formations such as copyright.

8 Minutes of the parliamentary committees and other parliamentary records are accessible at the website of the Parliamentary Monitoring Group, www.pmg.co.za.

9 A juristic person is an entity, which although not a person in the normal sense of the word, is recognised by the law as a person and thus capable of having legal rights and duties. The most common example is the company.

10 These comments are not reserved for indigenous cultural practices. Within popular culture, I am convinced that, for example, certain practices amongst participants in DJ culture and practices such as "tagging" amongst spray-can artists also constitute "rites of ownership".

11 For example, Serote expressly linked the legislative protection of indigenous knowledges with the affirmation of identities; see Serote (1998).

12 It is important that essentialist discourses of identity are not immediately assumed for all who claim Khoisan identity. Tomaselli (2002:215) discusses how for some "secret" San "constant shifting of identities, names, and ethnicities constitutes a survival strategy within larger populations which are ill-disposed towards them".

13 Saunders (1990) describes this intersection between copyright and obscenity laws in England.

References

Abrahams, Yvette. 1996. "Miscast" 43 *Southern African Review of Books* (July/August).

Abrahams, Yvette. 1996a. "Yvette Abrahams responds" 43 *Southern African Review of Books* (July/August).

Ballantine, Christopher. 2000. "Joseph Shabalala: African composer" in Nuttall, Sarah and Michael, Cheryl-Ann. *Senses of Culture. South African Culture Studies.* Cape Town: Oxford University Press.

Blakeney, Michael. 1999. "What is Traditional Knowledge? Why Should It Be Protected? Who Should Protect It? For Whom?: Understanding the Value Chain" delivered at the WIPO Roundtable on Intellectual Property and Traditional Knowledge, Geneva, November 1 and 2.

Boyle, James. 1997. *A Politics of Intellectual Property: Environmentalism for the Net?* Duke Law Journal, 47. 87.

Clifford, J. 1997. *Routes*. Cambridge, MA: Harvard University Press.

Coombe, Rosemary J. 1998. "Contingent articulations: a critical cultural studies of law" in Sarat, Austin and Kearns, Thomas R. *Law in the Domains of Culture*, University of Michigan Press.

Cotterrell, Roger. 1995. *Law's Community. Legal Theory in Sociological Perspective*. Oxford: Clarendon Press.

Davison, Patricia. 1998. "Museums and the reshaping of memory" in Nuttall, Sarah and Coetzee, Carli (eds.). *Negotiating the Past: The Making of Memory in South Africa.* Cape Town: Oxford University Press.

Dening, Greg. 1992. *Mr Bligh's Bad Language. Passion, Power, and Theatre on the Bounty.* Cambridge: Cambridge University Press.

Dowson, Thomas. 1996. "Reproduction and Consumption: The Use of Rock Art Imagery in Southern Africa Today" in Pippa Skotnes (ed.). *Miscast. Negotiating the Presence of the Bushmen.* Cape Town: University of Cape Town Press.

Friedman, Jonathan. 2002. "From roots to routes. Tropes for trippers". *Anthropological Theory* 2(1). 21-36.

Geertz, Clifford. 1983. *Local Knowledge. Further Essays in Interpretive Anthropology.* Basic Books.

Hunt, Alan. 1987. "The Critique of Law: What is 'Critical' about Critical Legal Theory?" *Journal of Law & Society* 14: 5.

Jabbour, Alan. 1983. "Folklore protection and national patrimony: developments and dilemmas in the legal protection of folklore". *UNESCO Court Bulletin*, XVII(1): 10.

Jacanimijoy, Antonio. 1998. "Initiatives for protection of Rights of Holders of Traditional Knowledge, Indigenous Peoples and Local Communities" presented at the WIPO Roundtable on Intellectual Property and Indigenous Peoples, Geneva, July 23 and 24, 1998.

Jolly, Pieter. 1996. "Between the Lines: Some Remarks on 'Bushman' Ethnicity" in Pippa Skotnes (ed.). *Miscast. Negotiating the Presence of the Bushmen*, Cape Town: University of Cape Town Press.

Klopper, Sarah. 2000. "Hip-hop Graffiti Art" in Nuttall, Sarah and Michael, Charyl-Ann (eds.). *Senses of Culture. South African Culture Studies.* Cape Town: Oxford University Press.

Kozain, Rustum. 1996. "Miscast" 43 *Southern African Review of Books* (July/August).

Kuruk, Paul. 1999. "Protecting folklore under modern intellectual property regimes: a reappraisal of the tensions between individual and communal rights in Africa and the United States" *American University Law Review*, 48. 769.

López, Atencio. 1998. "Initiatives for the Protection of Holders of Traditional Knowledge, Indigenous Peoples and Local Communities" presented at the WIPO Roundtable on Intellectual Property and Indigenous Peoples, Geneva, July 23 and 24.

Maddock, Keith. 1991. "Introduction" in Keith Maddock (ed.). *Identity, Land and Liberty. Studies in the Fourth World.* Nijmegen: Katholieke Universiteit Nijmegen.

Merry, Susan Engle. 1988. "Legal Pluralism" *Law and Society Review*, 1988. 869.

Morris, Alan G. 1996. "Trophy skulls, museums and the San" in Pippa Skotnes (ed.). *Miscast. Negotiating the Presence of the Bushmen*, Cape Town: University of Cape Town Press.

Nuttall, Sarah and Michael, Cheryl-Ann. 2000. "Introduction: Imagining the Present" in Nuttall, Sarah and Michael, Cheryl-Ann. *Senses of Culture. South African Culture Studies.* Cape Town: Oxford University Press.

Posey, Darrell. 1990. "Intellectual Property Rights: And Just Compensation for Indigenous Knowledge". *Anthropology Today* 6(4). 13.

Prins, Frans E. 1996. "Praise to the Bushman Ancestors of the Water. The integration of San-related concepts in the belief and ritual of a diviners' training school in Tsolo, Eastern Cape" in Pippa Skotnes (ed.). *Miscast. Negotiating the Presence of the Bushmen.* Cape Town: University of Cape Town Press.

Robins, Steve. 1998. "Silence in my father's house: memory, nationalism, and narratives of the body" in Nuttall, Sarah and Coetzee, Carli (eds.). *Negotiating the Past. The Making of Memory in South Africa.* Cape Town: Oxford University Press.

Rose, Mark. 1993. *Authors and Owners. The invention of copyright.* Cambridge: Harvard University Press.

Rossouw, Rehana. 1996. "Setting history straight – or another chance to gape?" *Mail & Guardian*, 19 April 1996.

Santos, Boaventura de Sousa. 1987. "Law: a Map of Misreading. Toward a Postmodern Conception of Law". *Journal of Law and Society* 14. 279.

Saunders, David. 1990. "Copyright, Obscenity and Literary History". *ELH,* 57(2). 431-444.

Schrire, Carmel. 1996. "Miscast" 43 *Southern African Review of Books* (July/August).

Serote, Mongane Wally. 1998. "Initiatives for the Protection of Rights of Holders of Traditional Knowledge, Indigenous Peoples and Local Communities Document" presented at the WIPO Roundtable on Intellectual Property and Indigenous Peoples, Geneva, July 23 and 24, 1998.

Skolnik, Peter. 1988. "Tribe as Colonial Category" in Boonzaier, Emile and Sharp, John (eds.). *South African Keywords. The Uses and Abuses of Political Concepts.* Cape Town: David Philip.

Skotnes, Pippa. 1996. "Introduction" in Pippa Skotnes (ed.). *Miscast. Negotiating the Presence of the Bushmen*, Cape Town: University of Cape Town Press.

Skotnes, Pippa. 1996a. "Pippa Skotnes responds" 43 *Southern African Review of Books* (July/August).

Suchman, Mark C. 1989. "Invention and ritual: notes on the interrelation of magic and intellectual property in preliterate communities" *Columbia Law Review*, 89. 1264.

Tomaselli, Keyan G. 2002. ". . . We have to work with our own heads" (/Angn!ao): San Bushmen and the Media" in *Visual Anthropology* 15. 203-220.

Watson, Stephen. 1991. *Song of the Broken String: after the /Xam Bushmen.* New York: Sheep Meadow Press.

Wiessner, Siegfried. 2001. "Sixth Annual Tribal Sovereignty Symposium: Defending Indigenous Peoples' Heritage: An Introduction" in *St. Thomas Law Review* 14. 271-4.

Wilmsen, Edwin. 1996. "Decolonising the Mind: Steps Toward Cleansing the Bushman Stain from Southern African History" in Pippa Skotnes (ed.). *Miscast. Negotiating the Presence of the Bushmen.* Cape Town: University of Cape Town Press.

WIPO International Bureau. 1999. "Protection of Traditional Knowledge: A Global Intellectual Property Issue" delivered at the WIPO Roundtable on Intellectual Property and Traditional Knowledge, Geneva, November 1 and 2, 1999.

WIPO Secretariat (2001) "Matters Concerning Intellectual Property and Genetic Resources, Traditional Knowledge and Folklore – An Overview", First Session of the Intergovernmental Committee on Intellectual Property and Genetic Resources, Traditional Knowledge and Folklore, Geneva, April 30 to May 3, 2001.

Woodmansee, Martha and Jaszi, Peter (eds.). 1994. *The Construction of Authorship. Textual appropriation in law and literature.* Duke University Press.

CHAPTER TWELVE

'Fugees': African Immigrants, Media and the New South Africa

Patrice Kabeya-Mwepu and Sean Jacobs

Introduction

Both popular as well as official discourses in post-apartheid South Africa that have to do with immigrants and refugees[1] from the rest of Africa are characterised by a marked degree of xenophobia. Given the increasing mediated nature of public debates in South Africa in the last five years or so, there have been growing interest in the role and impact of mainstream mass media on popular sentiment towards refugees and immigrants from the rest of Africa. In South Africa, the best known research has been produced by Reitzes and Dolan (1996), Peberty and Crush (1998), and Danso and McDonald (2000).[2] The general picture that emerges from these studies is that media coverage of immigrants and refugees is overwhelmingly negative and uncritically reproduces problematic statistics and assumptions about cross-border migration.

It is therefore not surprising that refugees and migrants express widespread distrust and pessimism towards local media. In fieldwork conducted among 120 refugees and migrants living in Cape Town's African townships by one of the writers, these sentiments were confirmed. Asked whether they would speak to the media about their daily lives, 60% of respondents answered no, 30% expressed reservations, preferring anonymity, and only 10% indicated they would reveal their identity if necessary.[3]

One set of responses to this state of affairs by journalists' organisations as well as human rights and, significantly, organised refugee groups has been to make the media (radio programmes and print media) challenge and counteract such stereotypes and assumptions. At its core, the aim with this media is to engage directly with the South African public. In particular two projects – one a series of radio documentaries broadcast on the South African Broadcasting Corporation (SABC) stations (as well as a number of community radio stations) and one a print media initiative by a refugee organisation – were developed by these groups. Refugees and migrants took an active part in the formulation and output of these media projects.

While suggesting that these media do impact the dominant discourse and perceptions about refugees and immigrants, this article wants to put forward two key arguments. The first intervention deals with the failure of such media to engage critically with the dominant human rights framework as it relates to refugees and immigrants. This is that it does not challenge the seemingly logical argument, based on research information – such as that foreigners do not take jobs, but create jobs – to explain why people should not be xenophobic or that there is no reason to be xenophobic. Secondly, it is assumed that, by appealing to the intellectual capacity of individuals or communities, behavioural changes will occur. In other words – it is assumed that if individuals or communities understand, agree with and accept the human rights framework and logical arguments, they will become less xenophobic.[4]

A second set of interventions relates to how outsiders (often with good intentions) see refugees and immigrants as an undifferentiated mass. In this case there appears to be scant reference to questions of power among individuals and groups of refugees and migrants, as well as the differential access of migrants and refugees to South African social and political institutions. It does suggest a kind of insularity that diverts attention away from the intimate patterns of daily social and economic interaction with citizens and host institutions that preoccupy most migrants. "Community" is taken for granted and these efforts appear to rely too much on the potential of social capital (e.g. transnationalism as a vehicle for resistance).[5]

Finally, most anti-xenophobia initiatives do not make room for the agencies of refugees and migrants which (wilfully and for strategic reasons) underplay tensions and differences among themselves.

This chapter is also an attempt to respond to new research challenges. The demise of formal apartheid has created "new and yet only *partially* [our emphasis] understood opportunities for migration to South Africa", as Crush and McDonald (2000:2) point out in an introduction to a series of studies on African immigration and "new migrant spaces". They even question how far their own work, based upon large structured questionnaires, can grasp the new developments, and suggest that "the more nuanced information . . . can [rather] be gleaned only from local case studies of an ethnographic, participatory and place-based nature". (Crush and McDonald 2000:3) They plead for a change of focus to buttress their survey and empirical research with more "qualitative" assessments of the "new South African migratory mosaic".[6]

The "New Wave" and the Media

Refugees and immigrants from north of the border are not new to South Africa. The country has a long history of African migration. Neighbouring Southern African states for a long time provided a pool of cheap labour to the national economy – both legal (mostly to the mines on the Witswatersrand) and undocumented migration (to farms on the northern borders of South Africa with Zimbabwe and Mozambique). In the 1980s large numbers of Mozambican refugees crossed the border into apartheid South Africa, fleeing the civil war between the Frelimo government and the South African-supported insurgency force, Renamo. An estimated 350 000 refugees entered South Africa at the time and less than 20% have since returned to Mozambique (Crush and McDonald 2000).

A new wave of wars and violent conflicts in West, Central and East Africa have brought a new wave of refugees to South Africa, from countries as diverse as Nigeria, Sierra Leone, Congo (both the Democratic Republic or former Zaire as well as Congo-Brazzaville), Angola, Somalia, Ethiopia and Eritrea. Similarly, the demise of formal apartheid has created new and as yet only partially understood opportunities for migration to South Africa. Legal migration from other Southern African Development Community (SADC) countries, for example, has increased almost tenfold since 1990, to over four million visitors per year. South Africa's re-insertion into the global economy has brought new streams of legal and undocumented migrants from outside the SADC region and new ethnic constellations within. The easing of legal and unauthorised entry into South Africa has made the country the new destination for African asylum-seekers, long-distance traders, entrepreneurs, students, and professionals (Crush and McDonald 2000; Simone 2000; Murray 2001).[7]

Most refugees are feeling the verbal and sometimes physical sting of rampant anti-foreign sentiment, which is particularly acute against Africans, as opposed to migrants or refugees from elsewhere (Human Rights Watch 1998; McDonald 2000).

Regular public opinion surveys bear out the rising anti-immigrant sentiment (Crush and McDonald 2000; Dodson and Oelofse 2000). Two recent national surveys (conducted in mid-1997 and early 1998) on public attitudes towards immigrants and immigration conducted by the Southern African Migrancy Project (cited in McDonald 2000) show that the overwhelming majority of South Africans oppose a liberal immigration regime. Fully 25% of the population want a complete ban on migration into the country and approximately half (45% in 1997 and 53% in 1998) call for a "strict limit on the number of foreigners allowed into the country". Only 6% said in the 1997 survey that the government should "let anyone in who wants to enter", a figure that dropped to a mere 2% in 1998. The remainder was "unsure" or said that people should be allowed in only if there were jobs available. These attitudes towards immigration were considerably more conservative than comparable survey results from seventeen other countries around the world for which similar data exists, including the United States.

The surveys also found that South Africans themselves hold strongly negative views about immigrants, especially concerning those from other African countries. African migrants are perceived to be responsible for stealing jobs, creating crime, and bringing diseases such HIV/Aids into South Africa. In the 1997 survey, 37% of South Africans felt that people from neighbouring countries that are now living in South Africa are a "threat to jobs and the economy", 48% believed they "bring diseases". By contrast, only 25% of the sample said they have "nothing to fear" from foreign migrants. McDonald (2000) points out that virtually every socioeconomic and demographic group in the country have these perceptions and assumptions. Men and women, whites and blacks, young and old, rich and poor, educated and uneducated, all hold the same generally negative stereotypes about immigrants and immigration generally in South Africa.

Crucially, McDonald suggests that perhaps the most interesting finding in the two surveys is that only 4% of the 3 500 people surveyed in 1997 and 6% of the 1 600 people surveyed in 1998 said that they have had a "great deal of contact" with people from other African countries. Almost one half said they had no contact with immigrants whatsoever, and an additional 17% in both years said they had "hardly any contact". This leads McDonald (2000) to conclude that clearly anti-immigrant sentiment in South Africa is not a result of personal experience with non-citizens, but rather a product of (mis)information from secondary sources such as schools, state agencies, friends and the media. As a result, research into the sources of this anti-foreigner sentiment have focused on state (both official and unofficial) and media discourses.

Government ministers and senior policy-makers in South Africa are notorious for their xenophobic comments (cf. Dodson and Oelofse 2000; Crush 1996). Minister of Home Affairs (since 1994) Mangosuthu Buthelezi has publicly made wild and unsubstantiated claims about marriages of convenience, false asylum claims, and the criminal tendencies of foreigners. By linking "illegal aliens" with drug trafficking, weapons smuggling, and spying for industrial secrets, senior police officials have lent legitimacy to unfounded beliefs that immigrants are primarily responsible for the rising crime rate in South Africa. Joe Modise, one-time military commander of the ANC's military wing (whose members were based in SADC states such as Angola, Tanzania and Mozambique) and also former Minister of Defence (1994-99), once threatened to switch on the 15,000-volt electrified fence on South Africa's northern and eastern borders "to lethal mode" as an effective means of discouraging and reducing clandestine border crossings (Murray 2000). These sentiments are also repeated in the technical language of government Bills and laws. In 1999 the draft White Paper on International Migration – effectively the government blueprint for future policy – referred to migrants and refugees as "problems and threats" that need to be resisted, rather than opportunities to be managed (Dodson and Oelofse 2000:126). It should be noted that South African President Thabo Mbeki has stated in an address to the opening of Parliament in February 2001 that migrants can, and do, make a contribution to the development of South Africa. However, this message has not been conveyed more strongly or consistently.

The role of the media in establishing or reinforcing a xenophobic discourse has received considerable attention from researchers both inside and outside South Africa (cf. Reitzes and Dolan 1996; McDonald et al. 1998; Pederdy and Crush 1998; and Danso and McDonald 2000).

The South African media carry extensive reports on harassment and violence towards non-citizens. These include sometimes graphic (and even sympathetic) articles which suggest that tens, if not hundreds, of non-citizens have been killed in South Africa simply because they are foreigners. Yet more systematic research has indicated that the South African media play a significant role in creating anti-foreigner sentiment. The research by Danso and McDonald (2000), for example, draws on a collection of over 1200 English-language newspaper clippings about migration from all South African newspapers between 1994 and 1998. It presents both a quantitative and qualitative analysis of this media coverage. Among the findings of most import for this essay is their observation that though not all reportage is negative, and newspaper coverage would appear to be improving over time, the overwhelming majority of newspaper articles, editorials and letters to the editor are negative about immigrants and immigration. The articles uncritically reproduce problematic statistics and assumptions about cross-border migration. A large proportion of the articles depicts, for example, Mozambicans as car thieves and Nigerians as drug smugglers. This criminalisation of migrants from other parts of Africa is made worse by the more subtle use of terms such as "illegal" and "alien", despite the fact that these terms have been roundly criticised by institutions such as the United Nations High Commission for Refugees (UNHCR) for contributing to misconceptions of an otherwise law-abiding group of people. Danso and McDonald conclude, that:

> . . . at best, the press have been presenting a very limited perspective of cross-border migration dynamics, and in the process leaving the South African public in the dark as to the real complexities at play. At worst, the press have been contributing to xenophobic sentiments in the general public by weaving myths and fabrications around foreigners and immigration (2000, executive summary).

The research findings have been taken on board by government agencies set up to protect and investigate human rights abuses (e.g. the South African Human Rights Commission) as well as media organisations (e.g. the South African National Editors' Forum). Both organisations appear to accept such findings and insist on including the media as a crucial area of work with regard to "rolling back" xenophobia[8] and are working together with organisations such as UNHCR and refugee and migrant activist groups.

Not all media reproduce stereotypes. More perceptive journalists – the exception – have also pointed to the xenophobia of their colleagues. Writing in the *Mail & Guardian* (June 26, 1998), journalist Angella Johnson, who is of Caribbean-British descent, implicated her colleagues in the "rising tide of xenophobia":

> They [xenophobes] are aided and abetted by media reports of police rounding up and arresting "illegal immigrants" – usually hard-working men and women eking out a living selling goods on the streets. The use of these terms by officialdom and the

> media to describe people from neighbouring states contributes to the growing xenophobia in the country.

Johannesburg-based journalist Emeka Nwandiko (of Nigerian descent) related the case of a former (South African) news editor of a Johannesburg daily newspaper:

> He [the news editor] wrote an article defending a mob that killed a Mozambican hawker by throwing him off a moving train. Two Senegalese men tried to escape by climbing onto the roof of the train: they were electrocuted. The mob, returning from a jobs rally in Pretoria, was of the mistaken belief that the hawkers were pinching their jobs (*Mail & Guardian*, July 23, 1999).

More recently, changes have been observed in the presentation of certain television programmes, breaking a lance for refugees and non-citizens.[9] However, such shows are still few and far between and at most (im)migration and refugee issues are handled in a sensational and emotive manner with stereotypes about migrants and refugees either repeated or left unchallenged by the shows' hosts.[10] Regular workshops have been organised countrywide for journalists on reporting about migrants. There are signs of changes (in individual cases), yet one observer who has conducted such workshops and worked closely with refugee and migrant groups concedes that "the media are usually awful about refugees/migrants. They often perpetuate stereotypes through clumsy use of language and bad sub-editing. They often rely uncritically on [official] statistics, or prejudiced opinions given to them by state agencies or police" (personal communication, Davidson 2002).

Making Media, Challenging Media Stereotypes

There are no systematic surveys of media produced by immigrant and refugee individuals, groups or organisations.

The existence of media among refugees and migrants came to public attention for the first time with news of a magazine aimed at the small community of Ethiopian exiles based in Johannesburg. In April 1999 two journalists of *Simosa,* with an estimated readership of 4000, received death threats, were assaulted, and their offices broken into, allegedly by security agents of the Ethiopian government (*Freedom of Expression Institute Action Alerts*, April 14, 1999). At the time a number of South African newspapers carried the story and the press freedom group Freedom of Expression Institute (FXI) made a number of public statements and requested the South African government to convey their protest to the Ethiopian government. The issue soon faded from the public view.

In the late 1990s, a group of immigrants and refugees based in Cape Town produced a weekly programme on the community radio station Bush Radio. That programme was later discontinued. There are doubts about the impact of that programme, given the lack of audience figures for Bush Radio (which nonetheless broadcasts on a sought-after FM frequency) and the fact that the programme relied on volunteers. More significantly, in 1999 and 2000, refugee groups working with SABC radio producers finished a series of short radio documentaries entitled *Voices of Refuge*, which was broadcast on the SABC radio station SAfm in early 2000. Some community radio stations also rebroadcast the programmes. A number of newspapers or newsletters aimed at refugees also exist. In Johannesburg, refugees and immigrants produce the newspaper *Botshabelo*, while in Cape Town a group of refugees launched the newspaper *Fugee* in 1998.

Most media attempts by refugees or migrants have as their primary aim to fulfil the informational needs of refugees and immigrants. However, *Fugee* and the *Voices of Refuge* are significant, as their aim was also to engage directly with South Africans. They appear to have two primary aims: challenging negative stereotypes and assumptions about refugees and immigrants is at the heart of such efforts, but more directly, they are aimed at improving journalists' coverage of refugee and migrant issues.

Voices of Refuge is part of a broader campaign, titled "Roll Back Xenophobia". This campaign is the result of collaboration between the state-funded SA Human Rights Commission (SAHRC), the local representatives of the UNHCR office and the National Consortium on Refugee Affairs – the latter consisting of a loose consortium of NGOs working primarily in Cape Town and the Gauteng province. South Africans largely drive the initiative, which includes projects in radio, television and print media. *Voices of Refuge* was conceived by an SABC producer and the head of the Roll Back Xenophobia campaign who works for the SAHRC.[11] Refugee participants – from Somalia, Ethiopia, Ivory Coast, Democratic Republic of the Congo, Rwanda and Sudan – were trained through a series of workshops to produce their own 5-minute radio documentaries. The documentaries were broadcast in early 2000. Its impact is not very sure. Brett Davidson, the key SABC producer, suggests there were "articles in two or three newspapers" mentioning the documentaries. He is not sure of its impact (personal communication, Davidson 2002).

In contrast, *Fugee*, while using the editing skills of South Africans, is very much the product of refugees in Cape Town. The Cape Town Refugees' Forum (CTRF) provides much of the copy for the magazine that appears every three months. The publication of *Fugee* seems to be a natural reaction of refugees vis-à-vis the media as a means of communicating information concerning their history and their new life conditions. According to Zoe Nkongolo, a refugee himself from Angola and a member of the editorial staff, "the purpose of the publication is to give refugees an opportunity to present their true situation, to explain to the South African audience the reason of their migration" (interview, 2001). The first issue of *Fugee* was published in October 1998. For Nkongolo the "correct information" is crucial for changing South Africans' attitudes to refugees and assisting refugees' integration into "local community life". As a result, the editorial in the inaugural issue stated somewhat optimistically: "Hopefully, this newsletter will fulfil the function of providing much-needed, updated information for both refugee and local communities, over which collective ownership would be fostered."

Media Is Not Enough

Based on his experience with anti-xenophobia work, Williams suggests that public awareness strategies only have very limited impact. While it does provide alternative information about refugees and migrants, it does not necessarily change attitudes and prejudices. He concludes that while public education/awareness programmes must continue, they must be reinforced by strategies that engage citizens more directly. His conclusions are important for future work on how to approach media strategies around refugees and immigrants.[12]

According to Williams it is evident that the collective and individual efforts of organisations involved in anti-xenophobia activities have had some impact at a broad level. In particular, the public discourse in the media and by officialdom has shifted from being negative, derogatory and hard-lined, to being more circumspect and balanced. However, it has not reached the point at which expressions of xenophobia and specifically random attacks on foreigners have been condemned as a violation of the rights of persons, and as contrary to the Bill of Rights (Chapter 2 of the new Constitution, 1996). If anything, government and official response to xenophobia has been conspicuous precisely because of its absence.

At a more substantial level, there has not been any major shift in the perceptions of, and attitudes towards, foreigners by citizens. On the contrary, negative attitudes are becoming more commonplace and widespread, and increasingly result in foreigners being victims of indiscriminate and violent attacks. Even when citizens have been exposed to alternative and more balanced information about migrants and refugees, this has had little impact on attitudes and perceptions. The typical response when attempting to change attitudes through the provision of alternative information amounts to: "Don't confuse us with your facts; our minds are made up. Even if what you say about foreigners (not taking jobs, being victims of crime and so on) is true, we still don't want them in South Africa."

Thus, while public education/awareness programmes may have contributed to the development of a more acceptable public discourse generally, it has not necessarily resulted in the changing of attitudes and/or perceptions. This is not to suggest that public education programmes (such as the media efforts) have failed, but merely to point out that it has only had limited success.

Williams argues that the limitation of current anti-xenophobia strategies is that it is based on two premises. Firstly, it makes use of South Africa's human rights framework and logical arguments based on research information such as "foreigners do not take jobs, but create jobs", to explain why people should not be xenophobic, or to argue that there is no reason to be xenophobic. Secondly, it is assumed that, by appealing to the intellectual capacity of individuals or communities, behavioural changes will occur (cf. Murray 2001). In other words – it is assumed that if individuals or communities understand, agree with and accept the human rights framework and logical arguments, they will become less xenophobic. However, he argues, experiences in conducting information or public education workshops suggest that, even when people agree with and accept that foreigners have rights, or that they may be ignorant about foreigners, this does not translate into any substantial reflection on the need to confront and modify their own behaviour. Williams suggests a combined set of strategies that includes lobbying around the orientation of legislative and policy frameworks, human rights education, more research into the attitudes of citizens to migrants, and actively challenging the public and official discourse in the media of government spokespersons and opinion-makers that migrants are responsible for the hardships suffered by South African citizens. He makes a strong case for increased interaction between migrants and refugees, and citizens.

Experience has shown that those citizens who have had opportunities to interact with migrants and refugees in a meaningful way, are less likely to be xenophobic. These processes of interaction, however, will only succeed if they are specifically constructed to allow for dialogue and meaningful interaction. By implication, this means that such interaction cannot just be coincidental, but needs to be organised and facilitated (personal communication, Williams 2002).

Finally, Williams pleads for "going beyond the debate(s)". He argues that much of the current anti-xenophobia work is focused on attempting to shift the debate(s) about migration. The starting point is usually in response to the belief held by South African citizens – that millions of poverty-stricken, illiterate migrants and refugees are invading the country and competing unfairly for access to social, welfare and economic opportunities. However, it is well known that many migrants and refugees bring with them significant entrepreneurial and other skills and expertise. Many are also well qualified academically. The problem is that South Africans are not easily persuaded to change their perceptions, based simply on what they are told about the profiles and potential contribution of migrants and refugees. Thus, the value that migrants and refugees add, and in particular the extent to which they can make a difference to the lives of South Africans, needs to be demonstrated in a concrete manner.

The Trouble with the "Refugee and Migrant Community"

It is easy – both for strategic reasons and on the part of human rights or refugee organisations, but also as a direct binary response to the attacks and stereotypes of such groups (as Williams points out above) – to present refugees and migrants as an undifferentiated mass. For the same reasons questions of power and access among these refugees or their access to and contact with South Africans and South African institutions are also underplayed. Foreign migrants (and refugees) who enter South Africa either legally or illegally do so under confounded conditions that defy simple classification.

As Murray (2001) argues, the conventional distinction between permanent migrants and temporary sojourners fails to capture the sheer complexity of the movements both in and out of the country. For many African migrants, South Africa after apartheid is a land where the potential rewards outweigh the potential risks. Immigrants have fled war in Angola, Burundi and Somalia, and broken economies in the Democratic Republic of the Congo, Nigeria and Zimbabwe. Some foreigners enter the country as itinerant traders, intending to stay only as long as necessary. The tendency to present them as an undifferentiated mass is largely an unintended response to the xenophobia they faced. Regardless of their different parts and trajectories, they are denounced – across the board and in one sweep – to embody a number of stereotypes. Like all stereotypes, these sweeping platitudes reduce and flatten the real complexities of disempowered and marginalised populations (Murray 2001). Simone (2000:428-431) makes a distinction between four kinds of immigrant communities in Johannesburg, for example: political refugees, economic opportunists, "brain-drains" and affiliates – each with its own evolving interests, national hierarchies, competition, differential access to South African institutions, motives and debates over permanence and impermanence. These distinctions are not bounded, as Simone points out, as migrants and refugees move in and between them.

This definitely has implications for the kind of responses on the part of refugees and their allies. As Crush and McDonald (2000:12) point out: there are networks of migrants with strong links back home and institutional support in South Africa through unions and nongovernmental organisations, but these networks tend either to represent a relatively narrow constituency (such as mine workers) or are very small and poorly funded (like the Cape Town Refugee Forum that produces *Fugee*). These are not unimportant organisations or initiatives for migrants and refugees, and they are likely to grow in importance in the future, but their current role in protecting and expanding the rights of migrants is very limited.

Another failure is the tendency not to acknowledge the formation of new kinds of identities among these groups. As Murray (2001) points out, immigrant transnational communities create new forms of vernacular cosmopolitanism whose manifestations no longer refer to the acquisition of an identity through full assimilation to a new cultural milieu, but rather to the maintenance of a hybrid, syncretic identity neither "here" nor "there". Religious affiliations provide new forms of solidarity (for example, Islam and charismatic Christianity), and help to ground identities amongst disparate individuals who are otherwise unknown or disconnected to each other. It also deforms old South African identities. What initiatives by human rights and refugee groups themselves must take into account is that the new identities are always fluid, provisional and impermanent.

Conclusion

This paper explored the neglected aspect of media in studies about refugees and migrants. It argues that media campaigns are not enough in dealing with attitudes about refugees and migrants in South Africa. It recognises that while lots of research seems to have been done on newspaper content, most South Africans get their information from radio and TV. The essay emphasises the limitation of an intellectual approach to combating xenophobia. We did not have the time to explore – what would bring up interesting results – how emotion could be brought in, and what such tactics would look like. One suggestion which researchers could explore would be to target a study aimed at the small percentage of South Africans who actually come into contact with refugees. Researchers could identify these people, and target them specifically for high-intensity campaigns first. For example, forums could be organised in communities where refugees live. After all, it's most important that those who come into contact with foreigners don't threaten them, or treat them with disrespect.[13]

We argue that it is definitely necessary to try to get officials and public figures to change the way they talk about refugees and migrants, and maybe a campaign could target them too. One criticism of our argument is that our insistence that there are definite divisions, alliances and power dynamics that are not acknowledged, does not count for much. It does not make much difference to an anti-xenophobia campaign. For example, people hostile to foreigners don't care who these foreigners are, where they come from and why – they even sometimes target South Africans by mistake. When you are trying to get a simple message of "don't hate foreigners" across, you may end up getting too complicated trying to treat each individual or group differently. However, on the other hand, it can help to focus on individual stories so that the public sees people and not a stereotypical group. These are the kinds of issues we feel should be explored further by researchers.

Notes

1 Unless otherwise indicated, the considerations in this essay will largely concentrate on the dynamics related to the migration and immigration of Africans from outside the Southern African Development Community (SADC) region.

2 Institutionally, the most consistent research on the media aspects of the immigrant/refugee debate has been that by the Southern African Migrancy Project (SAMP), a joint project of South Africa's Idasa and Queens University, Canada. As a result, the latter part of this essay relies for a large part on the insights of Vincent Williams, head of SAMP in Cape Town.

3 This research is part of an ongoing project into refugee and migrant livelihoods by Kabeya-Mwepu. The findings referred to here are based on interviews with 120

refugees and migrants living and residing in a number of African townships on Cape Town's Cape Flats. The interviews were mostly conducted in an informal manner. One example of how refugees and migrants' distrust develop can be gleaned from the following account. Albert Ilunga, an Angolan citizen and refugee in South Africa who also works for a welfare organisation, was interviewed by journalists of the Xhosa-language weekly newspaper aimed at the residents of Khayelitsha township, the largest (African) urban settlement in Cape Town. In a subsequent article (March 16, 2000), unrelated to the interview, a story appeared under the heading: "Kuvunjululwe iimpahala zobusela" (translated: "Stolen goods discovered"). Ilunga's photo was published next to the report, which implied that he was in possession of stolen goods. Given the hostility against migrants and refugees in the area, Ilunga feared for his life (interview by Kabeya-Mwepu, 2001). Some of the other reasons given by informants were that their appearance in the media could put them at risk of being prosecuted by their respective governments because they "have entered the arena of politics". They also cited the "reputation" of the local media to "misinterpret" statements by foreigners.

4 This set of criticisms is based on the notes of Vincent Williams, head of SAMP (personal communication, 2002).

5 It is assumed that refugees and migrants have access to networks outside South Africa, in their home country or in Europe, for example, that make it easier for them to negotiate their new circumstances. While such networks do exist, these networks tend either to represent a relatively narrow constituency (such as mine workers) or are very new and poorly funded (such as the Cape Town Refugee Forum, whose publication is discussed in this essay). These are not unimportant organisations for migrants, and they are likely to grow in importance in the future, but their current role in protecting and expanding the rights of migrants is very limited (Crush and McDonald 2000:12).

6 Peter Vale, in a critique of international relations approaches to Southern Africa, also makes a similar point. He calls for researchers to look into "the vast underbelly of Southern Africa, that vast interchange and exchange of people and ideas which is taking and has taken place" which is as or more important than state action in determining the realities of the region (Vale et al. 2001:23). He offers the examples of illegal migrant labour in South African border farming districts, the impact of South African liberation politics on neighbouring states, and informal economic activity among African migrants and refugees in Johannesburg's innercity. Up to now, Vale notes, these trends have been reckoned with only as "threats to security", and not considered important to the larger political scene. (see Peter Vale, Larry Swatuk and Bertil Oden [eds.]. *Theory, Change and Southern Africa's Future*. Hampshire and New York, NY: Palgrave.)

7 There are disputes as to the number of migrants and refugees in South Africa. Official

estimates on the number of undocumented immigrants living illegally in South Africa vary widely, ranging from fewer than one million to a truly phantasmagoric 12 million – a staggering number in a country of only 40 million people. Experts regard these wildly discrepant figures as hardly more than guesses, provocative conjectures that reflect more what various state agencies and officials want to believe, than what they actually know. The truth is that there are no reliable methodologies available for determining the actual number of foreign immigrants and migrants in South Africa. But what is not in dispute is that the number of illegal immigrants deported has dramatically increased, from an estimated 90 000 in 1994, for example, to around 200 000 in 2000 (cf. Murray 2001).

8 For example, on a series of pages describing its programmes to fight xenophobia, the SAHRC states: "The media's presentation of issues relating to refugees, asylum seekers and migrants significantly shapes public opinion about these groups. Hence, the media has massive responsibility in providing factual coverage that does not perpetuate myths, encourage generalisations or spread misinformation about refugees, asylum seekers and migrants. Unfortunately, accurate, truthful and factual coverage on refugees, asylum seekers and migrants is not the norm. There is a general tendency to lump together all foreigners into one big category."
(See http://www.sahrc.org.za/focal_issues.htm)

9 These include a number of current affairs and magazine shows on the public broadcaster South African Broadcasting Corporation (SABC) – which commands the bulk of the television audience – for example, the shows *Two Way* (SABC 1), *Special Assignment* (SABC 3; documentary insert), as well as *Felicia* (later broadcast on the rival e-tv channel). Although prone to sensationalism, the specific episodes on refugees and migrants attempted to be informative and included on-air panelists or as speaking subjects in background reports. This has also been extended to fiction television. The popular soap opera *Generations* has introduced an African immigrant character, so has *Soul City*, a drama series promoting basic health care. *Soul City*, incidentally, is partly funded by the government Department of Health.

10 Vincent Williams, who heads SAMP, has noted that journalists who have been writing about immigrant and refugee issues are now a bit more circumspect in terms of the language that they use and searching out contextual information, rather than just uncritically reporting whatever Department of Home Affairs officials or the police tell them (personal communication with Vincent Williams, head of SAMP, 2001).

11 An exhibition "Images of Refuge" was held in Johannesburg, where refugees had been given disposable cameras and asked to record their daily lives. Brett Davidson (then a senior SABC producer) "thought it would be a great idea to try something similar on radio" and approached the head of RBX (personal communication with Brett Davidson, head of Idasa Radio Democracy Project, 2002).

12 This section relies heavily on insights from Vincent Williams.

13 Thanks to Brett Davidson for this suggestion.

References

Crush, J. 2001. "Immigration, Xenophobia and Human Rights in South Africa". Cape Town, SAMP / SAHRC, Series No. 22.

Crush, J. and McDonald, D.A. 2000."Transnationalism, African Immigration and New Migrant Spaces in South Africa: An Introduction", in *Canadian Journal of African Studies*, Special Issue, Vol 34, No 1. 1-19.

Danso, R. and McDonald, D.A. 2000. "Writing Xenophobia: Immigration and the Press in Post-Apartheid South Africa". Cape Town, SAMP, Series No. 17.

Dolan, C. and Reitzes, M. 1996. "The Insider Story: Press Coverage of Illegal Immigrants and Refugees, April 1994-September 1995". Centre for Policy Studies, Research Report No. 48, April.

Dodson, B. and Oelofse, C. 2000. "Shades of Xenophobia: In-Migrants and Immigrants in Mizamoyethu, Cape Town". *Canadian Journal of African Studies*, Special Issue, Vol 34, No 1. 124-148.

McDonald, D.A. 2000. "We Have Contact: Foreign Migration and Civic Participation in Marcomi Beam, Cape Town" *Canadian Journal of African Studies*, Special Issue, Vol 34, No 1. 101-123.

Murray, M. 2001. "Alien Strangers in Our Midst: The Dreaded Foreign Invasion and Fortress South Africa". Unpublished Paper.

Simone, A. 2000. "Going South: African Immigrants in Johannesburg" in Nuttall, S. and Michaels, C. (eds.). 2000. *Senses of Culture: South African Culture Studies.* Cape Town: Oxford University Press.

South African Human Rights Commission. Roll Back Xenophobia Campaign: http://www.sahrc.org.za/.

Southern African Migrancy Project: http://www.queensu.ca/samp.

Williams, V. et al., 2000 "Losing our Minds: Skills Migration and the South African Brain Drain". Cape Town, SAMP, Series No. 18, 2000.

CHAPTER THIRTEEN

Taxi to Soweto and *Panic Mechanic*: Two Cinematic Representations of Whiteness in South Africa Post-1994

Melissa Steyn

> Contained within the plot structures, the characters and social practices they represent, working unconsciously at deeper levels of signification, are to be found the suppressed traumas, hopes, fears and preoccupations of Afrikaner culture (Tomaselli and Van Zyl 1992:396).

Introduction

The flux of history sees the fortunes of different groups of people wax and wane, and along with them the discourses that enabled, supported, enforced and perpetuated their power. Major discourses that helped to shape the second half of the last millennium clustered around the notion of "race", rationalising European global expansion, conquest and domination (Blaut 1993; Pieterse 1992). The belief in the superiority of the people who hailed from Europe, identifiable by their lighter complexion, circulated the globe along with the military, material and cultural power of Europe, and opened up a social space of privilege relative to "others". This is the ideologically powerful space of whiteness. Emanating from the centre of power, whiteness has been able to pass itself off as the "normal" way of being human. "White" people, generally, have displayed a marked tendency not to understand how their racial advantage is constructed in everyday life. Disadvantage is analysed and examined, but the lifeworld of quotidian privilege is not seen to require explanation, to the point, in some contexts, of becoming "invisible"[1] (Dyer 1997; Frankenberg 1993; Nakayama and Martin 1999).

The eurocentric constructions of modernity are increasingly being challenged, particularly in the postcolonial studies literature (Brah 1996; Goldberg 1994; Pieterse and Parekh 1995; Said 1994). It is not surprising, therefore, that a growing community of scholars emphasises that the critical examination of how "white" people experience their *own* racialisation, analyses which expose the inner workings of racially privileged positions, is crucial to the task of dismantling the power which "race" has to structure unequal societies (Delgado and Stefancic 1997; Fine et al. 1997; Frankenberg 1997; Kincheloe et al. 1998). This study responds to the call in whiteness studies to particularise whiteness in specific contexts (Nakayama and Krizek 1995).

The aftermath of South Africa's first democratic elections in 1994 did not only see the end of official white rule, but also the beginnings of processes of reconciliation and reconstruction. However, these are undertaken within a legacy of deep-seated intercultural and racial conflict, and societal deformation left by the structures of apartheid and 300 years of hegemonic colonial discourses. Major re-alignments are taking place and a new power balance between the cultural groupings in South Africa is being established. The African majority has gained political power, and for the first time in the history of the country, "white" people are losing the position from which they have been able to define both self and other.

The defence of the practices of whiteness – always somewhat precariously maintained in a country in which whites were numerically by far a minority – depends largely on psychological misrecognition, personal inflation and denial. Since the early 1990s, white South Africans have been adapting to a situation where white "self" and "other" constructions are challenged by the society that is evolving around them. The dominant societal dynamics are inimical to the perpetuation of privileged whiteness; a new sense of self has to be forged on different terms (Dolby 2001; Steyn 1999, 2001a; Zegeye 2001). Studying how white South Africans represent this new situation is therefore interesting for what it reflects of how the loss of racial entitlement is experienced subjectively (Steyn 2001b). And with South Africa now almost a decade into its new dispensation, such a retrospective glance helps us better to track the process of (mal)adjustment which whites have been making to living in a context where whiteness has been decentred, and may shed light on white identity in the future.

This chapter analyses two films that were screened on the popular film circuit in the period around the 1994 transition. The chapter examines the portrayal of whiteness in these films, and what these representations suggest about how the broader white society was responding to being socially repositioned. In respect of valorising white experience, these two films continue the canon as it has been for the full 100 years of the South African film industry (Blignaut and Botha 1992; Tomaselli 1997). Through most of this history, the film industry has been almost entirely in the hands of white producers, usually screened for segregated white audiences, and generally funded by government capital (Botha 1995; Tomaselli 1997). Consequently, it has reflected, largely uncritically, the worldview and ideological agendas of mainstream white population, particularly Afrikaans-speaking white South Africans (Botha 1995; Prinsloo 1996; Tomaselli and Van Zyl 1992). Films which interrogated white realities, and/or reflected the real-life experiences of black South Africans, have been few and far between, usually have been funded from elsewhere, and have not been screened in mainstream cinema (Botha 1995; Tomaselli 1997).

Botha (1995) argues that a development of the early 1990s was the consensus "from all sectors of the industry that cinema has a vital role in the forging of social cohesion and the process of democratisation and development that so urgently need[ed] to take place" (1995:10). Cinema was seen to be potentially "a liberating medium of mass communication" (1995:2) and "vital in South Africa's transition" (1995:1).

Both films analysed in this chapter can be situated within this moment in the development of the South African film industry. Both take as their subject matter the turmoil experienced within the white psyche at the time of transition. The first film is *Taxi to Soweto.* A human drama, *Taxi to Soweto* is the work of director Manie van Rensburg, producer of award-winning television dramas, as well as the internationally acclaimed film *The Fourth Reich* (1990). Van Rensburg's work belongs to the minority genre of domestic anti-apartheid films which have examined white racial attitudes (Tomaselli 1997), even to the point of his being regarded as "a chronicler of the Afrikaner psyche" (Botha 1995:12). *Taxi to Soweto* can be firmly placed within Van Rensburg's revisionist tradition, and forms part of the transformative agenda to which Botha refers:

> [A]s forms of popular fiction, films and videos such as *Taxi to Soweto* can explore the changes taking place in South Africa in a way that helps people to make sense of these dramatic changes (1995:2).

The second film, *Panic Mechanic,* came out in 1996, two years into the "new" South Africa. Directed by David Lister, this film belongs squarely in the tradition of "cheap-shot filming", using the "candid camera" formula – a formula that has been successful at mainstream white cinemas since the 1960s (Feldman 1996). Leon Schuster, the Afrikaans comedian who wrote the narrative and acts in the main role (Feldman 1996), is well known for his outrageous radio and television shows, which mostly follow the candid camera tradition. The tenor of his work is reflected in the name of his television series, *Hanky Pranky.* A South African box-office hit, *Panic Mechanic* self-avowedly purports to hold up a comic mirror to the country on the way in which it is coping with change, with a view to relieving tension.

Although very differently textured in their responses to the changes they depict, both films show the new South Africa to be a radical disjuncture from the "old order". As products of "white" South African consciousness, the films portray transition in terms of an inversion of the logic of the past. The old white certainties around which life had been built, while not equally problematised in these films, are shown in both to be decentred and destabilised. The advent of the new order is accompanied by psychological stress in the form of loss of potency, diminished control and agency, confusion of roles and lines of authority, and a sense of the collapse of order, of knowledge and even of a coherent self.

As postcolonial theorists remind us, white identity has depended largely on a bifurcation (Bhabha 1994; Lopez 2001; Memmi 1990; Nakayama and Martin, 1999; Steyn 1999,

2001; Werbner and Ranger 1996). In South Africa, "Africa", and what it was constructed to represent, was split off from the "European" and what that was constructed to represent: the cultured, the ordered, the rational, the centre of progress, the measure of cleanliness, of civilisation. As a signifier, "Africa" carried "otherness", everything not "European" (Mudimbe 1994; Memmi 1990; Pieterse 1992). One could argue that apartheid was a material and legal enactment of the psychological dynamic that attempted to keep Africa split off, separate, and to leave "whiteness" pure. For whites in this country the new South Africa can be understood as an encounter with Africa, with the "other" that it did not want to know except in terms of knowledge constructions that facilitated control. The fear of a reversal of position with the repressed "other" has always dominated the psyche of white South Africa, achieving apocalyptic proportions in the white imagination (Thornton 1996). The fear of a "black take-over", of the "black peril", has been the bogey that informed much of policy and action in South Africa. The new South Africa, then, which empowers this "other", heralds the return of the repressed (Steyn 2001a). In effect, both films deal with how white South Africans are coping with the encounter with Africa they had previously pushed away both psychologically and physically. This paper argues that both films, despite their attempts in different ways to perspectivise white South Africa's responses to this challenge, nevertheless affirm the ideological underpinnings of white South Africa, carried in the "dominant memory" of whiteness, submerged in the "secondary levels of meaning, operating connotatively and symbolically" (Tomaselli and Van Zyl 1992:401).[2]

The Old Order Slips Away: *Taxi to Soweto*

The first film, *Taxi to Soweto,* has as its main character a white woman, Jessica, from a privileged white area of Johannesburg. In the context of her protected white background, her only extended contact with the "other" is with servants, "tamed" Africa. She is forced to take a crowded "black taxi" after her car breaks down en route to the airport where she is to meet the husband with whom she shares a tired marriage. The taxi is hijacked, and instructed to reroute to Soweto, the heart of "otherness". Soweto – the sprawling black township outside Johannesburg – may be characterised as Johannesburg's "twin city" – its "black" counterpart. Whereas Johannesburg, built on gold mining, has been the seat of "white" wealth and establishment, Soweto has been a psychic hub from which resistance and struggle against the system emanated.

The scenes that follow portray her sense of bewilderment and alienation when she finds herself "dumped" in the township. The camera identifies with her white gaze as scene succeeds scene – poverty, chaos, criminality, overcrowding, filth, and strange (primitive) customs. Totally out of her depth, she is frightened and shocked at this different reality. The taxi driver, Richard, evincing a measure of disdain for her effeteness, provides some protection but not much guidance, which forces her into an encounter with herself. She is confronted by her ignorance, and the local people do not spare her. As one puts it: "You people know nothing about us; you couldn't care less about us" ["*Julle weet niks van ons nie; julle mense worrie nie van ons nie*," in the original Afrikaans dialogue of the film]. For the first time, she starts to see herself as the "other" sees her, or rather, as the "other" sees *through* her. In a jocular taunt, they continue calling her *Miss* Jessica, underscoring the uselessness of the false dignity of whiteness in this context. Her discomfort is acute, as she increasingly has to acknowledge her dependence on the "other".

In a scene that carries a great deal of the symbolism of the film, she finds herself caught up in the middle of a mass demonstration. Alarmed and terrified, she has no option but to blend in with the toyi-toying mass as she is propelled along, raising her hand in a black power salute. At this crucial point in the plot, Richard loses her in the crowd and she has to deal with feelings of abandonment as well as genuine danger.

Richard calls her home to see if she has managed to find her way back, and her husband interprets the message on the answering machine to mean that she has left him for a black man. The emasculating factor is the blackness of her assumed lover. It is an assault upon the entire construction of his identity, premised upon the illusion fostered by the old order of white male unassailability. He is thrown into confusion by the challenge the new South Africa presents to the white male phallus: once seemingly certain knowledge constructed from the position of, and in the service of, white male domination, can be, and is being, deposed. In a state of severe psychological disorientation, Jessica's husband seeks to make sense of her desertion, desperate to find her.

In the meantime, she has been drawn into the "life" and vitality of Soweto, where she finds the corrective to the sterility of her proper life in "white" South Africa. A turning point in her development is when she drinks too much alcohol in a jazz club, and passes out on the stage after making a fool of herself. This is a levelling experience. The loss of control and of pretences at superiority amounts to the loss of her old self. She breaks through white defences and denials, and emerges with a sense of solidarity with black Africans, a growing identification with their world and its hardships. Carried forward by events, she stands up to her husband's racist employer in solidarity with his striking workers, an act that gets her into confrontation with the legal system that has protected her "white" life. Her husband's name is disgraced by her behaviour, and he loses his job, further destabilising his "old" world.

Jessica's husband, Du Toit, has been going through his own dark night of the soul. The law, he has been informed by the police, no longer prohibits interracial relationships. Drunk and demented with pain, he sits in a bar. His delusional brain transforms the images on the television screen into those of his wife and a black man (acted by Richard), kissing passionately. The man breaks off kissing Jessica, turns to him, and says, "Welcome to the new South Africa. Peace, brother." "He's pitch black," Du Toit repeats senselessly to the barman, his worst imaginings now "confirmed" by his hallucination.

Eventually Du Toit traces Jessica to Soweto. They are romantically re-united, both having now outgrown their earlier limited selves. They spend a happy evening in the jazz club, the place of healing, harmoniously integrated with the Sowetan folk. The film ends as we see them leaving Soweto, this time in the back seat of a "white" taxi. They are the only passengers, in love again. A smiling Richard is driving.

Taxi to Soweto presents Jessica as having undergone a "hero's journey". She has ventured into the world of the "other", a kind of underworld, and has returned healed and wiser, reconciled with her psychic opposite. Her black taxi driver/chauffeur, in the role of a familiar, has acted as her guide through the dangerous territory, bringing her safely back to herself. And she has done all this for the good of her society – she brings healing wisdom to the sterility of her marriage and culture, which had become severed from the wellsprings of life. The film, it seems, intends us to see her courage in crossing boundaries and moving beyond her whiteness as holding the key to personal healing and social reconciliation, the way through the damage wrought by apartheid, and towards social reconciliation. "In many ways this film is the first filmic presentation of the dawn of a post-apartheid South Africa" (Botha 1992:176).

Yet the resolution of the story undermines this intention. Ironically, the most important thing about the film is the taxi *from* Soweto. The contrast between the entry into Soweto and the exit from the city reflects the "white" desire that the new South Africa, while temporarily uncomfortable, will not really require much permanent personal and material adjustment. The encounter with Africa that the new South Africa necessitates may be no more than a cathartic journey that ends, thankfully, back at "home". The fundamentals of the white world may yet remain intact. Jessica did not stay in Soweto; she did not really get involved with the black man, who is once again in his proper role; she returns to her privileged white suburb in her husband's arms. His phallus, though reprimanded, has been reinstalled.

Taxi to Soweto is a white fantasy at the end of an era. In the face of acute anxiety about what the future could hold, the fantasy is that the disruption to the old way of life and the troubling of its certainties will be no more than a temporary disturbance. The threat to old realities may be no more than a bad dream with a happy ending. In the failure to carry through the creative vision of the film, *Taxi to Soweto* repeats a similar loss of poetic integrity that Marx (1991) observed in Van Rensburg's acclaimed *The Fourth Reich*. Marx writes that the film *betrays* its own material, in particular in the manner in which the portrayal of the right-wing Afrikaners (and their language) lapses into the very stereotypes the film purports to problematise:

> It is to render the right-wing extremism that continues to rear its head merely another mad aberration of a rather odd lot of people. It is to make them safe, exotic, other unintelligible, thus repeating the mistakes of the colonial enterprise in its confrontation with dark continents, and subverting, precisely, the impact that the film . . . was meant to have . . . (1991:72-73).

A Bizarre World is Born: *Panic Mechanic*

The Leon Schuster film, *Panic Mechanic,* appearing two years into the new South Africa, exposes something of whites responding to their new circumstances. The film has a very thin story line. Schuster himself is the main character. He loses what he regards as a secure position with the South African state-owned television network, and ends up working for a dishonest, opportunistic foreigner, making a film for the new South African president, a black woman.[3] The film he is commissioned to make is supposed to help South Africans deal with the stress of transformation by laughing at themselves and the stressful situations occasioned by transformation, and consists of several candid camera pranks. *Panic Mechanic* then loosely interweaves the fortunes of Schuster dealing with his own encounter with transformation, with staged situations that he sets up in order to film his fellow South Africans' unguarded reactions to exaggerated stereotypes of change.

The most salient feature of the film is that it concretises what is already present in the "white" imagination, presenting these fantasies as achieved reality in unsubtle, "in-your-face" scenarios. Schuster then confronts people with these situations unexpectedly. The result is that their immediate reactions tend to be visceral, revealing a great deal about their emotional and psychological assumptions. The parallels between the experiences of Schuster, the character in the film, and the traumas of his "victims" in the "film within the film" then further correspond to topical situations and issues in the real society to which the film alludes. The effect of this internal and external intertextuality is to present uncertainty and shock as ubiquitous and inescapable – every which way we turn, we witness the same sense of confusion. The film takes us into a hall of mirrors in which the repetition and consistency of images of disorientation accumulate into what can rightly be called a portrayal of a pervasive and profound sense of panic.

The opening scene of the film aptly provides a metaphor for the loss of "white" control. Within the Union Buildings in Pretoria, Schuster, disguised as a furniture trucker, is supervising the removal of an enormous (fake) portrait of the cabinet of the former nationalist president, P.W. Botha (F.W. de Klerk's predecessor). With the old South African anthem playing in the background, Schuster cautions the workers carrying the portrait to the removal van about the value of their charge. In addition to its monetary value, the portrait represents "our past", and its removal from the corridors of power is "sad, sad but very true". The portrait is to be taken to the Wilderness, where P.W. Botha now resides. As they are carrying the portrait across the street, a motorcyclist, primed by Schuster, roars down the road and smashes through the canvas. The image speaks of the demise, or even demolition, of an era, the falling into disrepute of a once seemingly invincible regime, and the reversal of the fates of the powerful. It is an objective correlative for the feelings amongst many white South Africans at the time of being "dethroned", stripped of the authority and privilege that had once been regarded as their "normal" heritage and birthright.

Shots of Schuster driving in the streets of Johannesburg with his car radio playing follow. Both visually and aurally, we are confronted with the "new South Africa". The news bulletin carries report after report of corruption, financial decline, labour unrest, and the deleterious effects of affirmative action and of crime. The streets are lined with (yes, white) people holding placards announcing their unemployment and begging alms. Flea markets selling the goods of whites who have emigrated are flourishing. The implication is clear: South Africa has become "Third World". No longer kept at bay by white rule, Africa is "out". An expression of gratitude for his job at the broadcasting corporation scarcely off his lips, Schuster arrives at his office and sits down absentmindedly in his chair, and quite literally onto the lap of a black man. He has been ousted overnight, as has his boss to whom he appeals in his distress. The complacent new manager exhorts them to be mature. When Schuster finally manages to express what he now realises ("I'm fired"), the new boss confirms his worst fear with the dreaded word, "affirmative". In what approaches psychodrama of white male paranoia, the scene portrays in literal terms what white men subjectively believe is happening to them.

Images of the "rainbow nation" accentuate the extremes of disparity within the population and by implication the bizarreness of notions of current or potential unity. The queue outside the president's office consists of overtly right-wing militants, an African in traditional dress, a be-turbaned man, people in loincloths bearing placards demanding "higher prices for Khoisans and other 'interest groups'". The rainbow nation is an absurd nation. Disrepair and disintegration are everywhere evident, symbolically captured in the prank where a minibus pulls away, leaving the chassis behind, the bewildered schoolchildren still seated. The incapacity of the government to stem the acceleration of chaos is reflected in the reaction of the "minister of transport" when confronted with the news of further taxi violence. Harassed and out of his depth, he instructs: "Call in the army." The new South Africa is plummeting into a state of emergency. Violence and crime have become culturally normalised. For example, when a dinner party in a restaurant pops champagne, the entire restaurant clientele rises in unison, their response conditioned by the sound. They all simultaneously fire the guns they were carrying and sit down to continue eating as if nothing has happened.

It is in the context of this spiralling stress that the president recognises the "genius" of the Schuster approach, which claims to heal through outrageous exposure of the underlying conflict and disorder, rather than an attempt to placate: "Use the root of your stress as the route to recovery." The president then initiates the stream of the narrative that carries the "redeeming" strain in the film: the proceeds from the film to be made by the company for which Schuster now works, will establish a Children's Fund. This allows for the development of a clichéd and unconvincing story line that shows Schuster acquiring some appreciation for the lot of impoverished children, and engineering a slapstick vindication over his crooked employer.

The analytically interesting material in the film is contained in the scenarios which Schuster assiduously creates for the film within the film, all of which draw on the stereotypical thinking that abounds in "white talk".[4] In a rather cavalier manner, Schuster taps into highly contested areas in the process of South African reconciliation. Two examples follow.

A shabbily erected tollgate across a country dirt road in the heart of a white conservative farming area is guarded by Schuster, disguised as a black man. The slogan, "Better roads for a better future", on a billboard poster announces that this is a Reconstruction and Development Fund project. He demands R50 from the aggressive Afrikaner farmers who wish to continue along the road, whereas he allows a black man who speaks to him in an African language to proceed. When challenged by one of the irate farmers, he explains: "He's black, sir." They finally pay him the R50, whereupon he immediately calls a young child standing at the roadside and instructs him to "go and buy four litres of Coke and some smokes". He responds to their fury by candidly confirming the assumption which had informed all their reactions: "I've taken the money for myself, sir."

The scenario acts out the "white" belief that money used for reconstruction disappears into a bottomless pit of corruption within the ranks of the "newly advantaged". It surfaces as resentment against the intention on the part of the new government to "redistribute" wealth, and reveals a belief that disempowerment has simply been reversed under the new regime.

Another scenario draws on the contested area of land restitution. Schuster, again disguised as what he refers to as a "rainbow person", has set up "his own place in the sun" on a golf course in a wealthy area of Johannesburg. He explains to the indignant English-speaking golfers that this is his ancestral ground, and that his grandfather was buried under the nearby tree. When he stirs his porridge with one of the golf flags, the challenge as the white golfers would interpret it is clear: the "illogicality" of Africa is reasserting itself, and confronting the logic of Europe. In the face of their protestations about legal land ownership, he invokes the powers of the new state, "My president says the land belongs to everyone." His further embellishments bring into the fray more of the European stereotypes that abound about what africanisation entails: his brother is coming with the goats and kids (the cultivation effected by European influence will regress into primitive practices), he is accumulating trash (the country will become increasingly "Third World"), and he has cut a hole into the fence to get onto the fairways (Africa can no longer be contained through "normal" methods).

Scenarios such as the above act out the deep-seated belief that loss of European control inevitably ushers in the chaos, stagnation, poverty and irrationality that is the "essence" of Africa. The "white" imagination that is exposed in these encounters is structured by a profound Afro-pessimism, a pervasive negativity which actually accounts for a great deal of the stress experienced by white South Africans in a country now controlled politically by Africans.

The rationale expressed in the film is that viewing these provoked conflictual situations will be cathartic for South Africans, and somehow contribute towards more relaxed attitudes and therefore reconciliation. The problem, however, rests with Schuster's gaze and voice as scriptwriter and commentator. He presents an uncritical, ludicrous celebration of the interactions the scenes provoke. An element of collusion with the stereotypes of Africa and Africans out of which his dupes react, exposes his close identification with "white talk". Rhetorically, the film suggests that trenchant intercultural conflict centred on serious issues of competing interests can be reduced to benign fun. More particularly, it suggests that this conflict arises from the incompatibility of the groups themselves, that the absurdity is inherent in the attempt to create a new order. The socially constructed frames of reference that the "victims" bring to the incidents are not evaluated critically. Specifically the white imagination is not problematised, so that no further self-reflexivity is required of the white viewer.

In sum, therefore, the film itself ends up being one more example of what it portrays. It contributes to the white discourses of anomie and dislocation that accompany the displacement of the old centre, old certainties. Rather than showing the cathartic way to reconciliation, Schuster has produced a celebration of a society that is battling to cope with profound social and psychological reorientation. The element of vindication at being able to reflect difficulties under black government, as if whites could have "told you so", suggests that the deeper thrust of the film is to sabotage, rather than to further, reconciliation. As Prinsloo (1996) has argued, a representation of reconciliation in South African film that does not propose transformation, cannot "contribute in any significant way as custodian of popular memory" (1996:46).[5]

Conclusion

Both films analysed in this chapter engaged the new realities of "white" existence in South Africa, as they were being processed at the time. Both films purport to affirm the political change that removed the legalised and enforced privilege of the old order. Yet Van Rensburg's representation of a white woman's journey, while in all probability having earnest and progressive intent, finally reinstates the co-ordinates of "white" order it sets out to displace; Schuster's "nod in the direction of political change" (Feldman 1996) is plainly unconvincing. While they come from different positions within the historical development of the South African film industry, they finally converge in their difficulty of envisioning a transformed, yet successful, "white" positionality. Taken together, then, these films seem to reflect a deep-seated ambivalence and inner conflict in white society in relation to the changes to which whites were being asked to adjust. The impulse towards escapism, denial, withdrawal, and even passive aggression is evident, creating a tension that pulls against the need, whether idealistic or pragmatic in inspiration, to be reconciled with new realities.

This analysis suggests that the prognosis circa 1994 was that if white society was to contribute with commitment to reconciliation and reconstruction within the broader society, a great deal of emotional work would need to be done. While overtly supportive of the changes, when the moment of change was upon the nation, South African whiteness closeted fantasies of a future in which the status quo would endure in essential ways. The desire to keep whiteness as intact as possible has probably informed the generally less enthusiastic attitude whites displayed to the TRC process and to suggestions of restitutive measures, for example (Gibson and MacDonald 2001).

The tricky question is whether recognising this dynamic at work is able to shed light on how whiteness may unfold as the country moves forward into the new millennium. What is clear is that the longer and more ardently white South Africans hold onto "white" assumptions, particularly in relation to what Africa signifies, the more besieged they will feel as time goes on. Post-1994 there have been those for whom a realignment with Africa and its issues has proved to be profoundly meaningful, and who are redefining "self" and "other" in ways that can undercut "whiteness". Others, like Jessica giving the black power salute when she finds herself propelled forward by the marching crowd, have been letting go of some of the trappings of whiteness through sheer pressure of circumstances, and are finding that it is not all bad. For many, though, the nostalgia lingers for easier, more self-serving times. The general sense that they are enmeshed in circumstances that in some way aggrieve them inhibits these white South Africans envisioning a different mode of being in the society.

The seduction of whiteness, it seems, works on. The new millennium will not escape the legacy of the old. Within the country, discourses of whiteness, which used to ensure dominance, now often reconfigure into discourses of resistance (Steyn 2001), or reshape so as to become less detectable (Wicomb 2001). A steady stream of emigration continues to countries where whiteness is, as yet, less contested.

Yet whites elsewhere in the global community also find the "normality" of white privilege and entitlement are being eroded. One can surmise that, like white South Africans, they are unlikely to leap at the opportunity to self-deconstruct their fantasies of white entitlement, a surmise which is also anticipated by other studies (e.g. Gabriel 1998; Gallagher 1999). One of the major democratic challenges that faces our societies is for people of European descent to find ways to imagine what it would mean to "be white" differently – ways that would depart from cultures of entitlement and would transform fantasies of perpetual privilege into imaginaries of creative engagement in building a more truly equal world: The challenge that remains for such a narrative [of transformed whiteness] would thus come not from without, in the form of an angry, avenging other; rather, the final and most damaging obstacle to the psychic maturation of a postcolonial whiteness remains its own will-to-mastery – the lasting legacy, in short, of a colonialism that has left its ineffaceable mark on the postcolonial world, which continues even now to function as unacknowledged ideology. To systematically uncover and interrogate such colonial traces wherever they may surface is the proper work of a postcolonial discourse (Lopez 2001:118-119).

Notes

1 I am not attempting to address the question here of how whiteness in South Africa has differed from configurations elsewhere. It is clear, however, that several factors led to a whiteness that, while assumed to be appropriately advantaged, was not as invisible as this theorisation suggests (Steyn 2001a). Also see Wicomb (2001).

2 Tomaselli and Van Zyl (1992) show the continuities that have underpinned popular Afrikaans expression for the bulk of the twentieth century. While it is beyond the scope of this paper to analyse the genre in detail, the underlying colonial "structure of mind" which casts Africa as the anarchic, primitivistic "other" of white, European order and rationality is shown to be still central, still serving a hegemonic function.

3 South Africans will recognise two conflated allusions. The first is to former President Mandela's Children's Fund; the second to the financial controversy surrounding the film, *Sarafina 2,* commissioned by the former Minister of Health (a woman) for Aids awareness education.

4 A term I have given to a discursive practice prevalent in white middle-class South Africa that arises from the subjective experience of loss of privilege. (See Steyn 2001b.)

5 Prinsloo (1996) makes this comment in the context of her analysis of *Cry, the Beloved Country,* which her analysis shows does not serve to "illuminate and transform the present" (1996:47).

References

Bhabha, H. K. 1994. *The location of culture.* London: Routledge.

Blaut, J. M. 1993. *The colonizer's model of the world: Geographical diffusionism and Eurocentric history.* New York: The Guilford Press.

Blignaut, J. and Botha, M. (eds.). 1992. *Movies – Moguls – Mavericks, South African Cinema 1979 – 1991.* Cape Town: Showdata.

Botha, M. P. 1992. "The cinema of Manie Van Rensburg: Chronicles of the Afrikaner Psyche". In Blignaut, J. and Botha, M. (eds.). *Movies – Moguls – Mavericks – South African Cinema 1979 – 1991.* Cape Town: Showdata.

Botha, M. P. 1995. "The South African film industry: Fragmentation, identity crisis and Unification". *Kinema,* Spring, 1995. http://waarts.uwaterloo.ca/FINE/juhde/botha951.htm. Accessed 20/1/02.

Brah, A. 1996. *Cartographies of diaspora: Contesting identities.* London: Routledge.

Delgado, R. and Stefancic, J. 1997. *Critical white studies: Looking behind the mirror.* Philadelphia: Temple University Press.

Dyer, R. 1997. *White.* London: Routledge.

Feldman, P. 1996. "Cheap-shot giggles in the garbage." *Star Tonight.* 12 December

1996. Independent online. Film Reviews. http://164.88.55.4/online/star/tonight/film/Film_pqr/1998/panic.html Accessed on 28/02/1999.

Fine, M., Weis, L., Powell, L. C. and Wong, L. M. 1997. *Off white: Readings on race, power, and society.* New York: Routledge.

Frankenberg, R. 1993. *White women, race matters: The social construction of whiteness.* Minneapolis: University of Minnesota Press.

Frankenberg, R. 1997. *Displacing whiteness: Essays in social and cultural criticism.* Durham: Duke University Press.

Gabriel, J. 1998. *Whitewash: Racialized politics and the media.* London: Routledge.

Gallagher, C. A. 1999. Researching race: Reproducing racism. *The review of Education/ Pedgagogy/Cultural Studies,* 21(2). 165-91.

Gibson, J. L. and Macdonald, H. 2001. "Truth – Yes, Reconciliation – Maybe: South Africans judge the Truth and Reconciliation Process". Research report, Institute for Justice and Reconciliation. Rondebosch: Institute for Justice and Reconciliation.

Goldberg, D. T. 1994. *Multiculturalism: A critical reader.* Cambridge, MA: Blackwell.

Kincheloe, J. L., Steinberg, S. R., Rodriguez, N. M. and Chennault, R. E. 1998. *White reign: Deploying whiteness in America.* New York: St. Martin's Press.

Lopez, A. J. 2001. *Posts and pasts: A theory of postcolonialism.* Albany: SUNY Press.

Marx, L. 1991. "For queen and country: 'The Fourth Reich' and the great betrayal". *South African Theatre Journal, 5*(1).

Memmi, A. 1990. *The colonizer and the colonized.* (H. Greenfield, Trans.). London: Earth-scan Publications. (Original work published 1957).

Mudimbe, Y. Y. 1994. *The idea of Africa.* Bloomington: Indiana University Press.

Nakayama, T. K. and Martin, J. N. 1999. *Whiteness: The communication of social identity.* Thousand Oaks: Sage.

Pieterse, J. N. 1992. *White on black: Images of Africa and blacks in Western popular culture.* New Haven: Yale University Press.

Pieterse, J. N. and Parekh, B. 1995. *The decolonization of imagination: Culture, knowledge and power.* London: Zed Books.

Prinsloo, J. 1996. "South African films in flux: Thoughts on changes in the politics of identity in recent film productions". *South African Theatre Journal 10*(2).

Said, E. W. 1994. *Culture and Imperialism.* New York: Vintage Books.

Steyn, M. E. 1999. "White Identity in context". In Nakayama, T.K. and Martin, J.N. (eds.). *Whiteness: The communication of social identity.* Thousand Oaks: Sage.

Steyn, M. E. 2001a. *Whiteness just isn't what it used to be: White identity in a changing South Africa.* In Suny series, Henry Giroux (ed.). *Interruptions: Border testimony(ies) and critical discourse/s.* Albany: State University of New York Press.

Steyn, M. E. 2001b. "Whiteness in the Rainbow: The subjective experience of loss of privilege in the New South Africa". In Hamilton, C. V., Huntley, L., Alexander, N.,

Guimaraes, A.S. and James, W. (eds.). *Beyond racism: Race and inequality in Brazil, South Africa, and the United States.* Lynne Rienner Publishers.

Thornton, R. 1996. "The potentials of boundaries in South Africa: Steps towards a theory of the social edge". In Werbner, R. and Ranger, T. (eds.). *Postcolonial identities in Africa.* London: Zed Books.

Tomaselli, K. G. 1997. *Cinema on the periphery: South Africa (1910-1995).* Centre for Cultural and Media Studies, Durban. http://www.und.ac.za/und/ccms/articles/cinemasa.htm Accessed 04/03/1999.

Tomaselli, K.G. and Van Zyl, M. 1992. "Themes, myths and cultural indicators: On structuring of popular memories". In Blignaut, J. and Botha, M. (eds.). *Movies – Moguls – Mavericks – South African Cinema 1979 – 1991.* Cape Town: Showdata.

Wicomb, Z. 2001. "Five Afrikaner texts and the rehabilitation of whiteness". In Kriger, R. and Zegeye, A. (eds.). *Culture in the New South Africa. After apartheid – volume two. Social identities South Africa Series*. Cape Town: Kwela Books.

Zegeye, A. 2001. *Social Identities in the New South Africa: After Apartheid – Volume One.* Cape Town: Kwela Books.

CHAPTER FOURTEEN

Yizo Yizo and Essentialism: Representations of Women and Gender-based Violence in a Drama Series Based on Reality[1]

René Smith

Introduction: Contextualising "The Real Thing"

> Newspapers all over the country carried letters from irate parents and community leaders blaming the programme for setting antisocial trends, reviewers raved about the realism, and the black teenagers nodded their heads that someone understood the dilemmas they faced each day both inside and outside their classrooms (Oppelt 1999:14).

Yizo Yizo is a television drama series that was aired every Wednesday evening between 20:30 and 21:00, from 3 February 1999 to 28 April 1999, on the SABC1 channel of the South African Broadcasting Corporation. The hour-long (20:30-21:30) second series, *Yizo Yizo II* ("The return"), was aired on the same channel, every Tuesday evening from 20 February 2002 to 15 May 2002.[2] The story involves learners at a township high school, Supatsela High,[3] and includes events occurring within the timeframe of one academic year, which is constitutive of the "demise and subsequent transformation of the school" (COLTS 1999:1).

The production of *Yizo Yizo* began as an initiative of SABC Education, in partnership with the national Department of Education and its Culture of Learning, Teaching and Service campaign (COLTS), which commissioned a series dealing with the "culture of learning and teaching". Through their emphasis on research – as implicit in the process of production – Laduma Film Factory won the tender to produce "a drama series that would highlight the crisis in education, specifically in township schools in the country" (Gibson 2000). The research team consisted of five writers (four men and one woman): Peter Esterhuysen, Angus Gibson, Teboho Mahlatsi, Mtutuzeli Matshoba and Harriet Perlman.

One of the defining characteristics of *Yizo Yizo* is that "the story and characters are based on research and are all believable and authentic" (COLTS 1999:1). Issues relating to authenticity are particularly pertinent to any discussion on *Yizo Yizo*, which according to stakeholders of the series translates to "[i]t's the real thing" (Perlman and Esterhuysen 1999). This concurs with other interpretations/translations likening the phrase *Yizo Yizo* to "this is it" (Smith 2000). In this regard, it follows the ideology surrounding the use of the phrase "Yona ke Yona" featured in Yfm's marketing campaign during the radio station's inception (1997).[4] The prevalence of Yfm and the local music genre, kwaito, constitutes a deliberate effort on the part of the creators of the series to represent real township life experiences (Gibson 2000; Mahlatsi 2000).

Kwaito is part of the negotiation of cultural processes by black South African youth. It advances the success of the series' soundtrack (Ghetto Ruff et al. 1999), where the song "Yizo Yizo" contributed to creating a sense of identification with the programme. This illustrates the reciprocity between the series and the album that refers to it explicitly. This form of vertical intertextuality is also evident in the relationship between the series and supplementary material. The use of local black musicians (through the soundtrack and on-screen appearance of TKZee for example) is particularly pertinent as it contributes to the "authenticity" of the text. Viewed as a celebration of youth culture, as an indelible asset to black South African youth culture, and as a form of resistance, kwaito thus is an integral part of representations of "real-life" township experience (Mashego 2000).

Furthermore, within the context of this chapter, it is analogous to the use of African American rap and hip-hop musicians to cement the affiliation to "real-life" African-American experiences (Smith 1992). In attempting to address the crisis in education, the series exposes a barrage of issues impacting the learning process of many young people. These include rape, harassment, lack of educational materials, problems relating to motivation of learners and educators, corporal punishment, drug abuse, crime and corruption. Within the context of this chapter and this country, the synergy between "exposing" and "challenging" these issues is extremely contentious in itself. This is particularly problematic when assessed within the precise "real-life" context which *Yizo Yizo* purports to represent. That is, in relation to representations of violence against women, for example, the series exists within a context where "[t]hree out of every ten women in the south of Johannesburg experienced a severe form of sexual violence between 1998-99" (Soul City 1999). It is within this context that the concerns raised in this paper are situated. *Yizo Yizo* is an important text, which has contributed to, if not instigated, extensive debate around the crisis in South African schools (Gaser 1999).

The series attracted 13-, 16- and 25-year-olds, Nguni and Sotho language speakers primarily, with approximately two million people watching per episode, except for the final one (SABC Research 1999).[5] Creators and stakeholders are to be applauded for their attempts at addressing concerns that impact and hinder learning in South African schools. Furthermore, in creating dialogue, *Yizo Yizo* has begun the process of challenging what for many has been, and still is, a reality. Nevertheless, in achieving this aim, the series cannot be exempt from analyses of the very issues that inform it. This chapter is written within a cultural studies framework, acknowledging that meaning is implicit in language and that representations (texts) are inextricably connected to contexts (Tomaselli 1989; Hall 1997). In examining representations of gender-based violence, the chapter is informed by the history of this research on the relationship between violent behaviour and the viewing of violent programming (Gunter 1985; Schlesinger et al. 1992; Barker and Petley 1997).

Furthermore, in analysing representations of "real" township high school life in the local production *Yizo Yizo*, I am informed by the work of Valerie Smith (1992), Todd Boyd (1997) and Wahneema Lubiano (1997) who examine "representations of contemporary black popular culture" and the use of "facticity" in African-American cultural production. Moreover, my subjectivity, defined primarily in terms of race, gender and class, ensures that I remain vigilant with regard to the politics of re-colonisation. This is especially pertinent as issues relating to the portrayal of black life are determined, invariably, by historical constructions that legitimate representations that perpetuate myths and stereotypes of black people and black life (Hooks 1992; Smith 1992; Boyd 1997).

Representing Gender-based Violence: "Acts" of Violence against Women

> Because there are many different and conflicting ways in which meaning about the world can be constructed, it matters profoundly what and who gets represented [. . .] and how things, people, events, relationships are represented (Hall 1986:9).

There are various interpretations of what constitutes a violent act, and various forms of violence further contribute to this debate, including "physical, sexual, emotional, verbal, representational, cognitive" violence (Fawcett et al. 1996:1). For example, pulling or shouting at someone may be construed as violent by some and not by others (Hearn 1996). It is for this reason that it is imperative to attempt to define what is meant by violence. The importance of meaning is then embedded in interpretations by the creators, audiences and characters of the series. In other words, each stakeholder or viewer/consumer[6] approaches the series with individual interpretations of the definition or definitions of violence.

As mentioned earlier, subjective, personal interpretations of violence cannot be divorced from the socioeconomic and sociopolitical context within which these symbolic representations (in *Yizo Yizo*) occur. South Africa and the international community are also faced with continuing reports of youth as victims or perpetrators of violence. Mass media reports have included the following headlines: "KwaMashu pupils pack guns with their pens" (Ndiyane 2000), "Student tells of campus shooting" (Bisetty 2000), and "Sex: The shocking truth" (Ncube 2000). Reports about violence in schools in the United States, for example, aren't much different: "Class killing: all teachers ask, could it happen in my school" (Sapa-AP 2000), and "Schoolboy shoots teacher" (Associated Press 2000).

But what is violence? The first definition (recognisably functionalist) refers to "the application of force, action, motive or thought in such a way (overt, covert, direct, indirect) that a person or group is injured, controlled or destroyed in a physical, psychological or spiritual sense" (Van der Merwe in Thipanyane 1992:44). A second definition is one situated within the discourse of violence in television programming. In this regard, violence is perceived as: "the overt expression of physical force (with or without a weapon) against self or other, compelling action against one's will on pain of being hurt or killed, or actually hurting or killing" (Gunter and McAlleer 1990:80).

Based on the above definitions, there are indeed various acts that can be construed as violent portrayed in the series *Yizo Yizo*. These include criminal violence such as the rape of the characters Hazel and Dudu; the carjacking (also referred to as hijacking) perpetrated by Chester on two separate occasions; and the attempted murder of Mr Edwin Thapelo and Zakes, for example.[7] These forms of violence are otherwise referred to as "social violence" (as distinguished from political violence), inclusive of arson, assault and various forms of abuse (Thipanyane 1992). As such, sexual violence, or "unwanted sexual conduct", is included as an example of social violence.

Expressed violence and implied violence (sexual harassment and the prominence of the gun/phallus) is the subject of the final scenes of episode three, where violence is used as a "cliff-hanger". A netball match is taking place between Supatsela High and another high school. Chester and Papa Action are spectators, the latter appearing anxious as he has placed a bet on his school, and hopes for victory from his team. The following dialogue takes place:

CHESTER *(drives onto the netball court)*: <u>Hello my love . . . Get into the car and come and serve me. Am I talking or shitting?</u> [8]
CHESTER *(grabs Hazel)*: <u>Come here.</u>
MANTWA: <u>Leave me and my friend alone. What are you doing? Don't touch me.</u>
CHESTER *(to Mantwa)*: <u>What's with you?</u>
CHESTER *(to Hazel)*: <u>You come here.</u>

As this struggle continues, Sonnyboy (Hazel's friend who is a taxi driver) arrives. He gets out of the minibus taxi, and proceeds toward the court. The viewer sees that Sonnyboy is in possession of a gun, which he attaches to his belt.

CHESTER *(grabbing Hazel)*: <u>You come here.</u>
SONNYBOY *(swears)*: <u>Hey you shitty, wise guy, don't make me mad. Take your dirty hands off my girl.</u>
CHESTER: <u>You call this a woman? You know what? If you're a hero, come piss on my face.</u>

SONNYBOY: Don't point at me.
Chester turns direction and faces his back to Sonnyboy.
SONNYBOY: Hey boy! You're just a boy.
Chester walks away and then pulls out his gun. Everyone ducks.

Having established power by just showing his gun, Chester then puts the gun away and gets in his car; Sonnyboy – with gun in hand – has "rescued" Hazel and has defended his honour by saving "his girl/woman". This is confirmed by Mantwa's comment to Thiza (who is interested in Hazel) in the final scenes of episode three: "You're too late; she was saved by her boyfriend." The episode finally ends with the departure of the trademark red BMW transporting Chester and entourage in a blaze of dust.

The abovementioned scenes represent coherence (albeit general) between the narrative structure of *Yizo Yizo* and that of other texts. Todorov's analysis of the social is as applicable as Propp's analysis of the individual in examining the narrative of *Yizo Yizo* (Fiske 1987). With regards to the latter, the abovementioned altercation between Sonnyboy and Chester adheres to the "six sections" of Vladimir Propp's "thirty-two narrative functions" (Fiske 1987). In terms of the former, *Yizo Yizo* begins with a state of equilibrium, proceeds to a state of disequilibrium (characterised by disruption of the original state of harmony) until equilibrium is again achieved – preferable to the original state. This disequilibrium/chaos is evident at the end-of-term party where Thiza – in the company of Chester and Papa Action – is engaged in consuming alcohol and smoking marijuana. The following dialogue forms part of the scenes from the end-of-term party, which are achieved through quick, unstable camera movements, complementing the tension-inducing music.

HAZEL *(approaches Sonnyboy)*: How do I look in this dress?
SONNYBOY: It's beautiful.
HAZEL: Come let's go dance.
SONNYBOY: You know what? Let's go somewhere quiet. It'll be nice. Are you enjoying yourself? *(They proceed to his taxi.)*

This is followed by a montage including Thiza consuming more alcohol, Sonnyboy and Hazel proceeding to his taxi, the continuation of drugging and partying and the burning of a tyre.

SONNYBOY *(sits close to Hazel and is drinking)*: Is it nice here?
HAZEL: Yeah.
SONNYBOY: Are your friends gone?
(Hazel nods.)
SONNYBOY: When are you leaving? Did you tell them at home that you'll be late?
HAZEL: I didn't.

SONNYBOY: Okay.
SONNYBOY: I treat you nicely, don't I?
HAZEL: Ja . . .

This is followed by a shot of graffiti on the school wall, Papa Action (intoxicated) breaking down a classroom door with a hammer, and school desks being burnt.

SONNYBOY *(while trying to unbutton her shirt)*: Show me that you appreciate it.
HAZEL: Wait, I don't have condoms. I don't want to fall pregnant.
SONNYBOY *(continues advances towards her and tries to undress her again)*: It's not raining, or is it raining?
HAZEL: No, what are you doing?
SONNYBOY: Why must I wear a raincoat?
HAZEL *(continuously trying to fend off Sonnyboy)*: Wait!
(Sonnyboy forces himself on top of her and Hazel fights back and screams.)
SONNYBOY: Look here . . .
Hazel's screams are inaudible (lost in the chaos of the celebrations). Fire and shots of burning furniture interrupt the sequence.
SONNYBOY *(forces himself on her)*: Look at me. Look at me. I'm your boyfriend.
(Hazel is crying.)
SONNYBOY: You're killing me baby. Look at me. Why do you treat me like a stranger? You're mine, I'm your boyfriend. Don't behave like this. I love you. *(Sonnyboy rapes Hazel.)*

The final sequence of shots includes one of the end-of-term party, Thiza in a drug-induced state of sleep, and a shot of Hazel. Finally, a shot of the "controlled" fire on the school premises is followed by the end sequence of *Yizo Yizo*. Violence is used again as a "cliff-hanger" with images of Hazel's rape being intercut by the chaos of the party, thus contributing to the dramatic effect of the episode.

In following the sequence of events, it would appear that Thiza's dependence on alcohol, and his decision to keep company with Chester and Papa Action, are connected to Hazel choosing Sonnyboy, not Thiza, as a boyfriend. This association is illuminated in the abovementioned sequence of events and montage, which connects Thiza's "deviance" to Hazel's rejection.

Hazel is ideologically positioned as a product of exchange. She entered a relationship with Sonnyboy, who buys her clothes and pays for her to have her hair styled. Her comments (in an earlier episode) to Thiza about her relationship with Sonnyboy ("He cares for me, he's good-looking and he gives me money") perpetuate the myth of women entering into "agreement/s" with partners. Hazel's rejection is positioned to coincide with Thiza's relationship with Chester. Chester's advice to Thiza confirms Hazel's comments: "You dress shit! You must look good and they'll come."

Violence and the "Patriarchal Discourse of Gender"

The United Nations Declaration on the Elimination of Violence against Women defines violence against women as:

> Any act of gender-based violence that results in, or is likely to result in, physical, sexual, or psychological harm or suffering to women – including threats of such acts, coercion or arbitrary deprivation of liberty, whether in public or private life (Soul City 1999:5).

Sexual harassment as a form of gender-based violence "can take verbal, physical and non-verbal forms. It can include suggestive gestures or jokes [...] At worst, sexual harassment may result in rape" (Soul City 1999:26). There are numerous scenes in *Yizo Yizo* concerning sexual harassment, where the liberty of female characters is infringed upon, or where female characters are made to feel uncomfortable. For example, in episode one of the series, Nomsa is stopped by three male students and taunted about her uniform.

> STUDENT: Nomsa, did you repossess that skirt from your baby sister?
> NOMSA: Repossess . . . don't mess with me.
> STUDENT: If I could have those thighs . . . I would put pepper on them.

In another scene Papa Action points toward a group of women and addresses Chester.

> PAPA ACTION: It's time to claim your crown.
> PAPA ACTION *(grabs a young woman):* Come here. Kiss me . . . Voetsak.

Sexual harassment as a form of violence against women is also the subject of the following altercation between Papa Action and an educator at Supatsela High, Louisa, who is portrayed as a lazy, inefficient teacher willing to offer sexual favours for a "ride in a Pajero" (episode one). In episode three, Papa Action sends Louisa a paper aeroplane that reads: "I want to have you for breakfast, lunch and supper." Louisa's challenge to his offensive remarks (for her tone of voice and expression show that offence is taken) is overshadowed by the image of her already created. The representation of Louisa as elitist is maintained, instead: "Some filthy ghetto rat here is dreaming. I say to you, better wake up and go to the toilet and relieve yourself."

Episode one of the series, for example, includes various myths and representations of women, either as objects of gazing, or in stereotypical roles. Myth in this instance is seen as a culturally determined ideology (that is naturalised), constitutive of stereotypes which "reflect a prejudiced view of persons based on a single characteristic or set of characteristics" (Peach 1998:92). For example, the myth of marriage as central to the existence or life of women is presented in episode one when the young female learners are cleaning the female lavatories and Mantwa concedes to assisting Nomsa and Dudu by exclaiming that it is "good practice for marriage". This symbolic representation in *Yizo Yizo* perpetuates the dominant patriarchal discourse in which "television's fictional world apparently places greater emphasis on establishing the marital status of its female characters" (Gunter 1986:9).

To add to this, although the circumstances of Mrs Shai and Snowey, for example, are distinctly different, both portrayals emphasise the importance of the domestic domain – a nice home in the case of Mrs Shai versus a corrugated iron home/shack in the case of Snowey. The visibility of female characters on television internationally has been proven to be unrepresentative (Gunter 1986). Female characters occupy dialectic sites of struggle. To this end, women are positioned as either good or bad, as illustrated in the examples of Mrs Shai and Snowey. Mrs Shai is a hardworking nurse who is positioned as the matriarch, while Snowey is the alcohol-dependent, young, unmarried, unemployed mother representing the "welfare mother" (Peach 1998).

Representations in *Yizo Yizo* are particularly problematic, as they are hegemonic in so far as they elicit consent to the perpetuation of historical ideologies (Gramsci 1971). *Yizo Yizo* contributes to the myth of the maintenance of the nuclear family as a contributing factor to attaining success. For example, the Shai family includes hardworking parents (a mother who is a nurse and a father who is a traffic officer) and two children. Nomsa's strength of character, her values and belief systems are connected to her familial environment, and her parents' employment status merely contributes to her success and security. This representation foregrounds the lack of security and guidance in the case of Hazel. This in turn is seen as a contributing factor to her hardship and as a reason for her being seduced by Sonnyboy who offers material gain.

In addition, Snowey's position as a single mother is a result of absentee parenting. Within the context of the feminist discourse of gender, this representation is very problematic, as patriarchal guidance appears to guarantee that young men are successful. Javas' father and Mr. Thapelo are both instrumental in disciplining and encouraging him. His success (he proves to be a talented science student) and his strength of character (he negotiates an end to the hostage drama) are therefore implicitly connected to paternal influence, within a system that is patriarchal in nature.

Thiza's situation is different in that his brother Zakes assumes the responsibility of father, while their grandmother assumes a maternal role. The audiences of *Yizo Yizo* are never introduced to the parents of Chester and Papa Action, Dudu and Mantwa, for example.[9] This implies that their social maladjustment, naivety and insecurity (for example) are directly related to their absentee parents. In the case of Thiza, his brother's criminal activity contributes to him being "led astray", thus rendering his grandmother's efforts insufficient and inefficient. If Thiza's family life is viewed in relation to that of Javas, then a further reading is that the absence of a father/father-figure is a contributing factor to failure. This demonstrates how *Yizo Yizo* preserves the culture of patriarchy and the success of the series "reflects its power to confirm hegemonic family values" (Wallace 1992:125).

"The Madonna" and the "Deviant": Dudu versus Mantwa

> Women associated with the Madonna are idealised and sentimentalised as pure, good, modest, at once virginal and maternal (somewhat of a logical contradiction). In stark contrast, women associated with the whore are disdained and treated with contempt as sexually promiscuous and manipulated temptresses (Peach 1998:92).

It is my contention that representations of Dudu and Mantwa conform to stereotypes of women as either "ideal" or "deviant" (deviating from expectations of what constitutes the ideal or the "normal" behaviour of a woman), respectively. Dudu is the young woman who survives the second rape and Mantwa is positioned as her friend in the series. In episode three, the viewer gets a glimpse of Mantwa's opinions in her discussion with Hazel about Sonnyboy:

> MANTWA: Sonnyboy is in love with you, why are you so slow?
> HAZEL: What do you mean?
> MANTWA: He fell for you the first time you boarded the taxi [...] You know, taxi drivers have got money.

Mantwa appears to encourage the relationship between Hazel and Sonnyboy because (according to her) the latter appears to love Hazel. Mantwa proceeds to represent the myth of the "gold-digger" who cares less for love and more for financial gain. Furthermore, in episode four it is Mantwa who not only alludes to materialism or material gain (again) but also encourages Hazel to sleep with Sonnyboy.

> MANTWA: Friend! Have you slept with him?
> HAZEL: Mantwa, no.
> MANTWA: What are you waiting for? Make your move fast friend. Move fast when the economy is bad.
> HAZEL: Listen, if he truly loves me, he'll wait.

Mantwa is positioned as a complete contrast to Dudu, who appears to admire her and relishes her advice. In episode six, for example, the two discuss their proposed attire for the end-of-term bash and Mantwa suggests that she will be "noticed" because she'll "be wearing [. . .] hipsters and smoking a zol". To this Dudu responds, "I'll be doing the same". Later, they are harassed by Papa Action and Chester, who grabs Mantwa and kisses her neck. She reacts by first smiling and then pushes him away and asks to be left alone. Mantwa's smile, which is not seen by Chester – thus included for the benefit of the viewer – appears to suggest that she enjoys having her neck kissed by him. The seductive eating of Chester's apple can be interpreted on one level as symbolic of oral sex, and on another level, as a symbolic representation of the image of woman as responsible for man's banishment from the biblical Garden of Eden.

Although this image offers an alternative in so far as it is the man who offers the apple, it reinstates the myth of the seductive temptress. Furthermore, seen in relation to the rapes that occur in *Yizo Yizo* and within the context of South Africa, the image of Mantwa first enjoying the attention of Chester and then pushing him away perpetuates the myth that women who get raped, "ask for it". In addition, it fosters the myth of women saying "no" when they mean "yes", or of women meaning "yes" when they say "no". This particular scene between Mantwa and Chester includes Papa Action and Dudu. When Chester turns his attention to Dudu, it is Papa Action's presence, his hovering and stern, evil facial expressions which not only contribute to the "act" of harassment, but also to the overwhelmingly tense, uncomfortable atmosphere of the scene. Dudu's final comment concurs with Mikki van Zyl's (1990) assertion that: "Women are perpetually trying to predict whether men's sexual behaviour will lead to violence and because they cannot control men's behaviour, take appropriate avoidance measures to prevent the anticipated threat."

CHESTER *(referring to Dudu)*: Who's this little beauty? I'm going to bring you up myself and keep the wolves and little boys away from you. Do you hear me?

MANTWA: She's not your type.

DUDU: Please Chester, leave us alone.

(The young women attempt to move away.)

DUDU: We are no longer safe at this school.

And indeed, it emerges that Dudu's forewarning could not save her from Chester and Papa Action. In episode nine, Dudu is kidnapped by Papa Action, Chester and the gang. The music is fast: kwaito music in the background is infused with the *Yizo Yizo* score, which in this instance includes an ominous tone. In her attempts to escape, Dudu is overpowered, and dragged to their car. The scene (as with the first rape scene) is interrupted by another scene, of the Learners' Representative Council which is discussing the school's state of affairs and the general reactionary and tense atmosphere. The focus returns to those involved in Dudu's abduction. The mise-en-scene is a chicken warehouse where a general unpleasant, unclean and noisy atmosphere is created. Papa Action rapes Dudu and says: "Let her pay for her sins". This is followed by images of the other men present and the viewer is left to assume that she has been gang-raped.

It is clear from the above that there are various forms of gender-based violence. Representations thereof are pivotal to understanding and combating the "problem" of violence against women and to perceptions of and attitudes toward survivors. This includes contesting existing stereotypes and myths about women and in the process of representing gender-based violence. However, it is evident from discussions with directors of the series that reconceptualising gender relations (research is being done with rape survivors) will indeed play an important part in *Yizo Yizo II*.[10] For this and for their attempts to address rape within the context of intimate relations (e.g. Hazel and her boyfriend), the writers of the series must be commended. This story line challenges the common belief that "rape is something that takes place between strangers, and that rape between [. . .] a woman and her boyfriend, is not possible" (Smith 1999).

A booklet produced by Soul City (1999) focusing on violence against women states "the number of reported rapes has increased faster than population growth over the past few years, according to Central Statistics' latest report 'Women and Men in SA' (Central Statistics 1998:38)". It is therefore disconcerting that according to research conducted for SABC Education, "the issue around sexual harassment and rape" was prominent in the section on "low-scoring messages" (The Research Partnership 1999). That is, the message "must not harass or rape girls", was not regarded as "priority learning" by viewers of the series (The Research Partnership 1999).

"Representing the Real": Dramatising Gender-based Violence

> Members of the same culture must share sets of concepts, images and ideas which enable them to think and feel about the world, and thus to interpret the world, in roughly similar ways (Hall 1986:4).

Following insights into the production process of *Yizo Yizo* as alluded to earlier, it is possible to see the importance placed on establishing the "look", style or aesthetics of the programme (Mahlatsi 2000). Technical codes assist in representing the action, narrative and dialogue of *Yizo Yizo* where the aim is to reflect the lives of "real" people, in "real" townships, attending "real" township schools. To this extent, *Yizo Yizo* fulfils its role as a reality-based drama. Lubiano (1997) assesses the essence of representation as "truth", and examines the contradictions of authenticity and realism in the work of Spike Lee and locates this within the context of black popular culture. This position is similar to that of Smith (1992) who draws on Barbara Foley's assessment of the history of facticity in African-American narrative writing in relation to the impact of slavery.

The following section will interrogate *Yizo Yizo* in relation to these approaches. Examining issues of genre and "reality" is particularly important to this discussion, as perceptions of violence and gender, for example, are connected to opinions advocating these portrayals as reflecting reality. Realism is indeed contentious and at the root of mixed emotions. The disparity exists somewhere between opinions advocating that exposure of the crisis in our schools will shock audiences into action, and opinions about possible copycat actions as well as violence against characters (Miya 1999). Philip Schlesinger et al. (1992) confirm the view that there are other social and cultural experiences which impact the "fear" and apprehension of crime and violence. The authors' research on "women viewing violence" highlights the importance of personal experience (of violence) in relation to the fear of violence and crime. To this extent, women subjected to domestic violence were particularly disturbed by representations of similar scenes on television and indicated that "certain types of media tended to increase their anxieties about crime" (Schlesinger 1992:41). Furthermore, "when asked to choose from a list of those formats most likely to increase fear of crime, women were most likely to choose television news, television dramas and documentaries, television films, and the tabloid press" (Schlesinger 1992:41).

The option of warning mechanisms, indicating the nature and amount of violence in television programming, was articulated by respondents to research conducted by the national public service broadcaster, which was responsible for airing *Yizo Yizo* (SABC 1994). The SABC's concern with violence on television was highlighted about six years ago when the then chairperson of the board, Dr Ivy Matsepe-Casaburri, warned "that there is an unacceptable proportion of violence on television" (SABC 1994:15). The article in one of their in-house publications discussed research commissioned by Dr Daan van Vuuren, General Manager of Broadcasting Research. Some of the findings included:

> Real-life violence, such as in news programmes, had a greater emotional effect on viewers who were exposed to such situations (for example people living in strife-torn areas such as Thokoza), whereas fictional violence, as depicted in action programmes like *MacGuyver*, had a greater emotional effect on viewers who did not experience real-life violence . . . (SABC 1994:16).

However, the fact that *Yizo Yizo* is a drama and therefore fictional compounds this equation. Comments from stakeholders reveal that the series was based on real-life situations applicable to subjects of the series and audiences who were predominantly black South Africans. Clearly, asserting that *Yizo Yizo* has some relation to reality allows the series to assume an "authoritative perspective", for "[r]ealism poses a potential, longstanding challenge for counterhegemonic discourse" (Lubiano 1997:104).

Yizo Yizo is indeed a text of immense dexterity. The above section attempts to relate the impact of the generic construction of the series on representations of gender violence in particular. Recognising the increasing blurring of boundaries between fictional and non-fictional media violence, I concur with the assertion that research into violence on television "must leave the simplified notion of 'entertainment violence' aside and realise [. . .] that all kinds of media violence are cultural and symbolic constructions" (Carlsson and von Feilitzen 1998:99).

Concluding remarks

Yizo Yizo is a highly textured narrative that is open to multiple interpretations, which this chapter cannot interrogate. The primary concern, however, has been to examine representations of women and gender-based violence in particular in the series. In so doing, the chapter suggests that (mis)representations of young women in the series perpetuate the dominant patriarchal ideology, thereby obliterating the series' counterhegemonic potential. I argue, furthermore, that in neglecting to challenge the existing order and to interrogate issues relating to violence against women in particular (accepting that this constitutes a significant part of the series), *Yizo Yizo* contributes to naturalising existing gender relations and perceptions of violence against women.

Similarly, the series falls short of its (potential) counterhegemonic narrative in so far as it refrains from exposing the myth of the "conditions" of township high schools. In so doing, the viewer is left with the dominant ideological positioning of the forces of evil as responsible for a state of disequilibrium. The restoration of "equilibrium" is thus particularly relevant when viewed in relation to the substantial drop in audience ratings for the final episode, which epitomised a school in which the "culture of learning and teaching" is established or restored (depending on how the viewer views the original state of leadership). This relates to a more general assessment of the series not interrogating the socioeconomic and political context of education in South Africa. That is, "crisis" in education is paralleled with issues of delinquency at the expense of the socioeconomic inequities of an education system with a history tainted by the legacy of apartheid. In positioning itself as an essentialist narrative, *Yizo Yizo* should have exposed the myth of the conditions of township high schools as a problem of "forces of evil" disturbing the balance of "leadership". The exposition and/or exhibition of rape and the consistent and continuous harassment of school girls/young women in *Yizo Yizo*, however, is neither substantiated by social responsibility messages (helplines or contact details for rape counselling), nor solutions.

It is my contention that the contradictions of representing gender-based violence in the series lie at the precise moment of representation where violence is commodified in the process of representing the "real". In this regard, certain representations of violence within *Yizo Yizo* are substantiated by the dramatic intent of the series (violence as a "cliffhanger"). The analogous relationship between the series and the "real" (informed by, and confirmed by research) is used by stakeholders of the series to defend the legitimacy of representations of township high school life, as well as the public service broadcaster's fulfilment of its commitment to social responsibility (McQuail 1994). This chapter attempted to demonstrate that promulgating issues of authenticity illuminates the way in which the series – and dissidents thereof – choose to address issues that impact "the crises in education".

Notes

1 The research on which this paper is based was made possible through financial assistance from the National Research Foundation (NRF) towards an MA (Media and Cultural Studies) from the University of Natal, Durban (Smith 2000).

2 It is important to note that this paper focuses on *Yizo Yizo* – the first series – exclusively. However, I do recognise the significance of the second series, *Yizo Yizo II*, in addressing some of the issues/concerns raised in this paper. Furthermore, it is important to note that *Yizo Yizo II* constitutes an integral part of the *Yizo Yizo* "package" (inclusive of supplementary material such as the *Yizo Yizo* magazine, teachers' guide and compact disc recording, for example). Nevertheless, the first series predominates, while reference to *Yizo Yizo II* is included as anecdotal information.

3 Although fictitious, it is based on real-life occurrences emanating from research (COLTS 1999).

4 Yfm is a radio station "targeted at the 16-to-20-somethings that comprise South Africa's burgeoning black youth market" (Friedman 1997).

5 Episode thirteen was the least watched episode. This is due – in part – to the *Bafana Bafana* soccer match that was scheduled on SABC2 from 19:12 to 20:49.

6 The branding of *Yizo Yizo* confirms the series' position as a product with exchange value.

7 Protagonists of the series include THIZA (Grade 10 learner), HAZEL (Grade 10 learner), NOMSA (Grade 10 learner), JAVAS (Grade 10 learner), CHESTER (gangster) and PAPA ACTION (learner and gangster). Their colleagues include THULAS (older/mature learner), DUDU (Grade 10 learner), MANTWA (Grade 10 learner), STICKS (Grade 10 learner), BOBO (student), GUNMAN (Grade 10 learner) and LESEGO (Learners' Representative Council president).

Other characters include MR. MTHEMBU (first principal), KEN MOKWENA (second principal and history teacher), GRACE LETSATSI (third principal), THABO MAHLATSI (school advisor), ZAKES (Thiza's brother), SONNYBOY (taxi driver), SNOWEY (Hazel's sister) and BRA GIBB (drug dealer). Teachers include ZOE CELE (new, part-time English educator), EDWIN THAPELO (science educator), LOUISA (disillusioned educator, friend of Ken) and ZAZA (educator, Zoe's cousin).

8 Underlined text signifies subtitles. (The author wishes to highlight that attempts to obtain transcripts or original scripts from the producers proved unsuccessful; however, every attempt was made to present accurate transcriptions of the episodes.)

9 Audiences are introduced to Papa Action's mother, Mantwa's mother, and Dudu's father, in particular, in the second series, *Yizo Yizo II*.

10 The second series focuses on the survivors of rape, albeit superficially. Nevertheless, representations of women in *Yizo Yizo II* remain contentious (Smith 2001).

References

Associated Press (AP). 2000. "Schoolboy shoots teacher". In *Sunday Tribune*. 28 May 2000. 10.

Barker, M. and Petley, J. (ed.). 1997. *Ill effects: The media/violence debate*. London: Routledge.

Bisetty, K. 2000. "Student tells of campus shooting". In *Daily News*. 5 May 2000. 6.

Boyd, T. 1997. *Am I black enough for you? Popular culture from the 'hood' and beyond*. Bloomington: Indiana university Press.

Carlsson, U. and von Feilitzen, C. (eds.). 1998. *Children and media violence*. Nordicom: Unesco.

COLTS. 1999. *Yizo Yizo: A COLTS TV drama series*. Information Booklet.

Fawcett, B., Featherstone, B., Hearn, J. and Toft, C. (ed.). 1996. *Violence and gender relations: Theories and interventions*. London: Sage.

Fiske, J. 1987. *Television Culture*. London: Methuen.

Friedman, H. 1997. "Yfm goes for the gap". In *Weekly Mail & Guardian*. 1 October 1997. http://www.sn.apc.org/wmail/issues/971001/ARTS51.html.

Gaser, C. 1999. "Blaming Yizo Yizo is creating a scapegoat". In *Sowetan* (Letters to the Editor). 13 May 1999. 12.

Gauntlett, D. 1996. *Video Critical: Children, the Environment and Media Power.* Luton: University of Luton Press.

Ghetto Ruff, Universal Music, SABC Education & Laduma Film Factory. 1999. From the TV Series *Yizo Yizo*.

Gibson, A. 2000. Director/writer of *Yizo Yizo*. Telephonic interview conducted on 10/4/00.

Gramsci, A. 1971. *Selections from the 'Prison Notebooks' of Antonio Gramsci*. In G. Nowell-Smith and Hoare Q. (Trans. and eds.). London: Polity Press.

Gunter, B. 1985. *Dimensions of television violence.* Hartfordshire: Gower.

Gunter, B. 1986. *Television and sex role stereotyping*. IBA. London: John Libbey.

Gunter, B. and McAleer, J. L. 1990. *Children and television. The one-eyed monster?* London: Routledge.

Hall, S. 1986. "Media power and class power". In: Curran, J. et al. (eds.). *Bending reality. The state of the media*. London: Pluto Press. 1-12.

Hall, S. 1997. *Representation: Cultural representation and signifying practices*. London: Sage/The Open University.

Hearn, J. 1996. "Men's Violence to Known Women: Historical, Everyday and Theoretical Constructions of Men". In Fawcett, B. et al. 1996. 22-38.

hooks, b. 1992. *Black looks: Race and representation*. Boston: South End Press.

Lubiano, W. 1997. "But compared to what?: Reading realism, representation, and essentialism in School Daze, Do the Right Thing, and the Spike Lee discourse". In Smith, V. (ed.). *Representing blackness: Issues in film and video*. London: Athlone Press. 97-122.

Mahlatsi, T. 2000. Director/writer of *Yizo Yizo*. Interview conducted at *Shooting Party* on 23/3/00.

Mama, A. 1995. *Beyond the masks: Race, gender and subjectivity*. London: Routledge.

Mashego, G. 2000. "You can call me kaffir". In *Ymag*. April. 10.

Maslamoney, S. 2000. Programme Manager for Youth, Adult and Public Education. Interview conducted at *SABC Education* on 18/3/00.

McQuail, D. 1994. *Mass communication theory: An introduction*. (3rd edition). London: Sage.

Miya, S. 1999. "Abezemfundo bathi makubhekwe isifundo esisemdlalweni weTV 'iYizo Yizo' yodumo". In *Umafrika*. 9-13 March. 5.

Ncube, J. 2000. "Sex: the shocking truth". In *You*. 13 July 2000. 20, 21, 24.

Ndiyane, E. 2000. "KwaMashu pupils pack guns with their pens". In *Daily News*. 18 April 2000. 3.

Oppelt, P. 1999. "Interpreting the reel world". In *Sunday Times Magazine*. October 31, 1999. 12-14.

Peach, L. J. (ed.). 1998. *Women in culture. A women's study anthology.* Massachusetts: Blackwell.

Perlman, H. and Esterhuysen, P. 1999. *Yizo Yizo Magazine: A learning resource based on the TV series.* In Association with Laduma Film Factory, the Department of Education in support of the COLTS campaign, SABC Education and Coca-Cola.

SABC. 1994. "Violence on TV". In *SAUK Radio & TV*, Jul-Sep. 15-19.

SABC Research 1999. Audience Ratings (ARs) and viewership figures for *Yizo Yizo*.

Sapa-AP. 2000. "Class killing: all teachers ask, could it happen in my school?" In *The Star.* 3 March 2000. 4.

Schlesinger, P., Emerson Dobash, R., Dobash, R. P. and Weaver, C. K. 1992. *Women viewing violence.* London: British Film Institute (BFI).

Smith, G. 1999. "Rape Statistics". In *Elle SA*. August.

Smith, R. 2001. "Yizo Yizo prompts long overdue debate". In *The Sunday Independent*, 25 March 2001. 7.

Smith, R. 2000. "Yizo Yizo: This is it? Representations and receptions of violence and gender relations". MA Thesis, University of Natal, Durban.

Smith, V. 1992. "The documentary impulse in contemporary U.S. African-American film". In Dent, G. (ed.). *Black popular culture.* (A project by Michele Wallace). Seattle: Bay Press. 56-64.

Soul City. 1999. *Violence against women in South Africa.* (A resource for journalists). Johannesburg: Soul City Institute for Health and Development Communication.

The Research Partnership. 1999. *An evaluation of Yizo Yizo.* Conducted for SABC Education by The Centre for the Study of Violence and Reconciliation; Co-ordinated Management Consulting (Pty) Ltd; Helene Perold & Associates CC, The South Africa Institute for Distance Education.

Thipanyane, T. 1992. "Violence and its effects on Children". In Centre for Development Studies (ed.). *International Conference on the Rights of the Child.* Bellville: University of the Western Cape. 43-48.

Tomaselli, K. G. (ed.). 1989. *Rethinking culture*. Bellville: Anthropos.

Van Zyl, M. 1990. "Rape mythology". In: *Critical Arts*. 5 (2).

Wallace, M. 1992. "*Boyz N the Hood* and *Jungle Fever*". In Dent, G. (ed.). *Black popular culture.* (A project by Michele Wallace). Seattle: Bay Press. 56-64.

Yizo Yizo (Episodes 1-13). 1999. SABC & Laduma Film Factory/ Shooting Party.

CHAPTER FIFTEEN

Another Male Fantasy: Race, Gender and Advertising

Lene Øverland

Introduction

Given the fact that nonsexism and nonracism stand side by side in the South African Constitution, it is regrettable that critical voices are not able to theorise and argue race in relation to issues such as gender and sexuality. However, current South African advertisements that portray mostly white people, and more half-naked women than fully dressed women, do not seem to take notice of the Constitution anyway. Despite the formal commitment to gender rights in the new South African Constitution (which came into effect in 1996), gender is still being sidelined or seldom regarded as being as significant as race issues.

This chapter focuses on advertising content, and represents a snapshot case study into gender representations within contemporary post-apartheid South African advertising campaigns in the mainstream media. The main objective of this chapter is to investigate how advertising content reproduces and reflects gender and sexual stereotypes in post-apartheid South Africa. The chapter further elaborates on the following questions: Do race and class mediate messages that reflect gender and sexual stereotypes? How do members of various communities read and reflect around gendered and sexual stereotypes and what impacts do these messages make on people's lives? The chapter will be placed within a historical framework that explores the development and structure of the South African advertising industry.

A Note on Methodology

The chapter is based on audience research and perception analysis conducted on the basis of focus groups organised by the Women's Media Watch, a Cape Town-based media-monitoring organisation, during the second half of 2001.[1] Further data was produced by studying advertisements in the popular magazines *You, Drum* and *Huisgenoot* in October 2002.[2]

One of the reasons for the popularity of audience research is that contextual analysis seems impossible with textual analysis only. Audience research further challenges the power relationship between researcher and researched, and the process does not allow the researcher to claim access to the definitive ideological meaning of the research material or put herself in a situation of telling other women what is best for them. By using quotes I aim to break down the distance between the participants and myself, and make the reader sense the interaction and dynamic that took place within the groups (Gouws 1996). A third important reason for working with audiences is represented by the acknowledgement by feminist standpoint theory (Harding 1997) that as a researcher or a so-called "knower" I am shaped by my position in society, a position influenced by the privilege of belonging to the elite world of white Western academia. As the author I am in power of the text. Audience research hence represents a useful tool as it allows the visibility of multiple voices and knowledge of multiple cultural codes.

The participants for the study came from diverse backgrounds in terms of race, class, sexuality, geographical location, occupation and educational background. The participants consisted of one core group of members of Women's Media Watch (these are mostly working-class gender activists), a control group of professional media activists located in various countries in the Southern African Development Community, and one group of trained media monitors. Approximately half of the core group were either Women's Media Watch members who actively took part in several other Women's Media Watch projects focusing on issues of gender and sexuality, or people who had some connection to media and/or creative and artistic work.

The core Cape Town group was split into two groups, one male and one female, and made up of 15 participants, eight female and nine male. Their ages ranged between 19 and 25; however, two participants were over 40. In terms of race, nine participants were black, five white and three coloured.[3] Half of the participants were at the time of the research formally unemployed; others were students or freelancing as artists. Those who were employed worked mainly in the NGO sector or in academia. Eleven of the core group participants lived in peri-urban areas around Cape Town and six in rural areas in the Western Cape. The Western Cape Women's Media Watch group was made up of approximately 30 women and two men, mostly coloured and mostly living in peri-urban areas around Cape Town. The regional group was made up of five black women, ranging from ages 20 to 60.

A total of four meetings took place with the core group. The women met separately from the men and vice versa, and the groups twice met jointly. The Women's Media Watch members met for one full day and the regional participants for two full days.

The groups initially met to discuss and establish an understanding of sexuality in advertising. Tools such as recorded TV adverts and several magazines were used for this purpose. The second phase of the workshops included an investigation into gender representation in advertising. The groups looked at the use of gender stereotypes and particularly at sexuality as a means to promote products. Thirdly, the audiences were assisted in undertaking simple semiotic analysis. Several adverts were analysed in a formalised way and the groups entered into discussions on how single discursive expressions such as advertisements can evoke emotions, associations, fears, hopes, fantasies and even generate and construct meaning that affect people's lives. This step also included a critical debate around issues of race, class and cultural familiarity.

Several methodological challenges were encountered during the process. Separate from the audience research, I attempted to interview people who work in the advertising industry to test the responses of the Women's Media Watch audiences. Several attempts to conduct interviews with female and male employees in the advertising industry were unsuccessful. None of the women who were approached were willing to answer any questions, arguing that they had too little knowledge about the sector. All the men approached were either impossible to get hold of or they transferred me to someone else "better placed" to answer my questions. However, all the men approached were willing to help me with information in other areas of advertising.[4] With respect to the focus groups, two main challenges arose from the artificial set-up that focus groups represent. The various audiences interpreted messages according to the logic of their own social, cultural and individual circumstances. In addition, there appeared forced reflection and political correctness on the part of participants when the discussion was recorded. This changed when the recordings stopped. However, this is a general challenge attached to all research processes that involve audiences.

Historical Overview of the South African Advertising Industry

"Modern" advertising in South Africa dates back to the newspapers started by the first white settlers of the former Cape Colony. *The Cape Town Gazette* was founded in 1800, followed by the *South African Commercial Advertiser* and the *South African Journal* (Brewer 1989).

Prior to 1950 most South African advertising was produced overseas and confined to print; newspapers, magazines, billboards and cinema slides were mainly concerned with promoting imported products from England and the United States. American involvement was mainly with advertisements of motorcars, industrial and agricultural machinery, but also with Cadbury sweets. Other advertisers were financial institutions, which were offshoots of British banks and insurance companies. Local advertisers were state-owned corporations such as the South African Railways, and patent medicine manufacturers such as Lennon's and Norwood-Coaker. Advertising as an industry only really developed in the 1960s, as the media infrastructure developed. Commercial radio came first, and was followed by television in 1976. Under apartheid, advertising in South Africa was mainly aimed at the consumer needs of whites and sometimes served the cause of the whites-only regime. Whites also mainly staffed the advertising industry. Changes in the industry's approach to black people went hand in hand with the capital changing relationship to the black majority, particularly in the late 1980s, as racial capitalism embarked on its last-ditch reforms (Frederickse 1986).

The rapid political transition that dominated South Africa in the early 1990s also had profound effects on economic and social organisation. This had both an effect on the structuring of the industry, as well as on the types of products advertised for black audiences. A number of other sectors of South African society, outside of the white community, also benefited from the change in political power in 1994. A black middle class began to emerge, both through active state intervention (the black economic empowerment programmes) as well as capital's own strategic initiatives, in the face of possible anti-trust legislation and other dissatisfaction on the part of the state, to include some black presence in the economy. As a result of this emergence of a black middle class and a small black elite, a new market developed that had implications for the advertising industry, both internally and externally.

Since 1994 there has been an increase in black involvement in the advertising industry, mostly in the shareholding structure of agencies rather than in actual employment. For example, former trade unionist and senior ANC leader Cyril Ramaphosa's company holds 25% of leading advertising firm Hunt-Lascaris, and more than 50% of the South African subsidiary of Saatchi & Saatchi through a black-owned consortium. Another leading firm, The Agency, has a significant percentage of black ownership, and Herdbuoys McCann is a majority black-owned firm. Despite this, recent media reports highlight the racial disparities in employment and management practices in these agencies.

A report in a weekly business magazine, *Financial Mail* (May 18, 1998), suggested that the advertising industry was busy employing more and more women. Yet men still hold more than half of the professional positions, and while women are becoming more prominent in research, media, production and client service departments, the creative jobs remain in men's hands. "The industry is still dominated by white males, but there is a danger that it will be taken over by either a coalition of white and black males, or alternatively by black males solo" (personal communication, Di Paice 2001). Black employees make up about 31% of the total staff, 19% of the top management and 21% of the professional management. Women make up 22% of the top management and 56% of the professional team (Public Hearings into Racism in Advertising, November 6, 2001). The Advertising Association insists it is committed to increasing blacks on boards to about 30% by 2003. According to John Farquhar this will have to coincide with training of black advertising professionals so as to change the attitude with which brand communication strategy is developed. "Whites in advertising see blacks as one. To them there is no social hierarchy. They know there are middle-class blacks out there but they see them as whites in a black skin and they talk to them on this level. They ignore culture, language, environment, etc. To them a Xhosa, Zulu, Sotho, Tswana, etc. are all the same. They talk to them in English because they believe that they aspire to be white, and therefore will abandon their own culture in the process" (personal communications, John Farquhar 2001).

Do You Buy Because You Desire the Model?

Working definitions of terminology such as "gender" and "sexuality" were dealt with as preliminary matters before the participants started analysing adverts. The greatest challenge was to establish a common understanding of the term "sexuality". All the preliminary workshops started off with participants brainstorming notions of sexuality and the representation of sexuality in the media. In the first workshop we worked with very broad definitions. One exercise performed as part of the process to reach a definition of "sexuality" was to write down the first word that came to mind when one sees or hears the term "sexuality". These words were written down by the participants: *Hormones, nice body, vagina, penis, mind + body, joy, hedonism, happiness, horny, expressionism, art, rape, abuse, HIV, Aids, pleasure, passion, procreation, nature, relationship, emotions, orgasm.* At the last workshop a specific effort was made to combine individual definitions into a working definition.

The discussion of sexuality in advertising was kickstarted by looking at issues of power, hormones, men and women, and heterosexuality and homosexuality. The participants involved agreed that sexuality was a complex construction affected and mediated by several forces, institutions such as communications, religion and patriarchy and certain individuals. What contributed to the wider understanding was to relate sexuality as an abstract concept to the participant's own experiences of power, sexual preference, sexual fantasies, societal expectation and sexual pleasure. The participants concluded that sexuality was an expression of humanity and desire, that sexuality shaped human behaviour – not only intimate behaviour, but also the way we dress, walk, talk and in general relate to, desire and feel for other people. However, the discussion was not only related to positive emotions but also to issues of morals, taboo and abuse. The debates also entered a gendered generation discussion and identified a need to address the systems of myths and meanings that structure our imagination around issues of sexuality.

Having established a broad consensus on the term "sexuality", the next challenge was to create an understanding of sexuality in the media and eventually narrow the discussion down to sexuality in the advertising industry. Interestingly, both male and female participants spoke mostly about how women were portrayed in adverts and how female sexuality was used to sell products and to communicate to people about how one should look to be cool and popular. They also questioned whether the human body was no more a private construction but rather a public satisfaction and utility maximising machine.

> Everything seems to be advertised today with women. No matter whether it's matches or toothpaste, it's going to be some woman. Females think they need to look like and behave like the women in the ads, who are slender and wear lots of make-up. If these women are not white they are from some exotic origin. So it kind of tends to be unreal (Male participant in joint core group workshop).

> Advertising seems to operate in a way where it makes sexism a normal part of everyday life, and we become unable to imagine a different world of advertising. Advertising in South Africa represents an unreal world. We are not all white or exotic-looking (Participant in the Women's Media Watch 2002 media monitoring project).

Another participant stressed the differences in the manner male and female body images were portrayed in the media.

> They never use fat women in adverts. They show women in a very stereotyped slim body. That is what is seen as physically attractive by the media. Women are at times dressed up to look like men, in macho suits and the like. Women are always (shown) with make-up, they are never portrayed as natural. In adverts women often sell a natural product, but the woman looks unnatural. Women in adverts often have big breasts, they all have nice legs, and beautiful eyes and you will never see them with stretch marks or wrinkles. Men in adverts are presented as strong and most of the time he has clearly visible muscles. If his body isn't exposed he is portrayed as a professional, as a smart, sophisticated man that knows what he wants and how to get it (Participant from women-only workshop).

Models in the advertisements seem to represent role models; people do want to look like the people in the adverts, meaning white or exotic. Further, women want to look unnaturally beautiful, and men smart, sophisticated and muscular. These are some of the stereotypes, which also are closely related to body images reflected in South African advertising.

The groups critically studied several magazines, hunting for images of the nonstereotypical kind, but had to conclude that current advertising reveals containment, sexualisation, beautification and objectification of the white female body. They also observed that more women than men were portrayed in adverts; however, when men were portrayed they were more often than women portrayed in dignifying positions. The female body was often offered to the reader purely as a spectacle object of sight and a visual commodity to be consumed – in other words as a clothes rack and sex object. In the joint workshop one of the male participants questioned why women always looked good in advertising. "Do women look good so that men can look at them or do they look good so that women can look at women and aspire to look like them?" The groups further elaborated on this question when they analysed a Kellogg's Special K advert.

The issue of sexual preference was also raised, especially in terms of the media demonising other sexual choices than the heterosexual. With respect to advertising, one participant mentioned an advert she had seen some time back in an unmentioned woman's magazine. The advert promoted clothes for men from Markhams, a leading men's clothing retailer. In the background of the advert a lesbian couple was kissing and in the front a man was saying: "Markhams – the only brand truly dedicated to men!" What does this say about societal values and about what is accepted female behaviour? The advert can be interpreted in several ways. It can be interpreted as lesbian-friendly, as it allows the portrayal of two women who love each other. However, it can also be seen as homophobic, as it suggests, in an emotional way, that nothing much is left in the world for the man other than a few desirable clothing products. Are women on the one hand being integrated, but on the other exploited?

The question of race was also critically addressed within the groups. All groups stated from the first meeting that most adverts use white models. Messages of this kind that do not have a "natural" space not only communicate gender stereotypes, but also lack of cultural knowledge and race stereotypes. Far fewer adverts were found in South African magazines portraying black people than those portraying white people. The advertising content seems to be mainly directed towards the white consumer, as we could only find a few low-price products such as household products and a few status symbols such as cellphones using black models. Even in magazines such as *Drum*, *Pace* and *Y,* targeting black people specifically, it was hard to find adverts making use of black people as media targeting the black population in general carry very few adverts. Is it true that the advertising industry does not seem to be interested in the black target market? If so, it is a message that reinforces stereotypes of the black market as non-existent.

The dominant portrayals in South African advertising "normalise" forms of passivity, dependency, beauty and domesticity for women, and control, strength, intelligence, exploitation and access to power for men. This portrayal contributes to the stereotypical, racial and gendered system where beauty, often represented by slim bodies, blond hair and blue eyes, can be viewed as a normalised discipline. The production of normalised bodies through advertising is a practice that is imposed directly by men or by "male norms" on which patriarchal society is based. But more often than not, women are willing participants in these practices and might even experience them as empowering, as the objectification of women's sexuality has been economically profitable to models as well as to advertisers (cf. Haraway 1991; Bordo 1993; McDowell and Sharp 1999).

Consumers, on the other hand, have become so accustomed to the stereotypical representations in advertising that they hardly question that contemporary relations of dominance are sustained by allowing the advertising industry to tell people what and how they can be. This was illustrated when focus group participants began to argue that advertising images serve in our subconscious as role models, against which the self continually measures, judges, disciplines and corrects itself. One could also question whether the advertising industry uses sexual desire and images existing in our fantasies, and more so in the male creative director's fantasy than in our real lives, to appeal to people's emotions and hence create a sense of human desire for a product – the same desire people feel for other human beings close to them no matter whether she or he looks like the model used in the advert? In other words, do these adverts play on intimate human emotions that make people forget about everyday life, and hence create feelings of desire for products carrying emotions existing in our fantasies?

Has the Male Fantasy Become Normalised?

Throughout the research process the focus groups analysed several adverts. Only three of them will be analysed more closely in this essay: one promotes household products, another cereals and the third cars.

The first was an advert for Rhinowall household products in August 2001. The advert, which ran in the lifestyle magazines *Rooi Rose*, *Marie Claire*, *Men's Health* and *House and Leisure*, showed a (white) woman in black underwear, an unbuttoned pink shirt and black shoes sitting in a big leather chair in front of a peach-coloured wall. The advert text reads: "This illustrates two ways to keep warm. One cost R250 per hour, the other R85 per square metre. Rub up against a nice piece of drywalling this winter and you'll see why Rhinowall is your only real option of insulation."

Soon after it appeared, the Advertising Standards Authority (ASA) received several complaints about this advert. Some objectors began an email campaign complaining that the advert portrayed the woman as an object for sale, and on the same level as a drywalling product. The controversy soon surfaced in the press. When questioned on the advert's motives, Neil Gurney, the CEO of Saatchi & Saatchi, the agency behind the campaign, told *Business Day* newspaper (August 24, 2001) that the challenge was "to make walls topical, create excitement and hype". He went on to suggest that Saatchi & Saatchi chose to tackle the campaign with "humour, innuendo and controversy and never intended to offend". Also quoted was the marketing director for the company producing the drywalling systems: "We have tried to get drywall systems into the housing industry for 30 years and have not succeeded, and the ad was placed in consumer magazines targeting women to catch the decision-makers in the home." They said nothing of the fact that more than 100 readers found the advert so offensive that they wrote letters of complaint.

The second advert we looked at was that for Special K breakfast cereal made by the Kellogg's company. In South Africa, Kellogg's adverts are conspicuous for their use of long-legged, slim and beautiful women as their attraction element. Kellogg's had also begun to adjust their advertising campaigns to fit the political times since 1994, increasingly using black models (particularly black children) in adverts that appealed to a broader, cross-racial, South African audience.

This particular advert for Special K ran in several women's magazines in 2001, and took up two full pages. On the first page, a fully dressed adult male sitting on a sofa is watching something (revealed on the next page). The text on this page reads: "She does look great in that dress. Then again, she looks great without it." On the next page, a tall, blond woman dressed only in underwear is holding up a red dress in front of her as she is looking at herself in the mirror. The text on this page reads: "Decisions, decisions. She can never make her mind up. But not when it comes to her choice of cereal, it's always Kellogg's Special K. 'They're low in fat,' she says. If only everything was so easy."

Unlike the Rhinowall advert, this advert was not subject to the same level of public debate. The different focus groups, however, singled it out and the discussion regularly returned to its contents.

The third advert promoted a new model car, a 5-door Peugeot 206. The advert made use of a woman cut in two, photographed half-naked and out of focus. The figure almost resembled a paper doll. The advert used language easily associated with relationships and sexuality: "It takes a special car to make you feel this way . . . Of course, looks aren't always everything. When it comes to performance, both the 1.4 8V SOHC and the 1.6 16V DOHC engines deliver plenty of bite . . . So if you want more out of a compact car, take a 5-door Peugeot out on a date. It'll be the start of an unforgettable love affair." The pay-off line was "Stop liking. Start loving. Engineered to be enjoyed."

This kind of advert appeared out of touch with recent developments in car advertising. The car industry was one of the first industries to make use of modern advertising and has since its early days (even in South Africa) gone through several phases, from having half-naked women on the bonnet to eventually having them fully dressed and placed inside driving the car. The Peugeot advert triggered the participants at a monthly Women's Media Watch meeting to write a formal complaint to the South African Advertising Standards Authority.

The Peugeot and Rhinowall adverts clearly objectified the women in their respective pictures and alienated them from the product for sale. The women seem to be strategically placed to sell the products, and do not seem to be present in the advert for any other purpose than to awaken the consumer's sexual desire and appropriation. The Kellogg's Special K advert, on the other hand, allows the woman a voice, and a close connection to the product and its values.

Participants in the research project felt that the Rhinowall advert was distinctly sexist and degrading to women. They interpreted the advert as having clear associations to prostitution and hence explicitly legitimising women and women's bodies as sales objects. They further argued that the half-pornographic display undervalued women and communicated that women's bodies were legitimate and available subjects for sale and consumption. The pay-off line "One cost R250 per hour, the other R85 per square meter" could be seen as promoting prostitution, hence this advert legitimised prostitution and equated the sale of a woman's body with the sale of a commercial object. The message of the advert appeared to be: "A body and a wall will both give you the same service: warmth in the cold of winter."

The strongest comments were reserved for the Rhinowall advert. One of the male participants remarked: "After seeing this advert, Rhinowall has lost a potential customer in me" (Joint focus group meeting). A black woman participant, at the same meeting, remarked: "I would now really like to start campaigning against sexist advertising. We need adverts that we can relate to. As an African woman I cannot sit in my underwear in the living room looking sexy. I also don't think this image is representative for white culture, and I don't even think this represents how men would like to find their partners." The degrading and sexist nature of this advert and its trivialisation of prostitution clearly reflect a dominant ideology of women as submissive and available for men's consumption.

Participants were asked what their initial impression of the Kellogg's Special K advert was. The most common answer was: "It looks like the Kellogg's Special K advert is promoting a red dress." The second most common answer was: "It looks like the Kellogg's Special K advert is promoting a red dress and not Kellogg's 99% fatfree cereals. However, because I know Kellogg's advertising practice I know what the advert promotes." To the question whether there was any value attached to using a half-naked woman to sell cereals, one response was:

> Why isn't the woman wearing the dress rather than holding it up in front of the mirror, and why is nudity used to sell Kellogg's K? A dressed woman would serve the purpose of selling breakfast cereals. There is no need for nudity in this advert. The woman would look good if she was wearing the dress, and her body would be left to the consumers' fantasy (Regional gender activist).

The research groups also looked at how men were portrayed in the three adverts.

The Kellogg's Special K advert placed the man in a central position in the image, but it was still the image of the woman that caught the eyes of the participants first. One participant remarked: "The woman is the most important element in the advert. Without the woman the advert will carry a very different message, and you also see her first." This response came from both male and female participants. "The woman's half-naked body is the main attraction; her body is objectified and pacified to the extent that she is even spoken for."

The statements were followed up with discussion of the text used to communicate the message. This can be summarised as follows: The underlying message in this two-page advert seems to be that men look at women, and that women look at themselves. This is in line with Van Zoonen's (1999) argument that this has become a normalised action in a society which has defined masculinity as strong, active and in possession of the gaze, and femininity as weak, passive and to be looked at.

This argument is backed by the fact that all participants saw the woman long before they even noticed the man. However, his words also contribute to the statement: "She looks great in that dress. Then again, she looks great without it." This suggests that men look at women (with or without clothes) for their personal satisfaction. The image of the woman looking at herself in the mirror combined with the wording "they're low in fat" suggests that women look at themselves in relation to other factors, such as low fat content, thus offering men visual satisfaction. In other words, this advert reinforces common ideology, saying that a man will look at a woman when she adheres to the beauty ideals promoted, and maybe even invented, by the mainstream media.

This advert is using sophisticated methods to communicate the commercial myth of beauty and control: "A good figure is the slim figure." According to this myth a woman must be slim to be beautiful; a man will only look at her and admire her when she is beautiful, hence she must eat low-fat products. The advert plays on the emotions of the reader to manipulate her to buy the product. "When I look at this advert, I become dissatisfied with my own body and I get a feeling that I need to look like her to get an admirable look from the opposite sex" (Views of regional gender activist). Is it possible at this point to conclude that this advert plays on emotions in an opposite way to the Rhinowall advert? The Rhinowall advert sets off to create a positive feeling of warmth, whilst the Kellogg's Special K sets off to create a bad feeling amongst people who "need" to lose weight. Hence the two adverts are playing on feelings that can make the consumer take action.

One argument often advanced by participants as to why they first see the woman related to the choice and use of colours. "The advert cleverly makes use of colour. Red draws attention to the advert, but also to issues of sexuality, command, control and power. The red successfully attracts the consumer's attention. The red seems to be chosen to draw associations to sexuality and sexual desire. Red also associates availability and communicates that the woman says 'I want to be seen, I am available for desire and I look good because I eat Kellogg's Special K'" (Part of written submission from the regional gender activist).

The colour red does not necessarily need to symbolise availability; it can also symbolise control. In the case of this advert one might be able to say that it portrays a woman who is in control and aware of her own appearance, including her body. However, the woman seems to be controlled by hegemonic ideology exercised through her partner.

The first comment often made about the car advert was that it had a very human emotional and sexual overtone and that it communicated the need to crave for the one, the special. The car that is the object for sale is central in this advert. Two responses by women, the first from the first workshop, and the second by a regionally-based gender activist, will illustrate this.

> This advert communicates power; buying this car will get you a woman. The advert hence communicates the availability of both the woman and the car. Is the woman

placed strategically as an object to attract men to buy the car, is she a symbol of the kind of woman you can get if you buy a car or is this woman the potential buyer of the car? Obviously most people do not drive only in underwear, but maybe men dream about picking up a woman walking by the road wearing only underwear? (Local gender activist).

It is a common male dream to cruise around in a nice car, picking up a beautiful sexy lady. The woman is probably placed as an unfocused object in the advert in order to help the potential male buyer sort out his priorities and strategies: First buy the car then catch the woman. The image makes you associate to what a man could be fantasising about when he is planning to buy a car. We would say this advert communicates that any man who buys this car can get a woman like this (Regional gender activist).

However, a male focus group participant offered an alternative analysis:

This advert draws a parallel from the car to emotions and actions belonging in a human relationship; love and dating. The advert communicates: "Fall in love with the car rather than falling in love with a woman." This advert might be sexist towards women, because it communicates that women are unpredictable and that this car forever will remain faithful to you and it will behave exactly how you tell it to. The advert further plays on men's fear of women and especially on men's fear of not being able to attract a woman. This fear is complemented by the image portraying a desirable, but unfocused woman. This image communicates that the woman exists only in the fantasy of an average man, hence the advert communicates: drop the woman and go for the car! The car is as attractive as a woman is. On top of that the car is achievable, faithful and not dangerous. Buying this car will make your dream of a beautiful woman come true or if you buy this car you do not need to get into the challenge of forming a relationship with a dangerous woman. Buying these products can give you what you want no matter if it is a relationship with a car or a woman.

Again, a feeling for the desirable is what makes the buyer tick and act. No matter what the advert promotes, all participants who analysed this advert found it offensive and sexist. However, the regional group was more focused on the degrading portrayal of the half-naked body in this advert, whilst the local workshop participants focused more on the actual lack of clothes. Here are two samples of responses from the workshops:

There is no value attached to the use of the naked body in this advert, this woman is clearly placed here to please the target group of this advert, men (Women's Media Watch regional advert workshop).

> The presence of the half-naked woman is offensive. Why is the woman cut in half, wearing only underwear and not sitting inside the car? The unfocused image of the woman makes it seem as if she appears in a man's fantasy and not in his reality. Our first reaction to this ad is that it communicates that men place women as objects. The advert does not only construct females as oppressed, it also reflects males negatively. This advert constructs a male reality that is being occupied with material things and objects and not with human beings. It also communicates that a man can have a love affair with a car. All he needs is the finances to purchase the car. So as long as you have money you have a happy life! This advert is both sexist and classist (Women's Media Watch local advert workshop).

A general comment from the various groups was that this car was so desirable and could so easily have been sold in a nonsexist way. Why not rather be progressive and portray the woman as the driver of the car instead of as a passive sexual object? Again, the argument was brought back to the "normalised" communication of capitalist consumer culture where the image of the woman is primarily interesting as an eye catcher. This is clearly an ideology that does not accommodate gender transformation and hence offers no alternative ways of looking at human beings.

Discussions further brought to light that all the messages conveyed in these adverts promoted the same capitalist ideology. Advertising is therefore more than a way to extract money from unsuspecting people; it is also a vehicle for conveying the larger view of a confining, body-obsessed culture. The individual trained monitors of the Women's Media Watch 2002 monitoring project however also noted that as consumers they were not just passive recipients of capitalist consumer culture. Their awareness of the ideologies promoted by current advertising can be interpreted as a sign of resistance to the power of dominant forces of capitalist ideology, and an indication of the possibility for consumers to choose buying a product without buying into the ideology it promotes.

Media perception represents one of the practices in which the construction of gender identity takes place. The characters in advertising function as "textual constructions of possible modes of femininity and masculinity: as embodying versions of gendered subjectivity, these could be fantasy models of femininity and masculinity and hence offer opportuinities to the advertising agencies to try out different subjectivities that might encourage the consumer to buy their product (Van Zoonen 1999).

Advertising tells us, as do various other forms of media, that women don't matter very much except as housewives and mothers. This symbolically denigrates women. The challenge hence lies in getting the media to acknowledge the existence of the diversity of South African women and men. History, as Mthala (2000) argues, tells us that because of the historical position of black women at bottom of the social strata, the media, including advertising in South Africa, struggle to portray women differently.

Concluding Remarks

This essay is a reflection of the meanings generated by the participants through analysis of specific adverts. After analysing several adverts, the general feeling amongst the participants was that the depiction of beauty in the magazines had a significant effect on the way they viewed themselves as men and women. This can be illustrated by a comment from one of the Women's Media Watch monitors: "The adverts set the standard for what is beautiful according to exterior looks. The magazines cannot cover 'inner beauty', charm, intelligence and so on. The adverts usually make us think that for instance to be slim is to be beautiful."

All participants pointed out that it is rare to see men's bodies displayed in ways similar to the exhibition of women's bodies. The monitors observed several images of men, but they were seldom subjected to the gaze of the female, and it was very uncommon to see men more than slightly undressed. In all the magazines, women were portrayed as paying tremendous attention to their looks. It seemed as if their motivation was mostly related to attracting men.

The adverts in all the magazines presented limited diversity and hence gave women very few options. The ideal woman seems to be young, lean, heterosexual, sexually available and dressed to party. Women who do not look available are in most instances slightly older while subtly exhibiting the characteristics of the younger women. They are clearly distinguishable by the fact that they are wearing much more clothing and are usually positioned in a domestic context.

The monitors felt that the general public shared their observations and sentiments, but that most people did not voice these due to a lack of access to the channels of communication, as well as due to lack of awareness about the dynamics of advertising and the media industry in general. At the same time, some felt that adverts set the standards for beauty in society because the general public had been naturalised to passive interaction with the media.

From the advertisements that have been discussed in this snapshot case study, one would be able to ask further questions regarding the communications strategies that brought previously private bodies into the public sphere. It is further imperative to theorise about the way gender and the perception of popular culture and mass media are related.

The white young market seems to be the main target of the South African advertising industry, as evidenced by media images of Western sexy femininity and a money-boosted masculinity. One would be able further to investigate the ways in which this approach contrasts with other agendas aimed at transforming representations of race, class and gender in post-apartheid South Africa. Ongoing public debates regarding these issues could also serve to make media consumers more critically aware of the role advertising plays in the construction of gender identity. Subsequent studies will also have to deal with the ways in which commercial representation of gender links with representations of race and ethnicity in the mainstream media, and how this is related to ownership and market considerations.

Notes

1 The workshops were held during the second half of 2001: 23 August (women only); 28 August (men only); 1 September (joint men and women); and 13 October (local advert workshop). We also solicited written responses from gender activists within the Southern African region. I also relied on Internet sources to contextualise the audience responses, and conducted a number of interviews (both verbal and written) with people working in the advertising industry.

2 The history of studies of the media audience can be seen as a series of oscillations between perspectives which have stressed the barriers "protecting" the audiences from the potential effects of the message. The term "reception" analysis has come to be widely used as a way of characterising the wave of audience research which occurred within communications and cultural studies during the 1980s and 1990s. On the whole this work has tended to use qualitative research methods, and has tended one way or the other to explore the alternative choices, uses and interpretations made of media materials by their consumers (Van Zoonen 1999). The shift from feminist interpretative media to audience research and perception analysis reflects a fundamental paradigmatic shift that has taken place in feminist studies in general. Empirically the focus of attention moves from analysis of social and economic structures to the way people engage with these and how they construct meaning (ibid.).

3 This racial breakdown is necessary to distinguish within the South African milieu.

4 Chris Brewer and John Farquhar were helpful in my research.

References

Bordo, S. 1993. "Material girl: The effacements of postmodern culture". In Baehr, H. and Brewer, C. 1998. *Advertising in South Africa.* Cape Town, Media Association of South Africa.

Business Day. 2001. "Attempt to woo women backfires". August 24.

Fredrickse, J. 1986. *South Africa: A Different Kind of War: From Soweto to Pretoria.* Johannesburg: Ravan Press.

Gouws, A. 1996. "Feminist Epistemology and Representation: the Impact of Post-Modernisation and Post Colonialism." In *Transformation* 30 (1996).

Haraway, D. 1991. "A Cyborg Manifesto: Science, Technology, and Socialist-Feminism in the Late Twentieth Century." In *Siams, Cyborgs and Women: The reinvention of Nature.* New York, Routledge. 149-181.

Harding, S. 1997. "The Science Question in Feminism and the Privilege of Partial Perspective", in McDowell, L. and Sharp, J.P. (eds.). *Space, Gender and Knowledge.* London: Arnold.

McDowell, L. and Sharp, J.P. 1999. *A Feminist Glossary of Human Geography.* London: Arnold.

Media Monitoring Project. 1999. A Snapshot Report at the end of the Millennium. Cape Town Women's Media Watch, South Africa.

Mthala, P. 2000. "Gender the next step." *Rhodes Journalism Review*, August.

Van Zoonen, L. 1999. *Feminist Media Studies.* Sage Publications.

Øverland, L. and Lediga, K. 2002. "Monitoring Advertising in *You, Drum* and *Huisgenoot* through a Gender Lens." Women's Media Watch, South Africa.

CHAPTER SIXTEEN

Experts, Terrorists, Gangsters: Problematising Public Discourse on a Post-apartheid Showdown

Suren Pillay[1]

In late 1995 People Against Gangsterism and Drugs (Pagad) emerged from the Cape Flats, originating largely from neighbourhood watch groups. Its stated aims were to remove gangsters and end the sale of drugs in communities on the Cape Flats. Although it claimed a diverse support base, it had an overwhelmingly Muslim face.

The dramatic killing of one of Cape Town's most notorious gang leaders by a group of Pagad supporters immediately catapulted this organisation, and the presence of gangs, into the public space. This paper is an attempt to problematise representations of both Pagad and gangs in the media and academic studies. It seemed to me that the representations and studies were based on a set of politico-philosophical assumptions that led to the generic categorisations of these phenomena. From these categorisations derivative discourses offering programmatic solutions arose. The argument of this paper is that, firstly, the identity of the gangster in Cape Town – as derivative of poverty, as anti-social, as a result of the Group Areas Act – and that of Pagad – as representative of a homogenous Islam and as the local incarnation of a global "Islamic threat" – obscures their particularity and specificity. I argue that a richer grasp of their constitutive dynamics will be obtained if we explore their identities as nonstatic "processes". These processes involve locating identity formation within the interface of globality and locality: the symbolic borderlands of a structured contingency, which brings to the fore the constitutive conditions of ambiguity and hybridity.[2]

The paper is divided into two parts. Firstly, I explore the "construction" of the gangster in Cape Town. The second part of the paper problematises the "construction" of Pagad that emerged once it entered public discourse.[3]

The Making of the Gangster

> "The men on foot opened fire on the car. The driver lost control and it mounted the centre island; then a passenger jumped out of the back of the car and ran backwards

towards Chucker Road with the gunmen chasing him. It was like in the movies," said the witness (*Cape Argus*, May 14, 1988).

Conventional explanations of gangsterism in the Western Cape tend to be economically reductionist, essentialist and descriptive. They underplay the role and construction of cultural symbols and meanings, and the relationship between the local and the global in gang identity formation. I argue that there is a need to develop alternative approaches that incorporate a broader range of dimensions in attempting to understand gangsterism.

Of late, the phenomenon of gangsterism has been at the centre of much debate and discussion in the Western Cape – not that it had been absent for a long time. Responses to addressing the issue have ranged from appeals for an understanding of the socioeconomic reasons underpinning it, to coercion via ultimatums, to the meting out of violence by groups within civil society such as Pagad. Gangster leaders have become peace crusaders, and peace crusaders are seen as breaking the law and becoming fugitives. Political parties, community groups and nongovernmental organisations (NGOs) are all at pains to offer solutions, to the point where the issue has become highly politicised with the party politicisation of "crime".

There are relatively few formal academic studies which have been done on gangsterism in Cape Town. They fall overwhelmingly into two areas of scholarship: historical and sociological. The historical work is found in the study done by Seeraj Mohamed (1990). The sociological approach guides the work of Don Pinnock (1984, 1997), Wilfred Scharf (1986) and Lauren Nott (1990). The later work (Mohamed 1990; Nott 1990) draws considerably on a conceptual framework established by Pinnock's groundbreaking 1984 book *The Brotherhoods: Street Gangs and State Control in the Western Cape*. These studies share one conceptual starting point: marginalisation. This becomes the conceptual framework within which the mystery of gangsterism is unravelled: "The central concept around which these concerns turn is that of marginalisation. The theory has it that the surplus population seeks its survival in the informal sector, most of which falls outside the ambit of the law and regulations" (Scharf 1986:2). The studies then proceed to rather descriptive, anecdotal accounts of gang life, gang rituals and economic activities such as theft, drug sales and illegal alcohol trade.

It is at this point that they move into two different programmatic agendas. One is the Marxist-inspired approach of Pinnock, which sees the solution to gangsterism in the dissolution of racial capitalism. The other is the criminologist's concern for re-integrating the marginalised back into society (Scharf 1986; Nott 1990). This approach does not suggest radical structural change, rather the development of "opportunity" in the liberal sense, and therefore suggests developing the individual by enskilling him or her.

Here, questions emerged: How does this line of thought explain the behaviour of youth coming from relatively middle- and upper-class families who are committing crime or sitting in prisons? How does it explain the esteem and status gangsters are given by youth growing up with relatively little material discomfort? Or why gangsterism, if it is determined by economic conditions, is not such a prominent phenomenon in black townships? There is considerable correlation between socioeconomic conditions and gang formation. This is not necessarily my area of dispute. My dispute is that this is presented as the "master narrative" of Cape Flats youth culture, and "working-class culture". I would suggest that the analysis needs a more nuanced, less programmatic approach if it is to explore the complex landscape that is the Cape Flats, and the attraction of gangsterism for the youth who live there.

The bulk of the studies argue, for the most part convincingly, that gangsterism is a historical response of working-class communities to unemployment, poverty and loss of self-esteem. However, there are important silences, essentialisms and assumptions which warrant unpacking. Since most of the work done on gangsterism in the Western Cape draws on primary research done by Pinnock (1984, 1997), I will use his work to demonstrate possible shortcomings in existing studies.

For Pinnock, in Cape Town, the "Cape Flats" is portrayed as the geographical space in which gangsterism emerges. "It is here that one finds squatters, the overcrowding and the poverty of Africa. Most people on the Cape Flats do not own property or capital, and the majority are unskilled or semi-skilled labourers" (Pinnock 1984:3). He concludes that the solution to the problem of gangsterism lies in the "elimination of poverty and the redistribution of wealth [and] changes in the labour process [although] it is difficult to see how such changes can take place under the present system of racial capitalism"(Pinnock 1984:106). This is a conclusion that is arrived at after the study explores the origin of gangsterism in Cape Town as having its roots in the social engineering processes initiated spatially by the Group Areas Act, as well as the mode of production which racially excludes youth on the Cape Flats from the "formal economy". Pinnock links the Group Areas Act to the "disintegration" of family life by noting that "many of the families have broken up, most of the houses and flats are overcrowded, and the schools are packed to bursting point" (1984:4). Furthermore, he argues, "the collapse of social control over the youth was one of the major problems facing the working class, it was the almost intangible, but very real cement which held working-class culture together" (1984:56). He concludes that gangs are "in a sense defensive class organisations within the system" (1984:10).

Pinnock paints a picture of the Cape Flats as a vast expanse of belts, rows and columns of concrete "compounds" in which "on any day of the week the most noticeable feature is the many young people on the streets" (Pinnock 1984:4). These young people, as a result of the social fabric having been ripped apart by the group areas-inspired dislocation, mutate into the vicious street gangs which stalk the Cape Flats. Pinnock notes that "ganging is primarily a survival technique, and it is obvious that as long as the city is part of a socioeconomic system which reproduces poverty, no amount of policing will stop the ghetto brotherhoods" (Pinnock 1984:99). Following this argument, the answer would therefore lie in solving the socioeconomic problems of our society. Give people jobs, and they won't rob and steal and they won't sell drugs.

This picture may contain a considerable degree of validity, but it also obscures quite a bit. The Cape Flats is not just full of unemployed youth living in a "working-class culture", which is presented as a homogenous, coherent set of shared patterns of interactions. The "Cape Flats" is delineated by a range of important cleavages, which may be regional, religious, class, ethnic or gendered, with shifting combinations of these at different moments.[4] Pinnock's argument that moving to the Cape Flats disrupted a "working-class culture" – and that this created a loss of social cohesion and resulted in gang formation – is problematic for two reasons.

The first is tautological: For Pinnock, gangs emerge from working-class life. Yet he suggests that the movement from one "working-class" area to another is to blame for gangsterism. If gangsterism emerged from working-class culture, then it should have been there prior to the effects of the Group Areas Act. Certainly, the effects were negative, but in the interest of rigorous analysis we should be wary of simple causality arguments.

The second is the problematic of memory and remembering involved in discourses about, and of, the subaltern. Pinnock suggests that as the group areas removals took place, "the familiar social landmarks in the closely grained working-class communities of the old city were ripped up, a whole culture began to disintegrate" and, he goes on, "these spaces were both physical (the networks of streets, houses, corner shops and shebeens) and social (networks of kin, friendships, neighbourhood and work). They was a mixture of rights and obligations, intimacies and distances, providing a sense of solidarity, local loyalties and traditions" (1984:5). This form of eulogising is a common act of remembering that we see in artistic productions such as David Kramer and Taliep Petersen's *District Six: The Musical* and subsequent spin-offs they have created. These works are remarkably similar in approach to works about the "cosmopolitan" township of Sophiatown, which was also destroyed by the Group Areas Act.

"Cultures" are not fixed or static entities. They are constantly being "ripped up", constantly disintegrating, but also constantly being reconstituted. As networks are being "destroyed" new ones are being formed, just as the ones that were there have mutated from other bonds. I would argue that the construction of the "history" of areas such as District Six in hagiographic terms was a conscious political act, which works from an originary and imaginary "fixed" past, in opposition to a binary "fixed" present. The fixed past is the community with a social fabric which held subjects in a relationship to each other which was "good" (community) and its "ripping apart" destroyed the bonds which produced the "good" relations. The "fixed present" is the bleak, windswept Cape Flats, from Bonteheuwel to Mitchells Plain, riddled in popular perception with gangsters, crime and drugs. The fixed past is constructed through memory, fantasy, nostalgia, and from the vantage point of the present, related to relationships of power.

In every act of remembering there are acts of forgetting, "master narratives and slave narratives", processes of closure which privilege particular "pasts" from the "present". The present with all its socioeconomic problems becomes "explained" through recourse to a single moment of rupture. Are there not, we should ask, networks, associations, intimacies, in Lavender Hill, Steenberg, and Hanover Park, i.e. post Group Areas Act communities? Why is the neighbourhood church band not celebrated? The Saturday afternoon soccer matches? The softball teams? The Sunday evening karaoke? These are fragments of the current story which are excluded by the dominant discourse, which puts these "little moments" in the previously whites-only suburbs, when they occur, in the main daily papers such as the *Cape Argus* and *Cape Times*, and reports on the "social events" of the Cape Flats in free knock-and-drop papers, such as the *Athlone News*, which only circulates on the Cape Flats. Pinnock's simplification reinforces the perception that there are no "networks" on the Cape Flats, except those that traffic marijuana, alcohol and prostitutes. The suburbs and its concerns are universalised, while the Cape Flats and its concerns are particularised, pathologised and eulogised.

A scenario which problematises the reductionist argument is in the following anecdote by a former gang member of the legendary Globe Gang which was dominant in District Six in the 1950s:

> The Globe were the most decent and well-bred gangsters ever. All their parents were well-to-do businessmen with flashy cars and good clothes. The gang leaders were always beautifully dressed ... Mikey had silk shirts especially made for him. And he drove around in lovely cars. And the women! Mikey always had the best women around him (Pinnock 1984:7).

The Globe Gang is interesting because they do not conform to the narrative that locates gangsterism as a response to poverty and unemployment. The original members came from middle-class families, who were shopkeepers, traders and craftsmen. They are not, I would suggest, an anomaly. Gangs can be more ambiguous in their class identity than simply "working class". Many members of gangs may be, but where are they in the power hierarchy? How and why Mikey would feel "marginalised" is a question seldom posed by existing analyses because they tend to stop at the point of saying that gangs are "defensive working-class organisations". We cannot glean from this what is specific and particular to their emergence on the Cape Flats. The particularities of race, class and religious influences, which establish its form and organisation, are lost.

Bad Guys are Good Guys: Global Culture/Local Meanings

I have sought to problematise the economic reductionist argument by suggesting the incorporation of other dimensions, such as the notion of a "globalised" culture industry. It seems to me that an interesting way of trying to answer the silences is to incorporate this dimension into studies on gang identity. There is a ubiquitous presence of cultural systems that have globalised and commodified the celebration of a particular hero figure through various circuits and channels that involve the movement, reception and localisation of global symbols.

Stuart Hall has argued that communication involves four separate but interlinked moments: production, circulation, use and reproduction. He says that "it is in the discursive form that the circulation of the product takes place, as well as its distribution to different audiences. Once accomplished, the discourse must then be translated – transformed again into social practices, if the circuit is to be completed and effective. If no 'meaning' is taken, there can be no 'consumption'" (1980:128). I would suggest that it is in the moment of "translation" that what Appadurai calls "indigenisation" takes place – the process in which the text's polysemy[5] is funnelled into a "negotiated" reading.

The radical individualism of consumer culture celebrates and criticises the "anti-communitarian" rebel at different moments of ambivalence – the cold, heartless rebel who can pull the trigger. North American film director Martin Scorsese might seek to portray the mafia in a way that shows us how ruthless and brutal the power structure is in order to make it unattractive, but the multiplicity of perceptions appropriated by the audience might be the opposite, depending on where they situate it in their system of hegemonic and preferred meanings. These hegemonic and preferred meanings are embedded in the institutional, political and ideological order.

Images in and of themselves do not have meaning. Meaning emerges in the movement between representation, the viewer and the social formation. All texts have, according to Hall, preferred readings. He distinguishes between the "dominant-hegemonic", in which the preferred meaning of the text is read; the "negotiated reading", in which the "legitimacy of the dominant code is acknowledged", but the reader locates it within his/her social condition; and lastly, there is the "oppositional reading", which involves a "radical decoding" in which the preferred meaning is radically opposed (O'Sullivan et al. 1994:238-239). So whilst Scorsese's preferred reading may be seeking to say one thing, oppositional and negotiated readings may be saying something else.

The "culture industry" as Adorno put it, uses the modes of production and the methods of corporate industry to produce and sell symbols, transforming cultural products into cultural goods (1993:85-92). These cultural goods, which are so pervasive in our environment, such as newspapers, periodicals, film, television and recorded music, need to be critically consumed. Employing the concept of bricolage,[6] I do not necessarily agree that globalisation means that we are being "Disneyfied" by cultural imperialism in a smooth and unproblematic manner. Understanding local gangsterism in the age of an "exploded" national imagination involves carefully unpacking the complex matrix shaken together in the cocktail of media, techno and ideoscapes. A cursory glance at most of the output of American cinema is a useful example. Heroes like those portrayed by Van Damme, Stallone and Schwarzenegger are singularly violent and destructive characters. These heroes are not only violent, but more importantly, are highly individualistic and "antisocial". In hot pursuit of a notion of "justice", they would destroy half a town without a blink. The celebration of Hollywood hero figures is not confined to the slums of the Western Cape, as Celestin Monga points out:

> In the slums of Cameroon's large urban centres, and in depressed areas generally, young people have developed a Rambo culture, because a certain type of film is their only escape from local bars. In their eyes, Sylvester Stallone, Chuck Norris and Arnold Schwarzenegger are visionaries of freedom and have displaced Cesaire, Anta Diop, or Mongo Beti (1996:95).

They do however stand at the extreme. Even "good cop" genre movies will show an entire fleet of cars being run out of the way in the pursuit of a lone criminal, or a spectacular shoot-out in a busy centre crowded with civilians – nameless, faceless, shouting, hysterical people, slightly blurred, often out of focus. The audience's attention is focused on hero and/or villain and does not stop to consider the helpless mass.

A glance at cinema listings of the two main distributors is revealing. Cinemas located in working-class areas in Cape Town consistently screen movies of a particular genre. The fare is dominated by "skiet, skop and donder",[7] whilst theatres in the plush southern suburbs such as Claremont become the "art house cinemas" (for the "discerning filmgoer", says the promotional blurb).[8] Violence, it seems, sells cultural products. Most analysis of the media industry will show this trend. Yet it sells only where it has an audience. The debate has been raging about the effect that mediated violence has on actualised violence. It is illuminating to note that the Globe Gang, who by 1950 "were controlling extortion, blackmail, illicit buying of every kind, smuggling, shebeens, gambling and political movements in the District" were also "taking in large doses of American gangland experience at the cinemas in the District" (Pinnock 1984:28). This is also alluded to in other studies, particularly during the heyday of independent cinema ownership. According to Mohamed, "there were many different bioscopes to choose from in the District; there was the Star, the British, the Empire, the Avalon, the National and the Union" (1990:72). Gangs such as the "Stalag 17, the Killers, the Moguls, (which later became the Mongrels), were all names of films . . . a description of the members of the Globe Gang going into battle could have come out of a scene in a 1940s gangster film" (Mohamed 1990:72).

Since the 1960s studies have been conducted in the United States to establish if this relationship existed at all, by relying on stimulus/response methodology (Elliot 1974; Ewen 1976; Rosengren 1985; Morley 1980). The findings indicated a definite relationship between stimulus, in this case television violence, and the audience behaviour patterns (Lull 1995:88). The major networks all denied culpability in contributing toward violent behaviour. Blame was laid at the door of parents instead. Effects theory has subsequently been criticised for its behaviourist framework by work done in cultural studies (Brantlinger 1990; Bourdieu 1993; Fiske 1993; Turner 1990).

It would only be in the interests of the multimillion-dollar culture industry to say that there was no relationship between mediated and actualised violence. Is it just coincidence that more murders take place on the Cape Flats where audiences imbibe a staple diet of violent cinema, than in the suburbs? It seems, however, too mechanical to argue that viewers are simply a passive audience. Audiences are sifting out the probable from the improbable and are dealing with normative issues continuously. We appropriate and situate images, values and actions within our own environment. But our choices are configured at the nexus of various cultural and financial interests. Some might trivialise the violence as "escapism", but the values are much more difficult to decode. All media texts are highly polysemic.

Heroes are not only packaged on celluloid. They are also celebrated in that other big industry: sports. American sports in particular, such as basketball, are major sources of income for a whole series of subsidiary industries, from shoe and clothing manufacturers to network screening rights. Brandname advertising relies heavily on the consumer associating a hero with their product. Michael Jordan, Dennis Rodman, Charles Barkley and others are taken out of the court and put on sneakers, soft-drink cans, cereal boxes and all sorts of apparel. Young people in particular purchase these goods because they associate the product with their heroes. When they buy these goods, are they also buying associated values? "Just Do It" Nike tells us. Don't bother to think that it takes the average monthly salary, or that workers are being super-exploited in South Korea, Thailand, China, Indonesia and Vietnam to make them. Just do it – regardless of the conditions of production, or effects of excessive consumption. Nike admitted in a 1993 *Sports Illustrated* article that it actively pursued athletes with a "bad boy" attitude to represent its products.

The expropriation of the "attitude" through which marginalised sections of African-American youth have constructed themselves has become highly marketable and permeates the sports industry as well as the music scene. The profits reaped from "gangsta rap" are a useful illustration of this. The romanticised "hood" now becomes appropriated from the Bronx to Bonteheuwel. Rap artists in Cape Town now interpret their circumstances through the discursive constructs of African-American youth. The Cape Flats, the "township", fast gives way to a discourse that comes with an attitude that is backed by a wardrobe. The "attitude" of sections of African-American youth resonates on the Cape Flats and finds an articulation with local youth precisely because it speaks within a discourse of "alienation", but is given cultural power; it is globalised by media and financial interests who have appropriated its symbols. This has been occurring over a period extending well into the early gang formations in South Africa and their idealised American gangster heroes (Fenwick 1996; Nicol 1991; Sorfa 1992).

Gangsterism is not a new problem, neither does it regenerate itself simply through mechanistic economic motivations. It has taken on a dynamism that spans generations. It represents an identity which is often seen as articulating the values of absolute individualism which are posited as oppositional to collective and social responsibility, that speaks more to a Hobbesian state of nature where life is "nasty, brutish and short".[9] Different aspects of the messages of particular products of cultural industries find articulation with different groups in society, delineated and overlapping between race, class and gender. Whether you are urged to spend huge amounts on a sports car, or buy clothing to lend you status, these are used to signify particular constructions of the "good life" within different communities. These produce a melange of different local identities, and a globalised hybridity, which marries Tupac Shakur, Manchester United and the Red Bulls.

Images of the "gangster" in Cape Town will visually demonstrate this. The information flows within processes of globally broadcast clothing styles and mannerisms, not in a two-way process. To understand the process of identity formation we would need to ask why Cape Flats gangsters have appropriated the dress style of North American ghetto gangsters and not, for example, the clothing style of American and Australian surfing culture, which many white youth in Cape Town choose as a particular subculture. The appropriation of products from the global highway finds its articulation, its translation and indigenisation at the nodes of the local and global in which the global is both localised and globalised. The important point is that it must be able to find its local interface. In this sense, globalisation does not deterritorialise the national and specific dimensions of particular commodities. Rather, they become "re-territorialised" in local contexts. As Hall suggests, "if no meaning is taken, there can be no consumption" (Hall 1996).

Pagad and the Return to Source

> And if in the process we can dispose finally of both the residual hatred and the offensive generality of labels like "the Muslim", "the Persian", "the Turk", "the Arab", or "the Westerner", then so much the better (Said 1978).

Pagad as an organisation has come to feature in the landscape of the public memory quite strongly over the last few years. In some cases this is as Good Samaritan, and in others as public enemy. The overwhelming body of written words devoted to Pagad have their origins in journalistic accounts. Some of these accounts have presented Pagad in ways that casually repeat orientalist clichés about Muslims, Islam, and Pagad, even conflating the three as one and the same. This paper is also written in the shadow of a number of concerns that were spawned by the ways in which "expert" knowledge and predictions come to inform a whole range of policies and perspectives.

In 1993 the esteemed political scientist Samuel P. Huntington published a piece in the North American journal *Foreign Affairs*, in which he posed the question whether the post-Cold War security environment would be confronted by a "clash of civilisations".

Huntington's affirmative answer was that "the clash of civilizations will dominate global politics. The fault lines between civilisations will be the battle lines of the future" (1993:3). After tracing the histories of civilisations, Huntington suggests that the principal conflict is going to be that between Islam and "the West". Moscow had been replaced by Tehran.

Soon after Pagad had emerged publicly, the *Cape Argus*, owned by the Independent Group, ran a piece headlined "UK panic button on Pagad" (*Cape Argus*, 14 December, 1996). The article reported that an "influential British newspaper" was suggesting that Cape Town was "becoming an Iranian terrorist training ground". The article went on to suggest, "Pagad will act as Iran's eyes and ears in Africa." Some time afterwards, the same paper ran a piece headlined "Blasts bring terrorism close to home" (Josephs 1998).

The word "terrorism" is not innocent of a range of associations. The process by which "terrorism" often seems to be accompanied by this or that Islamic "fundamentalist" has been well documented by Edward Said in his work on *Covering Islam* (1997). Chomsky has suggested that we may look at terrorism "literally", or "propagandistically". The literal approach requires us to decide what constitutes acts of terror, identify them and attempt to address them. The propagandistic approach, he suggests, "begins with the thesis that terrorism is the responsibility of some officially designated enemy" (George 1991:12). It follows that if one uses this approach he who names the terrorist becomes important. The United States government, in its "Global Patterns of Terrorism" report named Pagad as an "emerging terrorist organisation". I am of course not disputing that what we have experienced in the Western Cape are literal acts of "terror". I am interested in the way in which this "terror" is reported as being *brought closer to home*. To suggest that it is "brought", spatially, is to suggest travelling, as if in some way it has an unstated originary point in our assumed public consciousness. The "expert" produces the knowledge, the "government" gives it power and legitimacy, the media gives it currency and before you know it we get letters from the public asking, "What is the real agenda behind Pagad?" The most fully developed academic study on Pagad in South Africa is in many ways representative of this problematic tendency to regard Muslims the world over as a homogenous group without individual agency or local particularities (Le Roux 1997).

Its seems to me that to see Pagad as the "eyes" of an officially designated external enemy is to say that the organisation does not have locally driven dynamics and agency. In order to begin to explore "the local" this paper takes as its focus the making of particular identities associated with Pagad and processes involved therein. It is informed by a notion of identity, which sees it as fluid, conjunctural and contingent, not outside of time, place and power. Stuart Hall (1993) argues that cultural identity "is a matter of becoming as well as of being", that "cultural identity is not a fixed essence", it is "not a fixed origin to which we can make some final and absolute Return", "it is always constructed through memory, fantasy, narrative and myth", and that "far from being grounded in mere recovery of the past, which is waiting to be found [. . .] identities are the names we give to different ways we are positioned by, and position ourselves within, the narratives of the past" (1993:394-395). Muslims in South Africa, as much as other social groups, are symbolically constantly creating and recreating a sense of community from diverse cultural traces which have fused to constitute a number of particular identities using the same cultural symbols.

It seems to me that contestations over Islamic "truth" are at the interface of the local and the global underpinning the endogenous battles unfolding within Pagad. Since Islam features strongly in a study on Pagad, let me make the following observation. Islam, as much as any other religion, is not a homogenous entity and does not entail a singular way of thinking, behaving and doing things. Maxime Rodinson (1979) has suggested that Islam (as well as other monotheisms) should be considered as a composite of three categories. Firstly, there is the Koran, the originary text. Secondly, there is the hermeneutic practice through which textual interpretation takes place. This gives rise to the range of different sects, movements and schools of thought.[10] Thirdly, there is the activity of translating the interpretation into an ideological praxis, a mode of organising the activities of social organisation (1979:51). The third cannot come about without the preceding two.

It is at the site of the second and third categories that the wrestle between narratives, the struggle for authenticity, or the "return to source" takes place. As Said suggests, "what we are dealing with here are in the very widest sense communities of interpretation, many of them at odds with one another, all of them creating and revealing themselves and their interpretations as very central features of their existence" (1993:45). Prominent intellectuals within the Islamic community in South Africa have dichotomised the distinction between "Islamism" and themselves, which I have parenthetically called "democratic Islam". Among the former, they label "Islamist" groupings as "fundamentalist", a concept I find too problematic to employ here (Tayob 1996a). This division is for me a manifestation of Islamic thought wrestling with meaning temporally and spatially in South Africa in the 1990s. The result is a struggle over "authenticity", which is a struggle within Islam internationally. The wrestle between narratives which are the "enunciatory present" of the nation, as Homi Bhabha (1990) argues, is in this case transposed to the global level where the supranational narratives of the Islamic *ummah* is constantly being written and re-written, in highly localised ways. The paper therefore proceeds with a discussion on the different trends in Islamic political thought. It then looks at Islamic political thought in the Western Cape and attempts to argue that the multiplicity of narratives interface with the particularity of location to produce specific, hybrid forms of identity. It suggests that one form of this Islamic narrative is the dominant "Islamist" narrative present in Pagad.

Global influences

Postcolonial Islamic movements seem to be influenced by a number of key individuals. One of the most significant of these is Hassan Al-Banna, who initiated the Muslim Brothers tradition in Egypt. Postcolonial Islamic states were to be influenced by the thought of Al-Banna, who argued that Islam offered a complete plan for social, political and economic policy (Bagader 1994:117). Another influential figure is Abul-Ala Maududdi (1903-1978), an Indian Muslim, who argued that Allah's sovereignty must be maintained over the state. The laws made known through the Prophet Mohammed must be the laws of the state, and all other laws are therefore unlawful and Muslims should not obey them. The divine origin of Islamic law therefore overrides any other law. The ideas of Ala Maududdi heavily influenced Sayid Qutab, who became one of the most influential leaders of the modern "radical" Islamic movements. His execution and subsequent martyrdom has further enhanced his influence (Bagader 1994:119; Kritchen 1995:551). These ideas on state and religion exerted a strong influence on Sudanese, Iranian, Algerian and Afghan Islamic movements in different ways at different times.

The political middle ground of modern Islamic thinking coheres around a different set of intellectual voices. Shaikh Qaradawi and Shaikh Gazali are two such voices who represent a strand of Islam which agrees that Islam is a necessary solution for all societies, but in a more "moderate" stance. This school objects to the violent means through which movements associated with Al-Banna and Qutab seek to effect this global transformation. Significantly, notes Abubaker Bagader, the 1980s saw the emergence of a new set of voices from amongst Muslims. These new voices, representing previously silenced narratives, not only criticised the methods of some of the "radical" groups, they "publicly announced their opposition to the rule of the laws of Islam over society" (1994:121). Faraj Foudah, for example, put forward what is regarded as a secular view, which is opposed to the application of Shari'a laws. Another intellectual, Hussein Amin, goes so far as to state that radical Islamic groups are "blood-thirsty, barbaric, violent, and un-Islamic" (Bagader 1994:122).

This account of some of the thinking in postcolonial Islam is but a cursory exposition of what are complex and varied issues. What are apparent are the resonances[11] between local contestations over Islamic narrative, which have emerged around the issue of Pagad, and its global dimensions, within the Islamic community. The debates reveal the challenges facing Muslims, as citizens of Muslim states and those who have to negotiate their identity in relation to alternative views of nationhood and citizenship. Whilst these schools of thought remain influential, they are not static, and the thinking and influence of the Muslim Brotherhoods, for example, has changed over time and between places. The resonances that they have today should be seen in the context of what they say about the peoples, places and contexts where they are invoked in the present, rather than in a pristine past. In a study which explores the relationship between the local and the global in Islam, John Bowen (1998) looks at North African, Turkish Cypriot, Bangladeshi and Tuareg identities, "with various degrees of attention to Islamic dimensions of those identities". He arrives at the conclusion that "these women and men are actively, through multiple channels, situating themselves along many dimensions of identity, with respect to gender, modernity, mobility, transnational communication, nationhood, and sexuality" (1998:261). In another study, which seeks to use the concept of "borders" to understand constructions of Muslim identity, Katherine Pratt Ewing (1998) suggests "Muslim conceptualisations of boundaries and nationalist conceptions of borders create different sorts of social spaces and organise identity differently" (1998:263). These debates are also occurring in a world in which "nation" increasingly cannot be conflated with "state". Movement, migration and travel establish the disjuncture between nation and state and have important implications for debates around plurality and citizenship.

Global Islam: South African Style

Farid Esack (1996:7) argues that Muslims in South Africa arrived from three geographical routes, during different historical moments. The first arrivals coincide with the Dutch colonial presence in the form of Van Riebeeck, and came as prisoners, political exiles and slaves from the East. This group became known as "Malays". Many of these people fell into the category of "Coloured" under apartheid laws. The second group came as part of the indentured labourers from India in 1860 and settled in Natal originally. There has been a great deal of fusion between these two groups, particularly within the current generation. The third group arrived between 1873 and 1880, "when about 500 slaves were brought to Durban", and this group has become known as the "Zanzibaris", stemming from the story that they were a group of slaves on their way to Zanzibar, who were shipwrecked off the Natal coast (Esack 1996:7).

Muslims from particular areas of the world have had to negotiate the challenges of diasporas like other groups who have moved, voluntarily or involuntarily, from one territory to another, particularly those in which different laws based on different philosophical assumptions are to be adhered to. It is the construction of these identities which I find interesting and see wrestling within Pagad as different strands of Islam compete within a politics of authenticity for the authority to interpret Shari'a law and issue *fatwas*[12], which "includes the problems of negotiating with other Muslims and agreeing with them on the meaning of Islam . . . the hyphen of hyphenated identities like that of British-Muslim or American-Muslim [or South African-Muslim], reflects and obscures the necessary conjunction of disparate cultural traces brought together in the act of "re-membering" and "re-creating" (Akbar and Donnan 1994:6).

The Muslim community in South Africa originates territorially from diverse points. The Muslim narrative is about the construction of a "universal community", which is the *ummah*, for "throughout the world Muslims share a very deep sense of belonging to the world community of Muslims" (Esack 1996b:26). According to Fatima Mernissi, "[o]ne of the most emblematic verses [of the Koran] . . . is verse 13 of sura 49, which the Prophet proclaimed in a speech in the Ka'ba: 'Oh mankind! We have created you male and female, and have made you nations and tribes, that ye may know each other.' This verse condenses and articulates two messages: that of the *ummah* formed of equals, and the *ummah* whose solidarity crosses borders and encompasses cultures, giving Muslims the beautiful sense of belonging, of universal communion" (Mernissi 1992:110).

It is this same global *ummah* that Pagad's Amir invoked when he remarked that "the government poses a definite danger to our community and the police are nothing but legal gangsters in uniform ... this is the same scenario to be found in Bosnia, Algeria, Egypt, and all over the world, where governments are discriminating against Muslims" (Oliver 1997). The term "our community" is used with reference to other Muslims in a transnational sense. It is this sense of a homogenous *ummah* that seems to me also to give life to the idea of a "global threat" to the West. This picture of homogeneity can be invoked for different strategic reasons, good or bad, depending on where you stand, but can detract from the particularity of Islam within different regions and countries of the world. The diversity of political positions taken by states in the Middle East on a range of issues, for example the Gulf War or responses to Salman Rushdie's *Satanic Verses*, is revealing of the differences amongst "the world community" and the importance of location and power (Ahmed and Donnan 1994:12).

The identity of being "Malay", which Esack notes is widespread, displays this symbolic locality of meaning. He notes that "despite the fact that less than one percent came from today's Malaysia", there are particularities to Malaysian Islam which are quite different from what has been constructed as "Malay" in Cape Town (Esack 1996a:7). One such issue is dance, which in the "Malay" community in South Africa is largely considered to be un-Islamic – primarily due to influences of Shi'ite Islam – but is very much a part of Malaysian constructions of Islam. This resonates with Homi Bhabha (1990) when he speaks of the splitting of the nation, the double time, of the nation "as pedagogical object and the people constructed in the performance of narrative, its enunciatory 'present', marked in repetition and pulsation of the national sign" (1990:299). Creating the community of Islam involves contestations between different voices manufacturing its "enunciatory present", and in the process centring itself, decentring others, through closure.[13]

Muslims, who comprise 1,3% of the overall South African population, have historically been politically active both as a religious community and through individuals who have formed part of political organisations which are populist oriented or have sectional interests (Esack 1996a:7). Most prominent of these has been the role of Dr Abdullah Abdurahman in the African People's Organisation, although according to Keith Gottschalk, exclusivist Muslim organisations with an overtly political agenda began with Imam Abdullah Haron's founding of the Claremont Muslim Youth Movement in 1957 (Gottschalk 1998:1).

Contesting the Mantle of "Truth"

During the mid-1990s the political dimensions of Islamic thought in South Africa were presented as Janus-faced: one version "modern" and looking forward, the other "traditional" and looking to the past. The one aligned itself to what became known as the "Charterist" organisations, as embodied in organisations such as the ANC and, particularly important in the Western Cape, the UDF (United Democratic Front). Organisations such as the Call of Islam, established in the early 1980s, and the older Muslim Youth Movement seem to represent what some call a "democratic" Islam, which refers more to a willingness to participate in secular movements, both as a group and as individuals. One of the leaders of the Call of Islam during the 1980s, Ebrahim Rassool, is now the regional leader of the African National Congress in the Western Cape. Abdulkader Tayob argues that this "forward-looking" trend can be viewed as "nationalist" and is a critique of "traditional Islam", which it sees as "utopian, un-South African, and hopelessly inadequate to address real social and political inequalities in South Africa" (Tayob 1996a:31). This trend of thought is influentially purveyed by a group of Islamic scholars, including Tayob himself, Farid Esack, Rashied Omar and Ebrahim Moosa, whose house was bombed in July 1998, allegedly by Pagad. He had incurred the wrath of the organisation by publicly condemning their modus operandi, and its attempt to hegemonise its Islam over the Muslim community in the Western Cape (Smith, *Cape Argus*, July 18, 1988). According to Moosa "in this vision Islamic values are to be shared with the community of nations. This vision can only flourish within a dispensation of political pluralism where diversity with integrity is maintained" (1996).

The other face of political Islam in the Western Cape is said to cohere around the rather faceless enigma of Achmat Cassiem, and the Qibla movement which he leads. Cassiem has taken on the leadership of the Islamic Unity Convention (IUC), which was formed prior to South Africa's first universal franchise election, and which urged Muslims to boycott the election. Qibla emerged in the early 1980s as a militant force, inspired, according to Farid Esack, by the 1979 Iranian revolution (1996b:24). Much of the discussion around Qibla involves a discussion of Achmat Cassiem.[14] Esack suggests, "the phenomenon of the charismatic and supreme leader is one which is quite common to Islam, particularly Shi'ah Islam". He goes on to say that whilst many of Qibla's followers may not identify themselves as Shi'ites, "the model of a Khomeini-ist charismatic figure is one to which they are deeply attracted" (1996b:24). If that is the case, then it seems that the "attraction" needs to be explored further. What makes that figure attractive may not be explained by it being of Shi'ite origin in and of itself. The current leader of Pagad, whose identity was withheld for a long time, and who features at meetings enigmatically draped in a Palestinian style scarf, is addressed reverentially as the *Amir* (leader).

The debate around the status of religious leadership in the Islamic community is concerned with the distinction between Shi'ite and Sunni Islam. According to Mernissi,

"From the beginning the power of the Shi'ite imam was quasi-supernatural, whereas Sunni Islam has been astonishingly pragmatic and hyper-rational. The Imam is never infallible in Sunni (orthodox) Islam. A Khomeini, an imam who claims to be infallible, a leader who cannot err, is not exportable to the lands of Sunni Islam. This does not mean that the regimes in power there [. . .] and opposition groups basing themselves on the sacred, don't dream about it" (Mernissi 1992:33). Tayob counterposes the "democratic" Islam that seeks to exercise its influence by operating within secular structures, to the "international Islamism"[15] of Cassiem, which seeks dominance of Islam in the world, embodied in the slogan "One solution, Islamic revolution" (Tayob 1996:31). This finds curious resonance with the theme of Pagad's first national convention, the title of which was "Pagad – The Only Solution". At this convention Pagad outlined that it had a "global vision to rid the world of drugs" (Van Zilla, 21 March 1997).

I find Tayob's idea of "the larger democratic movement" – to which the Call of Islam and Muslim Youth Movement aligned themselves – slightly problematic. The "democratic movement" he refers to implies the ANC and ANC-aligned organisations. The Qibla movement aligned itself to the Pan Africanist Congress (PAC), New Unity Movement and the Azanian People's Organisaton (Azapo) – organisations that were also part of the anti-apartheid movement. Tayob seems to be saying that the anti-apartheid movement as a "democratic movement" is only represented by the organisations to which his Islam is sympathetic. All anti-apartheid organisations across the ideological spectrum claimed to be part of a movement toward some kind of democracy in South Africa, in as much as they all wanted, at minimum, universal franchise. Nonetheless, his conjecture that the alliance of Qibla with these movements did not necessarily detract from its commitment to a global "Islamic revolution" does hold. According to B. Sayyid, Islamists seek to establish an essentialised Islam, they are "people who try and practise the politics of authenticity: they try and erase the hybrid, annihilate the playful for the rigour of orthodoxy. Islamism is the last of the meta-narratives" (1994:279). This trend in Pagad is borne out by statements from the organisation[16] and attacks on dissenters within the Muslim community.[17] Between these two interpretations the Muslim Judicial Council could be seen to represent the South African orthodoxy by legitimating particular interpretations.

On 4 August 1996 a large contingent of armed supporters of the People Against Gangsterism and Drugs descended upon the fortified London Road house of the Staggie brothers in the suburb of Woodstock.[18] In what are now familiar, if not horrific, images, one of the twins, Rashaad Staggie, was shot and set alight. The Minister of Justice remarked that the event "wakened the soul of the community" (Jeenah 1996:17). It was this event that seemed to catapult the activities, demands and issues that Pagad was raising to front-page news, moving it from the peripheries to the centre of news coverage, at least in the Western Cape.

The organisational impulses that led to the formation of Pagad seem to go back to 10 years before this event, with the formation of the Salt River Anti-Drug Community. Within a short time similar committees were established in the Bo-Kaap, Surrey Estate, Athlone and Wynberg. These formations are explained as reflective of a growing anger and frustration amongst communities on the Cape Flats with the proliferation of gang activity and drug sales and usage. In an interview with Fatima Schroeder, Pagad's national secretary, Abidah Roberts, recalled its formation, which started with six members: a teacher, a housewife, a businessman, two community workers, and herself: "I'll never forget that day. We were all sitting there thinking of a name, when he [teacher Ebrahim Francis] just came out with it. His exact words were: 'We are simply people against gangsterism and drugs.' All of us agreed. As a believer, I thought that people were not created to live like animals. Gangsterism and drugs were destroying the fibre of society and I wanted to make my contribution to ridding the city of them" (Schroeder 1998). In March 1996, during a march to Parliament, protesters chanting "Who are we? We are the people against gangsterism and drugs", announced publicly the birth of this new movement formally known as Pagad.

Territorially, Pagad has emerged from what is known as the Cape Flats. The "Cape Flats" in popular discourse seems to imply mainly areas that were previously created for residence by people classified as "Coloured". It is also essentialised as working class, poor and violent. I argue that this is a somewhat problematic generalisation. The Cape Flats may be largely "working class", yet it is highly heterogeneous culturally, socially, politically and economically. The Group Areas Act, which circumscribed the movement of middle-class Coloured and Indian people spatially, created many shared patterns of experience and activity between and within socioeconomic classes, problematising a reductionist claim to a "working-class culture" and a "bourgeois culture" in the Western Cape. The other important essentialism of the "Cape Flats" is that it excludes the areas to which black African people were confined, which are signified by reference to "the townships".

Within this heterogeneity there is a long presence of gangsterism, drug and alcohol abuse. As Shamiel Jeppie has noted, "Class and locality do not simply fit together . . . [T]he middle-class drug consumer market and gangster activity are connected and overlap." Peddlers are actually the "contracted distributors for much bigger drug-lords who are gang-bosses" (Jeppie 1996:14). From this heterogeneous matrix, laced with variations of class, religion and racial identity, emerges Pagad.

The majority of the people involved in and directly supportive of Pagad are Muslim.[19] This is a vital part of its identity. It has been argued that the consumption of drugs and involvement in the sale of drugs amongst Muslim youth has been on the increase over the last two decades and that there is a correlation between this trend and the emergence of Pagad (Jeppie 1996:14). It is commonly accepted amongst some Muslim youth that whilst drinking alcohol is expressly forbidden in the religious texts of Islam, it is *de facto* more acceptable to smoke marijuana (dagga), which is implicitly seen as the lesser of two evils. Marijuana is augmented by the addition of Mandrax tablets, which are largely produced on the South Asian subcontinent.

If one takes a closer look at the attire of Pagad members, particularly through the visuals which appear in the media, we see traces of a range of cultural symbols, fragments from the global, but each artefact from "local" Islamic narratives fused to form another "local" representation of Islam. This pastiche is read as the solidarity of a "universal" imagined community. Jeppie (1996) has observed that the "Afghan Mujahiddin-style caps [. . .] the red or black Makka doeke [scarves], the calligraphied headbands [. . .] come out of the distant and disparate worlds of Middle Eastern conflicts. The complex tribal, civil, and political contradictions of Afghanistan, Palestine, south Lebanon, and Iran are reduced to a single issue" (1996:16). The scarves that Jeppie refers to are also associated with different factions of the Palestine Liberation Organisation, but as worn in Cape Town's streets in the mid-1980s by student activists, and now by Pagad, they take on a different meaning that has more to do with an expression of solidarity with the Intifada and militant protest, and more pragmatically, to hide the identity of protesters, than with reflecting support for a particular faction of a distant movement.[20] The facilitation of the global flows of information and particularly images play an important role in the construction of these identities. Images on CNN and the BBC do not only globalise baseball caps and basketball attire, but also the attire of protesting youth in the Gaza strip, Algiers, Cairo, Karachi and Kabul. These become representations of global, or militant, fundamentalist, unruly Islam, decontextualised and delocalised, but re-territorialised in the space of a global mediascape.

Simultaneously, this polysemic mediated reality also globalises feelings of anger amongst some Muslims with regard to blatant misrepresentations and stereotypes, aggression toward Muslims (e.g. Israel), and lack of political will by the "international community" regarding issues which confront Muslims (e.g. Bosnia), whilst also globalising the local forms and modes of resistance to these practices.

There are those like journalist Na'eem Jeenah who represent Pagad and Muslims in South Africa as a somewhat homogenous, coherent grouping. For Jeenah (1996), the emergence of Pagad is part "of the tradition of resistance and struggle for the past three hundred years [. . .] From the arrival of Muslims on these shores, Muslims have been engaged in a struggle against oppression and dictatorship [...] Muslims have striven with might to achieve justice here [...] the Pagad phenomenon is just a continuation of this heritage" (1996:18). Although he does mention that Muslims were also part of the oppressive machinery, the essentialising of the historical narrative of Muslims as one consistent with protest against oppression obscures a whole range of other narratives, for example that many of the gangsters in Cape Town are from Muslim families, notably Rashid and Rashaad Staggie. Yusuf McKenzie, shot while guarding the home of wellknown gang leader Colin Stansfield, is another case in point. His mother lamented, "I think it was Pagad. We're Moslem, and they're Moslem. I really don't understand anymore what the truth is about anything" (Duffy 1998, January 16).[21] If the Muslim "community" is analysed as separate from other communities in South Africa, how and where do these strands of the story fit in? The construction of "the Muslim community fighting oppression" based on this dominant narrative, which some journalists have represented unproblematically, has also been taken on by some analysts, who further suggest that "Pagad has increased religious polarisation between working-class Christians and Muslims" (Gottschalk 1998:3).

There are other problematic binaries. One is class based: Pagad as "home-owners, car owners, fire-arm owners and gun owners" versus the "overwhelming majority of gangsters and petty street drug dealers who cannot afford to move out of working-class homes". The other binary division is ethnic: "[M]any Muslims in Pagad are at least partly Asian by descent, Indonesian, Indian, Sri Lankan or Bangladeshi" while "the majority of Core and other gangsters are Coloureds of Euro-African descent" (Gottschalk 1998:3).

The "polarisation" between Christians and Muslims seems to be based on a rumoured slogan that permeated some Cape Flats areas, which proclaimed: "one bubbie, one bullet" (one shopkeeper, one bullet). The inference is problematic for two reasons. Firstly, it assumes that this statement could only be made by a non-Muslim, and secondly, it does not historicise the particular perceptions of traders who have had small shops in working-class areas over many years, some of which are streetcorner institutions. The relationships between these shopkeepers and residents are not always harmonious, based on a complex matrix of racial/religious/class-based discriminations. It is quite possible that a shopkeeper could be disdainfully regarded by both Muslim and non-Muslim youth on the Cape Flats.

The class-derived binary is just as problematic. To represent "Pagad versus the gangsters" as "middle class versus working class" seems to ignore that the most ardent supporters of Pagad are from overwhelmingly working-class areas. Arrested Pagad members have typically come from Manenberg, Bonteheuwel and Grassy Park, among other areas.[22]

The "ethnic binary" too falters, as soon as one's analysis extends beyond the images portrayed on television news and press conferences. Muslims in Cape Town have largely straddled two racial classifications under apartheid laws, Malay (as Coloured), and Asian or Indian. If one were to indulge in racial and ethnic categorisation, we would see that the majority of Muslims in Cape Town would be racially classified as "Coloured". Superficially, gangs in Cape Town have proliferated in working-class areas, as they tend to around the world. Apartheid has managed to essentialise "Indians" as wealthy, and this stereotype is reproduced in superficial analyses which see Indian/Muslim individuals and assumes wealth, and sees gangsters who would be classified as "Coloured" and reads "poor", and then concludes that it is an Asian versus Coloured conflict, rich versus poor, or Christian versus Muslim.

The complexity internal and external to Pagad makes the conflict at different moments about rich and poor; Christian and Muslim; Indian, Coloured and Malay; about conjunctural permutations which are constantly forming and re-forming other multiple combinations of the self, each involving acts of remembering, with identities shifting continuously between and within these categories rather than fixed in convenient oppositional constructs. Individuals are negotiating multiple identities. Pagad members could be classified as "Coloured", by being Malay or Muslim; or "Pagad members"; or "rich" or "poor"; or "brothers", "fathers", "sisters" or "mothers", at different moments. Pagad is made up of people from both working-class and middle-class backgrounds.

The involvement of Qibla in Pagad has always been an issue of intense speculation. Pagad seems to have evolved as an organic outgrowth of various predominantly Muslim neighbourhood watches. The initial leadership which emerged seemed to represent that origin, since they did not include "activists" with any real political past. Ali Parker and Mansoor Jaffer[23] appeared to ride the crest of a spontaneous wave. Qibla leaders were notably absent from early Pagad activity. Parker and Jaffer have since been displaced, and now "those who form the core of Pagad's leadership are individuals with a long-standing commitment to Qibla" (Esack 1996b:25).

The tensions in Pagad seem to jostle between these two interpretations of "political" Islam, between Islam and state-power. The militant Islamism of Qibla effectively captured the anti-gangster, anti-drug impulse's militancy. Once the movement's protests transcended secular legality, leadership disputes flared.[24] The "democratic" strand argued for the protests to be focused on drugs and gangsters, and for it to remain within the state's law, using displays of popular support through marches and mass gatherings. The "militant" sections that make up the "G-Force" are more interested in paramilitary-style, cell-based operations, which use urban guerrilla tactics, and which is currently borne out by the spate of pipe bomb attacks on the Cape Flats.[25] They derive their rhetoric from "internationalist" Islam and their human resources from eager men, youth and women who favour a more violent approach, for a whole range of reasons that need to be analysed.

Tensions around the interpretation of Islam are borne out by accounts of the interactions between Pagad and the Muslim Judicial Council (MJC), which is by and large regarded as the official interpreter of Islamic law for Muslims in South Africa. Its leader, Shaykh Nazeem Mohammed, at a public meeting a week after the killing of Rashaad Staggie, announced the MJC's support for Pagad. Pagad committed itself to Islamic Shari'a law as a guide to its actions, and the MJC set about drawing up a set of "ethical codes" which would inform the actions of Pagad. Yet, according to Tayob, when he "asked [Pagad] leaders how they would regard policy documents and juridical viewpoints from the MJC", they responded by saying that "their executive represented a range of groups, and could not be committed to one Muslim organisation, including the MJC". He concluded that "Pagad was not committed to Islamic legal codes represented and jealously guarded by the Muslim Judicial Council". For Tayob, who accepts the legitimacy of the MJC, this showed a dubious commitment to Shari'a law "exposed by [Pagad's] ambivalence to commit itself to the guardians of Islamic law in South Africa" (Tayob 1996a:33).

The neighborhood watches out of which Pagad emerged were largely conceived in local mosques in various areas. Imams played a particularly important role in guiding the activities of these local watch groups, as they commanded considerable authority amongst their congregations. The struggle between Islamism and imams responding to specific social issues – drugs and gangsterism in this case – posed a potential threat to the control of imams over influence of followers (Tayob 1996a:33). Followers are largely caught between competing voices of authority, although in the final instance imams will be more highly regarded. The sentiments of imams are not homogenous: there are those who align themselves with the sentiments of Shi'ite Iran, whilst others distance themselves from this strand of Islam. It is well known amongst Muslims on the Cape Flats that different mosques have differing degrees of "conservatism" or "liberal" sentiments on a range of issues. The Gatesville mosque is known to be a place where Pagad has assembled, whilst they have been barred from others, such as the Claremont mosque.

It is the Claremont mosque that, in an unprecedented act, allowed a woman to preach to the congregation during the Friday *Juma'ah* prayer. Subsequently, attempts were made by followers from the Gatesville mosque to oust the imam of the Claremont mosque, resulting in physical confrontation and verbal abuse towards the imam. On another occasion, the imam of the Muir Street mosque, Shaykh Moerat, also not in favour of the modus operandi of Pagad, was threatened during *Juma'ah* (Esack 1996a:9; Tayob 1996a:34; Gottschalk 1998:2). In its desire not to alienate imams completely, since they are a significant channel of legitimacy, Pagad has had to tread warily in terms of maintaining as its mobilisational focus, the issues of drugs and gangsterism. The moment it transgresses this popular mandate, it raises the ire of important imams who further distance themselves from the movement.

This struggle for hegemony has taken on alarming proportions with the increasing number of pipe bomb attacks against members of the Muslim community, most notably intellectuals who have made known their objections to "Islamism" and who themselves favour a more "pragmatic" approach to secular political life, and wealthy Muslim businesspeople. There is speculation about the reasons for attacks on these businesspeople. Some reports suggest that Pagad is "extorting" financial support against the wishes of members of the community, and those who refuse to co-operate are having their businesses attacked. There is also speculation that the attacks are directed against those members of the Muslim community who may be involved in drug trafficking.

Pagad has brought this tension out in the form of the "democratic Muslim" strand, around intellectual figures such as Farid Esack, Rashid Omar and others, and the "Islamist" tradition of Al-Banna and Qutab (and Shariati), in the form of Qibla and Achmat Cassiem. It is the latter version of Islam which has been constructed in popular images in the West as the "other" of "freedom" (see Said 1993), and as the essentialised meaning of Islam that intellectuals such as Samuel P. Huntington ascribe to the post-Cold War era, concluding that it is about the "clash of civilisations", because "as the ideological division of Europe has disappeared, the cultural division of Europe between Western Christianity, on the one hand, and orthodox Christianity and Islam, on the other, has re-emerged" (Huntington 1993). It seems that Islamism has become the "terroristic" constitutive outside of "freedom" amongst some intellectuals, displacing the "red under the bed", but competing in Hollywood with aliens and extraterrestrial beings for celluloid space.

Conclusion

There are a great many complexities, many of them local, which need to be explored if we are to understand events in the Western Cape that have to do with Pagad and gangs. The organisation is made up of a diverse range of competing elements. Amongst these elements are contested meanings of Islam, its role in a plural society, party-political legitimacy, a normative disdain for drug abuse and gangsterism, and elements of gung-ho machismo. It is also one narrative within a wider range of Islamic narratives, which are being constructed using global and local symbols, which produce specific and hybridised Muslim identities. These are intimately connected to the "routes" of these symbols, produced within colonialism, globalisation and the post-apartheid era. It presents us with an assemblage of tensions which are intensely internal and local, while at the same time being external and global.

Poverty, unemployment, overcrowding and various social "ills" are contributing factors to the formation and proliferation of what we know as gangs. In Cape Town, gangsterism and its associated practices *are* pressing social and political issues. Current explanations are based on a one-dimensional causality link. I have not sought necessarily to break the link of causality. I have simply attempted to argue that single-factor analyses premised on economic determinism and linked to programmatic agendas of change do tend toward simplification and caricature. The simplified explanations are used in a universalising manoeuvre to capture and explain all social phenomena within its net. Yet within this catchall stand glaring differences. These differences are anomalised as "abnormalities". Middle-class youth on the Cape Flats who become gangsters may not be the abnormality, just as much as working-class youth do not all become gangsters.

These single-factor explanations abound, to the extent that they begin to constitute a discourse which, through the power-knowledge nexus, can constitute their very subjects. As Pierre Bourdieu notes, "It is easy to understand why one of the elementary forms of political power should have consisted, in many archaic societies, in the almost magical power of naming and bringing into existence by virtue of naming" (1994:118). This brings our attention to the relationship between "thought, culture and power"[26] and the material implications of these relations. As an example of this, I offer the following anecdote. Whilst collaborating on a newspaper article on gangs at schools in Manenberg, a teacher confronted the reporter I was with and told her that she (the teacher) was concerned about the impact of "yet another story" about gangs and school kids in Manenberg, and the effect this was having on the students. Her concern stemmed from the problem she was having in motivating her students to aspire to complete school and to see education as a mechanism for "upward" mobility. She complained that the stereotyping of the youth in the media and by "experts" had created the attitude amongst students that they were expected to become gangsters and dropouts, that the script for their futures was being written in the daily stories of murder, rape, drug addiction and alcoholism: They were being determined by institutional power and knowledge, and were resigning themselves to this fate.

Strategies to address gangsterism which are premised on the overthrow of capitalism are not in and of themselves magical wands which are a panacea to these problems, nor is the enskilling of individuals in and of itself going to change the situation. Both rely on an economic determinism that underplays the role of culture and power in identity formation. A more nuanced approach, which attempts to grasp the multiplicity of causality which underlies social phenomena will produce, in my view, a more textured knowledge of gangsterism and the reasons for its persistence.

Notes

1 This chapter draws on my earlier publication "Problematising the making of Good and Evil: Gangs and Pagad", *Critical Arts*, 16(2), 38-75. I would like to thank Tahirih Cook, Brenda Coughlin, Nadia Guessous and Muhammed Haron for their helpful comments on this paper, as well as the participants of the Contemporary African Identities panel of the 3rd Crossroads in Cultural Studies, University of Birmingham, the Contemporary History seminar series at the University of the Western Cape, and the seminar series at the Institute for Democracy, Cape Town, at which versions of this paper were presented.

2 Hybrid does not in my use suggest the possibility of a prior condition of purity – it suggests rather an interruption in a stable, or "motivated", relation of signified to signifier, and hence "ambiguous" condition.

3 My focus here is on Pagad during the period 1996-1998.

4 Although race, class, religion and gender feature, the reductive tendency to assert the primacy of the economic is still maintained in these analyses.

5 "Polysemy" refers to the property of signs to signify multiple meanings.

6 "Bricolage" here is used in the way Hebdige (1998) defines it: a cultural process of improvisation or adaptation whereby objects, signs or practices are appropriated

into different meaning systems and cultural settings and, as a result, are resignified.

7 An Afrikaans phrase used to describe violent action-type movies that literally translates into "shooting, kicking and beating up".

8 Two large groups dominate cinema ownership and distribution: Ster Kinekor and Nu Metro. There has been a steady decline in independent cinema ownership over the last 15 to 20 years. This may have something to do with the proliferation of malls, which house most cinemas today. Malls are located in mostly middle-class areas. Of the 16 cinema complexes owned by Nu Metro and Ster Kinekor, one is on the Cape Flats: Westgate Mall, and even this is on the border of the most middle-class section of Mitchells Plain. Art house movies are screened at Ster Kinekor's two Cinema Nouveaus, located in Cape Town's two most upper-class malls, Cavendish Square and the V&A Waterfront. Ster Kinekor on any one day has 140 screenings in its 13 cinema complexes. On 3 November, 132 of these were North American films. Nu Metro had 31 screenings in its 3 cinema complexes. On 3 November they were all North American in origin (*Cape Times*, 3 November 1998). This is not an unusual scenario. These indicators do not take into account trends in home video rentals, which should also yield interesting results.

9 This strong individualism exists simultaneously alongside a strict set of codes, ethics and laws that govern the organisational hierarchy of the gang and regulates the behaviour of members (Schrwink 1986). Gangsters may therefore be "anti" one particular construction of the "social" *and* be bound within a different social construction. It is therefore a misnomer to read the conflict as one between "community" and "individualism".

10 An example of these hermeneutic modes is the contestation between *ijtihad* (individual interpretation) and *taqlid* (reliance on authorities) as ways in which the Koran is interpreted.

11 Resonance here implies an articulation, a listening, incorporation and a deployment. That incorporation is a process, including the internally prior and the external "voice" which resonates. Some symbols resonate in the making of local imaginaries and others do not. Why this is so is a question the study of identity politics would seek to explore.

12 *Fatwas* are non-enforced legal clarifications "concerned with and based upon doctrinal texts (*adilla*), although it requires the specifics of an actual case as a point of departure" (Messick 1993:146).

13 Esack (1999) attempts in my view to deal with this "closure" through making a distinction between what he sees as "essential to the faith" and what is "cultural accretion".

14 Muhammad Haron has usefully suggested to me that it was the writings of the assassinated Iranian sociologist, Ali Shariati, with its emphasis on social justice that was particularly influential on the early thinking of Cassiem, more so than Qutab and al-Banna.

15 Tayob uses Fisher and Abedi's notion of Islamism which refers to "a fear of difference . . . [which] block[s] access to the ethics of difference. They are defensively anxious about manhood and subordinating women. They exhibit an anxious pattern of denial about the rights of minorities and are insistent on the eventual erasure of cultural, religious, class and national differences in the name of Islamic universalism. They are indifferent to the rights of individual conscience, due process of the law, and civil and human rights, and are insistent that social discipline and the imposition of Islam, as they see it, override all such rights" (Fisher and Abedi 1990:153).

16 According to Pagad "in Islam there are no moderates [. . .] you either take action to right a wrong or you stand back and do nothing. If that strikes you as fundamentalism, then we say thanks be to God that we are fundamentalists" (*Mail & Guardian* 1996, November 15).

17 Prominent Muslim community leaders attacked include Sheikh Nazeem Mohamed, MJC president (grenade), Imam Sadullah Khan (death threats), Ebrahim Moosa (pipe bomb) (Daniels 1998).

18 Rashid and Rashaad Staggie were the leaders of the one of the largest gangs in Cape Town, the Hard Living Kids (HLKs).

19 This point is contested by Pagad. In a press statement Pagad asserted, "We say Pagad consists of people from various communities. Muslims, Christians, Catholics, Hindus [. . .] Do not persist with this Qibla link" (*Mail & Guardian* 1996, November 15).

20 In a similar way Fanon (1967) showed us the polysemic nature of meaning involved in the wearing of the veil by women in his study of colonial Algeria.

21 There are numerous other incidents which disprove this binary. Abdus Salaam Ebrahim, Pagad national co-ordinator, was charged with the attempted murder of four gangsters: Saleem Bawa, Caswell Karim and Ismael "Bobby Mongrel" April, all "Muslim" (*Cape Times*, 18 September 1997).

22 The Booley brothers, arrested for the killing of Rashaad Staggie, were from Grassy Park. They were traced after attempting to sell a gold chain belonging to Staggie. Another Pagad member, arrested for possession of materials used in the manufacture of pipe bombs, is a flower seller from Manenberg (Van Zilla 1998).

23 There have been attempts on both their lives. Whilst Parker survived, Jaffer was murdered in 1999. Reports subsequently emerged that he had become a police informer after his growing dissatisfaction with Qibla influence on the organisation (Merten 1999).

24 This dispute over control of the identity of the organisation even prompted Jaffer and Parker to register Pagad as a company with themselves as "directors" in 1997. (http://archive.iol.co.za/archives/1997/9701/7%20Jan/sneakyPagad.html).

25 Pagad has consistently denied that it is involved in these operations. The most conclusive evidence to the contrary was the death of two Pagad members when the vehicle in which they were travelling exploded. Police speculate that they were on their

way to plant a bomb. In a separate incident, police found materials required for the manufacture of explosives at the house of a Pagad member. Within a 10-month period up until August 1998 there were more than 80 pipe bomb explosions in the Western Cape, which killed 11 people (Hess 1998). Between January 1998 and October 1998 there have been 165 incidents of "urban violence" attributed to Pagad. In the same period there have been 437 incidents attributed to gangs (SAPS 1998).

26 I borrow this phrase from Partha Chatterjee (1999:26).

References

Adorno, T.W. 1991. *The culture industry: Selected essays on mass culture*. London: Routledge.

Ahmed, M. (ed.). 1986. *State politics and Islam*. USA: American Trust Publications.

Ahmed, A.S and Donnan, H. 1994. *Islam, globalization and postmodernity*. London: Routledge.

Albrow, M. 1996. *The Global Age: state and society beyond modernity*. Polity Press: Cambridge.

Andah, B. W. 1997. *The local in the global and the global in the local: African identity in the 21st century*. Paper presented to HSRC conference, July 1997, Pretoria.

Appadurai, A. 1993. "Disjuncture and difference in the global cultural economy". In: P. Williams and Chrisman, L. (eds.). *Colonial discourse and postcolonial culture*. New York: Harvester.

Bagader, A.A. 1994. "Contemporary Islamic movements in the Arab world". In: Ahmed, A. and Donnan, H. (eds.). *Islam, globalization and postmodernity*. London: Routledge.

Balakrishnan, G. 1995. "The national imagination". *New Left Review, March-April* 1995, 210.

Bhabha, H. (ed.). 1990. *Nation and narration*. New York: Routledge.

Bourdieu, P. 1993. *The field of cultural production*. Cambridge, United Kingdom: Polity Press.

Bourdieu, P. 1994. "Social space and symbolic power". In: *The polity reader in social theory*. United Kingdom: Polity Press.

Bowen, J. R. 1998. "What is 'universal' and 'local' in Islam?" *Ethos, 26* (2), 258-261.

Brantlinger, P. 1990. *Crusoe's footprints: Cultural studies in Britain and America*. New York: Routledge.

Brown, R. 1995. "Globalization and the end of the National Project". In: Macmillan, J. and Linklater, A. (eds.). *Boundaries in question: New directions in international relations*. London: Pinter.

Brubaker, R. and Cooper, F. 2001. "Beyond 'identity'". *Theory and Society, February,* Vol 29/1.

Chomsky, N. 1991. "International terrorism: Image and reality". In: George, A. (ed.). *Western state terrorism*. United Kingdom: Polity.

Chatterjee, P. 1999. "Nationalist Thought and the Colonial World". In: *The Partha Chatterjee Omnibus*. India: Oxford University Press.

Dickens, P. 1992. *Global shift: The internationalisation of economic activity*. London: Chapman.

During, S. 1993. *The cultural studies reader*. London: Routledge.

Elliot, P. 1974. "Uses and gratifications research: A critique and a sociological perspective". In: Blumler, J. G. and Katz, E. (eds.). *The uses of mass communications: Current perspectives on gratifications research*. Beverly Hills, C.A: Sage.

Esack, F. 1996a. "Pagad and Islamic radicalism: Taking on the State?" *Indicator SA, Vol 13*(4).

Esack, F. 1996b. "Pagad: Its location in a new South Africa". In Galant, R. and Gamieldien, F. *Drugs, gangs and people's power: Exploring the Pagad phenomenon*. Claremont: Masjid.

Esack, F. 1997a. *Qur'an, liberation and pluralism: An Islamic perspective on inter-religious solidarity against oppression.* Oxford: OneWorld.

Esack, F. 1997b. *On being a Muslim: Finding a religious path today*. Oxford: OneWorld.

Esack, F. 1988. Three Islamic strands in the South African struggle for justice. *Third World Quarterly,* April 1988. 473-498.

Ewen, S. 1976. *Captains of consciousness*. New York: McGraw Hill.

Ewing, K. P. 1998. "Crossing Borders and Transgressing Boundaries: Metaphors for Negotiating Multiple Identities" *Ethos* 26(2).

Fanon, F. 1967. *A dying colonialism*. New York: Grove Press.

Featherstone, M. (ed.). 1990. *Global Culture*. London: Sage.

Fenwick, M. 1996. "Tough guy, eh? The gangster figure in Drum". *Journal of Southern African Studies,* December 1996, *22*(4).

Fisher, M. and Abedi, M. 1990. *Debating Muslims: Cultural dialogics in postmodernity and modernity*. Madison: The University of Wisconsin Press.

Fiske, J. 1993. *Power plays, power works*. London: Verso.

Foucault, M. 1986. "Power/knowledge". In: Rabinow, P. (ed.). *The Foucault Reader*. London: Penguin.

Galant, R. and Gamieldien, F. (eds.). 1996. *Drugs, gangs, people's power, exploring the Pagad phenomenon*. Claremont: Masjid.

Gallin, D. 1994. "Inside the new world order: Drawing the battle lines". *New Politics,* Vol v(1).

George, A. 1991. *Western State Terrorism*. Polity: Cambridge.

Giddens, A. and Turner, H.J. 1987. *Social Theory Today*. Polity Press: Cambridge.

Giddens, A. 1993. "The consequences of modernity". In: Williams, P and Chrisman, L. *Colonial discourse and postcolonial theory*. New York: Harvester.

Gottschalk, K. "Islamic mobilisations in the Western Cape – 1987-1997", (preliminary draft).

Gramsci, A. 1978. *Selections from prison notebooks*. London: Lawrence and Wishart.

Gupta, A. 1992. "The song of the non-aligned world: Transnational identities and the reinscription of space in late capitalism". *Cultural Anthropology, 7*. 63-79.

Gupta, A. and Ferguson, J. 1992. "Beyond culture: Space, identity and the politics of difference". *Cultural Anthropology, 7*. 6-23.

Hall, S. 1980. "Cultural studies and the centre: Some problematics and problems". In: Hall, S., Dobson, D., Lowe, A. and Willis, P. (eds.). *Culture, media, language*. London: Hutchinson.

Hall, S. et al. (eds.). 1992. *Modernity and its futures*. Cambridge: Polity.

Hall, S. 1993. "Cultural identity and diaspora". In: William, P. and Chrisman, L. (eds.). *Colonial discourse and postcolonial theory*. Great Britian: Harvester.

Hall, S. and Du Gay, P. 1996. *Questions of cultural identity*. London: Sage Publications.

Haron, M. 1997. *Muslims in South Africa: An annotated bibliography*. Cape Town: Centre for Contemporary Islam.

Hebdige, D. 1998. *Hiding the light, on images and things*. London: Routledge.

Hobsbawm, E. 1998. "The nation and globalization". *Constellations, Vol 5*(1).

Huntington, S.P. 1993. "The Clash of Civilizations?" *Foreign Affairs,* Summer 1993. 22-49.

Jeenah, N. 1996. "Pagad, aluta continua". In Galant, R. and Gamieldien, F. *Drugs, gangs and people's power: Exploring the Pagad phenomenon*. Claremont Masjid.

Jeppie, S. 1996. "Introduction". In: Galant, R. and Gamieldien, F. *Drugs, gangs and people's power: Exploring the Pagad phenomenon.* Claremont Masjid.

Jordan, G. and Wheedon, C. 1995. "The celebration of difference and the cultural politics of racism". In Adam, B. and Allan, S. (eds.). *Theorizing culture*. London: UCL Press.

Keohane, R. O. and Nye, J. S. 1989. *Power and Interdependen*ce. Glenview, Ill: Scott, Foresman.

Kinnes, I. 1995. "Crime, violence and security: The struggle for the hearts and minds of the Cape Flats". Paper presented at Idasa Conference, August 1995, Cape Town.

Kinnes, I. 1995. "Reclaiming the Cape Flats: A community challenge". *Indicator SA, 2*. 5-8.

Krichen, Z. 1995. "The Islamic fundamentalist movement in Tunisia, 1970-1990: History and language". In Mamdani, M. and Wamba-dia-Wamba, E. (eds.). *African Studies in Social Movements and Democracy*. Dakar: Codesria.

Laclau, E. (ed.). 1994. *The making of political identities*. London: Verso.

Laclau, E. 1994. *Emancipation(s)*. London: Verso.

LeRoux, C.J.B. 1997. People Against Gangsterism and Drugs. *Journal for Contemporary History, June 1997,* Vol 22(1).

Lull, J. 1995. *Media, communication, culture: a Global approach*. Cambridge: Polity Press.

Mazrui, A. 1998. "Shifting African identities: The boundaries of ethnicity and religion in Africa's experience". Paper presented at Shifting African Identities Conference, July 1998, Brackenfell, Cape Town.

Mernissi, F. 1992. *Islam and democracy: Fear of the modern world.* USA: Adderson Wesley Publishing.

Messick, B. 1993. *The calligraphic state: Textual domination and history in a Muslim society*. Berkley: University of California Press.

Mohamed, S. 1990. *They did not commit crimes that would harm people, but genuine crimes: Towards a history of gangs in District Six.* BA (Hons) thesis. University of Cape Town: Department of Economic History.

Monga, C. 1996. *The anthropology of anger, civil society and democracy in Africa.* London: Lyn Rienner Publishers.

Morley, D. 1986. *Family television: Cultural power and domestic leisure*. London: Routledge.

Nicol, M. 1991. *A Good Looking Corpse*. London: Seeker and Warburg.

Nina, D. 1996. "Popular justice or vigilantism? Pagad, the state and the community". *Crime and Conflict,* Spring 1996, 7. 1-4.

Nott, L. et al. 1990. *Gangs: The search for self respect*. South Africa: Nicro.

Nye, J.S. and Donahue, J.D. 2000. *Governance in a Globalizing World.* Cambridge, Mass: Brookings Institute Press.

Nzongola-Ntalaja, G. and Lee, M. (eds.). 1997. *The State and democracy in Africa.* Harare, Zimbabwe: AAPS.

O'Sullivan, T. et al. 1994. *Key concepts in communications and cultural studies.* London: Routledge.

Pinnock, D. 1984. *The Brotherhoods: Street gangs and state control in Cape Town*. Cape Town: David Philip.

Pinnock, D. 1997. *Gangs, rituals and rites of passage*. Cape Town: Africa Sun Press.

Rattansi, A. 1994. "Western racisms, ethnicities and identities in a 'postmodern' frame". In: Rattansi, A. and Westwood, S. *Racism, modernity and identity*. Cambridge: Polity.

Rodinson, M. 1979. *Marxism and the Muslim world*. London: Zed.

Rosengren, K. E. 1985. *Media Gratifications Research: Current Perspectives*. Sage: California.

Said, E. 1978. *Orientalism*. London: Penguin.

Said, E. 1993a. *Culture and imperialism*. London: Chatto and Windus.

Said, E. 1993b. *Covering Islam*. United Kingdom: Vintage.

Sayyid, B. 1994. "Sign o'times: Kaffirs and infidels fighting the Ninth Crusade". In: Laclau, E. (ed.). *The making of political identities.* London: Verso.

Scharf, W. 1996. *Street gangs, survival and political consciousness in the eighties*. Paper presented at Western Cape Roots and Realities Conference, July 1996, University of Cape Town, Centre for African Studies.

Shwrink, W. et al. 1986. *Number gangs in South African prisons: An organisational perspective*. University of Natal, Durban, ASSA 17th Annual Conference.

Spanier, J. 1987. *Games Nations Play*. CQ Press: Washington, DC.

Sorfa, D. 1992. "Theorising the criminal: Early Drum and the representation of the black gangster, or crime for sale". *Interaction*. University of Cape Town, Department of English.

Tayob, A. 1996a. "Islamism and Pagad: Finding the connection". In: Galant, R. and Gamieldien, F. (eds.). *Drugs, gangs and people's power: Exploring the Pagad phenomenon*. Claremont Masjid.

Tayob, A. 1996b. "Jihad against drugs in Cape Town: a Discourse-centred analysis". *Social Dynamics, 22*(2). 23-29.

Tayob, A. and Wiese, W. (eds.). 1999. *Religion and politics in South Africa*. Berlin: Waxmann.

Tandon, Y. 1998. "Globalization and Africa's options". In: *African Association of Political Science Newsletter,* January-April 1998.

Turner, G. 1990. *British Cultural Studies: An Introduction*. Boston: Unwin Hyman.

Weiss, L. 1997. "Globalization and the myth of the powerless state". *New Left Review,* September-October 1997, 225.

Newspapers and other sources

Aranes, J. (1997, March 19). Pagad: Marchers with a major mission. *Cape Argus*.

Aranes, J. (1997, July 30). Drug war seethes: Pagad and gangsters. *Cape Argus*.

Cape Argus. (1997, April 4). Core begins campaigning for end to Cape Flats war.

Cape Argus. (1996, December 14). UK panic button on Pagad.

Cape Argus. What is the real agenda behind Pagad's activities. Found at http://archive.iol.co.za/Archives/1997/9701/24%20Jan/Pagad17/html

Cape Times. (1997, May 30). Core hands rape suspect to police.

Daniels, D. (1998, August 28). Pagad's true colours revealed. *Mail & Guardian*.

Duffy, A. (1998, January 16). Death of a mother's Mr Majestic. *Mail & Guardian*.

Duffy, A. (1998, July 17- 23). Sheikhs stand up to Pagad. *Mail & Guardian*.

Ebrahim, A. (1998, October 22). Pagad vows to stay on. *Cape Argus*.

Friedman, R. (1997, January 15). Gangsters warn Pagad. *Cape Times*.

Hess, S. (1998, August 7). Pipe bombs: Just pop down to the hardware. *Mail and Guardian*.

Josephs, N. Blasts bring terrorism close to home. Found at http://archive.iol.co.za/Archives/1998/9806/18/pipebomb.html

Mail & Guardian. (1996, November 2). What Pagad has to say.

Merten, M. (1999, July 23). Murdered Pagad leader was informer. *eMail & Guardian.mg.co.za*.

Moosa, E. (1996). Groups like Pagad hurt Islam. Found at http://archive.iol.co.za/Archives/1996/9611/18/Pagad.html

Olivier, P. (1997, January 19). Amir defiant at march. *Cape Times*.

Qwelane, J. (1997, April). Crimebusters or vigilantes? *Tribute.* 48-52.
Salie, A. (1996, January 14). Muslim clergy attacks Pagad. *Cape Times.*
Schroeder, F. Part two: The rise of Pagad. Found at http://archive.iol.co.za/Archives/1998/9803/12/whosPagad1702.html
South African Police Services. Pipe bomb attacks and Pagad/gang attributed incidents: Western Cape Province: 1998-01-01 to 1998-10-31.
Smith, A. (1998, July 18). Pagad leader blasts bombed cleric. *Cape Argus.*
Thiel, G. (1997, January 24). Pagad is helping the gangsters. *Mail & Guardian.*
Van Zilla, L. (1997, March 24). Pagad to go global. *Cape Times.*
Van Zilla, L. (1998, February 14). Pagad sues the State. *Cape Times.*

CHAPTER SEVENTEEN

Covering the East – Veils and Masks: Orientalism in South African Media

Gabeba Baderoon

Introduction

Discussions of Orientalism often assume a European or American gaze, with the Middle East or Asia as object. In fact, Orientalist images are elaborated in varied contexts throughout the world. In this chapter I draw attention to Orientalist images in South Africa and their intersection with similar international discourses. Analysing such instances has value because the globalisation and intensification of discourses about the East render the lessons that emerge from specific contexts particularly important. Indeed, studies of racist images that emerged with colonialism have already alerted us to the importance of historical context, for instance, showing how the meanings of similar images vary in the United States and Brazil (Stam and Spence 2000:318). Elizabeth Poole's study (2000) of images of Islam in three British newspapers usefully examines the tropes that characterise images about Islam in Britain, and suggests that there are significant continuities in such imagery. While many recent studies rightly contest the notion of South African exceptionalism as a lingering effect of apartheid's racist project, an inverse reluctance to argue the resonance of insights emerging from the country's history with that of other sites in the world still needs to be countered.

In attempting to do so here in a discussion of Orientalism, I draw on the work of historian Shamil Jeppie, whose pioneering study of the construction of a discourse of "Malay" identity in South Africa provides an invaluable model (1986, 2001). I wish to build on this work by examining the features of a distinctly South African Orientalism in the media and art, and subsequently explore an instance in 1996 where South African and international discourses of Orientalism intersected.

The media always tell a particular story, they encode a particular way of looking at the world. I argue that amid the saturation of Western media perspectives, the following analysis of South African media holds critical lessons from the margins. An instance of Orientalism in South African media from 1996 illuminates global debates by showing the different paths and possibilities that exist in this context, providing possibilities that cannot be found elsewhere.

"States of Fantasy": the National and International Neighbourhood

In the magisterial *Orientalism,* first published in 1978, Edward Said showed that any analysis of the discursive processes through which the West produced its necessary other, the Orient, must address the question of representation. This is because Orientalism is crucially a matter of discourse; it is "the cultural representation of the West to itself by way of a detour through the other" (Yegenoglu 1998:1). In this chapter I analyse a series of South African newspaper articles from 5-12 August 1996 featuring stories on the Cape Town-based group Pagad (People Against Gangsterism and Drugs), in which, I argue, an intersection of South African and international Orientalisms occurs.

Why does representation – journalistic, scholarly, artistic – matter? Pierre Bourdieu reminds us that "words do things, they make things – they create phantoms, fears, and phobias" (1998:20). These layers of "phantoms, fears, and phobias" give depth and conviction to the things they create. One might say words (and other forms of representation) matter because they *make worlds*. Gayatri Spivak calls this tying together of text and territory "worlding" (quoted in Mutman 1994:35). In showing how the world is worlded into West and East through the discourse of Orientalism, Edward Said described the working of an "imaginative geography" of both historical and contemporary power (quoted in Steet 2000:37). A political charge results from this understanding. The worlding that results from representation lives with us and through us, and therefore its details require a sensitive and acute attention.

The effects of worlding operate at the level of the text and beyond. Said argues that Orientalism consists not only of a series of texts, but of a supple and comprehensive discourse which creates a world divided into West and East. Crucially, this is not a purely additive or subtractive model, in which the presence of the West simply overwhelms a pitiful and lacking East. In fact, the mechanism of Orientalism is more complex and significant, for it *produces the Western subject* just as much it creates the Oriental. An "imaginative geography" thus manifests itself in both territorial boundaries and subjectivities (Said, quoted in Steet 2000:37).

What are the mechanisms and details of this process and where may one see it at work? How does one discern the interstices of this system of knowing and being in the world? Spivak argues that "worlding" is central to the imperialist project and alerts us to specific sites of creation:

> As far as I understand it, the notion of textuality should be related to the notion of the worlding of a world on a supposedly uninscribed territory. When I say this, I am

> thinking basically about the imperialist project which had to assume that the earth that it territorialised was in fact previously uninscribed. So then a world, on a simple level of cartography inscribed what was presumed to be uninscribed. Now this worlding actually is also a texting, textualising, a making into art, making into an object to be understood (quoted in Mutman 1994:35).

Hence in this study, it is on these sites of creation, particularly the media and art, that I focus in determining how South Africa was worlded.

Islam has entered the gaze of Western media, and therefore public consciousness, in moments of crisis (Agha 2002:222). In his study of US media representations about the 1991 Gulf War, Mahmut Mutman cites Said in showing that little attention was paid to Islam "as such" until the oil crisis of 1973 (quoted in Mutman 1994:6). With the rise in oil prices in 1974, "Muslims suddenly became the news" and Islam emerged into abrupt prominence in the US media (1994:6). The vertiginous shift from obscurity to constant presence occurred in a context of perceived threat. This plenitude of images encouraged a sense of knowing Islam. However, as Said points out, this sense was based on an extremely constricted portrayal. Olfat Hassan Agha notes the Iranian revolution in 1979 as another crisis that generated intensive attention around Islam in the West (2002:222). Similarly, Poole notes the heightened visibility of Islam in Britain around crises such as the *Satanic Verses* controversy, featuring tropes such as the enraged Muslim crowd.

In South Africa, the interplay between invisibility and crisis is evident too, as I show in a detailed discussion of representations in Capetonian newspapers below. There is a lingering effect of the absence of genuine engagement with the complexities of Islam in its varied contexts. It is only in crisis that Islam is fully realised. In the absence of genuine knowledge, Muslims often become explicable through stereotypes – Muslim women through the veil, Muslim men through militancy. Because this well-elaborated portrayal does not arise out of any intimacy, it relies on familiar tropes, rich in "phantoms, fears, and phobias". Media theorist Dennis Davis believes that the media turns to art in times of crisis to help frame an explicable world. "At times of crisis, stereotyped representations may be more popular since they provide frames that are easy to understand and communicate. Old artistic representations could provide a storehouse of frames for media practitioners to draw on at such times" (Davis 2002). When Islam emerges through such mechanisms, it does so fully and compellingly, drawing on the power of oppositional thinking. Repeatedly, when the crisis is over, Islam goes back to obscurity, setting the cycle in motion again. In South Africa, this is also a familiar pattern, as I elucidate below.

In a political climate in the West formed around a crisis about Islam, the temptation is great to approach representations of Islam in the hope of correcting or explaining them. Yet, the dynamics of both correction and explicability seem to me symptoms of, rather than solutions to, the problem of representation and politics. Correction through careful explanation of the problems of existing texts and the substitution of more appropriate ones is an unsustainable aim, for, as Linda Steet notes, "[r]epresentations do not cancel one another out like a math equation" (2000:10). Similarly, to attempt to abolish the impenetrability of Islam through a careful elucidation of representations means yielding to the same desire for explicability of the "inscrutable" that underlies the repetitive and reductive kinds of representations that abound in the mainstream. These well-intentioned attempts to explain Islam, and particularly to explain its relation to violence (an explanation which always takes the form of a denial of the automatic linkage that is made between Islam and violence which is obvious in racist representations) repeat, inevitably, the very formula of linking Islam to impenetrability, or violence. They embody, in other words, the very anxiety that they are trying to alleviate, *symptomatic* of their problem in the psychoanalytic sense. In later sections, this particular challenge will be addressed more fully. So it should be redundant to point out that it is not my intention to provide a sympathetic view of the people represented in the newspaper texts analysed below. In fact, I shall show that both the group featured (Pagad) and the media representations about them mutually and symbiotically use regressive discourses about Islam.

While disavowing the above impulse, I concede that there *is* a politics to this chapter: that discourse is a crucial register of social and political change and thus to change discourses means to enable a critical practice of reading and writing, and consequently to challenge received ways of interpreting the world. It is therefore on the terrain of representation that this chapter will operate. I aim in examining texts from the media to examine closely the mechanisms of representation that bring into existence a specific form of *mediated* Islam in South Africa, and the ways in which some people who identify themselves as Muslim use these mechanisms.

Covering Journalism

To think of the media in the twenty-first century, one's concept must encompass a multilayered entity. Journalism is the practice which transforms the material of contemporary experience into the products of the media. As such, the media theorist John Hartley argues that the role of journalism in the contemporary world extends beyond providing information to allowing us to *understand* the world in particular ways. And therefore, he concludes, "[a]s the sense-making practice of modernity, journalism is the most important textual system in the world" (Hartley 1996:32). The media operates at the material terrain, being an industry that deals in information, yet, importantly, the media's relation to society lies beyond the production and distribution of information. Particularly because it is part of the domain of international capital, the media has a heightened political significance. Because of its transnational presence and the ubiquity of its outlets, the media has a vast and intimate impact in the arena of culture. And lastly, in its elaboration throughout society, in the forms which have come to articulate contemporary life, it has also become a mechanism through which to know the self. Jacqueline Rose elucidates in a lecture entitled "States of Fantasy" that today social relations and self-hood crucially imply the workings of the media (Rose 1996).

How does the media work? In his analysis of contemporary media, Pierre Bourdieu insists that the media has the power to create, rather than simply describe events. "We know that to name is to show, to create, to bring into existence" (1998:20). In order to create the news, information is shaped into a form. Journalism translates experience into a narrative of a specific kind. As Stuart Hall puts it:

> A "raw" historical event cannot, *in that form*, be transmitted by, say, a television newscast [...] the event must become a "story" before it can become a communicative event (1981:41).

As Hall points out, editors and journalists usually take a more functional view of the choices and emphases in their reports. They call on news values, in other words, those stories which are "newsworthy", to explain their choice of chapters and angles in the news. But such professional, neutral understandings of what is news are, in fact, *ideological*. "Behind the apparently formal dimension of its news values lie the ideological themes of the society in which the newspaper operates" (Hall 1981:234). Journalism always generates *particular, situated* ways of understanding the world. These ways of understanding are never without ideological value. It is in such tropes that one can read the ideological impulses at work in journalism.

By disseminating such storied truths in a complex and powerful circuit of production and readership, the media creates communities out of audiences. Because of this, theorists argue that the media is crucial to generating a sense of national belonging. In fact, Hartley asserts that "[c]itizenship and communal identity are not possible these days without journalism" (1996:39). Such identities are formed in the context of providing a "national, political fantasy" in the media through which a sense of community is generated (1996:45). In this way, newspapers and other media allow audiences to map their symbolic reality. In an important sense, our notion of locality, of neighbourhood, is shaped these days by our experience of media. With the rise of 24-hour international news organisations based in the United States and Britain, a powerful, though usually unarticulated geography is at work in world news. There is a symbolic centre from which a gaze is aimed with equanimity at the rest of the globe. Watching the news, an imagined global viewer is situated, at least symbolically, in this unarticulated place. What are the implications of this geography, and when does it run against other forces? When does its seamless construction of a point from which to gaze at the world – *the rest of the world* – unravel? In the analyses below, instances of such tension will be explored.

The media helps to configure the boundaries of society – we might call this a "social map" – and thus who is inside and who is outside of (national) communities, an "us" and "them" formula. Yet, too rigid a distinction between our stories and those of "others" may cast the world into inflexible categories. Hartley's theory of the relation of readership to citizenship has an interesting corollary. If it is true that "[re]aderships are part of the intricate communicational machinery of modern journalism, produced by it and actively driving it", then it is also the case that *oppositional* readerships can provide an instructive commentary on the role of media. The responses of audiences may be particularly interesting in the light of this "us" and "them" formula. Inevitably there are members of the media audience who find themselves on the "outside" of this community. Examples of such an "outside perspective" may include foreigners who are the target of overt or covert xenophobia, the youth, environmentalists and political activists. Ironically, such people can provide a critical perspective which reveals the mechanisms of inclusion and exclusion at work in the media. Since journalism generates a sense of communality and insiderness, the "outsiders" – often misrepresented in the media – can provide a critical perspective that reveals journalistic mechanisms of inclusivity and exclusivity. In fact, Hartley says that "[a]n outside perspective [. . .] is sometimes most valuable in making journalistic practices and its assumptions visible".

An increasing reliance on advertising, and hence the imperative to attract audiences, often means an excessive focus on the most eye-catching or obvious stories and angles. One can, however, view the predictable appearance of such stories in a different way. Beneath the frequency of stories of transgression or disaster in the news (such as sex and corruption scandals, natural disasters, the decline of stock markets), one may detect a "deep structure" to news stories – the stability or precariousness of the social order. This imperative generates the most visible news stories, and, one may argue, creates an investment in the *renewal* of order and sense of community. In this way, the media "translates the legitimation of the social order into faces, expressions, subjects, settings and legends" (Hall 1981:234).

By focusing on discourse, I argue that an unacknowledged level of fantasy informs journalism. Christopher Lane argues that "fantasies organising the meaning of racial and ethnic identities" are reflected in the discourses that structure the reporting of "race" in the media (Lane 1998:1). My aim in the following analysis is to reveal the fantasies that underlie different representations of Islam in South African media. Building on work by Shamil Jeppie (1996, 2001) and others, I wish to move towards a theory of South African Orientalism by reading its manifestations in the media. In this light I wish to analyse South African newspaper coverage from the period 5-12 August 1996, of stories about the activities of the Cape Town-based Pagad (People Against Gangsterism and Drugs), which was distinguished from the many similar groups operating in South Africa at the time by drawing on Islamic iconography in its public profile.

A History of Images of Islam in Newspapers in Cape Town

Before I examine in some depth the coverage of these stories from the Capetonian newspapers, the *Cape Argus* and the *Cape Times,* I will provide a context for the analysis by looking at the history of Islam in South Africa. Islam entered the Cape with slavery. The first Muslims arrived in 1658 – slaves were brought from East and West Africa, Madagascar, India and South East Asia, until their importation was banned in 1808. Emancipation was proclaimed in 1834. The legacy of slavery, colonialism and apartheid has impacted on the experience of Islam in South Africa, as shown in studies by Abdulkader Tayob, Shamil Jeppie, Yusuf da Costa and Achmat Davids. Early leaders of Muslims at the Cape during Dutch rule included Sufist scholars such as Sheikh Yusuf. The high rate of conversion meant that the practice of Islam took hold under the trepidations of slavery and enserfment. As a result, while South African Muslims view themselves as part of an international community, there is nonetheless a specifically local definition to Islam in South Africa, manifested, for instance, in practices around language, food and other areas of culture. Beyond questions of religion, Muslims feature actively throughout the history of the country. This is critical when considering the importation in 1996 of anachronistic images of Islam drawn from the Middle East in the South African media portrayals of Islam discussed below.

In order to provide a context for the discussion of this coverage, in this section I examine earlier patterns of representation of Muslims in these newspapers. The South African National Library holds the entire newspaper archives of the *Cape Argus*, first published in 1857, and the *Cape Times*, which first appeared in 1876. These media organs are the largest English-language newspapers in Cape Town, and both have a significant Muslim readership. While other aspects of the South African media landscape, such as Afrikaans as well as specifically Muslim media, deserve attention, the extensive archives of the *Cape Argus* and the *Cape Times* provide a useful point from which to initiate broader analysis. Their continuous record of local media representations from the mid-nineteenth century provides a valuable research resource. They remain the most important English daily newspapers in Cape Town today. Research into representations of Muslims in these newspapers' archives provides an illuminating basis from which to read later portrayals.

Scanning four decades of coverage in these two newspapers, from 1940 to 1980, I found that during this time they showed a strikingly consistent, and narrowly circumscribed, image of Muslims. Almost all coverage falls into only six categories:

1. Pilgrimage.
2. Special occasions: Ramadan, Eid, weddings.
3. Mosques scandals (election of imams, controversies about the amplification of sound, and, during the apartheid era, the threat of forced removals of mosques).
4. The fate of the "Malay Quarter", an area settled by former slaves.

5. The "Malay" identity of Muslims, often portrayed as endangered by change.
6. Ratiep or khalifa – displays of "mystical" powers to tolerate pain.

Within these parameters, South African Muslims during this period were portrayed as largely "peaceful" and "law-abiding". They appear in these accounts to be respectable, though, with prominently reported Malay choirs and ratiep or khalifa, also quaint. The mystical or occult powers attributed to the latter activities gave them an exotic air, but this was usually seen as entertaining.

Very occasionally, another view would emerge. Reports showed "the usually placid Moslems of the Peninsula", as the *Cape Argus* put it on 24 July 1965, would sometimes become "insane" or "vicious". An 1898 obituary in the *Cape Argus* for Abdol Burns spoke admiringly of his leadership of the Muslim community (and his partly Scottish heritage). "His speeches contained more solid sense than those of many persons better placed in life." However, a negative note was struck by memories of his involvement in an 1886 protest by Muslims against the closure of their cemeteries in the city environs. The *Cape Argus* described the uprising in a later article in 1950 as "probably the only occasion in the history of Cape Town when the Malays rose in revolt". The language in which this story is told is familiar from other genres which tell of the inflamed passions of Orientals: "His one mistake was in leading the Moslem riots when Cape Town started to find that it might have to deal with Oriental fanaticism in the mass." Another article reported that "Police arrived while the child was being buried. By this time the law-abiding Malays had become fanatics." A report from November 1970 takes up this language, referring in a headline to "Fanatical Moslem Mahdists".

Traces of the polarity between ordinariness and respectability on the one hand, and fanaticism and decay on the other, can be found in other articles through the years. The limitations of the discourses that encapsulate Muslim life are evident, even, it sometimes seems, to the authors of these articles. On 31 August 1960 the *Cape Argus* reported: "At yesterday's City Council meeting, the Malay Quarter was described as a festering sore, complete with opium dens and brothels. In reality, the place is dull and suburban."

During the apartheid era, there was an evolution in this vocabulary for talking about Muslims in the media. Aside from the familiar stories, almost timeless in their repetition, of conflicts around mosque succession, there now also appeared stories such as "Sheikh angrily denies Security Police connection" (22 April 1975, *Cape Argus*). Notably, an article articulating a rare sense of a connection with international news involving Muslims appeared in the *Cape Herald* of 4 November 1972. The article reports that "Cape Town's major Moslem organisations reacted strongly this week after word was spread that they were being used by Arab terrorists in a plan to kidnap Israeli diplomats' children." Quoting a response from the Muslim organisations, the chapter continued: "We strongly refute any connections with any of the overseas Arab terrorists." Despite the long history of portrayals as generally harmless, this article and others referring to "Moslem fanaticism" suggest that the equanimity of Muslims is perceived as tenuous. Interestingly, in this case, the source of the disturbance is seen to be a conspiracy or infiltration by "overseas Arab terrorists". Thus, the judgement of placidity is seen here to be dependent on whether Muslims are perceived to be associated with an international Muslim community, portrayed here through the discourse of terrorism.

Having set this context, I will now consider stories from the same newspapers in August 1996, over the course of one week, 5-12 August 1996. The reason for the specificity of the period chosen is that this was a week of profound crisis in South Africa. The crisis was experienced on many levels, all of them interwoven with one another – a crisis of violence in poor black communities in Cape Town, a crisis in legitimacy for the criminal justice system in South Africa, and a crisis in the media. This period was initiated by the public murder on 4 August, captured on film by local and international media, of Rashaad Staggie, the co-leader of a powerful criminal gang in Cape Town.

It is clear that by focusing only on this small number of media outlets for such a brief period, and by not referring to broadcast media, the following analysis is limited. Nonetheless, the study remains of value. I have balanced its focus by situating the analysis in a larger study by researching the archives of the same newspapers, by interviewing journalists and academics, and by relating it to Orientalist images elsewhere. In the following section, I will analyse in some detail the images I collected from that period of coverage.

In the week of 5-12 August 1996, one pattern of images became strikingly evident. On 5 August 1996, *The Argus* coverage of the story included a prescient image on page 3. In the right-hand corner of the page is a small picture of an unidentified man whose face is masked by a scarf, known in Cape Town as a "Palestinian" or "Arafat" scarf. In subsequent coverage of the story, this masked figure, and others like it, would move from the side of the page to the centre, and would become ubiquitous. Even in coverage of other protests by people unrelated to Pagad and an analytical article by the academic Ebrahim Moosa, the image of a masked figure was appended. Wherever Muslims appeared in the public sphere, so did this masked figure. Before proceeding with the analysis of these images, let me provide a basis for understanding this pattern by considering the historical legacy of Orientalist images.

Images of Men and Women under Colonialism

"A photograph is a secret about a secret. The more it tells you, the less you know." (Diane Arbus quoted in McClintock 1995:124)

Pierre Bourdieu reminds us: "The world of images is dominated by words. Photos are nothing without words" (1998:19-20). And indeed, as one means to anchor potentially dangerous evidence of ideology and narrative, journalism calls upon news photography to secure an alibi of transparency and immediacy. News photographs as a genre draw on the discourse of clarity, transparency and naturalness towards which all realisms aspire; in addition, their sense of immediacy and truth is bolstered by their use in the media, which itself is driven by a discourse of professional access to truth. Photography gained power through the history of realism to which it lay claim, a history of telling the "truth of the world" (McClintock 1995:124).

The use of photography in colonial contexts provides useful lessons in thinking about news photographs. In European colonies, the relation of the gaze to gender and subjectivity was replicated and intensified by photography. There, the framing metaphors of scientific veracity that anchored photography's claims to truth were exposed to a different context. Examining photography in the colonial age, Anne McClintock shows how fantasies in the dominant culture, underpinning the discourse of science, were invoked "to tell the truth of the world" (1995:124). As with Orientalism and its production of Western subjectivity through the generation and subjection of the Oriental, the colonial relation was the site and occasion to exercise the expertise of the Western gaze. McClintock argues that:

> Colonial photography, framed as it was by metaphors of scientific knowledge as penetration, promised to seek out the secret interiors of the feminised Orient and their capture as surface, in the image of the harem woman's body, the truth of the world (McClintock 1995:124).

In fact, the colonial site intensified the opportunity to realise the access of the dominant gaze to the object, which was practised in the metropole in photographs of poor and working-class women. In a fascinating study, Linda Steet reports that the editorial guidelines that have governed photographs in *National Geographic* have for over a century decreed a rule of "*absolute accuracy*" (2000:17, emphasis in original). Yet, in her study, Steet found that photographs of Arab cultures published in the magazine were in some cases made by the same studio which produced the pornographic French postcards analysed by Malek Alloula in his 1986 study, *The Colonial Harem,* and in fact some of the same photographs sold as pornographic postcards were featured in *National Geographic* (Steet 2000:42). The transferability of pornographic and ethnographic photographs like these suggests how dominant fantasies inform the "truth" of a particular time and place.

Images thus have a history. The significance of history is evident in examining images of slavery in the United States. Michele Wallace analysed the occurrence of the myth of the "rapacious, inexhaustible Black penis" in the United States. This image of threatening male sexuality gained currency particularly around the time that slavery was abolished in the United States, when fears of black men's entry into political and economic life were translated, at the level of myth, into the fear of the rapacious black phallus. The myth invited and justified a brutal response toward black men, which took the form of widespread lynching, often accompanied by mutilation of the genitals. In contrast, myths about the sexual *availability* of black women predated the end of slavery, when it sustained the economic imperative to force slaves to have children and expand the slave population (Badoe 1991). Mahmut Mutman explains the connection, pointing out that "sexual and political economies are never separate from each other" (1994:11). Looking at the context of European colonialism, where a similar myth that white women were in danger from black rapists obtained, Mutman posits that this narrative was appropriate to its particular political economy. That is, it was the result of "the transition from a mode of exploration to a mode of administration in the history of colonialism", when white women entered the colonies in proportionally greater numbers, and the men of the empire focused on sustaining the white family (Mutman 1994:11).

In South Africa fantasies of black sexuality developed differently. The system of slavery and serfdom in South Africa generated fulsome discourses about black bodies, whether Khoi, San or slave (Gqola 2001:48). As in the United States, from the earliest encounters in the Cape, such discourses were undergirded by fears of miscegenation. Cheryl Hendricks delineates the evolution of these discourses in the Cape during the colonial era, finding that the licensing of white men's access to black women's bodies was accompanied by a continual anxiety about maintaining the boundaries of whiteness. Governed by such imperatives, the meanings of black sexuality varied across time, and the regulation of sexual relations between blacks and whites were enforced more or less strictly at different times. Gradations of female attractiveness were measured by proximity to whiteness, which placed women from Asia and "mixed-race" women further along the spectrum of attractiveness. However, Hendricks points out that "black men in all slave societies were severely punished for any presumed liaison with white women. White women were also usually viewed as mentally insane if they fraternised with black men" (Hendricks 2001:39). These insights indicate that it is important to note when certain kinds of images attain prominence.

Contemporary images of Islam in South Africa carry these legacies. Gqola shows that the laudable aim in Rayda Jacobs' *The Slave Book* (1998) to imagine the lives of slaves absent from usual accounts of the country's history is undercut by the replication of notions of attractiveness based on proximity to the ideal of whiteness (Gqola 2001:59). Alex Dodd, in a compelling article on "The Women of Pagad", originally published in *Cosmopolitan* magazine, notes the impact of "manufactured notions about Muslim women" in her initial understanding about their role in the group (2001:65). Among these is the assumption that Muslim women are "silent", "submissive" and "oppressed" (*ibid.*). Dodd acknowledges that these notions may be due to the fact that "I have relatively natural contact with Muslim women" (*ibid.*). As I argued above, in the absence of true exchange, Muslims often become explicable through stereotype.

In order to understand the power of these stereotypes, I revisit images of women and men under colonialism through the role of photography. One can deduce from studies by Rana Kabbani, Ania Loomba and Linda Steet, among others, a number of recurring myths about the Orient. In its view of the Orient, the West places an emphasis on the perceived "inherent violence" and "lascivious sensuality" of Orientals (Kabbani 1986:6). This is accompanied by a fascination with the "closedness of the society, the secretiveness of all its significant aspects" (1986:126). These aspects combine to produce the fantasy of the "exotic" Orient. The term has a specific meaning, for the Orient is "exotic in the special nineteenth-century sense of the term (that is, barbaric, different, other) [. . .] attractive precisely because it remains incomprehensible" (1986:122). Here is the exemplary myth of the Orient: the "inscrutability" of the East. Whatever is revealed stands paradoxically as a sign of mystery. To the bearer of the imperial Western gaze, "[t]his enclosed society [. . .] sublimates what it hides, transferring the qualities of all that is hidden onto exposed objects" (1986:127).

The Veiled Woman

The exemplary exposed-yet-mysterious object is the veil, and through it, the veiled woman. The veiled woman of the East is a fetish of both the colonial and contemporary eras. As Mutman notes, "the moment of fetishism is also a moment of *ambiguity* and *displacement*" (1994:21). A fundamental anxiety results for the colonial subject from the vacillation between certainty and elusiveness. As a result, Homi Bhabha argues, Orientalist stereotypes are *constantly repeated* in order to produce the "colonised as a social reality which is at once an other and entirely knowable and visible" (1994:70-71). It is the combination of mystery, with *knowingness* and *clarity*, and its use in media coverage, which I would like to address below. The anxiety to which Bhabha refers is visible in the subjection of the veiled woman to intense fascination and scrutiny. The imperial gaze obsessively studies the scene of its potential failure – an object that refuses to be looked at (Yegenoglu 1998:39). Such objects have an unerring allure, because the outcome of the Orientalist discursive system is the production and "*the centering of the Western self*" (Mutman 1994:3, emphasis in original). Thus, in the relation of the Western gaze to the Orientalist image lies the production of the centred Western subject.

There is a prolific association in the Western imagination between Islam and the veil. However, this association has a specific gender emphasis: it is about veiled Muslim women. The image of the veiled Muslim woman has heavily symbolic meanings. According to Helen Watson, this image is one of the most common methods in the West of portraying the "problems of Islam" (1994:153), central among these, the oppression of Muslim women. Yet she points to an important ambivalence in the reaction to the image: "outrage at its signal of oppression, or a romanticised view of the veil as part and parcel of the exotic, sensual Otherness of oriental traditions" (1994:153). Robert Young notes that in the colonial image of the East, there was much "vacillation evident [. . .] between Western contempt for the East's familiarity and delight or fear at its strangeness and novelty" (1994:143). This takes a particular turn when it comes to gender. Shahnaz Khan points out:

> While much Orientalist discourse focused on the liberation of Muslim women from Islam there was also an aspect of Orientalist/colonialist discourse that pointed to the availability of Muslim women (Khan 1998:467).

In his analysis of US media coverage of the 1991 Gulf War, Mutman found that "during the war, the woman was everywhere, as the veil, as the metaphor of truth, and as the truth" (1994:21).

This paradoxical appeal of the veiled woman points to the suppleness of Orientalist fantasies, which include both revulsion and allure. The image has a history of ambivalence. In the imperial imagination from the sixteenth century, Eastern women were represented in colonial literature and art as mysterious and knowing, yet, importantly, also convertible and assimilable. There is in fact, an obsessive "association between *the veil and the Western man's sexual fantasies*" (Mutman 1994:13, emphasis in original). The projected availability and vulnerability of Eastern women sustained a strong Orientalist fantasy: the desire of the European coloniser to enlighten the Islamic world, and to deliver its women from oppression. For instance, in British colonial imagery about India, "the stereotype of the libidinous Eastern woman [...] justifie[d] the need to govern her (and by implication also the Indian man)" (Loomba 1989:26).

In South Africa, the repertoire of images of women of the East includes the construction of the Eastern woman as sexual object along a spectrum of images of black women's bodies during the time of slavery (Hendricks 2001:36). The early twentieth-century painting "Malay Wedding" by Irma Stern shows a colourful, stylised view of veiled Muslim women, echoing the interest in rituals and performance evident in newspaper images of Islam at the time. Alex Dodd's 1996 article on women in Pagad cites the contemporary South African version of the imperial myth of Muslim women: "Shame, poor Gadjia – so voiceless and oppressed. She's never had the chance to sample the fruits of liberation" (Dodd 1996:65-66).

Examining the literature, Meyda Yegenoglu finds that the "practice of veiling and the veiled woman thus go beyond their simple reference and become tropes of the European text" (1998:39). Indeed, Watson points out the *consistency* of the meaning of the veil in the Western imagination: it "remains an icon of the otherness of Islam and is denounced as a symbol of Muslim women's oppression" (1998:142). Yet, in the literature about the veil that comes from inside societies in which it is worn, one finds varied narratives of the veil that show its complex meanings, changing across time and place. Writing about and from within societies in which the veil has varied and supple meanings, are Lila Abu-Lughod (*Veiled Sentiments: Honour and Poetry in a Bedouin Society*), Frantz Fanon

("Algeria Unveiled"), and Meena Alexander ("Alphabets of Flesh"). Fanon wrote about the context of the anti-colonial struggle in Algeria, where war was waged at an ideological level as well as on the bodies and under the veils of Algerian women. Such women found in the veil "a subversive entry into public space" (Alexander 1998:152).

The Other Half: Men of the East in Western Media Stories

If the women of the East are beautiful and vulnerable, from whom are they in danger? Again, Mutman's use of masking and sexual ambiguity in his analysis of the male figures in Western coverage of the Gulf War in 1991 proved a richly productive source in looking at images of men of the East in South Africa. I gathered images which spanned a number of years and different geographies. Among the images are those of Ayatollah Khomeini or Iran, Saddam Hussein of Iraq, Atal Bihari Vajpayi of India and Osama bin Laden. The first three follow almost eerily a pattern of extreme close-up, characterised by the glowering visage of Khomeini, the lazy eyes of Vajpayi shaped into a mushroom cloud for a story on India's nuclear tests, or the threatening, black-browed face of Hussein, partially blocked by the haloed figure of Bill Clinton in a 1997 story in *Time*.

Of this group, Osama Bin Laden is different. In contrast to the three above, Bin Laden looks calm and almost beatific. One of my students argued that in contrast to the evident threat of the other photographs, that of Bin Laden was perhaps more insidious. In this view, Bin Laden looked like an average turban-clad man. The very transferability of Bin Laden, as opposed to the singularity of the other men of the East, made this image of him a dangerous emblem of Eastern men. The incarnation of Bin Laden as the face of the East coincided with the evolution of Orientalist images after 11 September 2001 and during the war in Afghanistan in 2001. A new name was introduced for Muslim terror in the West: sleeper, that is, the deliberate adoption of a pose of normality as part of a disguise aimed at terrorist activity, or "trained Islamic terrorists awaiting orders from their faceless masters" (Karacs 2001:3). In conditions where the adjective "Muslim" was already a negative one, if normality could be interpreted as a sinister pose, then the presumption of innocence became even more tenuous. The result at a popular level was the default presumption of suspicion of all people, especially men, who "looked Muslim" (Kurtz, 2001). This logic also led to institutionalised racial profiling, what Said called "law enforcement efforts directed against Arabs, Muslims and Indians" (Said 2001:6).

As with Saddam Hussein, the question was asked: "What does Osama bin Laden want?' The answer: "[the] chilling conclusion was [. . .] nothing the West had to offer" (Johnson 2001:9). The threat in this formulation is the absence of reciprocity, which breaks the very contract by which the Orientalist object confirms the Western subject. This may be the psychic apparatus behind the power of the Oriental man, the reason that the black-masked figures which Said mentions must be so relentlessly disposed of, and why the

Oriental women become part of the fantasied triangular structure which justifies, at a rational level, the presence and intervention of the (male) Western subject (Said 1997:xxv).

With this background, I will return in the following section to a discussion of the Pagad story.

The Pagad Stories, 5-12 August 1996

To start, let me say something on the South African media landscape in August 1996. Under apartheid, the South African government was hostile to both the internal and international press, over which it did not have control. Internally, media ownership, audience profiles and the political sympathies of the press in South Africa were themselves a product of apartheid and as a result were highly racialised. During the transition and after 1994, the new political order was sympathetic to international investment in the previously insulated South African media market. This entry of global capital into South African media, including ownership of local media companies and titles, inserted the country into the dynamics of globalised media. This had an impact not only on content but led to the introduction of a globalised media culture into South Africa. At the time, foreign ownership was looked on by some journalists as a way to shore up the independence of the media in the post-apartheid era, since there was widespread anxiety about the attitude of the ANC towards media freedom. Yet, such concerns, based on assumptions that the media operates in the public service, appear anachronistic in the globalised culture of media, with its emphasis on the market (Webster 2002:120). Globalised media has very different dynamics, and the result of the insertion of South African media into this culture led to an intensification of market-driven pressures. For reasons only glancingly related to political sympathies within the country, the entry of South Africa into global media has had severe consequences for editorial independence and job security for journalists.

Another result is that South African audiences now increasingly receive their stories from international media. However, it is not just the content which the international media provide. Such stories carry a cultural idiom along with the stories themselves. This is one of the dimensions that I consider in my analysis of the Pagad stories below. When the Pagad story broke in 1996, South Africa provided the content. However, this was partly because this had been the first large-scale occasion after the elections in 1994 (and stories about a serial killer around that time) that South Africa was the source of a story which compelled international attention. It was also the first time that there was a story ostensibly about Islam in South Africa, about which there is a strong discourse in international media, as well as a well-established, internal South African discourse. The challenge of telling this story of international scale to a local audience, as well as an international one, fell to a South African media in turmoil. Crucially, international news provided the language, the idiom, and the concepts for a uniquely South African story.

The disjuncture between form and content, context and medium, became one of the reasons, I would argue, that this episode is one of the most illuminating in the history of the media in South Africa.

I will now return to the Pagad coverage in the *Cape Argus* and the *Cape Times*. On 4 August 1996, Rashaad Staggie, the co-leader of the Hard Livings gang, was murdered in Salt River, a suburb of Cape Town, after a march by the group People Against Gangsterism and Drugs (Pagad). This is how that event was portrayed in the *Cape Times* (Cape Town's most significant morning daily) and the *Cape Argus* (then *The Argus*, an afternoon daily) from 5 to 12 August 1996. On 5 August 1996, on its front page the *Cape Times* carried graphic pictures of the slow death the previous night of Rashaad Staggie, taken by the photographer Benny Gool. (The photographer would later be the subject of an attempt by police to subpoena his photographs as evidence in the prosecution of the Staggie murder.) Judging by the extent of the coverage in *The Argus*, the scale of importance of the events is clear. The front page of the *Cape Argus* of 5 August 1996 was composed of several articles and photographs about the murder, and large parts of the crucial third page were devoted to the story.

The *Cape Times* cover, which conveyed through the concreteness of news photographs the slow, tortured death of Rashaad Staggie, attracted national and international attention. *The Argus* composed its story of the murder in a different way. This newspaper too used photographs of the murder, though added other shots from the scene. The top half of page 3 to the story, under the headline "Staggie died as he lived", was devoted to the story, and included four photographs. The largest, in the centre of the page, is of the murder, with the caption "Drug War: Police surround a mortally wounded Rashaad Staggie after he was shot and petrol-bombed in a street in Salt River last night". To the left of this shot is a picture of two women, with the caption, "Distraught: A policeman tries to calm hysterical relatives". To the right are two photographs: one of a man with the caption: "Breaking point: An angry man, believed to be a relative of Rashaad, at the scene of the attack". Just above is a fourth photograph, with the caption: "Masked: One of the anti-drug vigilantes conceals a fiream under his jacket". This was the first appearance of the figure of the masked man in this story. In the coverage of this story in the days following, this figure would move to the centre and become an indispensable part of telling the story. In my argument below, I suggest that the prominence given to the image of the masked man would provide both a severe problem of meaning, and an indication of the connection of the local coverage with an international vocabulary with which to talk about Islam.

On Wednesday 7 August, *The Argus* carried the story on its front page under the headline "Mass action on gangs". The story occupies almost the entire top half of the front page, above the fold. To the left of the page is a photograph of a masked man at a rally called by Pagad. The man is shown reading a Quran and next to him lies a shotgun. The caption reads "Armed with a Prayer: A Pagad member reads the Quran while a shotgun lies within grabbing distance during the protest against gangsterism".

On guard: A member of Pagad – his face masked and his shotgun at the ready – stands guard during the Pagad rally at the Vygieskraal Stadium. Photographer: Thembinkosi Dwayisa.

On 12 August, the sister newspaper of *The Argus* in the Independent group, *The Star*, based in Johannesburg, has front-page coverage, headlined "Vigilantes declare 'holy war' on gangsters". *The Star* coverage continues: "Following last night's clash, chief Pagad commander Ali 'Phantom' Parker declared a 'Jihad' holy war against drug lords and has also 'declared war' on the police. He claimed Pagad had the support of the Iranian-backed Hezbollah and the Palestinian Hamas organisations" (*The Star*, 12 August 1996:1).

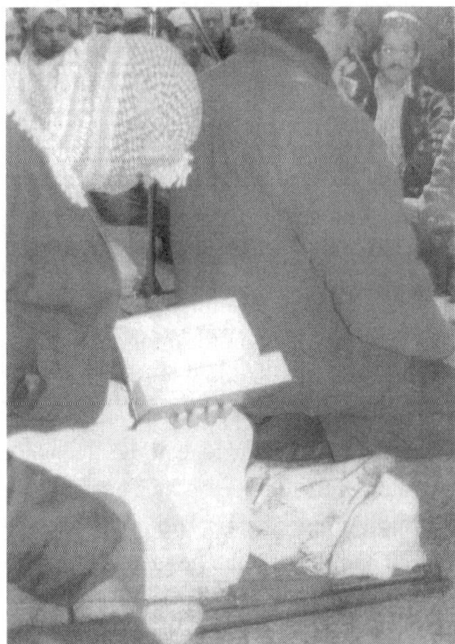

Armed with a prayer: A Pagad member reads the Quran while a shotgun lies within grabbing distance during the protest against gangsterism.
Photographer: Obed Zilwa, *Cape Argus.*

By 12 August, the figure of the masked man had become indispensable to telling the story of Pagad.

Part of the challenge of discussing the material is that South Africa was in the position of providing the content of the story told in a disjunctive vocabulary. It was a rare case of the authority of a powerful international Orientalist discourse being used in a country relatively new to such international patterns of images. Moreoever, as a result of the experience of colonial and apartheid media institutions, South Africa had a consistent Orientalist discourse of its own. Audiences were new to having South African stories told to them in an international idiom. The Pagad story represented the first time that the complicated politics and economics of international media had clashed with well-established local stereotypes. It internationalised a local story and also demonstrated the exercise by a South African group of the corollary of Orientalist stereotypes in the media – the use and manipulation of such imagery by some Muslim groups themselves.

The Politics of Pagad

This study does not include a sociological approach to Pagad, nor can I claim to have researched its publications in any systematic way; nonetheless, the agency and agenda of its members are relevant to this study, to the extent that they were active participants in the discourse around Islam which compelled attention and newspaper coverage in South Africa in 1996. In an article published in the South African edition of *Cosmopolitan* in November 1996 Alex Dodd attempted to deal with the clear attraction that certain aspects of Pagad's platform and behaviour held for the media in South Africa (1996:65). The machismo of certain members of Pagad, which dominated their public communications, resonated with the visual appeal of guns and inflammatory language. The lower-profile aspects of this and other anti-crime forums gained scant attention. Moreover, the emphasis which Pagad spokespeople contradictorily placed on Islamic iconography easily displaced the similarity between Pagad and other vigilante groups operating in South Africa at the time. In fact, Pagad could not easily claim either a Muslim identity or universal support among Muslims. It had an uneasy relationship with the established Muslim leadership. The Pagad stories demonstrated also a disparity in media and political attention given to crime in middle-class and formerly white areas of the city, and those in poorer, less powerful areas. The events were therefore a potent and complicated challenge. In many ways, the media can be faulted for its coverage. Yet, they were also on the receiving end of an unusual combination of pressures. Pagad conveyed a sense of suspicion about the motives and impact of the media, and journalists reported hostility from members of Pagad. Yet, in dealing in the same language of symbol and gesture, they collaborated uneasily with each other. They were each other's calibration of visibility and power. Pagad argued that the media was in fact a site and conduit of gang agendas. One of the primary sources of outrage about the gangs' imperviousness to prosecution cited by Pagad was the screening in South Africa of *Cape of Storms*, the 1993 documentary by Daniel Reed, in which the co-leaders of the Hard Livings gang, Rashied and Rashaad Staggie, acknowledged committing murders and selling drugs. No prosecutions resulted.

The media was faced with the task of contextualising Pagad's use of Islamic iconography. In many ways, the group itself was a creature of the media, partly because it learned the advantages of playing to the stereotypes which drew the most attention. These familiar images too it learned from the media, adopting, in Shamil Jeppie's coinage, a "bricolage" of themes associated with Islam. The largely uncritical way in which the South African media reported this complex performance was due to the paucity of its resources in dealing with the subject of Islam. Indeed, "What is this Islam thing?" – a question posed by a South African journalist to Shamil Jeppie – suggests both an illuminating bewilderment but also perhaps a perception of the performativity of the "thing" called Islam revealed in the constructedness of Pagad's evocation of the religion.

As argued above, the Capetonian media had historically little experience of dealing in complex ways with Islam. The expertise it did draw upon, such as the views of academics and politicians, was subsumed under the more powerful international Orientalist discourse. Under such conditions of tension and crisis, the media's reliance on a readymade discourse with the authority of international precedent seems inevitable.

In the midst of such complex representational politics, articles in the *Cape Times* and *The Argus* of that week referred to "holy war", "suicide bombs", "militant", "extremist", "jihad", "death threats", and "vigilante group" in potent combination with images associated not only with Pagad, but with Islam. An example of this knitting together of associations into a pattern of representations can be seen in an article in *The Argus* of 7 August 1996, titled "Mass action on gangs". The piece was accompanied by an image of a man masked with an "Arafat" scarf sitting on the ground reading a Quran. The caption reads "Armed with a prayer: A Pagad member reads the Quran while a shotgun lies within grabbing distance during the protest against gangsterism".

The newspaper coverage was not monolithic. The newspapers did print reflective pieces, such as the article by UCT academic Ebrahim Moosa, "Govt failure led to rise of Pagad" in the *Cape Times* of 19 August 1996. Moosa's subsequent article, "Groups Like Pagad Hurt Islam", appeared in various newspapers around the country. In *The Argus* (as it was then known), the piece was published under the title "Islam against the world: flawed radicalism will hurt the Muslim faith" (*Saturday Weekend Argus*, 16/17 November 1996). Ironically, however, even such pieces were accompanied by images of masked men. Strikingly, in the *The Star* of 12 November 1996, the same article published as "Groups Like Pagad Hurt Islam" too was accompanied by an image of a masked man. In a reduced vocabulary, the connection of Pagad to Islam, Islam to violence, and violence, therefore, to all Muslims, was made.

The Pagad stories showed the susceptibility of news about Islam to persistent stereotyping, in which gender plays a central role. The prototypical image conveyed in photographs was of men masked with "Palestinian" scarves, using the visual grammar familiar from international images of the Middle East – in extreme close-up, deadly and interchangeable. A similar visual pattern can be seen in images of the war in Afghanistan in 2001. In the Pagad story, the interplay of the global and the local was specific: the presence of international media images in a performance of the local changed the way stories of Islam could be told in South Africa.

The consequences were significant. The figure of the masked man in these articles serves as a vehicle for an anachronistic discourse of Islam. The dominant Western view that sees Islam as Other overrode and erased the specificity of context in South Africa. Significantly, since they felt excluded by this coverage, a section of the Muslim audience subsequently boycotted the two newspapers, and transferred their custom to Muslim media, particularly the community radio stations, Radio 786 and Voice of the Cape, which enormously increased their audiences. Yet, there may have been a larger loss than the Muslim audience. Shortly after 1994, the challenge existed for the media to redefine a new kind of *South African* audience. According to the journalist Yazeed Fakier, by reaching for the easy language of sensationalism the two newspapers lost a crucial opportunity to deal with the complexities of a changing South Africa. To Fakier, such lapses were due to the inadequacy of the post-apartheid media apparatus, which combined habits of thinking conditioned by apartheid with the loss of senior journalists due to rationalisation and cost-cutting - the "juniorisation" of the newsroom.

Men of the East: The Anxiety of Reciprocity

The anonymous masked men of Pagad provided an unprecedented opportunity for stereotype to parade as explanation in the media. Here was embodied the most famous and intractable of stereotypes, the inscrutability of the East. There are lessons to be learned from etymology. The word "inscrutable" comes from Latin: *in* [not] *scrutari* [to examine], hence not capable of being examined (*Concise Oxford Dictionary*). Inscrutable means "unknowable, incomprehensible, indecipherable, mysterious, mystifying, inexplicable, past comprehension, beyond research, enigmatic, elusive, unreadable, unrevealed, secret, veiled, masked, impenetrable". The opposite of inscrutable is "obvious, plain, clear, evident, penetrable, understandable, familiar, revealing, transparent, lucid". This set of binary meanings was set into motion by the mediated figure of the masked Oriental man.

The stereotypical unknown ability of this masked figure is a false one, of course. The colonial image of the inscrutable native ensures that the necessarily *penetrating* gaze was the preserve of the male European coloniser. As in the case of the colonial images, the blankness of the masked figure is a blankness upon which cliché could be written more clearly, definitively, and inerasably.

It is here that the discourses of covering and masking come suggestively together. The ways in which veils and masks are read despite different contexts tie together the local and the global. The journalistic use of the word "coverage" denotes description, analysis, and broadcasting. Further, "to cover" implies to include, embrace, comprehend. Yet "to cover" also connotes to sheathe, to envelop, to wrap; beyond this, to hide, obscure, veil, mask, disguise. The masked Pagad figure came to serve discursive needs for both the media and the group itself. In these stories, the entire explanation lay in the act of "covering" and "uncovering" the mask. And what the mask hid was, as Bhabha alerts us, already known. For, through the use of a readymade, decontextualised vocabulary, we were reading an *already covered* story. Harder to articulate in the light of this seductive Orientalist account was a historically informed analysis which showed complexity and depth, such as the use of drugs and gangs as political instruments by the apartheid regime in the 1980s, longstanding nonvigilante anti-crime initiatives within black communities, and complex responses within Muslim communities about Pagad.

The newspapers later recognised the failures of the initial Pagad coverage, and have attempted to change their strategies when it comes to matters of identity and culture. One response by the *Cape Times* was its "One City Many Cultures" initiative in 1999. This was an expensive campaign which devoted extensive space in the newspaper each week to exploring the "many cultures" of the city. Often, these explorations focused on the visible aspects of those cultures, and in some ways the coverage resembles the smorgasbord approach through which Muslim food, dress and customs had become familiar over the years. Nonetheless, it was a response which attempted to move away from crisis and to discuss culture in an indigenous vocabulary.

Conclusion: Muslim as Adjective

> We etch ourselves into . . . culture, in complex palimpsests of knowledge and desire (Alexander, 1998:152).

In this chapter I have provided a critical reading of images of Islam in South Africa in an attempt to counter notions of Islam as monolithic, unyielding, and unshakeably other. In an evocative article from the *New York Times* in 1995 an American Muslim, Al-Haaj Y. Khankan, notes "the media always put an adjective to the accused bad guy and the adjective is 'Muslim'" (26 March, 1995). As long as Islam appears encoded into language as other, and as long as some discourses that counter Islamophobia replicate the binary oppositions of "us" and "them", a necessary complexity about the topic will remain elusive.

In the neighbourhood mapped by media, we are circumscribed by a cultural geography that would pit us against one another. As audiences and citizens of an interconnected world, we are left with the massive intellectual and political challenge of *locating* ourselves, and telling other stories, in which our words and contexts count equally. In some discourses, Islam remains, like a woman, a mystery and perhaps a threat, but like an Oriental woman, also redeemable. Yet, there are other ways of speaking, ways of speaking which undercut the binaries that would oppose Islam and modernity, Islam and the West, Islam and humaneness. Who are "we"? Who are "they"? In a new geography, there may be space to contemplate not *already knowing everything* about Islam.

References

Abu-Lughod, Lila. 1986. *Veiled Sentiments: Honor and Poetry in a Bedouin Society.* Berkeley and London: University of California Press.

Agha, Olfat Hassan. 2002. "Islamic Fundamentalism and Its Image in the Western Media". In: Hafez, Kai (ed.). *Islam and the West in the Mass Media: Fragmented Images in a Globalized World.* Cresskill, New Jersey: Hampton Press. 219-33.

Alexander, Meena. 1998. "Alphabets of Flesh", in Shohat, Ella (ed.). *Talking Visions: Multicultural Feminism in a Transnational Age.* New York: New Museum of Contemporary Art, and Cambridge, MA and London: MIT Press. 143-59.

Bhabha, Homi. 1994. *The Location of Culture.* London and New York: Routledge.

Bourdieu, Pierre. 1998. *On television.* Translated by Priscilla Pankhurst Ferguson. London: Pluto Press.

Davis, Dennis. 2002. Email communication with the author. 4 July.

Dodd, Alex. 1996. "The Women of Pagad". In: Galant, Raashied and Gamaldien, Fahmi (eds.). *Drugs, Gangs, People's Power: Exploring the Pagad Phenomenon.* Claremont, Claremont Main Road Masjid.

Fanon, Frantz. 1965. *A Dying Colonialism.* Translated by Haakon Chevalier. New York: Grove Weidenfeld.

Frankenberg, Ruth and Mani, Lata. 1993. "Crosscurrents, Crosstalk: Race, 'Postcoloniality' and the Politics of Location". *Cultural Studies* 7.2 (May). 292-310.

Gqola, Pumla. 2001. "Slaves Don't Have Opinions: Inscriptions of Slave Bodies and the Denial of Agency in Rayda Jacobs' *The Slave Book*", in Erasmus, Z. (ed.). *Coloured by History, Shaped by Place: New Perspectives on Coloured Identities in Cape Town.* Cape Town, Kwela Books and SA History Online. 45-63.

Hall, Stuart. 1981. "The Determinations of Newsphotos". In: Mast, Gerald and Cohen, Stephen, (eds.). *The Manufacture of News.*

Hartley, John. 1996. *Popular Reality.* London and New York: Routledge.

Hendricks, Cheryl. 2001. "'Ominous' Liaisons: Tracing the Interface between 'Race' and Sex at the Cape", in Erasmus, Z. (ed.). *Coloured by History, Shaped by Place: New Perspectives on Coloured Identities in Cape Town.* Cape Town, Kwela Books and SA History Online. 29-44.

Jeppie, Shamil. 1996. "Introduction". In: Galant, Raashied and Gamaldien, Fahmi (eds.). *Drugs, Gangs, People's Power: Exploring the Pagad Phenomenon.* Claremont: Claremont Main Road Masjid.

Jeppe, Shamil. 2001. "Reclassifications: Coloured, Malay, Muslim", in Erasmus, Z. (ed.). *Coloured by History, Shaped by Place: New Perspectives on Coloured Identities in Cape Town*. Cape Town, Kwela Books and SA History Online. 80-96.

Johnson, Reed. 2001. "Elusive and Unknown Anti-hero Osama bin Laden's Frightening, Yet Compelling, Myth Expands", *Cape Times*, 10 October, 11.

Kabbani, Rana. 1986. *Europe's Myths of Orient: Devise and Rule*. Basingstoke and London: Macmillan.

Karacs, Imre. 2001. "Germany Centre of 'Sleeper' Network". *Sunday Argus*, 15/16 September 2001. 3.

Khan, Shahnaz. 1998. "Muslim Women: Negotiations in the Third Space". *Signs: Journal of Women in Culture and Society*, Vol 23(2). 463-94.

Kurtz, Howard. 2001. "CNN Chief Orders 'Balance' in War News: Reporters Are Told To Remind Viewers Why U.S. Is Bombing". *Washington Post (online)*, October 31.

Lane, Christopher. 1998. In: Lane, Christopher (ed.). *The Psychoanalysis of Race*. New York: Columbia University Press.

Loomba, Ania. 1989. *Gender, Race, Renaissance Drama*. Manchester: Manchester University Press.

McClintock, Anne. 1995. *Imperial Leather: Race, Gender and Sexuality in the Colonial Contest*. New York and London: Routledge.

Moosa, Ebrahim. 1996. "Groups Like Pagad Hurt Islam", *The Star*, 12 November.

Mutman, Mahmut. 1994. "Pictures from Afar: Shooting the Middle East". *Inscriptions*. Santa Cruz, California: Group for the Critical Study of Colonial Discourse.

Said, Edward. 1991 [1978]. *Orientalism*. London: Penguin.

Said, Edward. 1997. *Covering Islam: How the Media and the Experts Determine How We See the World*, Vintage.

Said, Edward. 2001. "Insidious, unthinking clash of ignorance", *The Sunday Independent*, 14 October. 6.

Spivak, Gayatri. 1988. "Can the Subaltern Speak?". In: Nelson, Cary and Grossberg, Lawrence (eds.). *Marxism and the Interpretation of Culture*. University of Illinois Press.

Stam, Robert, and Spence, Louise. 2000. "Colonialism, Racism and Representations: An Introduction" in Hollows, Joanne; Hutchings, Peter; and Jankovich, Mark (eds.). 2000. *The Film Studies Reader*. London: Arnold.

Steet, Linda. 2000. *Veils and Daggers: A Century of National Geographic's Representation of the Arab World*. Philadelphia: Temple University Press.

Watson, Helen. 1994. "Women and the Veil: Personal Responses to Global Process". In: Ahmed, Akbar and Donnan, Hastings, (eds.). *Islam, Globalization and Postmodernity*. London and New York: Routledge. 141-59.

Webster, Frank. 2002. "Global Challenges and National Answers", in Chan, Joseph M. and McIntyre, Bryce T. (eds.). *In Search of Boundaries: Communication, Nation-States, and Cultural Identities*. Westport, Connecticut and London: Ablex Publishing. 11-128.

Yegenoglu, Meyda. 1998. *Colonial Fantasies: Towards a Feminist Reading of Orientalism*. Cambridge: Cambridge University Press.

Young, Robert. 1995. *Colonial Desire: Hybridity in Theory, Culture and Race*. London and New York: Routledge.

Young, Robert. 1990. *White Mythologies: Writing, History and the West*, London and New York: Routledge.

Index